WINGS OVI
THE GLEN

CW00827973

Reminiscences of Northern and Scottish Airways Limited, Western Isles Airways Limited,
and Scottish Airways Limited, and their Founder and Managing Director at Renfrew,
George Nicholson.

CONTENTS

Front and rear cover: The painting 'Wings over the Glens' , by Edmund Miller, G.Av.A.

"Wings over the Glens"

ISBN 1 870384 35 0

First published 1995
by GMS Enterprises 67 Pyhill, Bretton
Peterborough England PE3 8QQ
Tel & Fax 0733-265123

Other titles by the same Author:
'A Flying Start to the Day '. First published July 1986.
'Flying Against the Elements' . First published August 1987.
'Rivals in the North'. First published May 1988.
'The Quiet Test Pilot'. First published June 1989.
'Sword in the Sky'. First published May 1990.
'Roy Chadwick - Lancaster Designer'. To come.
'Avro Test Pilots 1907 - 1994'. To come.

Printed and bound for GMS Enterprises by
Woolnough Ltd Express Works Irthlingborough Northants.

INTRODUCTION

This is the fifth booklet in the series covering the origins and growth of Scotland's early scheduled airline industry from 1933 to 1947, when all the independent airline companies' routes were simultaneously taken over by the newly formed State corporation, British European Airways, leading to the inevitable bowing out of the original airline pioneers.

The series has now covered the activities of the man who started it all (John Sword in Glasgow) and of those who followed close at hand (Ted Fresson in Inverness, and Eric Gandar Dower

in Aberdeen), and is now completed by this account of George Nicholson, who came from Consett, Co. Durham to take over where John Sword left off in Glasgow.

George came from obscurity (his early life and family have proved difficult to trace), and went into far off retirement in South Africa, after a lifetime of avoiding any great personal publicity. Yet he set up his company to carry on many of John Sword's early creations - principally flying to the remoter islands and towns in the West (more of a social service, rather than a profitable occupation), and operating and expanding the Scottish Air Ambulance Service.

Eventually, like Ted Fresson in Inverness, George merged his company into the financially strong United Airways Group in the South (later itself merged into the larger British Airways Group), and his scarcely profitable Renfrew operation was later combined with Fresson's more profitable Inverness company into a new, all-embracing airline for Scotland - Scottish Airways.

The history of Ted Fresson's Inverness-based airline has been documented in two previous booklets in this series - *A Flying Start to the Day* (published in July 1986) and *Rivals in the North* (published in May 1988) - both by the same author.

Inevitably, as Fresson's airline merged with George Nicholson's in August 1937, and the combination continued for a whole decade until nationalisation in February 1947, a certain amount of detail from these two booklets have been repeated here. But as far as possible, the duplication of material has been kept to the essential facts - and to the events precipitated by Ted Fresson (the most dominant and publicity-conscious of the two airline founders) which had a direct bearing on matters affecting Scottish Airways in the countdown to nationalisation.

A good deal of new material is published here for the first time - much of it coming from the Fresson archives (held now by his son Richard) and from the old British European Airways archives (now part of the British Airways historical collection). Such is the historical importance of some of the material that it has been reproduced here, even though it is of poor quality.

This shows how the combination of the two airlines' skills prospered and made profits right up to Nationalisation on February 1st 1947. Such profits were never seen again in the North for many years, which makes the study of the life and work of these pioneers well worth the documentation. They succeeded because they gave the Public what it needed - aerial transportation at the times they wanted, where they required it - and at the prices they could afford. We do well to keep those objectives in mind today !

Peter V Clegg
'Squirrels Leap'
9 Park Chase
Godalming
Surrey GU7 1TL
May 21st 1995.

George Nicholson (1905 - 1950)

Brought up in Consett, Co. Durham by his family , George founded Northern Airways in 1934 at Newcastle-on-Tyne, then Northern and Scottish Airways at Renfrew in December the same year. His airline grew in size and stature, through a series of mergers and acquisitions over the next twelve years, to become Scotland's all-embracing air carrier.
(Henry Vallance)

PART I

START OF A NEW CAREER

CHAPTER 1

A small Airline at Newcastle

Born on April 15th 1905, George Nicholson was brought up by his family in Consett, County Durham, and sent away to boarding school at Sedbergh at the end of the Great War.

His father was a Chartered Accountant, who had developed his own practice at Midland Bank Chambers, Consett, and about the time his son George was leaving school is thought to have also been involved with the financial side of operating a local bus and coach operation in the Newcastle-on-Tyne area, as well as with import and export shipping interests in Newcastle.

George started work in his father's office as soon as he had finished at Sedbergh, training as an accountant, and later had his name added to the letter heading of his father's practice - but without being able to describe himself as 'qualified' at that stage. The name of the firm was therefore just kept to: "J. M. Nicholson & Co."

Becoming an accountant himself was either not very easy for George however, or perhaps an ideal he soon discarded in favour of something else far more exciting !

Working with his father's firm for some 12 years after leaving school George found himself much more interested in the idea of running a transport undertaking, than sitting at a desk adding up client's ledger columns. He had already come into contact with the legendary John Cuthill Sword and his bus and coach operations centred on Kilmarnock, Ayrshire, and had watched how John Sword had suddenly in 1933 branched out into scheduled airline operations with his "Midland & Scottish Air Ferries".

Other bus operators, led by the unforgettable Edward Hillman in Essex, had instigated this move into airline operations across the length and breadth of the British Isles and George Nicholson was suddenly very interested in this trend. Why not start his own airline along similar lines, he mused, and base it at Newcastle-on-Tyne?

Accelerated acquisition

George had already seen how popular the coach services out of Newcastle were in mid-summer, to the coastal resorts in the West like Blackpool, Morecambe, and the Isle of Man. The last-named resort was more up-market, and involved a sea-crossing from Heysham too, and George reckoned an aircraft was the ideal means of transport in this case (he had noted how John Sword had opened up air services to the Isle of Man from Renfrew (Glasgow), Speke (Liverpool) and Stanley Park (Blackpool) during 1933 and early 1934).

So, in Spring 1934 he started to plan an operation, based at Newcastle's civil airport at Cramlington, which would call also at Carlisle's Municipal Aerodrome and terminate in the Isle of Man. He was really looking to begin the service in the summer of 1935, but by May 1934, with his planning only half completed, George suddenly became aware - through his contacts with John Sword and in the bus business generally - that the latter's airline, Midland & Scottish Air Ferries, was going to have to stop operating on July 14th that year. This was through no other reason than a 'conflict of interest' between Sword's personal involvement with his rapidly expanding aviation company, and his position as General Manager of the huge 'Western S.M.T,' bus operation - itself a subsidiary of 'SMT' in Edinburgh and owned by the LMS Railway Co., which was now backing the rapid expansion of its own airline operation 'Railway Air Services'.

Sword could not continue to compete against his own masters in the aerial sphere, and so was told to either "close down his airline, or leave S.M.T. forthwith". He had chosen to stay with the buses, and so George Nicholson was now in a quandary. He could accelerate the start of his own company, or risk others moving in to take over Sword's route network, and perhaps his own planned air service. On the other hand what better time to start his own company, and try to take over some of John Sword's old routes himself?

So George contacted John Sword, and started to negotiate to take over several services. At the same time he moved rapidly to acquire an aircraft from the De Havilland Aircraft agents, and bought the DH 84 Dragon, G-ACFG, which had been built and first certificated on June 28th 1933.

One of Sword's pilots at Renfrew, Edward F ('Ted') Palmer had been looking around for another position, when he knew

The bleak skyline of Cramlington Aerodrome at Newcastle-on-Tyne was broken only by the outline of the single, large hangar in which Connie Leathart's aero-engineering company overhauled the aircraft of many famous fliers, including Ted Fresson, John Sword, Eric Gandar Dower - and George Nicholson's Northern Airways. (Connie Leathart)

what was going to happen, and immediately agreed to join George at the end of May 1934 as his one and only pilot at Cramlington. And George contracted for the aircraft overhaul concern, 'Cramlington Aircraft Ltd' to house and maintain the Dragon for him at Newcastle's Airport. This company had the only hangar at Cramlington, and had been formed in October 1929 to combine together the aircraft maintenance skills of Miss Constance R Leathart (a licensed aero-engineer), and Mr (later Lord) W Leslie Runciman. It operated to look after many privately-owned aircraft and to overhaul the machines of several airlines in the North, including John Sword's M&SAF and Ted Fresson's Highland Airways at that time. (When the new Newcastle Airport opened at Woolsington in 1935, Cramlington Aerodrome, and Cramlington Aircraft Ltd, were both closed down. 'Connie' Leathart went on flying privately, and in the wartime Air Transport Auxiliary until 1958, dying in 1993 at the age of 89).

Miss Constance ("Connie") Leathart - the famous pre-war British aviatrix who not only overhauled aircraft for all and sundry at her works at Cramlington Aerodrome (she was a qualified aero-engineer), but also won trophies in many U.K. and continental air rallies. In WWII she joined the A.T.A. and ferried aircraft from factories and storage depots to the squadrons (Connie Leathart)

Northern Airways formed

George now hurriedly registered the name of his airline, Northern Airways, with its address at 'The Aerodrome, Cramlington, Newcastle-on-Tyne', on July 1st 1934. The company was wholly owned by George himself, and the only other employee at that stage was Ted Palmer the pilot.

Because of the undue haste in which he had to get everything organised and because he made the early decision to fly his first Cramlington - Carlisle - Castletown (I.O.M.) service on Monday July 30th 1934, George did not have time to invite the Lord Mayor of Newcastle or the Mayor of Carlisle to fly on the inaugural. He decided instead to invite the Press, and had five requests from Reporters, to take them on the first flight - which he did. He decided, however, to write to the Town Clerks of

Newcastle and Carlisle to ask the Mayors on a future occasion, and to explain his haste on this.

George set the timings of the inaugural flight to leave Cramlington at 10.00 on Monday July 30th, arrive Carlisle at 10.33 and proceed onwards to the Isle of Man. The aircraft would also fly as far as Carlisle on Tuesday 31st, but then stay in Carlisle to give 'special joy flights' from 11.30 until 15.30 in the afternoon. From August 1st the flight would be daily, and the timing as follows:-

09.30	Dep.	Cramlington	Arr. 17.00
10.00	Arr.	Carlisle	Dep. 16.30
10.25	Dep.	Carlisle	Arr. 16.05
11.30	Arr.	Castletown (I.O.M.)	Dep. 15.00

The inaugural, flown by Ted Palmer with George Nicholson and five newspaper reporters on board, evidently went off well, and George gained some instant publicity for his service - which as it had started late in the Season, it badly needed at that stage.

The fares were initially set at:

	(Single)	(Return)
Cramlington to Carlisle	£1.0s.0d.	£1.15s.0d.
Cramlington to I.O.M.	£2.10s.0d.	£4.10s.0d.
Carlisle to I.O.M.	£1.11s.0d.	£2.16s.6d.

There was a free luggage allowance of 25lbs per head, and the booking agents were Fenwick's Travel Bureau of Northumberland Street, Newcastle; Messrs Thurman's of 11 English Street Carlisle; and Mr W H Chapman of 63 Athol Street, Douglas (I.O.M.). The hand bills for the service also stated that bus connections were available to and from Cramlington and Castletown aerodromes, from Newcastle and Douglas respectively.

The daily service settled down after August 1st and George did start to publicise the fact that his aircraft's arrival and departure in the Isle of Man made connections with Hillman Airways flights to and from Belfast. Hillman had taken over the Stapleford - Liverpool - Isle of Man - Belfast service from John Sword on July 16th - just two days after the latter's M & SAF had closed down most of its routes. But George was premature with his promotion of interline connections - by early August Hillman had withdrawn the service !

When George realised this had happened, he tried to plan for his own service to fly on from Castletown (I.O.M.) to Newtownards (Belfast) on Mondays and Fridays, starting on Friday August 17th, and he publicised this again - but once more he had to call off the arrangement at the last moment. In fact by August 23rd, and with disappointing traffic results, he dropped the frequency back from daily, to just a Tuesday, Thursday and Saturday operation.

After September 3rd George reduced the frequency still further, operating now on Mondays and Saturdays only, with departures from Cramlington as before at 09.30 but with return flights leaving the Isle of Man at 12.30 (after a one hour turn - around).

By the end of October, George's airline had flown some 11,000 miles altogether, but its single Dragon (G-ACFG) had only carried a total of 182 passengers in all ! The last flight was made on Monday, October 29th and then George called it a day for the Winter.

A change of plan

By now George was not entirely satisfied with the results of his first airline service and as the Summer of 1934 had passed by, he had been in extensive conversations with John Sword in Ayr, about the break up and take-over of parts of the network operated

ing ✠ Chronicl

INCORPORATING THE "EVENING WORLD"

885 | NEWCASTLE, MONDAY, JULY 30, 1934. PRICE ONE PEN

BUILD AIRCRAFT IN N

A TOAST TO CRAMLINGTON - Isle of Man air service inaugurated today.

Left: Although of poor quality, this is one of the very few photographs of George Nicholson's first aircraft - DH 84 Dragon G-ACFG. It appeared in Newcastle's Evening Chronicle to mark a historic occasion - the inaugural flight to the Isle of Man on July 30th 1934. Interestingly, the name of George's company on the aircraft nose is ' Northern Airways Ltd' - yet all other documents in existence indicate the company was never 'Limited' in status.

Below: A map of Cramlington aerodrome as it existed in Summer 1934 as the airport for Newcastle-on-Tyne. It was closed in 1936, as by then Newcastle's Woolsington Airport had opened in July 1935, and has remained the region's civil airport to the present day. Cramlington has long since reverted to grass fields, and no trace of the single large hangar now remains. (Author)

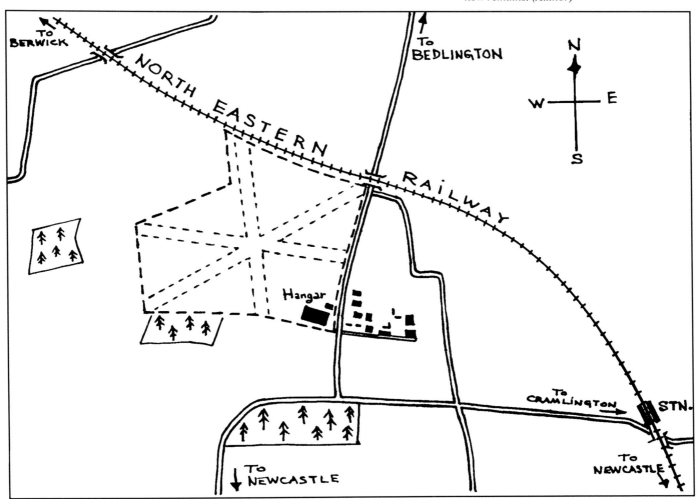

NORTHERN AIRWAYS.

Telephone:
CRAMLINGTON 9.

GN/LF/148.

THE AERODROME.

CRAMLINGTON.

NEWCASTLE-ON-TYNE.

26th July 1934.

The letter to the Town Clerk of Carlisle from George Nicholson , dated July 26th 1934, proposing giving joy flights at Carlisle's Kingstown Aerodrome with the DH 84 Dragon G-ACFG. Note that "Northern Airways" is not a "Limited" company. (Peter Connon)

Dear Sir,

    We propose to advertise the fact that our aeroplane will give special joy flights at Carlisle Aerodrome from 11.30 a.m. on Tuesday 31st instant, until 3.30 p.m., in order to introduce the machine. If there are any objections to this proposal will you please be good enough to let us know.

    Yours faithfully,

    FOR NORTHERN AIRWAYS,

    Geo. Nicholson.

\- Webster, Esq.,
Town Clerk,
Town Clerk's Office,
CARLISLE.

J.M. NICHOLSON & Co.

J. M. NICHOLSON,
CHARTERED ACCOUNTANT.

C. NICHOLSON.

TEL: CONSETT 48.

GN/LF/148.

Midland Bank Chambers.
Consett.

C° DURHAM.

26th July 1934.

Dear Mr. Webster,

    Further to our conversation of 24th instant regarding the trial trip to the Isle of Man there are five reporters who have expressed a wish to make this trip and I propose to run it as a press trip. As the time is so short I thought it would be difficult to make all the necessary arrangements with the Lord Mayor of Newcastle through the Town Clerk, and the Mayor of Carlisle through yourself.

    I hope the service will be used, and later perhaps we could make full arrangements for the formal inauguration ceremony.

    We propose to leave Cramlington on Monday 30th instant at 10 a.m. and arrive at Carlisle at 10.33 and then proceed to the Isle of Man. If you can see your way clear to come up to the Aerodrome I am sure the Reporters and myself will be delighted to see you.

    Yours faithfully,

    Geo. Nicholson.

\- Webster, Esq.,
Town Clerk,
Town Clerk's Office,
CARLIS-LE.

This letter from George Nicholson to the Town Clerk of Carlisle explains why the Mayor has not been invited on the inaugural flight! It has been written on notepaper used by George when working at his father's firm of accountants in Consett, Co. Durham. (Peter Connon)

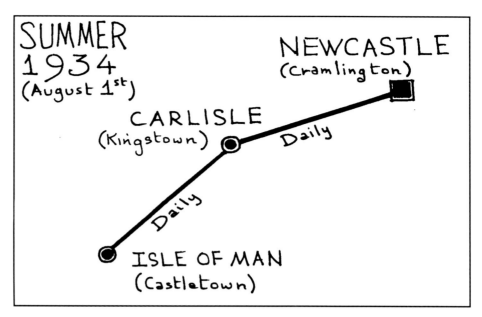

Northern Airways' route network in Summer 1934, as at August 1st. A daily frequency is now being flown in the DH Dragon G-ACFG between Cramlington, Kingstown and Castletown aerodromes. (Author)

SUMMER 1934 (August 1st)

NEWCASTLE (Cramlington)

CARLISLE (Kingstown)

Daily

Daily

ISLE OF MAN (Castletown)

by the latter's defunct Midland & Scottish Air Ferries concern.

George agreed with John Sword that he would take over the latter's Glasgow (Renfrew) - Campbeltown - Islay route, and had been negotiating with the owners of the landing fields at The Strath (Campbeltown) and Duich Farm (Islay) to rent them at a suitable figure. These negotiations dragged on through August and September, however, and John Sword (who had kept the Campbeltown/Islay services operating up to then with his last 'Chief Pilot', Charles F Almond) was finally forced to stop the twice daily flights on September 29th (the last Saturday in the month).

George was also thinking ahead to the following Summer about his Isle of Man service, and wondering how to combine the Renfrew service with his Newcastle route. He decided to drop Cramlington altogether for 1935 (partly because of airline operations having to transfer to the new Newcastle Airport at Woolsington in July 1935, in mid-season) and started a correspondence with the Town Clerk of Carlisle, Frederick G Webster, with a view to trying to get the Council to erect a permanent hangar there for his Dragon (there not being one in the Isle of Man), and also to ask for a rebate in the landing fees. If he could get these items, he planned to start the Isle of Man service from Carlisle on May 1st 1935, and would extend the flights through Castletown (I.O.M) to Renfrew (Glasgow), to link up operations there.

Finally, George was also interested in taking over the new Air Ambulance flights started by John Sword's airline in 1933, and using a specially-equipped D.H. Dragon and highly qualified pilot. John Sword was still supporting this service out of Renfrew and paying Charles F Almond (who was now a Flying Instructor at the Scottish Flying Club) to fly his stretcher-equipped Dragon (G-ACJS) on demand.

Ted Palmer, George's pilot and only other employee, once the frequency of the I.O.M. service had wound down in September/October, had begun to fly with M&SAF again down at their last surviving base at Blackpool's Stanley Park. He used to motor down from Carlisle and join Jimmy Orrell and Thomas Thomlinson there, running John Sword's Flying Club, and instructing pupils how to fly on the ex-M&SAF DH Fox Moth and Avro Cadet. This lasted through into November, with Ted taking up newspaper photographers on the dark nights to photograph the "Illuminations" along the Front at Blackpool.

Meanwhile, George Nicholson decided to finalise his arrangements with John Sword and the various landowners - including negotiating use of Renfrew Aerodrome and its hangars and Clubhouse facilities (and an office). He now registered a new airline company to start afresh in December 1934, and begin using Renfrew in a big way. The curtain had come down on the first Act.

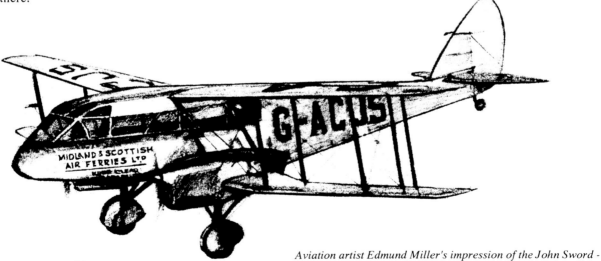

Aviation artist Edmund Miller's impression of the John Sword - supported DH84 Dragon G-ACJS as flown by Charles Almond on the early Air Ambulance flights,

George Nicholson, founder of Northern Airways and later Northern and Scottish Airways Ltd (centre) with his two right-hand men who joined him in NSA and helped build up the organisation - William Cumming (left) the Company Secretary, and William Gairdner (right), Operations Director. (Henry Vallance)

NORTHERN AND SCOTTISH AIRWAYS, LTD.

Directors :
Geo. Nicholson.   C. F. Almond.
A. E. Nicholson.   W. Gairdner.

TELEPHONE NEWCASTLE 24613.

GLASGOW OFFICE :
HOPE STREET, GLASGOW.
TELEPHONE : CENTRAL 594

MIDLAND BANK CHAMBERS,

CONSETT,

CO. DURHAM.

EXCHANGE BUILDINGS,

QUAYSIDE,

NEWCASTLE-ON-TYNE.

GN/LF/148.   23rd March 1935.

Dear Sir,

               Municipal Aerodrome. Ref. JAB/HH

        I am much obliged for your letter of 20th instant stating that the Air Base Committee has agreed to recomend the Council to make a charge to our company of 6d per passenger upon embarkation and disembarkation, instead of the usual charge in respect of the aeroplane itself, this arrangement to remain in operation for one year from 1st May 1935.

        Will you please be good enough to convey to the Air Base Committee my best thanks for the courteous consideration they have given our proposals.

               Yours faithfully,

               For and on behalf of
               NORTHERN & SCOTTISH AIRWAYS LTD.

               Geo. Nicholson.
               MANAGING DIRECTOR.

Fredk. G. Webster, Esq.,
Town Clerk
Town Clerk's Office
CARLISLE.

A letter from George Nicholson, this time on his new airline's notepaper, to the Town Clerk of Carlisle about the implementation of a passenger - rather than aircraft - landing tax.

Northern and Scottish Airways Ltd has its address at Exchange Buildings, Quayside, Newcastle-on-Tyne, but George has written from his Consett office!

Directors of NSA are shown to be: George Nicholson, his wife Ada E.Nicholson, C. F. Almond and W. Gairdner.

(Peter Connon)

CHAPTER 2

Northern and Scottish Airways

On November 21st 1934 George Nicholson registered a new airline company, Northern and Scottish Airways Limited, to be the vehicle for expansion into Scotland and which would control all his future network. He still kept the old company in existence - Northern Airways (not a 'Limited Company') - and it came in useful at a later date, as we shall see.

Northern and Scottish Airways Ltd was registered as a 'Private Limited Company', with a Capital of £7,000 in £1 shares. Its objectives were stated to be: *"To establish, maintain, work and carry on lines of aerial communication by means of aeroplanes, seaplanes, flying-boats, airships and other aerial conveyances, etc".*

The first Directors of the new company - referred to henceforth in its advertising as 'NSA' - were: George Nicholson (Managing) of Midland Bank Chambers, Consett, Charles F Almond of 66 John Street, Sunderland (the instructor at the Scottish Flying Club at Renfrew who was on 'call-out' for John Sword's Air Ambulance Service), and George's wife Ada E Nicholson, of Derwent Hill, Ebchester, Co. Durham.

The address given for Charles Almond was in fact, that of the Solicitor appointed by George to look after the company, Mr Eric W Moses, and the company's Memorandum of Association also stated that George would be 'permanent' Managing Director - as long as he held 500 shares (or the equivalent percentage of capital issued). The printed address of NSA was now given as: Exchange Buildings, Quayside, Newcastle-on-Tyne, although for some months after, correspondence was still conducted from George's old office at his father's firm in Midland Bank Chambers, Consett. A new Glasgow office address was however, shown - at 153 Hope Street, Glasgow (just north of St Vincent Street) - which had now become the town terminal (and the only place) where passengers could book for flights from the new base at Renfrew Aerodrome.

Services out of Renfrew

George had Ted Palmer back in November as his pilot, and Ted positioned the Dragon G-ACFG up to Glasgow's Renfrew aerodrome by the end of the month, for restarting the ex John Sword route Renfrew-Campbeltown (The Strath)-Islay (Duich Farm).

George Nicholson had employed Charles Almond as a Director of his new airline company, and so it was Charles who inaugurated the revived Campbeltown-Islay service on December 1st. This route was flown initially on a three times weekly basis - on Tuesdays, Thursdays and Saturdays, with the six-seat DH Dragon G-ACFG.

The timings were:

09.30	Dep.	Glasgow (Renfrew)	Arr.	14.40
↓ 10.05	Arr.	Campbeltown	Dep.	↑ 14.05
10.20	Dep.	(The Strath)	Arr.	13.50
↓ 10.45	Arr.	Islay (Duich Farm)	Dep.	↑ 13.30

George set the fares at:

Glasgow to:	Campbeltown	19s. 6d.
	Islay	£1. 10s. 0d.
Campbeltown to:	Islay	15s. 0d.

and he also announced that he had applied to the Post Office for permission to carry mails.

The resumption of services on this route was welcomed by the communities concerned as by now they had become used to the air service provided since April 18th 1933 (Campbeltown) and May 16th 1933 (Islay) by John Sword's old airline Midland & Scottish Air Ferries Ltd. (but suspended since September 29th 1934 due to its demise). The Renfrew - Campbeltown service was in fact, Scotland's very first scheduled service, and it was fitting that it should now be back in operation, albeit under 'new management' !

On the same day that George started his first Renfrew service, Hillman Airways in Essex started a weekday London - Liverpool - Belfast - Renfrew service in each direction, also carrying mails, and this provided a connection of sorts for the NSA service.

Also in December, the famous De Havilland Aircraft sales agents, Brian Lewis of Heston and Hooton Park, sent one of their directors up to Renfrew to open a sales agency there. His name was William ("Bill") Gairdner, and initially he busied himself with trying to find new customers to buy John Sword's old fleet of 17 aircraft in all.

Rival concern set up

George Nicholson had just got into Renfrew in the nick of time, for another gentleman had arrived there by December with the same ideas - but perhaps not the same financial backing. He was Mr J Glyn-Roberts who had been a joy-riding and display pilot for S.M.T. (Scottish Motor Traction) and had been based all that Summer and Autumn of 1934 at Ettrick Bay on the Island of Bute, just west of Rothesay.

He was after taking over the defunct M&SAF services also, but was just too late to negotiate the Campbeltown run. He did, however, set up a company in Scotland registered as "West of Scotland Air Services Ltd" (or WSAS), and acquired a couple of DH 83 Fox Moths at first (G-ACCT, ex -M&SAF; and G-ACDZ, ex-SMT), a hangar and an office at Renfrew (telephone number: Renfrew 140) and by December 1934 was advertising charter flights to all and sundry. As the Scottish Flyer magazine stated at the time: *"Messrs West of Scotland Air Services maintain at the aerodrome a Fox Moth available at anytime for any destination at exceptionally reasonable rates".*

J. Glyn-Roberts kept his charter company going for the next few years, however, and in 1935 he acquired another DH 83 Fox Moth (G-ACEC) from the old SMT organisation and continued to fly joy-rides at Ettrick Bay, Bute and opened a Greenock - Arran service on demand in the Summer, charging 25s. 0d. single and landing near Shiskine, Torbeg, on the west side of the island. His flights were popular, but ran mostly at the weekend. For the time being, therefore, he did not pose much of a threat to George's ambitions.

Taking over the Air Ambulance

From January 1st 1935 George agreed to assume responsibility for operating the Air Ambulance service originally set up at Renfrew by John Sword in May 1933 with his DH 84 Dragon I, G-ACCZ. Scarcely had George done this than Charles Almond flew NSA's first Ambulance flight from the Western Isles to Renfrew that January, in the Dragon G-ACFG.

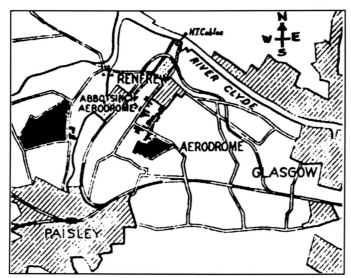

The position of Renfrew aerodrome (centre) compared with Abbotsinch (left centre) as shown in the 1937 edition of Air Pilot.

John Sword had funded the operation of the service himself until the turn of the year, but now George Nicholson managed to take things a step further - and during the early months of 1935 he concluded a proper contract with the first of the two County Councils covering his area - Argyll. Between Argyll and Inverness County Councils, these two covered the whole of Kintyre and the Western Isles (in those days), and George eventually concluded the same agreement with Inverness the following year - 1936. In these two years, the two Councils included the Air Ambulance Service for the first time in their respective schemes of Public Health and Hospital Facilities throughout the Islands. The local Medical Officers of Health were empowered to avail themselves, at their discretion, of the facilities provided by the Air Ambulance Services, and by arrangement with the Department of Health for Scotland the respective County Councils accepted financial responsibility, recovering from the individual patients a proportion of the cost in cases where financial circumstances of the patient allowed.

Up to 1938, it was the practice for the local District Nurse to fly with the patient to the City Hospital at Glasgow, but this deprived the district of her services until such time as she could fly back, or get back by surface means. So after 1938 arrangements were made with the Dept. of Health for Scotland whereby a nurse from the Glasgow area was then always on call to fly out with the air ambulance and attend to the patient on the way back in (up to February 1942 these nurses were supplied by the Trained Nurses Association of Paisley, but after this date, they came from the Southern General Hospital in Glasgow where a large number of nurses volunteered for this duty).

As Charles Almond had already been called out in January, he began to make reconnaissance flights over the next few weeks around the Inner Hebrides and Argyll, to pinpoint possible airstrips for use in an ambulance emergency. One example of this came on April 8th 1935 when Charles landed on the Island of Colonsay (north of Islay and west of Jura), finding a large and flat enough space for the Dragon to alight (he was following in the footsteps of Jimmy Orrell, one of John Sword's pilots who had pioneered landing at all kinds of isolated places, including the hilly Island of Muck!). Details of all the known ambulance flights flown by NSA and Scottish Airways between January 1935 and January 1947 have been taken from pilots' log books and are given in Appendix 3.

A very graphic description of how it all worked was published in Scottish Airways sales brochure in January 1939. Penned by one George Blake, it is worth reproducing here for its rapid conveyance of the arrangements that went on behind the scenes of an air ambulance call-out:

"HULLO! Is that Renfrew 230?"

"This is Renfrew 230 Scottish Airways speaking."

"This is Dr M-, of Tiree. I have a very urgent case for hospital. When can you let me have the Air Ambulance?"

"Right away. Can you get your patient comfortably to the Reef Airport? Good. Western Infirmary, Glasgow. Righto, doctor! Expect the plane in about an hour's time and have your patient ready."

And within three hours, that so far nameless patient in Tiree will be in an operating theatre in a highly-equipped Glasgow Infirmary, safe in the care of a specialist surgeon.

Six years ago, the doctor will reflect, that life would almost certainly have been lost. A diseased appendix, a shooting accident, or a bicycle smash would have meant, at the best, a makeshift operation by a general practitioner in a rarely-used cottage hospital. In remoter parts it would probably have meant just doing the best to ease the agonies until the inevitable end came.

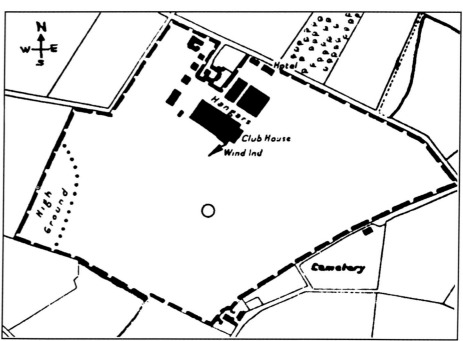

The layout of Renfrew aerodrome, with the large four-bay hangars and Scottish Flying Club clubhouse (and office for NSA).

Aircraft parked by the clubhouse, and the post WWII Terminal was built on that site. (Air Pilot - 1937)

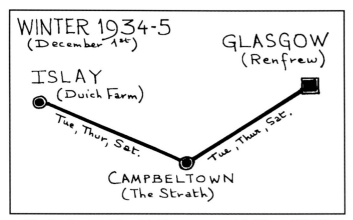

The Northern and Scottish Airways network in Winter 1934-35 consisted solely of the one ex -M&SAF route. (Author)

Now the most remote crofter of the Outer Isles has as fair a chance of speedy and expert treatment as a Lanarkshire miner.

The use of a plane for ambulance work started in 1933. The then operator of the Western Isles services was generous in giving the use of his machines to an occasional urgent case. One of the ambulance associations presented a special stretcher.

In 1935, however, the Argyll County Council entered into a regular arrangement with Northern and Scottish Airways - now SCOTTISH AIRWAYS LIMITED - in connection with the Highland Medical Service under the aegis of the Health Department for Scotland. Inverness County Council followed suit.

Power to call out the air ambulance is vested in certain doctors in the Highlands and Islands Medical Service of the Health Department. Of these Scottish Airways possesses a check-list. The costs of a flight - which work out at about £10 per flying hour - are divided between the department and the county council concerned in cases where the patient is unable to contribute.

From January 1935 to January 1939 the Air Ambulance Service as officially recognised had carried some 300 cases. The vast majority of these recovered - lives saved that would almost certainly have been lost six years ago.

An ambulance call is the signal for a positive fret of activity at the Renfrew Airport. Sometimes it may be possible to pick up the patient on the ordinary service run. The pilots can show you logbook entries telling how, over the Firth of Lorne, say, they were wirelessed to divert from their course to pick up a patient dangerously ill.

In the early days, it was usually a case of bringing the district nurse back with the patient. This took those invaluable public servants away from their areas, and now the practice is to send a nurse with the Air Ambulance.

Meanwhile, our pilot and wireless officer are on the airfield. The plane is being serviced according to a hard-and-fast schedule, for there must be no possibility of error or mishap.

Petrol tanks are filled. The stretcher is fitted. The nurse in her blue uniform takes her seat. The wireless officer sits at his instrument, waiting. The pilot climbs in.

" Contact! "

The engines, already heated by 10 minutes free running, roar into life as the mechanics swing the propellers. Away she taxies across the field for a fair take-off into the wind. She 'gets the gun', as the airmen say; she rears and rises and heads nor'-west. Another race for a life has started.

But they are still busy in the offices of Scottish Airways. Somebody has arranged for a St. Andrew's surface ambulance to be waiting the plane's return. Somebody has 'phoned an E.T.A. to the anxious doctor in the Isles - E.T.A. being simply expected time of arrival. Somebody has mobilised the ground staff to run out the flares if a return in darkness is expected.

At the Air Ministry Control Station, men wearing headphones, are listening to Morse messages from the ambulance, giving bearings and special weather forecasts in return. Each message is passed to Control Officer who transmits by phone to the company.

Then a great responsibility rests mainly on the pilot for a time.

Probably it is the Chief Pilot—Captain David Barclay, small, brown-faced, clear-eyed, He is wrestling all the time with the dirty weather of the western seaboard.

Naturally, the air ambulance tries to pick up its helpless passengers at an organised landing place. But sometimes the Pilot has to use a mere strip of wet beach, a runway indicated by the doctor himself, or even to discover a small field that will serve in the emergency.

Every Scottish Airways' Aerodrome has its own emergency stretcher for ambulance work. And Captain Barclay has been so long on the job that he knows every conceivable landing place from the Mull of Kintyre to the Butt of Lewis.

The air ambulance has never had a flying mishap.

Behind the pilot sits the wireless officer. The whole safety of the machine is depending as much on the quickness of his mind as on the pilot's skill.

He reports his position from time to time - over Lochgilphead, over the Ross of Mull, over Gigha - and QBG 3,000: that is, "flying above cloud at 3,000ft". And Renfrew is feeding him back, perhaps, another special weather report.

But it is only too easy to lose your bearings over the West Coast of Scotland. And Renfrew gives back at once a true bearing from that point.

If there is any doubt they give back "a cut" - that is, two or three bearings from different wireless stations: Renfrew, Sollas in North Uist, Perth, or Newtownards in Ulster. Where the lines of the compass bearings intersect on the map before him - well, that's where he is.

They even give him barometric pressure. That affects the instrument that tells him his altitude.

Then the last signal of all from the plane - QAL. "About to land". The pilot sees below him tiny dots in the grey light of dawn or the ruddy mirk of a winter sunset, the pathetic party - doctor, district nurse, relatives, and the white-faced patient he has flown perhaps 150 miles to succour. The plane banks, lands and taxies along the sand or turf, and comes to rest.

It doesn't take long nowadays to get the stretcher in. They have mastered the tricky art of edging it through a plane's narrow doorway. It is securely clamped on one side normally occupied by single seats for passengers.

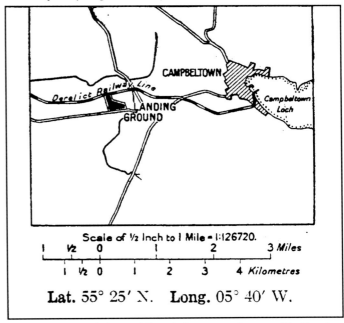

The location and shape of Campbeltown aerodrome at The Strath, as depicted in the 1937 Air Pilot.

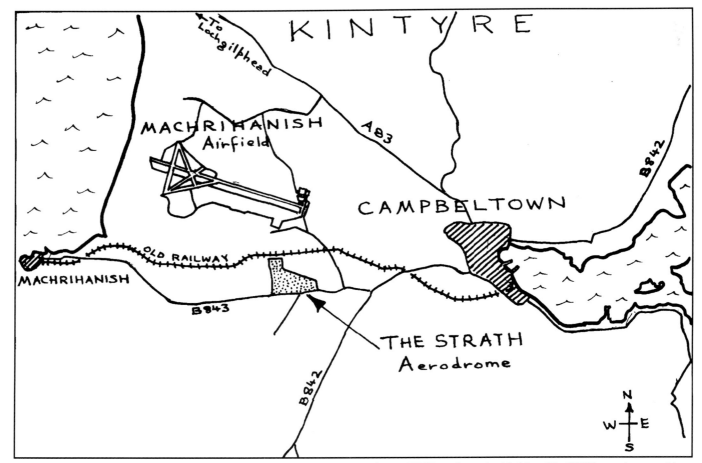

Above: The position of Campbeltown's aerodrome at The Strath, as used up to WWII, is shown in this Map. The WWII aerodrome, with long runways, was laid down at Machrihanish to the north, and is used today as the civil airport (and for NATO purposes).

Below Right: The various aerodromes used on Islay are shown here, starting with Bridgend Sands and Duich Farm (in M&SAF days), and from WWII on, Glenegedale with its hard runways (Author)

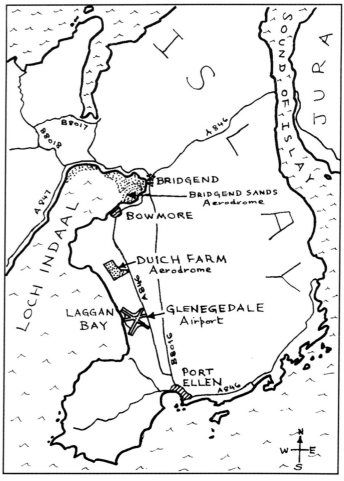

"Contact."

It has taken only five minutes. Barra - or Coll - or Tiree is a patchwork of fields far below. The Nurse is calmly taking the temperature of her new patient and explaining how simple and comfortable this flying business is, and what good doctors they have in Glasgow.

The Wireless Officer is back at his panel. The sharp rasping of the vigilant Morse signals is always in his ear. He gets a reassuring message that all is clear in the troublesome Clyde weather area and passes a chit to the Pilot.

The surface ambulance is waiting at Renfrew. There is an empty bed with aired sheets in a big Glasgow hospital. A surgeon is ready to diagnose and act.

The men in Radio Control on the airfield get through the headphones the plane's letters of identification and then a bold 'dah dah dit dah dit dah dit dah dit dit' - QAL in Morse - which means winding in aerial to land.

The Air Ambulance has been out and back for nearly the 300th time.

Preparing for the Summer schedules

Up to the start of the New Year 1935 George had only had the one aircraft to house at Renfrew - his old Dragon. And he had arranged for the routine maintenance to be carried out by the Scottish Flying Club engineers during this time.

From February 1st 1935, he increased the frequency of the popular Renfrew - Campbeltown - Islay service up to five times a week (Monday to Friday), extending the flights beyond Campbeltown to Islay on Mondays, Wednesdays and Fridays. Then, by mid-March, as traffic seemed so good, he upped it to a twice daily service to both points (Mondays to Fridays) from

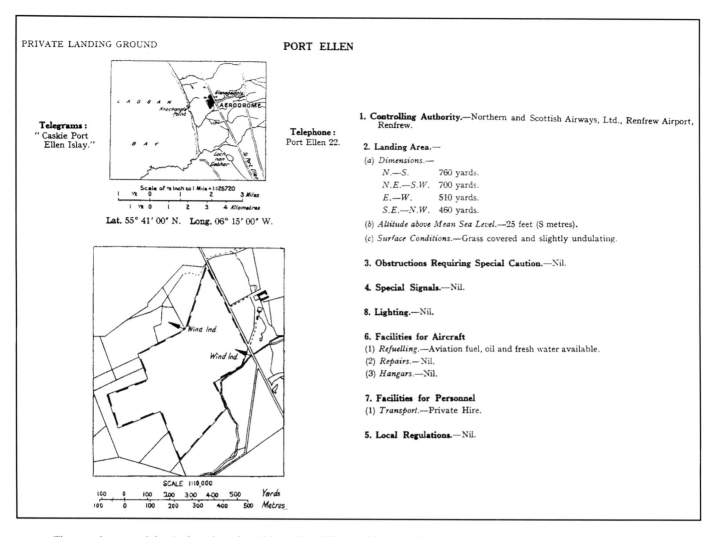

PORT ELLEN

Telegrams :
" Caskie Port
Ellen Islay."

Telephone :
Port Ellen 22.

Lat. 55° 41' 00" N. Long. 06° 15' 00" W.

1. **Controlling Authority.**—Northern and Scottish Airways, Ltd., Renfrew Airport, Renfrew.

2. **Landing Area.**—

(a) *Dimensions.*—

N.—S.	760 yards.
N.E.—S.W.	700 yards.
E.—W.	510 yards.
S.E.—N.W.	460 yards.

(b) *Altitude above Mean Sea Level.*—25 feet (8 metres).

(c) *Surface Conditions.*—Grass covered and slightly undulating.

3. **Obstructions Requiring Special Caution.**—Nil.

4. **Special Signals.**—Nil.

8. **Lighting.**—Nil.

6. **Facilities for Aircraft**

(1) *Refuelling.*—Aviation fuel, oil and fresh water available.

(2) *Repairs.*—Nil.

(3) *Hangars.*—Nil.

7. **Facilities for Personnel**

(1) *Transport.*—Private Hire.

5. **Local Regulations.**—Nil.

The aerodrome on Islay (referred to after 1936 as Port Ellen, or Glenegedale rather than Duich Farm) shown here as depicted in the Air Pilot of 1937. The layout of the fields has changed slightly.

March 15th onwards.

Before the start of the Summer schedules in May, there were several other developments of note, the first concerning Carlisle Airport. As mentioned earlier George had originally been thinking of re-starting this Newcastle - I.O.M. service again in 1935, but cutting out Cramlington altogether and basing the aircraft at Carlisle instead. During the winter Carlisle Corporation, through the medium of its Air Base Committee, had discussed the erection of a hangar to house George Nicholson's aircraft, and had invited tenders, and subsequently accepted one putting in train the construction process. Some time in March, George let the Corporation know that he had now re-based his operation at Renfrew instead, but would still try to fly the Carlisle - I.O.M. sector by scheduling a Renfrew - I.O.M. service and continuing the aircraft across to Cumberland. He had changed his mind for a very good reason, as we shall see. He said, however that he would not now be needing the hangar at Carlisle as the aircraft would return to Renfrew in the afternoon. This did not go down well at all with the Corporation, as their Town Clerk, Frederick G Webster put on record in a series of letters to George!

At the same time the Corporation had agreed to charge NSA's future services at Carlisle by asking for a fee of 6d. per passenger embarked and disembarked - rather than the normal method at this time of charging a fee based on the aircraft weight (on a 'landing' basis only).

George thanked the Town Clerk for the latter and asked him to convey his gratefulness to the Air Base Committee. But he had upset them over the question of the hangar, although they would soon realise why.

In the early part of the New Year, George met Bill Gairdner (who was Brian Lewis' De Havilland aircraft sales agent at Renfrew) during negotiations to take over some of John Sword's aircraft. He liked Bill so much that he invited him to become a Director and Air Superintendent of NSA - which Bill readily accepted - and hence forward Bill acted as Deputy Managing Director in effect, and looked after the aircraft acquisition and passenger marketing side. Being a good pilot, he would often 'fly the line' too when needed.

And so as April approached, the growing airline was getting ready for its first Summer season of scheduled services.

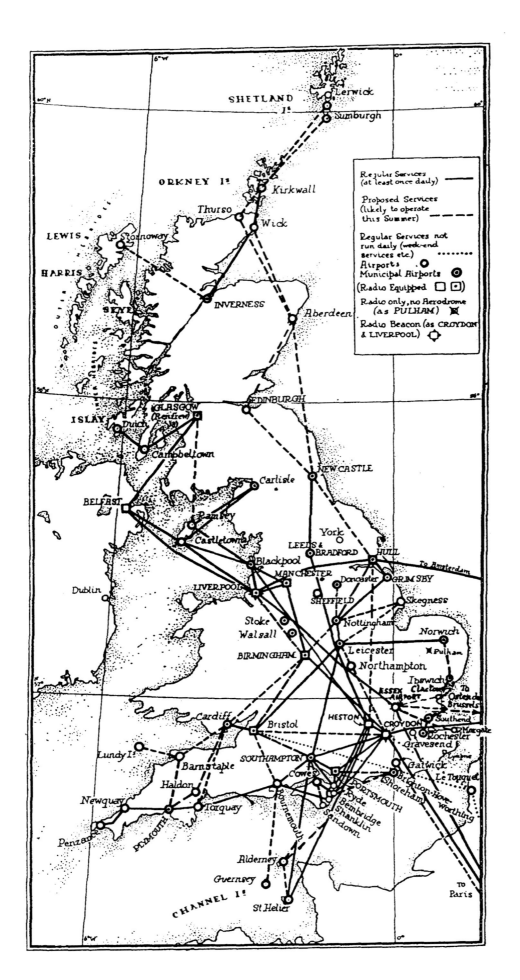

This Map shows the scheduled air route network of U.K. airlines in the Spring of 1935.

In Scotland, the only routes being flown were George Nicholson's Glasgow - Campbeltown - Islay service, and Ted Fresson's Inverness - Wick - Kirkwall run.

CHAPTER 3

Merger with United Airways

As George Nicholson was beginning to put the finishing touches in March to his idea of the Summer Schedules it may well have been Bill Gairdner, his new Deputy with his expansive knowledge of all the UK airlines and in particular, Whitehall Securities and other aviation finance companies who brought a startling idea to him.

Whitehall Securities Ltd was part of the great Pearson organisation built up by the first Lord Cowdray, and was the finance and investment arm of the group. Run by the Hon. Clive Pearson, Lord Cowdray's second son, the decision was taken in the early '30s to start to invest in civil aviation - both the manufacturing and airline side. Control of both Spartan Aircraft Ltd and its subsidiary, Spartan Air Lines Ltd., and Saunders-Roe Ltd was acquired in 1930, and on December 1st 1934 it was revealed that it had also taken a one-third stake in a new holding company (Channel Islands Airways Ltd) formed to operate both Jersey Airways and Guernsey Airways in combination.

Whitehall Securities then began to look around for other possible airlines to buy into, and conceived the idea of amalgamating as many as possible into one new nationwide group. And so a holding company, United Airways Ltd which was intended to be the centrepiece of the scheme, was formed in Blackpool on April 4th 1935 with a capital of £50,000.

United was set up for Whitehall Securities by W.L. Thurgood, the original founder (in December 1933) of Jersey Airways, and the three other Directors were all Whitehall Securities men - J de C. Ballardie, Capt H H Balfour M.C., and W.D.L. Roberts (Capt Balfour later became The Rt. Hon. Lord Balfour of Inchrye, P.C. M.C. M.P. and was Under-Secretary of State for Air from 1938 to 1944).

The Hon. Clive Pearson told Capt Balfour and Co. to start looking now for other possible airlines to merge into United Airways Ltd., and the news rapidly spread 'around the grapevine', bringing in requests for information from small airlines all around the country.

Ted Fresson of Highland Airways Ltd in Inverness saw in it a means of acquiring more funding, whilst still being allowed to operate under his own name. And George Nicholson started

negotiations at the same time - in March 1935 - on the same basis. While talks progressed between the Pearson organisation and George Nicholson, the company set up in Blackpool on April 4th - United Airways - went ahead to develop some local services of its own - under the dynamic leadership of Walter L. Thurgood (who was now running United Airways as well as his own company, Jersey Airways).

United Airways Network

Thus United Airways started a twice daily London (Heston) - Blackpool (Stanley Park) service on April 30th 1935, using four-engined De Havilland DH 86s borrowed from Thurgood's own Jersey Airways. The same day they started a daily Liverpool - Blackpool - Isle of Man, and a three times daily Blackpool - Isle of Man service using Spartan Cruiser aircraft (made by the Spartan Aircraft Co, also owned by Whitehall Securities). Two of the three Blackpool - I.O.M. services were also extended to Carlisle each day. This service was in fact, operated to suit George Nicholson, and to retain the backing of Carlisle Corporation, despite not using their new hangar overnight. George had been negotiating this service with Whitehall Securities during his talks with them between early March and late April.

The aerodrome selected for use in the Isle of Man was a new one, in the north of the island, close to Ramsey. It was called Hall Caine Aerodrome, after the famous Manx novelist Sir Hall Caine, and funded in 1935 by his two sons (both M.P.s) Ralph and Sir Derwent Hall Caine.

Whitehall Securities had appointed a Wing Cmdr. Monk to be their Technical Adviser and Chief Pilot of United Airways. Ronald Cecil Howe Monk has a place of his own in British Civil Aviation because on March 18th 1932 - at the age of 29 - he had started the first domestic scheduled service anywhere in the British Isles using a 4 - passenger Saro Cutty Sark amphibian between the sands at Blackpool and the Bay at Douglas. His firm, British Amphibious Air Lines Ltd., operated without incident to the end of September 1932, and again through the Summer of 1933. He attempted to buy a larger 8 - passenger Saro Cloud

A rare photograph of United Airways' DH84 Dragon G-ACMJ taken at Blackpool's Stanley Park aerodrome in the summer of 1935.

A sister Dragon, G-ACMC, was later transferred to NSA that summer.

amphibian for 1934 - but Whitehall Securities had bought Saunders-Roe (Saro) and were planning a Blackpool - I.O.M. service themselves in the future, and blocked his purchase. By Spring 1935 they had now set up United Airways and took on Monk themselves - holding out the possibility of both land and sea-plane services to the I.O.M. - if Monk could justify them !

Hall Caine aerodrome was selected by Monk as their new landing field in the I.O.M., probably because he was able to negotiate a better overall deal with the Hall Caine family than he could have obtained at Castletown with the operator there - Isle of Man Air Service (bearing in mind he had avoided using them previously by landing his amphibian in Douglas Bay!).

United Airways had inaugurated all its services on April 30th 1935, and Blackpool Corporation had lavishly entertained the VIPs on the first direct flights up from London and in from the I.O.M. and Carlisle - Lt. Col. F. C. Shelmerdine (Director General of Civil Aviation), the Mayors of Heston and Blackpool, Capt. Lamplugh (British Aviation Insurance Corp.), J de C Ballardie, W.D.L. Roberts, Capt H. H. Balfour, W.L. Thurgood, and the Mayors of Carlisle, Douglas and Ramsey, etc. It was competing strongly with the already established Railway Air Services' route London (Croydon) - Birmingham - Manchester - Blackpool, and charging a lot less - £3. 12s. 0d. return (versus the £5. 5s. 0d. of RAS). And United took vicious head-on competition on Blackpool - I.O.M. and Liverpool - Blackpool - I.O.M., with the newly formed 'Manx Airway' - a tripartite agreement between the LMS Railway, The Isle of Man Steam Packet Co. (wary of air competition to its steamers), and RAS, whereby the latter mounted by May 1935 as many as six flights daily on Blackpool (Squire's Gate) - I.O.M ! United was truly struggling hard from the word "go"!

Merger agreed

While all this was commencing, both George Nicholson and Ted Fresson were in steady negotiations about a merger with United Airways Ltd (using the latter merely as a holding company). Whitehall Securities eventually agreed to take them both over, pumping fresh capital in, and providing more aircraft for the carefully approved expansion plans each had put forward to the Pearson organisation.

George had agreed the merger in principle by the end of April (as had Ted) and had been guaranteed the necessary additional aircraft from the Whitehall Securities group (to come from Jersey Airways in fact) for the expanded network he proposed to fly from Renfrew after May 17th. He would have to accept J de C Ballardie from Whitehall Securities as his Chairman, however, but could continue as Managing Director, and operate still under the name of "Northern and Scottish Airlines Ltd". He would have to increase the Capital to £12,000, and allocate all of the increase (of £5,000), plus £2,248 previously unissued (i.e. a total of £7,248) to United Airways' nominees (leaving George and his fellow Directors with £4,752 between them, all in £1 Shares).

The news of the finalisation of all these arrangements was not officially made public until May 23rd 1935, although some 'leaks' to the Press had occurred, and meanwhile George could now concentrate on his expanded Summer scheduled service programme.

More aircraft, more staff

On January 8th 1935 the NSA fleet had expanded from its single original DH 84 Dragon I (G-ACFG) to two, by the purchase from John Sword of his personal DH 84 Dragon I, G-ACJS. This had a toilet and radio fitted to it, and Charles Almond had used it for infrequent Air Ambulance flights until George took it over in January (John Sword having agreed to continue the Air Ambulance at his own expense - as it had been all along - until taken over by someone else).

Knowing of the likely favourable conclusion of the merger talks as April went by, George had taken on more staff to run his airline, and rented the entire four-bay hangar at Renfrew that John Sword's Midland & Scottish Air Ferries had occupied the year before. "Northern and Scottish Airways Ltd" was now painted in large white letters on the hangar walls, in their place.

The staff taken on now included a Chief Engineer, William ("Bill") Mann (who would stay for many years and build up a

Newcomers to Northern and Scottish Airways in the Spring of 1935 included Capt. David Barclay (left) who became Chief Pilot on August 1st (after Charles Almond left on April 30th, and stand-in Tom McNeill on July 31st); William Mann (centre) the Chief Engineer; and John Swann (right) the Traffic Manager. All three stayed on with BEA after 1947. (Henry Vallance)

reputation for engineering excellence and safety second to none); a ground engineer called Ronald Rae, and various young Apprentice ground engineers (of whom the first was a young lad called Gilbert Rae, who would qualify not only for this, but later also as a pilot, flying for NSA and eventually becoming a Senior Captain with B.O.A.C.). There was already an experienced ex RAF pilot, who had flown briefly for M&SAF under Charles Almond on the Renfrew - Campbeltown - Islay service the previous September - Capt. David Barclay (David was to eventually become one of the handful of legendary Scottish pioneer pilots, alongside Fresson, Starling, and Vallance, as we shall see).

The new schedule started on May 17th, when NSA opened a three times weekly service from Renfrew to Hall Caine aerodrome (I.O.M.) on Fridays, Saturdays, and Mondays, using its DH Dragons. Flights left Renfrew at 09.45, and Hall Caine at 11.30. The trip took 75 minutes, and fares were £1. 17s. 6d. single or £3. 5s. 0d. return. (The Renfrew - Campbeltown - Islay service continued on its twice daily basis, as before). Extra I.O.M. flights were also made on demand (usually on Sundays).

On May 23rd, news of the merger of Northern and Scottish Airways with United Airways Ltd was released to the Public, as it was also of the merger of Capt. E.E. Fresson's Highland Airways (of Inverness) with United. Both airlines were allowed to continue under their original names, however, and the promise of expanded route networks and more aircraft was given by these two airlines to their local markets.

The Renfrew - Hall Caine service proved so popular that by May 31st, George Nicholson had upped the frequency to a daily flight. And by the end of June he doubled it again, to twice daily including Sundays. For this he needed more aircraft, and so United Airways supplied him with two more DH 84 Dragon IIs, G-ACMO and G-ACNH, by the end of May, and they were both flying schedules on June 1st 1935. A third Dragon, a Mk I (G-ACMC) arrived a little later in mid-August. All three of these aircraft had originally been bought by Jersey Airways, but recently replaced by more modern aircraft. The last, ('CMC) had been modified by De Havilland's into the prototype Mk II . The first ('CMO) had been the first production Mk II and this series differed from the Mk I by having individually framed windows, faired-in undercarriage struts, and better performance figures.

All this meant that NSA had acquired five Dragons altogether by August 1935, and at the beginning of June George had also bought a DH 83 Fox Moth (G-ACED) from the SMT fleet, and had this fitted out for Air Ambulance work to less accessible places. He had by now completely replaced the old Midland & Scottish Air Ferries at Renfrew, and a new generation had thus taken over from John Sword.

United Airways' Summer 1935 route network based at Blackpool, before being largely transferred to NSA .(Author)

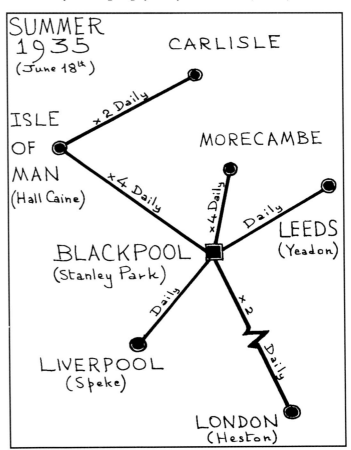

David Barclay's log book page showing (left) joy-riding with M&SAF, and (right) beginning flying with NSA on the Renfrew - Campbeltown run. Note Charles Almond's signature on the left page, David's seven month break between flying for M&SAF and NSA, (and on the right) under the NSA stamp, George Nicholson's signature with the comment: 'A new era!' (Mrs Sheila Harper)

Capt. Charles Bernard ("Tug") Wilson joined NSA in December 1935 for the Western Isles services, later transferring up to Inverness. (Henry Vallance)

Capt. John Annesley Hankins joined NSA in March 1936, later transferring to Inverness. (Henry Vallance)

Another rare United Airways picture - the ex-Imperial Airways Armstrong Whitworth Argosy 2, G-AACJ seen at Blackpool (Stanley Park) in 1935. The aircraft was later to appear in full British Airways colours!

CHAPTER 4

A Grand Consolidation

United Airways continued to expand during that Summer, and it started a four times daily service between Blackpool and Morecambe at the end of June, and a daily service (Sundays included) between Blackpool and Leeds on June 18th (fares £1. 4s. 0d. single, £1. 16s. 0d. return). As well as using two De Havilland DH 84 Dragons, it operated two DH 89 Dragon Rapides, three Spartan Cruisers, and even a single, old, ex-Imperial Airways Armstrong Whitworth Argosy airliner (G-AACJ). Carrying 28 passengers this three-engined, box-sectioned monster with a triple tail and high - perched pilot in the bulbous nose flew joy rides at Blackpool, but also frequently flew to Hall Caine, Ramsey where it created quite a stir !

As the Summer went by a radio station was installed at Renfrew by the Air Ministry, and so at last George had all his aircraft equipped to be able to use air-to-ground radio ('CJS, of course, already had it on board from the John Sword era).

Whitehall Securities was meanwhile planning how to integrate even more airlines together. As George later recounted:
"In those days no subsidy was derived from the Government, but in spite of this and the somewhat low takings in passenger fares, it was a very happy team with a pioneering spirit, and the support given to me at that time was of the highest standard, the staff realising that I was carrying the financial responsibility on my own shoulders. However, we were all prepared to 'sink or swim' and we were still weathering the storm in October 1935 when we merged our interests with four other pioneer air transport companies in Britain".

Highland Airways joins the fold
In the meantime the merging with United Airways had brought immediate benefits to Highland Airways in Inverness, too, and Capt. Ted Fresson was able to give newspaper reporters some idea of other future possibilities as well. The *Scottish Daily Express* for Friday 7th June 1935 stated:

"SCOTTISH AIR MERGER
FLYING BOATS TO BE USED FOR STORNOWAY ROUTE
HIGHLAND COMPANY JOINS £4,000,000 COMBINE
by Gordon Bishop

Flying boats for Scottish passengers.
Stornoway as an airport of international importance
New air mail route from Aberdeen to Wick, Kirkwall, Orkney, and Shetland. Services to start from Ullapool across Great Minch.

This was yesterday's development - which I forecast exclusively a month ago - in civil aviation when United Airways effected a merger with Highland Airways, Inverness.

United Airways are now the biggest internal air route operators in Britain. They are backed by Whitehall Securities Corporation with £4,000,000 capital.

Highland Airways are pioneers of aviation in the North of Scotland and although now members of the giant air combine, will still be controlled by Captain E. E. Fresson and a local board of directors.

Big developments are planned, including the use of a giant amphibian for the first time on any Scottish air route.

Captain Fresson told me yesterday that considerable expansion was to take place immediately. Soon a new air service will be tried between Inverness and Stornoway via Ullapool, Ross-shire.

Car Journey
In the initial stages the journey from Inverness to Ullapool will be by car. Passengers will then join the new land and water air lines for the Great Minch sea crossing.

Plans to build an airport at Stornoway are to be considered.

The completion of Sumburgh airport, Shetland, is to be hurried on and as soon as the Air Ministry wireless installation is completed Aberdeen will be linked with Shetland.

Next year it is expected that a direct service between Aberdeen and Stornoway will be run.

Up-to-date ground and aircraft wireless will enable Highland Airways to use a blind flying route. After the air liners cross the mountains, and are well above the ocean, they will be able to descend to sea level and their destination by wireless control.

A new air mail contract is to be entrusted to Highland Airways. It is from Shetland to Kirkwall and Aberdeen.

New southbound routes are to be considered only if time and money can be saved.

Meanwhile, the company have arranged their exisiting services to co-operate with the main railway services from Aberdeen.

Mr W.D.L. Roberts and Mr J de C Ballardie effected the merger on behalf of United Airways yesterday in Inverness and immediately left for Glasgow, where further conferences will take place.

Northern and Scottish Airways, also members of the air combine, will now consider plans for the linking up of Glasgow, Oban, and the Outer Hebrides."

The *Press and Journal* for June 8th 1935 contained more details and illustrated how Ted Fresson had entered into the combine in order to fight off competition from Eric Gandar Dower's Aberdeen Airways (based at Dyce, Aberdeen where he steadfastly refused to allow other airlines to use the same facilities). Fresson in fact, had been approached by Gandar Dower for a possible merger between the two, but feeling aggrieved by some of the Aberdeen - based airline's antics, had opted for the larger resources of the Whitehall Securities group:

"NEW PHASE IN NORTH AIR ROUTE 'WAR'

Highland Airways Merged With Great London Concern.
New Services Coming.
Aberdeen to Lerwick: Inverness to Lewis:
Shetland Mail Contract

The "war" between Highland Airways and Aberdeen Airways in connection with the Aberdeen-Orkney service has entered on a new phase.

An important merger which will result in extensive developments of air routes in the North-East and Highlands is announced in Inverness.

Highland Airways Ltd., pioneer of air travel in the North-East, has merged with United Airways, an influential company backed by the Whitehall Securities Group with its huge resources .

Among the new routes which will be developed is an Aberdeen-to-Shetland service via Kirkwall.

A Service between Inverness and Stornoway will also be started. The merger will ensure co-operation with subsidiary companies with considerable benefit to the public. Highland Airways will still retain its name, and the organisation will remain under the management of Captain E.E. Fresson.

Details of the merger were fully explained to me to-day by Captain Fresson, managing director of Highland Airways, Ltd.

Particular Significance.

The merger, said Captain Fresson had particular significance. It would place the south in direct contact with the north, but routes would only be developed where a distinct saving of time and expense could be effected through air travel.

Thus, for the moment, the Company's route from Kirkwall to Aberdeen would connect at Aberdeen with the express trains leaving and arriving from the south.

Obviously, when passengers could leave London at night by a comfortable express train, arriving at Aberdeen in the early morning, they would be better served by being able to make direct connection by air from Aberdeen to Kirkwall and Shetland than by flying the whole way from London at considerable extra expense.

Airways Time Table

Mr Fresson explained that the time-table of his Company's Kirkwall-Aberdeen service enabled passengers to leave Kirkwall in the morning and be in London the following morning, whereas if the whole journey were made by air, passengers would arrive in London on the evening of the day on which they left Kirkwall, but would have to make an all night stay in London at extra expense before they could start business on the following day.

The same applied to persons travelling north from London; passengers leaving on the night express from London could be in Kirkwall just after lunch, thus saving a night's stay in Aberdeen.

Future Expansion

In regard to future expansion of services, Captain Fresson assured me that considerable expansion would take place on routes which offered possibilities of development.

The first move, he said, would be to connect Aberdeen with Shetland via Kirkwall. The Company's landing ground at Sumburgh was nearing completion, and as soon as the wireless station, which the Air Ministry had promised to provide, was available, the Aberdeen service would be extended to Lerwick.

"The next route to be developed through the merger " continued Captain Fresson, "will be between Inverness and Stornoway.

A trial service will in all likelihood be operated next month with an Amphibian seaplane operating from Ullapool to Stornoway, the connection between Inverness and Ullapool being by road.

Ullapool Landing Ground

"Should this service prove that there is a demand for an air service from Inverness to Stornoway, an aerodrome will be built at Stornoway with an emergency landing ground at Ullapool. A direct service would then be run next year with land machines in conjunction with the necessary radio ground organisation.

"By this means", Captain Fresson explained, "the route can be operated as a blind flying route, the aircraft flying either in or above the clouds across the Wester Ross mountains and being directed down on either side of the mountains by radio control".

Asked whether Highland Airways contemplated running farther south, Captain Fresson said that it was felt that the company's time-table in conjunction with that of the railway was so good that only a little time could be saved, at extra expense, by connecting the cities in the South of Scotland by air.

Mail from Shetland

The Aberdeen-Wick-Kirkwall service which has recommenced from the Company's new aerodrome at Kintore, with the Aberdeen base at the Palace Hotel, is operating smoothly, and negotiations have now been completed by which Highland Airways will be entrusted with the Shetland mail contract over the Kirkwall-Aberdeen section. "

Hillmans Airways' DH84 Dragon G-ACAN is seen here parked tail on to a stiff breeze in front of the magnificent Scottish Flying Club offices and accommodation built on the east side of the main hangars at Renfrew. John Sword, and now George Nicholson, rented offices here. (Eric Starling)

RECORD OF FLIGHTS.

Date.	Aircraft. Type.	Reg. No.	Journey.	Time in Air. Hrs.	Min.	Remarks.
			Brought forward ...	513	45	
24·8·35	DH84.	G-ACJS	Renfrew – Islay	2	30	
25·8·35	DH84	G-ACJS	,, – Islay	1	15	
	,,	G-ACFG	I.O.M – Renfrew	1	10	
26·8·35	,,	G-ACJS	Renfrew – Islay	1	35	
27·8·35	,,	G-ACJS	Renfrew – Islay	2	40	
28·8·35	,,	G-ACJS	Renfrew – I.O.M	2	20	
29·8·35	,,	G-ACFG	Renfrew – I.O.M	2	10	
30·8·35	DH83	G-ACED	Renfrew – Balmoral	1	45	KGV.
			Balmoral – Dyce		45	
			Carried forward ...	529	55	

Whitehall Securities trump card

Whitehall Securities now played a trump card in their search for a united nationwide grouping of airlines under their control. As the Summer went by, rumours abounded of moves at Hillman's Airways in Essex to expand dramatically by merging their interests with others, and flying to new European capital city destinations.

Hillman's real company name was Hillman's Saloon Coaches and Airways Ltd., and it had been set up by the subsequently legendary Edward Hillman on November 12th 1931. It had begun its first scheduled service on April 1st 1932 between Romford (Maylands) and Clacton (Essex). This was the nation's second scheduled operation, following Wing Cmdr R.C.H. Monk's Blackpool - Douglas start on March 18th 1932 - (see earlier).

Hillman had gradually expanded his air network, linking it up with John Sword's Midland & Scottish Air Ferries in 1934 to give a London - Belfast/Glasgow service, and a Glasgow - London - Paris through connecting service (an imaginative step forward in air services). With the demise of M&SAF, his airline had consolidated services on the London - Liverpool - Belfast - Glasgow route and in 1935 opened new Liverpool - Manchester - Hull, Stapleford (its home base) - Ostend - Brussels - Antwerp, and Stapleford - Ramsgate - Le Zoute routes, and began to consider opening a London - Amsterdam - Berlin and Oslo service.

Edward Hillman had died suddenly from a heart attack on December 31st 1934, just when his airline was in the midst of its expansion, and his son Edward ("Sonny") Hillman succeeded him briefly as Managing Director. But Edward resigned on July 21st 1935, after becoming disheartened by strictures the financiers behind the airline were now imposing (due to heavy losses being incurred), and later became a professional airline pilot (and RAF pilot during WWII) himself.

The financial adviser behind Hillman's Airways Ltd. (the new name since a re-capitalisation on December 12th 1934, just before Edward Hillman Senior's death) was the d'Erlanger merchant banking business founded by its Chairman, Baron Emile Beaumont d'Erlanger, whose son, Gerard John Regis Leo d'Erlanger was also on the board (and had trained as a Chartered Accountant). The latter now became closely involved with running Hillmans Airways Ltd.

The airline had been planning to move into the brand new Gatwick Airport later in 1935, but the d'Erlanger bank now approached Whitehall Securities in August 1935 to see whether the two groups could combine. Hillman's was now the second largest British airline, (after Imperial Airways), and Whitehall Securities and the Pearson organisation now thrashed out an agreement which would produce the largest British domestic and North European carrier to date.

By the end of August formalities were being rapidly agreed for United Airways and Spartan Air Lines (the two wholly - owned subsidiaries of Whitehall Securities) to merge together, and then absorb Hillman's Airways into the same organisation. To do this Whitehall Securities registered: "Allied British Airways Ltd". as a new holding company on September 30th 1935, then on October 1st this then took over both United Airways and Spartan Air Lines.

The merger of Hillman's Airways was meantime being agreed in detail, and so the next step was to change the name of the holding company on October 29th 1935 to simply " British Airways Ltd" (dropping the word "Allied"). By the time all the details of taking over Hillman's had been worked out, it was December 11th 1935, and on this date Hillman's Airways Ltd., was completely absorbed into the main vehicle of Whitehall Securities Ltd - British Airways Ltd.

This grandly titled huge new combination of UK airline companies thus embraced the operations now of: Highland Airways Ltd., Northern and Scottish Airways Ltd., Spartan Air Lines, Channel Islands Airways Ltd. (controlling Jersey Airways and Guernsey Airways), United Airways Ltd. and Hillman's Airways Ltd. W.L. Thurgood still had an interest in Jersey Airways and only in July 1939 did he sell this to Whitehall Securities, to give them 50% control (the other 50% was held by the Railways).

Both Whitehall Securities and the d'Erlanger banking interests each put up £50,000 of capital into the new British Airways Ltd., giving it a starting base of £100,000. As *The Aeroplane* magazine said at the time: *"This seems to be a further guarantee against the swamping of air transport in this country by a monopoly dominated by the railways!"*

The routes of the new airline now formed a system extending over 2,200 miles in length, serving more than 25 cities in Britain and Western Europe, and the resources of British Airways now exceeded £200,000 in tangible assets (aircraft and equipment), and cash.

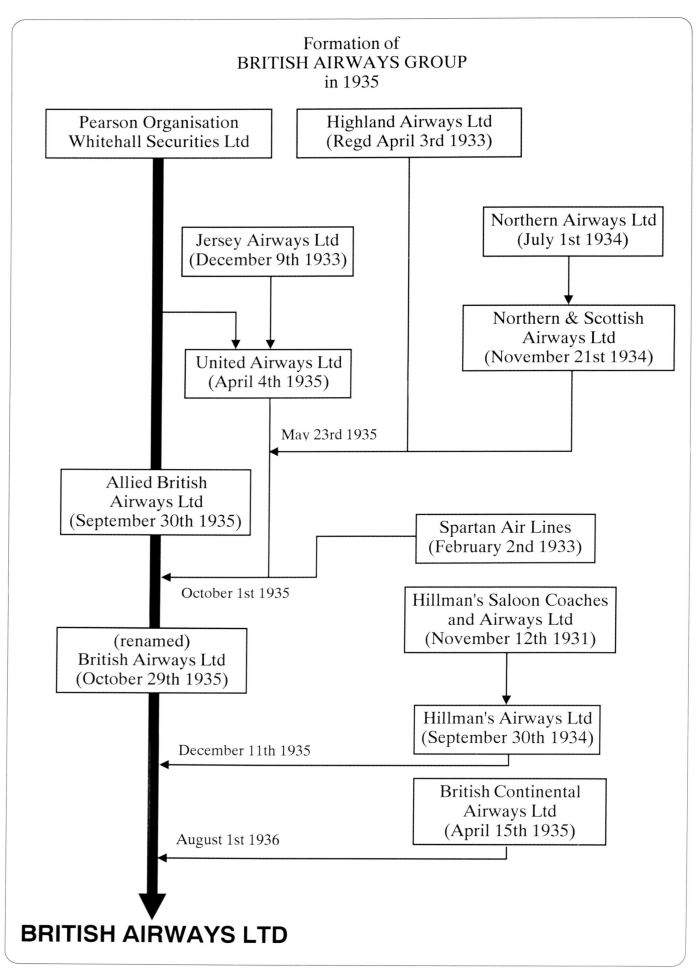

Formation of
BRITISH AIRWAYS GROUP
in 1935

CHAPTER 5

Expansion to the Western Isles

With the full backing of firstly United Airways Ltd., and by the end of the year the new 'parent' company, British Airways Ltd., George Nicholson now planned further extensions to his routes from Glasgow.

Like the other sister companies in the group, his airline was still allowed to use its original name to trade under - at least for another two years. (The only exception to this was Hillman's, whose name was now completely replaced by "British Airways", and henceforward traded under this name, concentrating on international services to Europe, flying out of its new base at Heston after January 1st 1936).

During 1935, George had tried to get away from his desk with David Barclay - who from August 1st had been promoted to Chief Pilot of the airline (Charles Almond having left) - to make some survey flights of the Western Isles. David Barclay had flown a number of charter flights during the summer, and on September 2nd 1935 he took the DH Fox Moth G-ACED on another, this time to bring a passenger back from Skye. He left Renfrew at 0400 after getting Gilbert Rae (the Apprentice ground engineer) up to see him off and eventually landed in a field behind the Broadford Hotel. He stayed there overnight and left next day to fly the customer back to Glasgow.

Then, coincidentally on September 9th, David had to fetch an Ambulance patient from Skye, and so he took the Fox Moth to Broadford again for the pick up.

Having seen something of the area around Broadford by now, he took George Nicholson there in the Dragon G-ACMO on September 11th, and landed it on the sands just to the north-east of Broadford Pier. This was probably only the second time a DH Dragon had landed in Skye (the first being by Jimmy Orrell on an ambulance flight to Uig for M&SAF on July 19th 1933).

On October 4th David took George up again, this time across the Island of Mull in Sword's old Dragon (G-ACJS) to Tiree, where, after considerable low flying around the island, he eventually made a landing on the beach in Gott Bay. After a survey by road around the small island, they flew back to Renfrew later in the day.

Next came a rather longer survey trip, on October 14th -17th, when they flew in 'CJS again, firstly to Skye, then two days later to Harris (the southern end of the Isle of Lewis whose main town was Stornoway), and down to South Uist in the afternoon of October 16th, returning to Skye in the evening. After another night in Skye they finally returned to Renfrew on the 17th.

This trip had been much longer for two reasons. George had spent a lot of time in Skye surveying more possible landing strips with David Barclay, as they were not entirely happy with the area around Broadford - at least for regular landings for a scheduled service operation. In the event, they had visited a number of sites across Skye, but they had settled on a large field at an unusual spot - just below Glen Brittle House at the head of Loch Brittle on the south-west coast of the island. This sheltered inlet was right in the shadow of the Cuillin Hills, but (surprisingly) was almost equally distant from all centres of population on the island - Uig, Portree, and Dunvegan, to the north, or Broadford, Kyleakin and Armadale to the east. But above all, its situation allowed for an uninterrupted approach by air over the sea from the south-west and creeping-in under the lip of any overcast which covered the Cuillins or the rest of Skye (particularly Broadford). There was far more area for a clear let-down here, than there was anywhere else in Skye in bad weather (which was usually blowing from the south-west anyway).

Secondly, the shorter visits to Harris and South Uist were to try to establish points to extend the projected Skye service to, at a later date. The site where they had landed in Harris was at Northton, again on the south-west corner, and on a large field just north of the village to the west side of the A859 road. This proved to need no more surveying, as it suited their requirements, as did the field they landed on at South Uist - between Askernish House and the beach, on the west side of the A 865 road at the south end of the island, and just 4 miles north of Lochboisdale.

They did not visit Stornoway at this time because their competitor at Renfrew, J. Glyn-Roberts and his West of Scotland Air Services Ltd had recently negotiated a deal with the Stornoway Trust (which controlled the rights to the local land

David Barclay's first landing on the beach at Gott Bay on the isle of Tiree at 06.00 on October 4th 1935 in Dragon G-ACJS is recorded in this page of his log-book. Interestingly, on 16th September - at the top of the page - David flew Lord and Lady Londonderry and party from Inverness to Dornoch and return. (Mrs Sheila Harper)

RECORD OF FLIGHTS.

Date.	Aircraft.		Journey.	Time in Air.		Remarks.
	Type.	Reg. No.		Hrs.	Min.	
			Brought forward ...	572	10	
16·9·35	DH. 84	G-ACFG	Inverness - Dornoch	-	20	Lord & Lady Londonderry + party.
··	··	··	Dornoch - Inverness	-	25	
··	··	··	Inverness - Renfrew	1	45	
30·9·35	DH 87A	G-ADBF	Local.	-	20	
1·10·35	DH 87A	G-ADDF	··	-	15	
2·10·35	DH 84	G-ACJS	Renfrew - Islay	2	25	
3·10·35	DH 84	G-ACMC	·· Local	-	20	Wireless Trials.
4·10·35	DH 84	G-ACJS	Renfrew TIREE	1	05	TIREE
··	··	··	TIREE - RENFREW	1	-	Beach Landing
		Gott Bay	Beach Landing			-6AM,
			Carried forward ...	580	05	

25

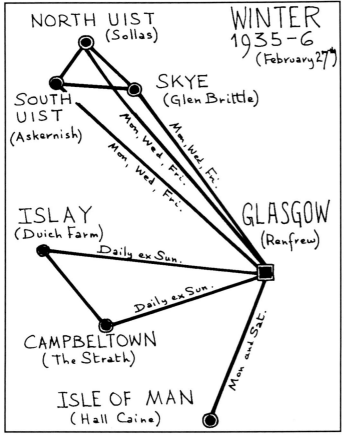

NORTH UIST
(Sollas)

WINTER
1935-6
(February 27ᵗʰ)

SKYE
(Glen Brittle)

SOUTH
UIST
(Askernish)

Mon, Wed, Fri.
Mon, Wed, Fri.
Mon, Wed, Fri.

ISLAY
(Duich Farm)

GLASGOW
(Renfrew)

Daily ex Sun.

Daily ex Sun.

CAMPBELTOWN
(The Strath)

Mon and Sat.

ISLE OF MAN
(Hall Caine)

NSA's 1935-36 winter network of services shows the airline in mid-development to the Western Isles, with the focus on Glen Brittle, Skye (Author)

and use of the harbour there) giving him a 5 - year exclusive right to start a Glasgow - Stornoway air service, much to the detriment of George Nicholson's NSA. (This did not apply to an Inverness - Stornoway service, however, and it was left to Ted Fresson in the North to try to organise an aerodrome at Stornoway).

Finding suitable airfields was one thing, but negotiating for the right to use them for scheduled services, was quite another, of course. When the landowner's permission had been secured, it

was frequently necessary to consult the 'local grazing committee', consisting of anything up to a dozen or more local crofters, all of whom had to give their unanimous decision in favour. This resulted in many meetings, spread over a long period of time, and sometimes a satisfactory conclusion was only reached with the sudden appearance of a few bottles of single malt - thoughtfully provided for such an occasion !

Schedule to Skye

Having completed negotiations for the first of these new airstrips NSA started a twice - weekly return service between Glasgow (Renfrew) and Skye (Glen Brittle) on December 5th 1935. Radio Transmission (R/T) facilities had just come into use at Renfrew on October 26th and David Barclay was now able to make use of these whilst flying out to the islands, or back into Glasgow, which was a step in the right direction.

The service was planned to operate on Tuesdays and Thursdays, leaving Renfrew at 09.30 and arriving at Glen Brittle at 11.00; returning at 12.00 from Skye, and arriving back at Renfrew at 13.30. Fares were set at £3. 5s. 0d single, or £6. 10s. 0d. return.

As *The Aeroplane* magazine for December 11th said:
"The distance by a direct route across Loch Linnhe and close by Ben Nevis is about 125 miles, but the journey takes most of 2 days by surface transport.

"As soon as landing grounds can be found in North and South Uist, the service will be extended to these islands. Rather an interesting point showing the cost of travelling in these islands is that to go from Lochbosidale, South Uist to Lochmaddy, North Uist by car and pony takes practically all day, a distance of 40 miles, and the cost is £5. 5s. 0d. for the journey.

"Communications are pretty bad from the islands to the mainland, and the ridiculous situation arises that Mr Nicholson's booking agents will have to communicate with each other by using carrier pigeons - unless someone can think of a brighter idea. Thus does one have to operate aeroplanes in this year of grace !

"Now that Mr Nicholson's company is associated with Highland Airways Ltd and the other three companies of the British Airways group, he will have the resources to build up the services which his part of Scotland needs".

David Barclay's log-book shows his official inauguration of Glasgow - Skye services on December 5th 1935, carrying Lord Inverclyde in Dragon G-ACFG. (Mrs Sheila Harper)

RECORD OF FLIGHTS.

Date.	Aircraft.		Journey.	Time in Air.		Remarks.
	Type.	Reg. No.		Hrs.	Min.	
			Brought forward ...	620	20	
2.12.35	DH84	G-ACNH	Renfrew - Islay	2	25	R/T. Snow storms
4.12.35	DH84	G-ACMO	" "	1	55	R/T.
5.12.35	DH84	G-ACFG	Renfrew - Skye	1	35	R/T Inauguration of
--	--	-	Skye - Renfrew	1	35	R/T Skye service Lord Inverclyde
7.12.35	DH84	G-ACNH	Renfrew - Islay	2	5	R/T.
10.12.35	DH84	G-ACFG	Renfrew - Skye	1	5	R/T.
--	--	--	Skye - Renfrew	1	25	R/T
11.12.35	DH83	G-ACED	Renfrew - Prestwick	-	20	
--	--	-	Prestwick - Renfrew	-	20	
			Carried forward ...	633	00	

26

One of the most evocative photographs ever taken of George Nicholson's airline, showing Capt. David Barclay flying Lord Inverclyde and his party in Dragon G-ACFG on the inaugural service to Skye (Glen Brittle). The picture, taken from a sister Dragon over the hills north of Helensburgh, looks south to the Isle of Arran. (John Stroud Collection)

So Thursday December 5th dawned, and David Barclay took George Nicholson, Lord Inverclyde and the VIPs in Dragon G-ACFG, taking 1 hour 35 mins for the trip to Glen Brittle, and exactly the same time for the return. A second Dragon was flown to take a load of fare-paying passengers there, just behind 'CFG.

Both pilots were able to use the new R/T at Glasgow for most of the trip, and David Barclay flew the service the next Tuesday and Thursday in the same aircraft.

On Tuesday December 17th 1935, (the fourth time of operating), Barclay extended the service for the first time to Askernish in South Uist, flying a triangular route and returning directly from Askernish to Renfrew, and using both R/T and W/T (Wireless Transmission) this time. This was by way of a practice run, carrying an Air Ministry official to check and license the field for them.

On Thursday and Friday, January 2nd and 3rd 1936, David Barclay and George flew around the route again, but staying over-night at South Uist and then visiting North Uist next day, looking for an airfield there. They decided a field at Sollas, on the north side of the A865, and just east of the hamlet of the same name (in the north of the island) was the most suitable, and so on Saturday January 4th David flew the Air Ministry Inspector out around the complete route, to make sure everything was satisfactory and ready for licensing, and, checking himself on the arrangements for handling passengers.

On January 14th 1936 David flew around the full circuit again - the last time prior to the official inaugural to South Uist. But on the way back he called in addition at a field at Oban - looking again for another possible scheduled service airstrip. He was not very satisfied, however, with the terrain at Oban, or the difficult approaches in bad weather.

So, on January 21st, David took the Dragon 'CFG around the Renfrew - Skye - South Uist - Renfrew circuit, inaugurating the passenger service to South Uist (Askernish). From here on, the service operated twice weekly, on Tuesdays and Thursdays around this circuit, always routeing back directly from Askernish to Renfrew. But George was trying to get Sollas into operation as soon as possible in North Uist, and had designs on linking up Barra as well.

On Wednesday, February 5th 1936 David Barclay took George and they flew off on another 3 - day survey, this time flying to Skye, South Uist, and then across to Barra, where they landed 'CFG on the sands at Tàigh Mhór, in the sheltered bay on the north-east end of the island. Afterwards he flew back to South Uist, then Skye and Renfrew. The round-trip took them 6 1/2 hours flying over the 3 - day period.

David repeated the exercise in one day on February 11th, making the six stops this time, in a period of 3hrs 55 mins. and using R/T and W/T communications.

Spartan Cruisers and North Uist.
Back on October 23rd 1935, David Barclay had been introduced to one of the new Spartan Cruiser III aircraft in the joint Spartan Air Lines/British Airways fleet, when David was down at Heston. It had been piloted by one of United's Senior Pilots, P.W. Lynch-Blosse, and David had made eight landings in it, under Lynch-Blosse's careful eye. This particular Spartan Cruiser, G-ADEL, was one of three of the latest Mk III types that had been delivered to Spartan Air Lines, but re-allocated later to British Airways. David had conveyed his liking of it to George Nicholson and there was no doubt that this metal 8-seat low-wing, three-engined airliner would be ideal for speed, comfort and safety purposes, over routes such as NSA's coming Western Isles routes.

On February 19th 1936, therefore, a Spartan Cruiser II (G-ACYL) arrived at Renfrew from the Group's combined fleet, allocated now to NSA to place on their expanding Hebridean services. David flew it for an hour, then next day, Thursday February 20th he operated the Cruiser II on a Renfrew - North Uist (Sollas) - South Uist (Askernish) - Skye survey flight with an Air Ministry official, Mr Campbell, to check the suitability of the Spartan for the difficult approaches to those airstrips and the effectiveness of its different Marconi radio installation. They returned from Skye next day.

David landed at another potential strip, at Skeabost, Skye in the Dragon 'CFG on February 25th. He flew there after landing first at Glen Brittle on the normal Tuesday schedule, to see whether Skeabost might provide a better site. But evidently it did not, possibly because of difficulty with getting permission to use it regularly, although it was closer to Portree and just off the Uig road, to the north of the town.

The official inaugural to North Uist (Sollas) occurred on Thursday February 27th, and all three stops - Skye, North and South Uist - were included from now on. But in order to provide an equal measure of speed to the different stops, on Tuesdays the service ran: Renfrew - Skye - North Uist - South Uist - Renfrew; and on Thursdays; Renfrew - South Uist - North Uist - Skye - Renfrew!

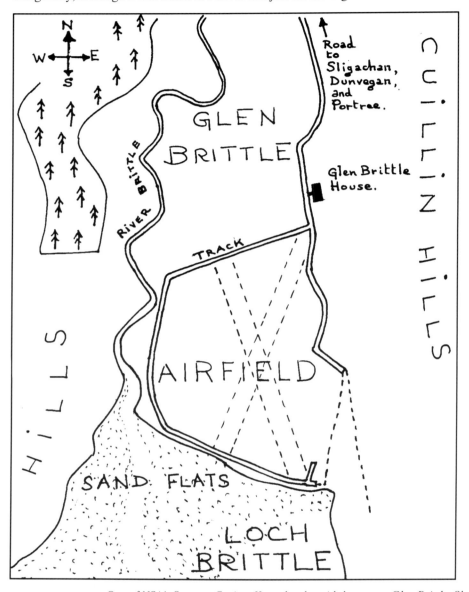

Map of Glen Brittle aerodrome, which became the focal point of NSA's route development to the Western Isles.

Landings were normally made from the north-east end of the waterside field, the airliners having to fly up the Glen and turn carefully onto final approach. (Author)

One of NSA's Spartan Cruiser IIs under the mid-day sun at Glen Brittle, Skye, in the summer of 1936. The hills behind lie to the north west of the airstrip. (John Stroud Collection)

SKYE MISCELLANY

Left: Ewen MacRae was NSA's Aerodrome Manager at Glen Brittle. His family lived in the large house nearby, and he cleared the field, organised passenger transport, and fuelled the aircraft from a tank on the rear of his 1927 Morris Oxford car. (Ewen MacRae)

Below: The NSA Dragon G-ACMO, snapped at Glen Brittle by Ewen MacRae on a spring morning, looking towards the north-west of the airstrip. (Ewen MacRae)

Arriving passengers at Glen Brittle airstrip wait whilst NSA Dragon G-ACMO is prepared. Judging from the heavy clothes and long shadows, these two snapshots show the morning service on arrival directly from Glasgow. (Ewen MacRae)

Ewen MacRae's 1927 Morris Oxford with fuel tank on the back to replenish aircraft, seen at Glen Brittle with arriving passengers. (Ewen MacRae)

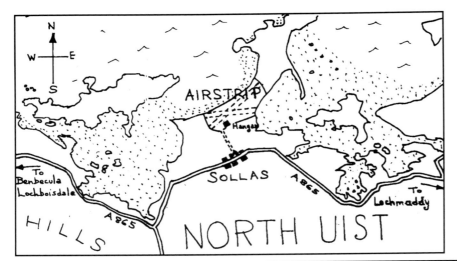

Left: Map showing the position of Sollas aerodrome, North Uist, as used by NSA. A hangar and radio station were erected there, and aircraft kept overnight. (Author)

Right Map giving position of the beach on Barra where NSA began scheduled services. The receding sea left a very firm sandy bay, and is used even today by the airlines. (Author)

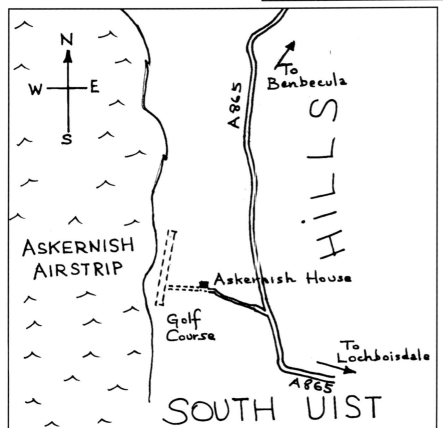

Left: Map showing the location of Askernish airstrip on South Uist, as used by NSA. (Author)

CHAPTER 6

A re-allocation of Group Routes

George Nicholson had by now set up most of the necessary infrastructure which any successful airline must have in order to properly cater for its passengers. Thus he had opened a sales and ticket office at 153, Hope Street, Glasgow (just north of St. Vincent Street), which also doubled as an airport check-in office, as his literature stated: *"This is made necessary, because the point of air departure or arrival is uncertain owing to the frequency of fog during the winter months at Renfrew Aerodrome, the official airport for Glasgow".*

Thus he insisted that no bookings could be made at Renfrew itself, nor passengers join the services there without previous arrangement (and checking -in) at the Hope Street Office.

NSA provided motor car transport to/from Hope Street, passengers having to check-in 15 mins before departure of the car - which was given on the air time-table (and was generally 45 minutes before Renfrew flight departure). Cars into town from Renfrew generally only took 30 mins.

In the Isle of Man, check-in was at the Hall Caine airport itself, to which several local bus services ran from all parts of the Island. At Campbeltown, cars ran between Kintyre Aerodrome (re-named from its original title of The Strath) and the White Hart Hotel in town, taking 10 minutes for the journey each way. It was free of charge. Also, local buses ran past the Aerodrome, between Campbeltown and Machrihanish. But NSA also offered private cars to be at the Aerodrome to meet passengers, if booked in advance, for a fee of 1s. 6d. for telegraphic costs, and 2s. 6d. hire deposit. (The deposit of 2s. 6d was credited by the driver on surrender of the voucher when the passenger settled with him at his destination).

Bookings in Kintyre could only be effected at No. 11 Union Street, Campbeltown, as could check-in on the day, unless ticket and baggage weights were previously reported - when passengers could report at the Aerodrome. In Islay, bookings, ticketing and check-in were all made only at the Duich Farm aerodrome itself.

Air Mail contract; Barra etc, added.

In February, Northern and Scottish Airways was awarded an Air Mail contract to carry mails on the Isle of Man - Liverpool route. The mail had originally been carried by Railway Air Services on this route for the two months of August - September 1934, but had then passed it on to Blackpool and West Coast Air Services from February to October 1935. From November 1st 1935, United Airways had secured the Post Office contract, but now, they prepared to pass it on to NSA under the re-grouping that was taking place since amalgamation. In the event NSA operated the service between Hall Caine and Speke from July 1st 1936 (see later).

In April 1936, David Barclay flew the Cruiser II, G-ACYL into Barra on the 9th on the way back from South Uist to Renfrew, and on May 26th he visited both Barra and Benbecula on an inspection of landing grounds, in the Spartan Cruiser II G-ACSM (just acquired from the group's pool of aircraft). The call at Barra this time evoked a request to air ambulance a patient out - which he did.

Barra then seems to have been added 'on demand' as a call on the routine triangular Western Isles route as from Wednesday June 10th (with Thursday June 18th being the next call). David Barclay had also landed on Harris on June 2nd in G-ACSM , for the first time adding this 'on demand' call there to the schedule around the Isles. Harris (Northton aerodrome) was always advertised hence-forward as an : *"Extension from North Uist on demand",* but it would not be long before Barra would go into the Winter 1936-37 time-tables as a proper advertised stop.

Tiree was added to the Renfrew - Islay service to form a triangular route on July 1st 1936, David Barclay flying a newly acquired DH Dragon Rapide, G-ADDF on the inaugural. And Benbecula was finally added to the Western Isles service 'on demand' at first, on July 2nd1936. David inaugurated this service on the Spartan Cruiser II, G-ACSM.

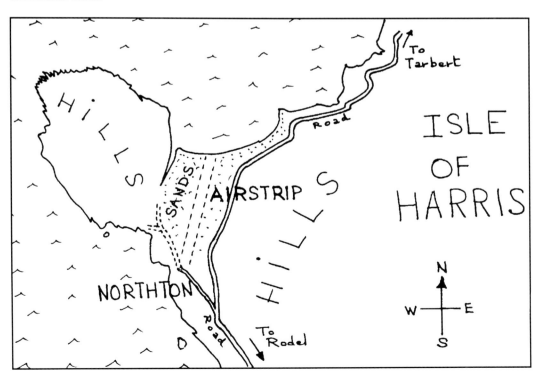

The Map shows the location of the landing strip at Northton, Harris, used by NSA. This was on a sandy bay, alongside low-lying marshes. (Author)

| | | | | | Time carried forward : | 1719 hr 5 min | | |

Date and Hour	Aircraft Type and No.	Pilot	Passenger(s)	Height	Hours	Mins	Course	REMARKS
23 June	G-ACSM	Self	Hughes W.T.O	6000	5	55	Renfrew - Skye - Barra - Uist - Renfrew	
24 ~	G-ADBU	..	—		2	5	Renfrew - Islay - Renfrew	
26, ~	G-ATDV	~	G. Rae		2	-	Renfrew - Kulross - Renfrew	
24 ~	S-ACSM	~	—		—	20	Local Wireless Test	
27 ~	G-ACAC	~	—		—	30	Local Airframe Engine + Wireless Test	
29 ~	G-ACDF	~	—		1	45	Renfrew - Islay - Renfrew	W.T. and R/T.
30 ~	G-ACSM	~	F.H. Hughes W.T.O		5	45	Uist - Skye - Renfrew	D Barclay Chief Pilot
			Total		1737	25		
							30.6.36.	NORTHERN AND SCOTTISH AIRWAYS LIMITED, RENFREW AERODROME
July 1	G-ADDF	~	—	4000	1	30	Renfrew - Islay Renfrew	R/T.
1	S-ADDF	~	—	3000	2	25	Renfrew - Islay Renfrew - ISLAY - Renfrew	R/T.
2	G.ACSM	..	F.R Hughes	—	4	20	Renfrew - N.Uist Benbecula S.Uist Skye Renfrew	W/T. + R/T.
3	G-ADBU	~	—	—	1	35	Renfrew - C'Town Islay - C'Town Renfrew	R/T.
3	G-ADBU	"	—		1	10	Renfrew - Islay Renfrew	R/T.
3	G-ADBU	..	—	4000	1	30	Renfrew - C'Town Islay - C'Town Renfrew	R/T.
4	G-ADBU	~	—	3000	1	5	Renfrew - C'Town Renfrew	R/T.
4	S-ADBU	..	—	4000	2	20	Renfrew - Island Tarbert Renfrew	R/T.
5	G-ADBU	~	—	3000	2	-	Renfrew - N'Uist Renfrew	R/T.
6	9-ACEM	~	F.R Hughes	4000	3	45	Renfrew - Skye Uist - Renfrew	W/T. + R/T.
6	G-ACEM	~	~	4000	3	-	Renfrew - N. Uist Renfrew	R/T. + W/T. Ambulance
					TOTAL TIME :—	1762 - 05 min		

The inaugural services to Tiree and Benbecula are shown on July 1st and 2nd respectively on this page of David Barclay's log. The Rapide G-ADDF was used to Tiree, and Cruiser II G-ACSM to Benbecula. (Mrs Sheila Harper)

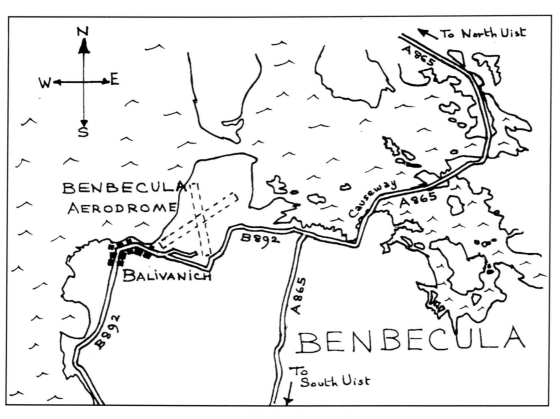

Map of Benbecula (Balivanich) aerodrome, which was developed later in WWII to have hard runways, and is currently up to NATO standard. (Author)

Summer 1936 schedules

NSA had expanded its core activities on the Renfrew - I.O.M and Campbeltown/Islay services for the summer schedules starting in May 1936. The I.O.M. route was now operated three times daily, the times being:

10.00 14.15 17.15 dep. Glasgow arr. 12.45 1700 20.00
↓ ↓ ↓ (Renfrew) ↑ ↑ ↑

11.15 15.30 18.30 arr. I.O.M. dep. 11.30 15.45 18.45
(Hall Caine)

The fares remained the same as they had been in Summer 1935, but the marketing of them, and the ease with which they could be obtained now - through the vastly increased medium of the British Airways group outlets - had increased out of all proportion.

Not only NSA's offices and its expanding list of travel agents in Scotland, but British Airways and all the usual Travel Agents, Clubs, and Hotels sold the tickets too. NSA itself had added four main travel agents in Glasgow to its sales promotion list - D. Mackenzie, Thomson's Tours, David Lawson Ltd., and John Mackay & Co - all in Hope, or Bath Streets. And their local managers around the islands were; J. MacGeachy in Union Street, Campbeltown; T. Caskie at Glenegedale Airport, Islay; Ewen MacRae at Glen Brittle, Carbost, Skye; A. F. Martin at Lochmaddy Hotel, North Uist; and F. S. Mackenzie at Lochboisdale Hotel, South Uist. In addition NSA now had a travel agent in Paisley (Andrew Duncan) and two in the Isle of Man (W H Chapman, and "Travel House") actively selling their tickets, not to mention British Airways' sales offices at the latters airports (Newtownards, Belfast; Stanley Park, Blackpool; Speke, Liverpool; Croydon, Heston and Gatwick, London) etc.

NSA used a funny little slogan at this time in their advertising: *"You won't hesitate a second time - you will be convinced it is the only way to travel. There in no time - without fuss or fatigue. Think it over !"*

Present from British Airways

On July 1st however, soon after the planned NSA summer schedules were in full operation - including the new Skye/Western Isles services flown in opposite directions on alternate days - the group decided to re-allocate the North of England schedules of British Airways (ex United Airways) to allow Northern and Scottish to take them over, operating from a consolidated base at Renfrew. And so George Nicholson now found himself asked to operate:

1. Liverpool (Speke) - Belfast (Newtownards) - Glasgow (Renfrew).
2. Liverpool (Speke) - Blackpool (Stanley Park) - I.O.M. (Hall Caine) - Glasgow (Renfrew). (Daily).
3. Belfast (Newtownards) - Glasgow (Renfrew). (Daily).
4. Belfast (Newtownards) - I.O.M. (Hall Caine). (Daily).
5. I.O.M. (Hall Caine) - Carlisle. (Daily).

On the same day (July 1st 1936), the Managing Director of the new British Airways company, Major J.R. McCrindle, was appointed to the Board of Northern and Scottish Airways. The group was fast pulling all its new subsidiaries together to work in commendable harness - and without a lot of fuss. The Air Superintendent of United Airways Ltd., the famous Australian aviator P.W. Lynch-Blosse, had also recently been round to see George Nicholson's outfit at Glasgow, as well as Ted Fresson up in Inverness. His mission had been to try to standardise all the various forms used by the airline subsidiaries - the Aircraft logs, traffic and maintenance records, even passenger tickets, etc. Whether or not George went some way to altering any of NSA's paperwork is not known, - but Lynch-Blosse certainly got short shift from Ted Fresson at Highland Airways, and being the nice fellow he was, quietly dropped the idea of pursuing the question with Ted!

It was because of the sudden allocation of these routes to NSA that extra aircraft were obviously needed as part of the package - hence their re-allocation to NSA at Renfrew.

Thus, during May and June more aircraft had arrived from the new group 'pool' to enable the expansion to take place, and these aircraft included; Spartan Cruiser II G-ACVT (newly restored at Prestwick after a prang in the Isle of Man); Spartan Cruiser II G-ACSM; and two newer De Havilland DH89 Dragon Rapides, G-ADBU and G-ADDF. These were joined by a DH83 Leopard Moth, G-ACUO in mid-May, which was often thereafter used for quick flights around the Western Isles, or to new landing sites, or for general charter work. And in July and August two more Rapides (G-ADAG and 'DAH) were put into use, with a Spartan Cruiser III (G-ADEM) and another Cruiser II (G-ACZM).

Taking over the North of England network like this pushed the company's fleet up to 15 aircraft in all, with 14 pilots and 100 other staff employed by NSA now. And from July 1st NSA also finally started the Air Mail contract between the I.O.M. and Liverpool. To do this, the Post Office collected all the mail from the northern half of the I.O.M. (including Ramsey) at Hall Caine, and all that from the south (including Douglas) at Castletown (now called Ronaldsway Airport). So NSA had to fly from Hall Caine to Ronaldsway with one lot of mails, then combine them onto the Liverpool flight there with the rest of the mails.

At times during this summer, the local traffic staff of NSA at Hall Caine aerodrome could be handling as many as 28 different flight departures daily. And amongst NSA staff based there were the Station Superintendent, J.W.S. Spinner, Base Engineer D.L. Robertson, traffic staff John Swann, A. Kelly and C Collister, and resident pilot Capt G.E. Mustard.

The first departure of the day from Hall Caine was the air mail

Taken from a Northern and Scottish Airways brochure, this shows an interesting line-up at Renfrew: two DH Dragons, including G-ACOR, Dragon Rapide G-ADAH (centre) and Spartan Cruiser II G-ACYL. The three De Havilland aircraft are still in the British Airways Group blue colour scheme, prior to being doped silver.

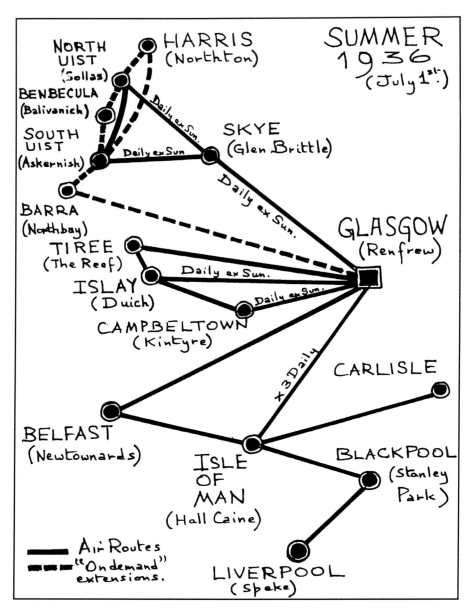

Maximum development - the NSA Summer 1936 network, showing the combined NSA/United Airways network after consolidation at Renfrew. (Author)

service at 07.30 (to Ronaldsway). Usually one traffic man had to fly on this as far as Ronaldsway to complete the load sheets there for the combined mails to Liverpool. Then the 09.00 arrival from Liverpool was the next event, followed throughout the rest of the day by 26 more departures or arrivals ! Although the number of passengers might not seem large (an average load of 3 per flight was good!) the day's total of some 70 passengers, over 600 lb of mail and 1,400 lb of baggage was quite respectable in those days.

Benefits of a mixed fleet

From August 7th 1936, as the Air Ministry had now granted a licence for the use of the sands at Barra's Tràigh Mhór (now called Northbay in NSA's literature), the call there became a regular scheduled occasion. In fact on many occasions the loads proved too great to combine islands together on the usual triangular routes, and David Barclay would often fly a return trip to Tiree or Islay or Campbeltown alone, and then follow up with another trip to the second point and back. (No doubt telegraphic details kept the intending passengers informed of timings!)

So varied was the fleet of aircraft now, that to some extent - at least at Renfrew - NSA could adapt the size and type of aircraft to suit the passenger loads on each route, day by day. The route with the largest loads could therefore be allocated the Dragon Rapide (8 seats) or Spartan Cruiser III (8 Seats) or Cruiser II (6 seats), etc. Thus David Barclay, the Chief Pilot, could find himself

flying a Dragon Rapide one day, a Dragon the next, followed by a Cruiser III or II, and even the Leopard Moth, all to the same point during the course of one week ! In the tricky weather conditions of the West of Scotland and the tricky landing fields, this required extreme versatility - which is why David only entrusted the Western Isles routes to himself, and the best of the other pilots. The less accomplished were scheduled on the Liverpool, I.O.M. and Belfast services, etc !

Stornoway and Perth

George Nicholson was forever looking for pastures new upon which to land his aircraft, and with his airline frequently being asked to extend the service from one of the Uists up to Harris (Northton), he tried again and again to get rights to land at Stornoway. As we have seen, J. Glyn-Roberts and his West of Scotland Air Services had a 5-year concession on Glasgow - Stornoway, but never did provide an air service.

So between August 24th - 26th 1936, George went with David Barclay on another trip in the Dragon G-ACFG to call on all the local NSA staff, landlords and Councils about the running of his aerodromes. But he also got David Barclay to extend this 'round-the-houses' flight to Stornoway, too.

On August 31st he flew with David in the Rapide G-ADBU to the new Perth Aerodrome at Scone (opened officially on June 5th 1936 by Viscount Swinton, Secretary of State for Air). So far

GLASGOW~ISLE OF MAN

				FARES.
GLASGOW (Central Hotel)	dep. 09.00	13.45	16.30	
RENFREW AIRPORT ...	dep.10.00	14.15	17.15	Single - 37/6
HALL CAINE AIRPORT ...	arr. 11.15	15.30	18.30	Return - 65/-
*RAMSEY (Parliament Sq.)	arr. 11.35	15.50	18.50	
*DOUGLAS	arr. 12.15	16.30	19.30	* Express Coach
(Central Bus Station)		From 1st July		Service to and from Hall Caine Airport.
*DOUGLAS (Central Bus Station)	dep. 10.30	14.45	17.45	Ramsey - 3d.
*RAMSEY (Parliament Sq.)	dep. 11.10	15.25	18.25	Douglas - 1/-
HALL CAINE AIRPORT ...	dep. 11.30	15.45	18.45	Reservation must be made in advance.
RENFREW AIRPORT ...	arr. 12.45	17.00	20.00	
GLASGOW (Central Hotel)	arr. 13.15	17.30	20.30	

DAILY (INCLUDING SUNDAYS).

Head Offices :

NORTHERN & SCOTTISH AIRWAYS LTD.
AIRPORT FOR GLASGOW, RENFREW.

Telephone : Renfrew 230. (Four lines). (24 hour service).
Telegraphic Addresses : "Northscot, Renfrew." "Airambulance, Renfrew."

MAIN BOOKING OFFICES :

GLASGOW.
D. Mackenzie, 153 Hope Street.
Thomson's Tours, 263 Hope Street.
David Lawson Ltd., 7a Bath Street.
John Mackay & Co., 21a Bath Street

CAMPBELTOWN.
J. MacGeachy, Union Street.

ISLAY.
T. Caskie, Glenegedale Airport.

SKYE.
Ewen M'Rae, Glen Brittle, Carbost.

NORTH UIST.
A. F. Martin, Lochmaddy Hotel.

SOUTH UIST.
F. S. Mackenzie, Lochboisdale Hotel.

EDINBURGH.
All usual Travel Agents, Clubs and Hotels.

PAISLEY.
Andrew Duncan, 4-6 Orchard Street.

ISLE OF MAN.
British Airways Ltd., Hall Caine Airport, Ramsey.
W. H. Chapman, 63 Athol Street, Douglas.
W. H. Chapman, 40 Parliament Square, Ramsey.
"Travel House," Prospect Hill, Douglas.

BELFAST.
Ards Airport, Newtownards.

BLACKPOOL.
British Airways Ltd., Stanley Park Airport.

LIVERPOOL.
British Airways Ltd., Liverpool Airport, Speke.

BRITISH AIRWAYS LTD.

Terminal House, 52 Grosvenor Gardens, London, S.W.1. Telephone : Sloane 0091.

And all the usual Travel Agents, Clubs and Hotels.

SPECIAL CHARTERS.

For Fox-Moth 3-Seater Taxis, 1/- per mile to anywhere.
Twin-Engined 7-Seater Air Liners, 2/- per mile.

MAP SHOWING SERVICES OPERATED BY NORTHERN & SCOTTISH AIRWAYS LTD

Above Left: The NSA Summer 1936 Isle of Man Timetable. Above Right: The NSA Summer 1936 Route Network.
Below: A fine photograph of NSA's DH89 Dragon Rapide G-ADDF at Belfast (Newtownards) Airport. (John Stroud Collection)

only Airwork's Civil Training School was operating there (having been established for some months before the official opening), and George was looking at Perth as a stop on a service northwards, to link up to his sister company Highland Airways Ltd in Inverness.

When the Harris stop was requested but the weather was bad, David Barclay could get permission to drop in on the golf course at Stornoway, or on the sand at Melbost, and he did this for the first time on September 12th in 'CFG. The weather, of course,

could also be bad back at Renfrew despite having R/T and W/T fitted now to most of the aircraft - so in this case the pilots would divert to land at Prestwick (a frequent occurrence in Winter).

Another change in NSA's capital took place on September 8th 1936 when the nominal capital was increased from £12,000 to £38,000 by the issue of £26,000 in £1 shares, allocated as fully paid to British Airways Ltd in consideration for the purchase price. The legal address of NSA was now given as: 51 Westgate Road, Newcastle-on-Tyne.

Northern and Scottish Airways Ltd
Traffic Statistics

Passengers carried:	
Period December 1st 1934 - December 31st 1935	5,006
January 1st - December 31st 1936	13,024
Total to date:	**18,030**

Northern and Scottish Airways Ltd

Aircraft Fleet - Summer 1936

1	De Havilland DH84 Dragon I	G-ACFG
2	De Havilland DH84 Dragon I	G-ACJS
3	De Havilland DH84 Dragon II	G-ACMO
4	De Havilland DH84 Dragon II	G-ACNH
5	Spartan Cruiser II	G-ACYL
6	Spartan Cruiser II	G-ACVT
7	De Havilland DH85 Leopard Moth	G-ACUO
8	Spartan Cruiser II	G-ACSM
9	De Havilland DH89 Dragon Rapide	G-ADBU
10	De Havilland DH89 Dragon Rapide	G-ADDF
11	Spartan Cruiser II	G-ADEM
12	De Havilland DH89 Dragon Rapide	G-ADAG
13	De Havilland DH89 Dragon Rapide	G-ADAH

Above: NSA's Isle of Man leaflet, with its timetable for the summer of 1936. Telephone number for Hall Caine Airport was Kirk Andreas 7! (John Stroud Collection)

"Go By Air" - an advert used extensively by NSA in many Scottish magazines. (John Stroud Collection)

CHAPTER 7

Last year as NSA

The Winter schedules for 1936-37 were published by Northern and Scottish Airways in time for their start on October 4th 1936. As usual, Carlisle - Isle of Man services were dropped for the winter, but the rest of the services continued at reduced frequencies.

Liverpool was the most southern point on the network, services connecting at Speke with a free Company car to make specific connections with London trains at Lime Street Station. There were basically two flights daily between Glasgow and Belfast (Monday to Friday, with one on Sundays), the services then splitting, one to go direct to Liverpool, the other routeing via the Isle of Man.

Then there was the usual triangular Glasgow - Campbeltown - Islay service, and the Western Isles services on alternate days routeing around in opposite directions (Glasgow - Skye - North Uist - South Uist - Barra - Glasgow, and v.v.)

British Airways - the group parent company - was also prominently displayed in the NSA Winter timetable, advertising its London (Gatwick) - Paris service (20 flights a week to Le Bourget, with train connections from Victoria Station, and First Class Rail fares included in the air fare). (Special mid-week day return fares on this route were stated to not need Passports). Its new Gatwick - Amsterdam, Hamburg, Copenhagen and Malmo services were similarly advertised (showing local and GMT times - Holland 20 minutes ahead, rest of the routes 1 hour ahead of GMT).

NSA's simple slogan was: 'Go by Air', and effective November 9th it issued a revised and streamlined version of its trunk route timetable showing both daily services southbound now calling at all points (Glasgow - Belfast - I.O.M. - Blackpool - Liverpool), and northbound one daily service doing the same, another originating in the I.O.M. in the morning, and an afternoon flight originating in Liverpool and terminating in the I.O.M. (obviously to provide an air mail aircraft at night from the I.O.M. back to Liverpool). For the lunchtime services, 'portable snack lunches' could be obtained at Renfrew, if wanted !

Accidents; and a radio station

On November 20th 1936 the Spartan Cruiser III G-ADEM was written off at Blackpool (Stanley Park) when taking off in a dense mist. The pilot mistakenly took off on a wrong orientation on the grass field, due to losing his bearings in the fog, and instead of taking the longest run, in fact travelled down the shortest one. Barely airborne at the end he flew into a hangar, crashed and caught fire. Both he and his single passenger were killed, and the hangar and its contents were burnt out.

Earlier on in the year, Northern and Scottish Airways had written off another Cruiser Mk II in Skye on July 25th 1936. Here G-ACVT was lost in the accident at Glen Brittle, but no one was badly hurt.

Through the winter, months, NSA was busy putting in a radio station and hangar at its airfield at Sollas, North Uist. Up to January 1937 the company had operated to all its airfields in the Western Isles with a high percentage of regularity, although no radio facilities were then available locally. Negotiations with the Air Ministry proved abortive, so NSA decided to install its own direction-finding radio station and this went 'live' in January 1937. Its was sited there not only as a guide for purely Scottish Air traffic, but with an eye to the time when aircraft would need bearings when making the North Atlantic ocean crossing. (This foresight was amply justified several years later when long-range aircraft streamed across the ocean from the New World, to the aid of war-torn Britain).

So the radio station at Sollas soon began to give NSA pilots useful bearings on their approaches to the Western Isles. But another helpful service then developed from all this progress - air to ship (or rather, lifeboat) transmissions. Because NSA aircraft had recently been flying to and fro while two lifeboats from a wrecked ship were being tossed about somewhere down below (and couldn't be found) George Nicholson asked if the Campbeltown lifeboat could be fitted with a radio receiver to pick up messages broadcast from the NSA airliners. It could, and it was, in February 1937, and successful trials started with it that month to bring air-sea rescue services up to a greater state of efficiency!

About this time, another development occurred in the Air Ambulance field. This time it was the formation of a new 'patient care plan' by the Campbeltown Co-operative Society, whereby a small quarterly subscription from enrolled members entitled them, if they needed specialist treatment, to free transport by Air Ambulance to Glasgow (on doctor's instructions), and also back again, with a nurse if necessary.

Left: The Radio Hut and station that NSA itself paid for at Sollas aerodrome, North Uist; and right, the kind of interior equipment used - in this case, the Air Ministry Radio Station at Sumburgh, Shetland, installed for Fresson's Inverness-based pilots. (E.E. Fresson, John Rae)

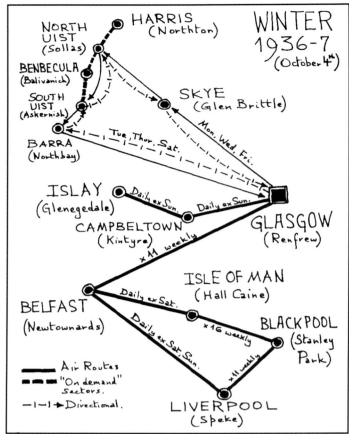

NORTH UIST (Sollas)
HARRIS (Northton)
WINTER 1936-7 (October 4th)
BENBECULA (Balivanich)
SOUTH UIST (Askernish)
SKYE (Glen Brittle)
BARRA (Northbay)
Tue., Thur., Sat.
Mon., Wed., Fri.
ISLAY (Glenegedale)
Daily ex Sun.
Daily ex Sun.
GLASGOW (Renfrew)
CAMPBELTOWN (Kintyre)
x14 weekly
ISLE OF MAN (Hall Caine)
BELFAST (Newtownards)
Daily ex Sat.
Daily ex Sat. Sun.
x16 weekly
BLACKPOOL (Stanley Park)
x11 weekly
LIVERPOOL (Speke)

——— Air Routes
■■■ "On demand" sectors.
—I—I—▶ Directional.

Left: NSA's Winter 1936-37 route network - showing the regular call at Barra now. (Author)

Opposite page: The NSA Winter 1936-37 time-table shows the new permanent stop at Barra, revised Hebrides routeings, and the fact that "Tea and Sandwiches, etc., can be obtained at Glenbrittle House (Skye) at usual prices"! (John Stroud Collection)

move. And almost immediately it put in hand a constant series of upgrading route equipment and the opening of new international services from Croydon, that went on unabated.

Its interest in domestic services thus took second place, and to this effect, it began negotiations with Railway Air Services to withdraw some of its own group company routes where they clashed with RAS. These principally involved the Northern and Scottish Airways' network around the Isle of Man, and so, as from May 20th 1937, NSA agreed to give up the operation of it's Liverpool - Belfast, Liverpool - Isle of Man, Blackpool - Isle of Man, Belfast - Isle of Man, Belfast - Glasgow and Carlisle - Isle of Man services.

Its summer operations therefore ceased on these routes on that date, and arrangements were made between British Airways, the LMS Railway Co. and Coast Lines (the last two being the operators of the Railway Air Services) to transfer all forward passenger bookings to RAS from May 21st.

NSA had interestingly already issued a summer-style timetable to cover just the Easter weekend of March 25th - 30th inclusive, but they never did issue a Summer 1937 timetable for the routes now handed over to RAS.

The Easter weekend timetable included re-starting the Carlisle - I.O.M. (Hall Caine) service just for those six days, and increasing to a three times daily service on the Liverpool - Blackpool - I.O.M. - Belfast sectors, and twice daily on Belfast - Glasgow.

NSA's Summer timetable proper, thus now confined itself purely to the Campbeltown/Islay service (upped to 18 flights a week to Campbeltown and 21 to Islay); the Western Isles triangular (three flights a week in each direction on alternate days), plus an extra Glasgow - Skye - Glasgow on Saturdays; and a Glasgow - I.O.M. (Hall Caine) service from June 1st to October 2nd, upped to 23 flights weekly.

The Western Isles run involved the usual Glasgow - Skye - North Uist - South Uist - Barra - Glasgow circuit, with Benbecula and Harris as extensions 'on demand'. The Isle of Man services were the last to be operated into Hall Caine airport, as the other routes that Northern and Scottish Airways had given up to Railway Air Services were transferred to using Ronaldsway Aerodrome this Summer (at Blackpool, RAS transferred its own services from Squires Gate to Stanley Park, however, when it picked up NSA's services from May 21st).

Traffic and the Maybury Committee

NSA released details of its traffic carryings at the ends of the first two years, and these showed that the total for 1935 - its first full year - had been 5,006 passengers, and that for 1936, 13,024 passengers. (These included the carryings on the ex-United Airways network taken over in the Summer).

The Maybury Committee had reported finally on December 9th 1936 about the whole system and future of British Civil Aviation. It had been set up under the chairmanship of Brig. Gen. Sir Henry Maybury, G.B.E., K.C.MG, C.B.: *"To consider and report upon measures which might be adopted by H.M. Government or by local authorities for assisting in the promotion of civil aviation in the U.K. and their probable cost. The Committee will take into account the requirements of the Post Office for air mails and the relation between aviation and other forms of transport".*

In the event it had looked very carefully at all these matters, and its recommendations were to have a lasting and dramatic effect upon the airlines in the United Kingdom. One of its key recommendations concerned the setting up of a licensing system for all internal air routes 'to avoid uneconomical and wasteful competition', and 'to ensure the most effective service for the Public'. Others included the operation by the Government of all radio, meteorological and air traffic control facilities, to secure the safety and regularity of air communications, and the setting up of a system of subsidies to airlines.

As the New Year 1937 started, therefore, airlines began already to look at their forthcoming plans for 1937 Summer schedules to try to eliminate some of the existing 'wasteful duplication'.

British Airways, the main group company, had decided to concentrate on cross-channel routes, and to move its base back from Gatwick to Croydon Aerodrome on February 7th 1937 - a combination of better navigation facilities and traffic catchment area (plus closeness to Central London) helping to dictate the

Running up - Spartan Cruiser II G-ACYL runs it's engines up on the chocks at Renfrew. (Henry Vallance)

NORTHERN AND SCOTTISH AIRWAYS LIMITED
AIRPORT FOR GLASGOW, RENFREW.

GLASGOW—SKYE—NORTH UIST—SOUTH UIST—BARRA—BENBECULA—GLASGOW.

MONDAYS, WEDNESDAYS, FRIDAYS.

			a.m.
GLASGOW	Grosvenor Restaurant	... dep.	9-00
	RENFREW AIRPORT	... dep.	9-40
SKYE	*GLENBRITTLE AIRPORT	arr.	11-25
		... dep.	11-40
NORTH UIST	SOLLAS AIRPORT	... arr.	12-25p
		... dep.	1-00
SOUTH UIST	ASKERNISH AIRPORT	... arr.	1-40
		... dep.	1-50
BARRA	NORTHBAY	... arr.	2-00
		... dep.	2-10
GLASGOW	RENFREW AIRPORT	... arr.	4-10
	Grosvenor Restaurant	... arr.	4-30

GLASGOW—BARRA—SOUTH UIST—NORTH UIST—BENBECULA—SKYE—GLASGOW.

TUESDAYS, THURSDAYS, SATURDAYS.

			a.m.
GLASGOW	Grosvenor Restaurant	... dep.	9-00
	RENFREW AIRPORT	... dep.	9-40
BARRA	NORTHBAY	... arr.	11-40
		... dep.	11-50
SOUTH UIST	ASKERNISH AIRPORT	... arr.	12-00
		... dep.	12-10p
NORTH UIST	SOLLAS AIRPORT	... arr.	12 50
		... dep.	1-25
SKYE	*GLENBRITTLE AIRPORT	arr.	2-10
		... dep.	2-25
GLASGOW	RENFREW AIRPORT	arr.	4-10
	Grosvenor Restaurant	... arr.	4-30

Connection to Harris for Stornoway from North Uist on demand.
Connection to Benbecula from South or North Uist on demand.

* Tea and Sandwiches, etc., can be obtained at Glenbrittle House at usual prices.

To allow for re-fuelling, maximum times are shewn from point to point.

FARES and BAGGAGE.

	Single	90-Day Return	
Glasgow/North Uist	...£4 0 0	£7 17 6	**BAGGAGE**
Glasgow/South Uist	... 4 0 0	7 17 6	
Glasgow/Harris	... 4 15 0	8 10 0	**ALLOWANCE**
Glasgow Benbecula	... 4 0 0	7 17 6	
Glasgow/Barra	... 4 0 0	7 17 6	25 lbs.
Glasgow/Skye	... 3 0 0	5 15 0	
Skye/North Uist			
Skye/South Uist			
North Uist/Barra	1 7 6	2 15 0	**EXCESS**
Benbecula/Harris			
Skye/Barra			**LUGGAGE**
Skye/Benbecula			
Skye/Harris	1 15 0	3 5 0	4d. per lb.
Barra/Harris			
North Uist/South Uist			
North Uist/Benbecula			
North Uist/Harris	1 2 6	2 5 0	
South Uist/Benbecula			
South Uist/Barra			
South Uist/Harris	... 1 10 0	3 0 0	

FREIGHT and TRANSPORT.

Freight.

Ground Transport.

Same as Excess Baggage, with a minimum of 1 6, but the Company reserves the right to charge on c.c. at 1 - per cubic foot.

Provided by Company between Glasgow Renfrew only.

(This cancels Schedule shewn on page 4 of Time Table issued 4th October, 1936.)

NORTHERN & SCOTTISH AIRWAYS LIMITED
AIRPORT FOR GLASGOW, RENFREW

Phone : RENFREW 230.   Grams : "NORTHSCOT"

Effective from 9th November, 1936

GLASGOW-BELFAST-ISLE OF MAN-BLACKPOOL-LIVERPOOL
SOUTHBOUND

		W.O.	W.O.	S O
GLASGOW—				
Grosvenor Restaurant, -	dep.	8·10 a.m.	11·30 a.m.	9·15 a.m.
Renfrew Airport, - -	dep.	8.45	†12·15 p.m.	9.45
BELFAST—				
Ards Airport, - - -	arr.	9·45	1·15	10·45
Grand Central Hotel, -	arr.	10·25	1·55	11·25
Grand Central Hotel, -	dep.	9.5	12·50	10·20
Ards Airport, - - -	dep.	10·0	1·30	11·0
I.O.M.—				
Hall Caine Airport, -	arr.	10·30	2·0	11·30
Ramsey, Parliament Sq.,	arr.	10·55	2·20	11·50
Douglas, Cent. Bus Stn.,	arr.	11·30	3·0	12·30 p.m.
Douglas, Cent. Bus Stn.	dep.	9·30	1·0	12·50
Ramsey, Parliament Sq.	dep.	10·10	1·40	1·30
Hall Caine Airport, -	dep.	10·45	2·10	2·0
BLACKPOOL—				
Stanley Park Airport, -	arr.	11·30	2·55	2·45
Stanley Park Airport, -	dep.	11·40	3·5	2·55
LIVERPOOL—				
Speke Airport, - -	arr.	12·5 p.m.	3·30	3·20
Adelphi Hotel, - -	arr.	a12·30	b4·0	c3·50

LIVERPOOL-BLACKPOOL-ISLE OF MAN-BELFAST-GLASGOW
NORTHBOUND

		W O	W.O.	W.O.	S.O.
LIVERPOOL—					
Adelphi Hotel, - -	dep.		d8·45 a.m.	e1·30 p.m.	9·35 a.m.
Speke Airport, - -	dep.		9·15	2·0	10·10
BLACKPOOL—					
Stanley Park Airport, -	arr.		9·40	2·25	10·35
Stanley Park Airport, -	dep.		9·50	2·35	10·45
I.O.M.—					
Hall Caine Airport, -	arr.		10·35	3·20	11·30
Ramsey, Parliament Sq.,	arr.		10·55	3·50	11·50
Douglas, Cent. Bus Stn.,	arr. a.m.		11·30	4·20	12·30 p.m.
Douglas, Cent. Bus Stn.,	dep.	8·5	9·30		12·50
Ramsey, Parliament Sq.,	dep.	8·45	10·10		1·30
Hall Caine Airport, -	dep.	*9·15	10·55		2·0
BELFAST—					
Ards Airport, - -	arr.	9·45	11·30		2·30
Grand Central Hotel, -	arr.	10·25	12·10 p.m.		3·10
Grand Central Hotel, -	dep.	9·5	2·0		2·0
Ards Airport, - -	dep.	*10·0	2·40		2·40
GLASGOW—					
Renfrew Airport, - -	arr.	11·0	3·40		3·40
Grosvenor Restaurant, -	arr.	11·30	4·25		4·25

W.O.—Daily except Sundays.   S.O.—Sundays Only.

† Portable Snack Lunches obtainable at Renfrew.

* Calls at Campbeltown on request.

a—Connects with 2-15 from Lime Street to London.
b—Connects with 5-25 from Lime Street to London.
c—Connects with 4-25 p.m. from Lime Street to London
d—Connects with 2-30 a.m. from London arr. Lime Street 6-55 a.m.
e—Connects with 7 a.m. from London arr. Lime Street 12-27 p.m.

Northern and Scottish Airways' southern routes flown in winter 1936-37 are shown in this timetable with rail connections from Liverpool to London. (John Stroud Collection)

From October 4th 1936, NSA had changed its Glasgow City Terminal to 'The Grosvenor Restaurant', 74 Gordon Street, C2, and an additional ticketing outlet in Glasgow was advertised from June 1937 - 'The Royal Restaurant' at 10 West Nile Street. It also advertised a new Travel Agent at Newcastle-on-Tyne, Charltons Ltd, - The Haymarket Travel Bureau, which was not taken on merely to sell tickets from Carlisle to the I.O.M. - but for other reasons as well!

Stornoway still not available

Now that Northern and Scottish Airways had handed back the southern routes to another airline, it was time for George Nicholson to concentrate once more upon the local Scottish scene. His often threatening competitor J. Glyn-Roberts and his West of Scotland Air Services, which had the 5-year concession for Glasgow - Stornoway services, had still not started this route, but was very nicely keeping NSA off it ! Now, in May 1937 Glyn-Roberts began to advertise a new way of opening the service - by using a number of Short Scion Senior airliners (four Pobjoy Niagara engines) fitted with floats. He proposed to fly from Greenock's Great Harbour to land on the water at Tobermory (Mull), Portree (Skye), and Stornoway's Broad Bay. The Harbour Trustees were to install slipways, sheds and a crane, and a floating petrol station at Stornoway, and launches would transfer passengers to shore. Two of the 8-seat aircraft were on order (he announced), and the service would start at the end of June. In time, he said, he hoped to add services to Oban and Fort William. But if there were any real intentions on Glyn-Roberts' part, they certainly came to nothing in 1937, and it was Summer 1938 before any floatplane appeared on the scene - and then not for very long.

Since the beginning of 1937 George Nicholson had been meeting his sister company's Managing Director (and Chief Pilot) from Inverness - Ted Fresson - more frequently, with an eye to trying to finally join their respective networks together in the near future, and David Barclay, George's Chief Pilot, had been up in January 1937 to fly Fresson's Rapide G-ADAJ to the Orkneys to gain experience of the route. Ted Fresson had been planning to operate this service for more than three years, from Renfrew to Inverness and through to the Northern Isles, and return, using his own aircraft. Competition with the London, Midland and Scottish Railways had led to the delay as Ted had

Ready to Go! Spartan Cruiser II G-ACYL prepares to depart Renfrew on a murky Glasgow morning. (Henry Vallance)

not wanted to upset his arrangements at Inverness and Aberdeen with the railway connections. Now that the LMS were being invited to be partners in the Scottish companies being 'hived off' by British Airways, Ted and George got together to see how they could start this link-up in partnership.

Aircraft replacements

Another DH Dragon II (G-ACNG) arrived at Renfrew on February 17th to join the fleet, and was to be followed by Dragon II G-ACOR in April, and the Spartan Cruiser IIIs G-ACYK and G-ADEL in June.

With the handing back in May of the Liverpool/Isle of Man/Belfast routes of course, NSA did not need the extra fleet of aircraft which had been used on these services, and for the second half of the 1937 Summer season it consolidated on using the D.H. Dragon IIs G-ACMO, 'CNG and COR, Spartan Cruiser IIs G-ACSM and 'CZM and Cruiser IIIs G-ACYK, 'CYL and 'DEL - a fleet of nine altogether, including the small D.H. Leopard Moth G-ACUO. The faster, newer D.H. 89 Rapides were handed back with the routes, together with the remaining aircraft.

Talks on merging in Scotland

Handing back these routes in May 1937 was only part of the equation however, as talks were on-going within the British Airways group as the summer began, on how to further consolidate the subsidiaries, and weld a network together free of too much competition from other airlines - where profits could best be made.

At a meeting called by British Airways in London in March both George Nicholson and Ted Fresson from Inverness had attended, to hear about the parent company's plans. With them were their own company secretaries, William Cumming of NSA, and William Hamilton from Highland Airways (who was Director and Company Secretary of Macrae & Dick Ltd, the town's largest firm of motor engineers).

British Airways board, including W.D.L. Roberts (Vice Chairman), who was also Chairman of both NSA and Highland Airways, and Major J.R. McCrindle O.B.E. M.C., (Managing Director), had discussed the intention of trying to form both NSA and Highland into a combined Scottish unit and to introduce a share-holding from the LMS Railway Co. - representing its own Railway Air Services (RAS) operations.

It is evident that a previous approach to the LMS Railway had been made, but the Railways had obviously demanded a majority, or controlling stake - which British Airways had rejected. They were proposing to stand firm (they told George and Ted) on not allowing the LMS to take more than a 50% share, retaining 50% themselves in British Airways.

However, at the end of this meeting both George and Ted said they could see no real reason for British Airways wanting to dispose of a 50% share-holding in their companies to LMS, and neither wanted to see the LMS Air Superintendent, a Wing Cmdr. Measures, taking control away from them of the thriving little airlines they had each built up with so much hard work! They left the matter to W.D.L. Roberts to try to resolve. 'Old Man Roberts' - as they referred to him - contacted them both early in May and along with Wing Cmdr. Measures from the RAS visited George's airline and its facilities at Renfrew making a careful note of all the departments and what the staff did, day to day. They then went up to Inverness to see Ted Fresson's operation.

Several more meetings followed, with Wing Cmdr. Measures coming up to visit every one of NSA's airports or airstrips, and to inspect all the facilities at the outstations (with the same in the North). Measures made a very thorough inventory of all their assets, and queried many of the operating or engineering procedures - betraying (as Ted Fresson remarked) the impression that everything would have to be turned around - if only for any new London controlled set-up to assert its own authority!

A fine view of NSA's Spartan Cruiser II G-ACVT, at Glen Brittle aerodrome, Skye, with the Cuillin Hills visible behind through the haze.
(John Stroud Collection)

*Left: One of NSA's Spartan Cruiser IIs at Renfrew Airport taking on passengers and Royal Mail for Campbeltown .
(John Stroud Collection)*

Below: An Air Mail cover flown on NSA's Spartan Cruiser II G-ACSM from Campbeltown to Renfrew on March 12th 1937 (it is postmarked 8.10pm on the 11th). Capt. David Barclay and Radio Officer F.R. Hughes have signed the cover, and the charter flight was laid on to Islay and Campbeltown as the mail boat was disabled (Dr. J. Forbes)

*Below: Looking north from Glen Brittle airstrip on Skye towards Glen Brittle House (in the trees). The 'dot' in the centre of the picture is a Spartan Cruiser circling onto 'finals' in the distance before landing towards the camera. NSA's local Aerodrome Manager, Ewen MacRae lived in Glen Brittle House with his parents and brother and even provided "Tea and Sandwiches" for the passengers!
All NSA aircraft were restricted to 60% payload out of Glen Brittle, because of the terrain.
(Ewen MacRae)*

PART IV   A COMBINATION FOR SCOTLAND

CHAPTER 8

NSA and Highland form Scottish Airways

During May 1937, negotiations between British Airways, the LMS Railway Co. and the David MacBrayne Co., began to reach a conclusion on how best to combine Northern and Scottish Airways Ltd and Highland Airways Ltd together as an operating unit, which would then be 50% owned by British Airways, 40% by the LMS, and 10% by the David MacBrayne organisations.

Organising the operational merger was simple but deciding on the way in which the combination could be legally effected on paper, under the Companies Act, was a great deal more exacting.

Northern and Scottish Airways Ltd had been set up by George Nicholson and his fellow directors on November 21st 1934 with an initial authorised capital of £7,000. This had subsequently been increased to £12,000, and later £38,000, after its takeover firstly by United Airways Ltd., and later the British Airways Ltd takeover of United in turn.

When United Airways first took over NSA, it had been allotted the whole of the new increase in capital (5,000 x £1 shares) plus 2,248 x £1 shares that had been previously unissued. United therefore at that stage had acquired £7,248 of the £12,000 capital. George Nicholson, Charles Almond and Ada Nicholson had originally held the balance of £4,752 between them, joined in Spring 1935 by Bill Gairdner. When British Airways was created to take over the group, the additional capital created (£26,000) was apparently still allocated to United Airways Ltd., raising its stake in NSA to £33,248 (out of £38,000 in total).

Thus, on paper British Airways Ltd. controlled United Airways Ltd., which in turn controlled Northern and Scottish Airways Ltd.

Highland Airways Ltd had been treated in the same manner, when taken over by United Airways in May 1935. Thus, after British Airways Ltd had taken over United the latter's shareholding in Highland Airways had risen to £11,150 out of the £16,000 issued share capital, leaving £4,850 being held by other parties. These 'other parties' are believed at this time to have included Capt. E.E. Fresson, Robert Donald and William Hamilton of Macrae & Dick Ltd., Col. J. J. Robertson of Wick, Robert Wotherspoon of Inverness, and The North of Scotland & Orkney & Shetland Steam Navigation Co Ltd.

Scottish Airways Ltd was now to be set up to function operationally from August 1st 1937, and legally as soon as financial and legal requirements could be completed thereafter. It was created by the simple expedient of registering the company with an Authorised and Issued Share Capital of £80,000 £1 "A" Shares.This capital was then issued as follows:-

Company buying the shares:	Amount
Northern Airways Ltd	£25,515
Highland Airways Ltd	£14,485
Total on behalf of British Airways:	**£40,000**
LMS Railway Co. Ltd.	£32,000
David MacBrayne Ltd.	£8,000
Total:	**£80,000**

Northern Airways and Highland Airways between them therefore controlled 50% of Scottish Airways (the majority stake) while LMS held 40% and David MacBrayne 10%.

NSA's Spartan Cruiser II G-ACVT, which skidded through the boundary wall on landing at Glen Brittle on July 25th 1936. The reason was the usage of smooth tyres up to then - treaded ones were subsequently fitted. The pilot and passengers were only bruised, but 'CVT was written off and parts taken back to Glasgow by "puffer-boat". (Ewen MacRae)

Ernest Edmund Fresson O.B.E.

Managing Director of the Northern Section of Scottish Airways Ltd. in Inverness (and Founder there of Highland Airways).

(Northern's individual share was in fact, 31.9% while Highland's was a smaller 18.1%). It will be noted that the name of the company now controlling a stake in Scottish Airways was referred to as just "Northern Airways Ltd" - not George's originally registered "Northern and Scottish Airways Ltd". The reason for this was purely to avoid confusion with the "Scottish" part of the name and the new "Scottish Airways", and George's company was henceforward referred to in its abbreviated sense, at all times.

Western Isles Airways Ltd

There was another slight complication, over the David MacBrayne shareholding. The Ministry of Transport required David MacBrayne Ltd to segregate the financial results of its participation in services to and from the Western Isles from the rest of its results. Because of this, therefore, another company had to be set up, called Western Isles Airways Ltd., of which Scottish Airways Ltd held 50% of the shareholding and David MacBrayne Ltd held the other 50%. Scottish Airways then undertook to operate the services on behalf of Western Isles Airways.

Negotiations were completed by June 10th 1937 subject only to the consent of the Government (which was given soon after). As for the management, it was agreed that Mr W.D.L. Roberts (Vice-Chairman of British Airways) would be Chairman of Scottish Airways Ltd., and that the airline would be split into two operating divisions - the **Western Section,** whose Managing Director would be George Nicholson; and the **Northern Section,** whose Managing Director would be Ted Fresson. Both these persons (or their successors as Managing Directors of the Sections) would be co-opted as members of the boards of Scottish Airways Ltd and Western Isles Airways Ltd.

Bill Gairdner was co-opted as a member of the Board of Western Isles Airways, and was to continue with his normal duties now, looking after the specific area of the Western Isles and Argyll.

Wing Cmdr Arthur Harold Measures C.B.E. (or "Daddy" to his colleagues) had become Superintendent of Railway Air Services on May 21st 1934, having previously been Divisional Engineer, East Africa, for Imperial Airways and later their Operations Manager in India. He was now appointed by British Airways and the LMS Co. to the boards of both Scottish Airways and Western Isles Airways as an independent member (not representing any of the other parties concerned with the formation), and he was to act as Managing Director of both companies on a part-time basis (whilst retaining his post in Railway Air Services). The directors brought into these two airlines from the LMS Co included W.P. Bradbury and W.

Yeaman (LMS Scottish Region Manager), and from David MacBrayne, J.W. Ratledge.

The headquarters of the two new Companies was to be at George Nicholson's offices at Renfrew (unfortunately for Ted Fresson in Inverness), and most of the meetings would be held there in future.

Objects of the merger

The objects of the merging of these two Scottish airlines, the one at Glasgow and the other at Inverness, were summarised in a Memorandum put before a Committee of Enquiry into Civil Aviation in February the following year - 1938. They were stated to be:

"The companies (Scottish Airways and Western Isles Airways) are to continue operating the existing routes of Northern Airways and Highland Airways.

Additional routes are planned, amongst others being Glasgow - Perth - Inverness - Stornoway.

The development of air services along the west coast of Scotland is being continued.

The operation of present and future routes by Scottish Airways aims at achieving reduction of losses which have been incurred and are at present being incurred and will have to be incurred with the development of the west coast system.

In order to operate these routes, adequate aerodromes, complete with essential facilities are required. At present Northern Airways and Highland Airways lease certain aerodromes, which though adequate for their purpose, are in many cases incapable of development or only after further heavy expenditure.

The Company must now face the possible enlargement of existing facilities or the acquisition of new aerodromes. The area to be served is sparsely populated, and Local Authorities cannot afford to consider incurring expenditure from Public Funds for the construction of airports, in spite of the fact that they depend to an increasing degree on air communications.

The Company foresees capital expenditure of some £33,000 to provide adequate facilities to comply with Air Ministry requirements."

It was really the latter problem that had confronted the separate companies, and even now the newly merged operation. And even British Airways wrung its hands when it came to providing these monies for aerodrome improvements. Thus the plea was put to the Committee of Enquiry in February 1938, for Government Support to be granted to the aerodromes directly, or by granting

Wing Cmdr. Arthur Harold Measures C.B.E.

Managing Director of Scottish Airways Ltd and Western Isles Airways Ltd at Renfrew (and Superintendent of Railway Air Services Ltd.)

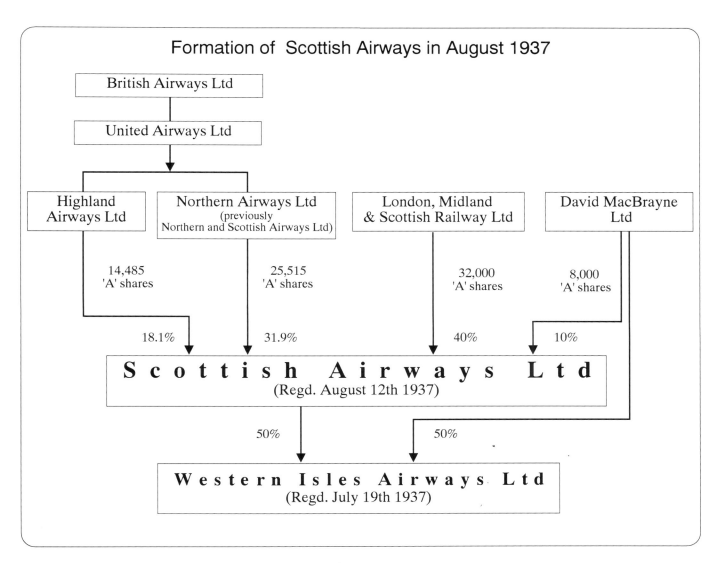

Formation of Scottish Airways in August 1937

British Airways Ltd → United Airways Ltd

Highland Airways Ltd — 14,485 'A' shares — 18.1%

Northern Airways Ltd (previously Northern and Scottish Airways Ltd) — 25,515 'A' shares — 31.9%

London, Midland & Scottish Railway Ltd — 32,000 'A' shares — 40%

David MacBrayne Ltd — 8,000 'A' shares — 10%

S c o t t i s h   A i r w a y s   L t d
(Regd. August 12th 1937)

50%   50%

W e s t e r n   I s l e s   A i r w a y s L t d
(Regd. July 19th 1937)

---

extra assistance to Local Authorities so the latter could provide the necessary facilities. The Maybury Committee Report had recommended that airlines should not own airports, and also that Government subsidies should not be paid to them. But the uneconomic case of airports in the Highlands and Islands ran counter to this norm, and hence Scottish Airways were requesting Government help for the airports as soon after the merger as February 1938.

Projected Routes

At the time of the merger the projected new routes included:
1. Renfrew - Perth - Inverness
2. Renfrew - Oban - Tiree
3. Renfrew - Tiree - Barra
4. Renfrew - Stornoway
5. Inverness - Stornoway
6 Harris - Stornoway
7. Inverness - Thurso - Kirkwall

Aerodromes needing lengthening were:
1. Campbeltown
2. Islay
3. South Uist (Askernish)
4. North Uist (Sollas)
5. Sumburgh
6. Westray

And new aerodrome sites needed urgently were at:
1. Oban
2. Tiree
3. Coll
4. Benbecula
5. Stornoway
6. Thurso
7. Kirkwall

So there was much to be done, and much capital needed for the expansion of services to suit the population.

Results to date

The individual results of the two airlines from their start to the end of July 1937 were impressive. George's NSA in its two years and 8 months' existence since being founded in November 1934 had carried a total of 23,796 passengers altogether (including the considerable boost from taking over the ex-United Airways services to and through the Isle of Man).

Highland Airways in Inverness in the four years and three months since it had started flying in May 1933, had carried 18,560 passengers.

So jointly, the two airlines that had now merged together had flown a combined 42,356 passengers altogether, in their short existence. Now they were to go on as a single unit, expanding their traffic by constantly improving the frequency and efficiency of their services.

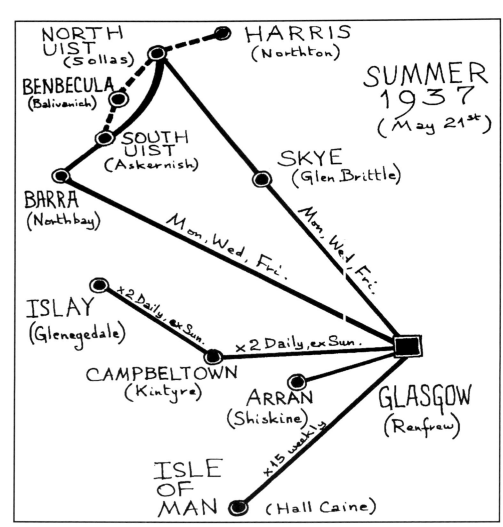

Above: Capt. John ("Jock") Young, who was one of Scottish Airways' safest pilots, and well known for his 'smooth flying'. (Henry Vallance)

Above: This map shows NSA's route network at the start of its 1937 Summer season (just three months before the formation of Scottish Airways Ltd. Arran was an 'on demand' call. (Author).

Right: A timetable that must hold some sort of record for the shortest period of issue ever! NSA issued this special time-table for just the six days of Easter 1937 (March 25th - 30th). This was the very appropriate cover drawing! (John Stroud Collection)

Left: Capt. Gilbert Rae, who started with NSA as its first Apprentice Engineer, later learning to fly and becoming a Captain. (Henry Vallance)

CHAPTER 9

Under New Management

One of the first accounts of the merger appeared in *The Glasgow Herald* of Wednesday, August 18th 1937. It stated:

"AIR TRANSPORT IN BRITAIN
Proposed Merger of Companies.
Under one central control.

As mentioned yesterday by our London Correspondent a merger of air transport companies within the British Isles is pending.

Negotiations, which have been proceeding for three months, are likely to result in the amalgamation of the principal internal air lines in Britain under Railway Air Services, Ltd., in association with Imperial Airways.

Mr George Nicholson, director of Northern and Scottish Airways at Renfrew airport, told a representative of *The Glasgow Herald* yesterday that while no official statement had yet been issued it was permissible to state that negotiations were nearing completion.

The effect of the proposal, which aimed at the elimination of duplication and competition on British trunk air routes, he said, would be to bring the principal internal air lines under one control.

Scotland to benefit

"Scotland" he added, "will benefit greatly under the new scheme. It is not too much to prophesy that hundreds of miles will be added to existing air lines, and that many new routes will be pioneered.

"Ground organisation and the extension and modernisation of airports - an important feature of air transport development - will benefit and progress under the direct control of the Air Ministry".

Two new companies, Scottish Airways and Western Isles Airways, have been formed. They will have complete control of the principal Scottish air routes under the merger. The L.M.S. and David McBrayne Ltd., Glasgow, will have an interest in these Scottish groups.

One Control

The Maybury Committee's report, issued last January, indicated the desirability of development on the lines adopted by the promoters of the merger. The Committee observed that future progress in building up a network of air services was dependent on the creation of one controlling group, the Air Ministry providing wireless stations and ground organisation and the Post Office granting air mail contracts.

The proposal under consideration is that there should be a pooling of finance, organisation, and experience with a view to development. Independent operators, while they will not lose their identity, will be absorbed in the merger and will become shareholders in the governing company.

Railway Air Services, formed in 1934 by the four railways in association with Imperial Airways, operated services over the territories of the Great Western, the Southern, and the L.M.S. companies. Their principal air line is that between Glasgow and London by Belfast, Liverpool, Manchester, Stoke-on-Trent, and Birmingham.

Avoiding Duplication

The chief object of the merger is to prevent unnecessary duplication on the more important British air routes. Until recently as many as three different companies were fighting for control over one route.

That position, deprecated by the Maybury Committee, resulted in the possibility of a merger being first considered.

Air transport companies involved in the negotiations with Railway Air Services include British Airways (London), their Scottish subsidiaries - Northern and Scottish Airways (Renfrew) and Highland Airways (Inverness) - North Eastern Airways (Aberdeen), and West Coast Air Services (Blackpool)."

As Ted Fresson later stated :

"On August 12th 1937, Highland Airways and Northern and Scottish Airways lost their identity and the two companies became welded together under the name of Scottish Airways Ltd with registered offices at Renfrew. The amalgamation brought powerful backing, but we lost a lot of our independence.

"On Thursday August 12th we held our first Board Meeting at Renfrew, and after our Chairman, Mr Roberts, introduced us all to the new members of the Board, we got down to work. Wing Cmdr Measures was appointed Managing Director of the new company. I would have preferred that George Nicholson and myself should have become Joint Managing Directors as I could not see how a newcomer could possibly cope with the complexities of the operations Nicholson and I myself had grown up with. After all - the routes operated were organised by us.

"As it was not to be so, we had to make the best of a difficult job. The major issue discussed was the *Modus Operandi* of the new company. It was agreed that George would carry on as before with the Southern Section, and I would remain 'boss' of the Northern Section.

Cruiser at Barra! NSA's Spartan Cruiser II G-ACSM at Barra on the sands of Tàigh Mhór. The salt water corrosion generated by landing on the beach eventually led to 'CSM being prematurely scrapped in July 1940. (John Stroud Collection)

NORTHERN AND SCOTTISH AIRWAYS LIMITED
THIS TIMETABLE CANCELS ALL PREVIOUS ISSUES

LINE 111

RENFREW—CAMPBELTOWN—ISLAY.
1st July to 2nd October, except where otherwise stated.
Sundays excepted.

			a.m.	a.m.	p.m. A†	p.m. *	p.m. *
GLASGOW	Grosvenor Restaurant	... dep.	9.00	10.00	1.30	4.30	6.00
	RENFREW AIRPORT	... dep.	9.45	10.45	2.15	5.15	6.45
	KINTYRE AIRPORT	... arr.	10.30	11.30	...	...	7.30
CAMPBELTOWN	White Hart Hotel	... arr.	10.45	11.45	...	...	7.45
	White Hart Hotel	... dep.	10.15	...	...	...	7.00
	KINTYRE AIRPORT	... dep.	10.35	...	...	...	7.35
ISLAY	GLENEGEDALE AIRPORT	arr.	11.00	...	3.05	6.05	8.00
	Port Ellen	... arr.	...	...	...	...	...

NOTES.—A—Friday, Saturday and Monday only. * Operates one hour earlier from 1st September. † Service discontinued 1st September.

ISLAY—CAMPBELTOWN—RENFREW.
1st July to 2nd October, except where otherwise stated.
Sundays excepted.

			a.m.	a.m.	a.m.	p.m. A†	p.m. *
ISLAY	Port Ellen	... dep.	...	8.15	...	11.40	4.00	6.45
	GLENEGEDALE AIRP'T	dep.	8.15	...	11.40	4.00	6.45
	KINTYRE AIRPORT	... arr.	8.40	...	...	...	7.10
CAMPBELTOWN	White Hart Hotel	... arr.	8.55	...	...	...	7.25
	White Hart Hotel	... dep.	8.25	11.30	...	...	7.00
	KINTYRE AIRPORT	... dep.	8.45	11.45	...	...	7.15
GLASGOW	RENFREW AIRPORT	... arr.	9.30	12.30	12.30	4.60	8.00
	Grosvenor Restaurant	... arr.	10.00	1.00	1.00	5.30	8.30

LINE 222

GLASGOW—ISLE OF MAN.
1st July to 2nd October, except where otherwise stated.
Daily unless otherwise stated.

			a.m. NS †	a.m.	p.m. C‡ SO	p.m. NS *
GLASGOW	Grosvenor Restaurant	... dep.	9.00	10.00	1.30	6.00
	RENFREW AIRPORT	... dep.	9.40	10.45	3.45	6.45
ISLE OF MAN	HALL CAINE AIRPORT	... arr.	10.55	12.00	5.00	8.00
	Ramsey	... arr.	11.15	12.20	5.20	8.20
	Douglas	... arr.	11.55	1.00	6.00	9.00

ISLE OF MAN—GLASGOW.
1st July to 2nd October, except where otherwise stated.
Daily unless otherwise stated.

			a.m. NS *	a.m.	p.m. NS †	p.m. C *	p.m. SO ‡
ISLE OF MAN	Douglas	... dep.	8.15	1.15	4.15	5.45	4.15
	Ramsey	... dep.	8.55	1.55	4.55	6.25	4.55
	HALL CAINE AIRPORT	dep.	9.15	2.15	5.15	6.45	5.15
GLASGOW	RENFREW AIRPORT	... arr.	10.30	3.30	6.30	8.00	6.30
	Grosvenor Restaurant	... arr.	11.00	4.00	7.00	8.30	7.00

NOTES.—NS—Sunday excepted. C—Friday, Saturday, Sunday and Monday only. † Service discontinues 1st September. * Operates one hour earlier from 1st September. SO‡—Sunday only from 5th September.

LINE 333

GLASGOW—SKYE—NORTH UIST—SOUTH UIST—BARRA—GLASGOW.
1st July to 2nd October, except where otherwise stated.

			a.m. P †	p.m. S ‖
GLASGOW	Grosvenor Restaurant	... dep.	9.00	3.00
	RENFREW AIRPORT	... dep.	9.50	3.45
SKYE	GLENBRITTLE AIRPORT	... arr.	11.20	5.15
	GLENBRITTLE AIRPORT	... dep.	11.25	6.15
NORTH UIST	SOLLAS AIRPORT	... arr.	12.05 p.m.	...
	SOLLAS AIRPORT	... dep.	12.40	...
SOUTH UIST	ASKERNISH AIRPORT	... arr.	1.10	...
	ASKERNISH AIRPORT	... dep.	1.20	...
BARRA	NORTHBAY	... arr.	1.30	...
	NORTHBAY	... dep.	1.40	...
GLASGOW	RENFREW AIRPORT	... arr.	3.20	7.45
	Grosvenor Restaurant	... arr.	4.00	8.30

GLASGOW—BARRA—SOUTH UIST—NORTH UIST—SKYE—GLASGOW.
1st July to 2nd October, except where otherwise stated.

			a.m. M	p.m. S ‖
GLASGOW	Grosvenor Restaurant	... dep.	9.00	3.00
	RENFREW AIRPORT	... dep.	9.50	3.45
BARRA	NORTHBAY	... arr.	11.30	...
	NORTHBAY	... dep.	11.40	...
SOUTH UIST	ASKERNISH AIRPORT	... arr.	11.50	...
	ASKERNISH AIRPORT	... dep.	12.00	...
NORTH UIST	SOLLAS AIRPORT	... arr.	12.30 p.m.	...
	SOLLAS AIRPORT	... dep.	1.05	...
SKYE	GLENBRITTLE AIRPORT	... arr.	1.45	5.15
	GLENBRITTLE AIRPORT	... dep.	1.50	6.15
GLASGOW	RENFREW AIRPORT	... arr.	3.20	7.45
	Grosvenor Restaurant	... arr.	4.00	8.30

Connections to Benbecula from North Uist or South Uist, and to Harris from North Uist, on demand.

NOTES.—M—Tuesday, Thursday and Saturday. S—Saturdays only. P—Monday, Wednesday and Friday. ‖ July and August only.

FARES

GLASGOW to		Single	90-Day Return
Campbeltown	...	20/-	40/-
Islay	...	30/-	60/-
X Isle of Man	...	40/-	75/-
Skye	...	60/-	115/-
North Uist	...	80/-	157/6
South Uist	...	80/-	157/6
Barra	...	80/-	157/6
Benbecula	...	80/-	157/6
Harris	...	95/-	170/-
CAMPBELTOWN to			
Islay	...	15/-	30/-
SKYE to			
Benbecula	...	27/6	55/-
Barra	...	27/6	55/-
Harris	...	35/-	65/-

SOUTH UIST to		Single	90-Day Return
Barra	...	22/6	45/-
Benbecula	...	22/6	45/-
Harris	...	30/-	60/-
Skye	...	27/6	55/-
BARRA to			
Harris	...	35/-	65/-
NORTH UIST to			
Skye	...	27/6	55/-
Barra	...	27/6	55/-
South Uist	...	22/6	45/-
Benbecula	...	22/6	45/-
Harris	...	22/6	45/-
HARRIS to			
Benbecula	...	27/6	55/-

X Cheap mid-week return 65/- available Tuesdays, Wednesdays and Thursdays, validity 30 days.

Baggage Allowance	Line	Excess Baggage Rates	Freight
25 lbs. ←	111	→ 2½d. per lb.	Same as excess baggage, with a minimum of 1/6, but the Company reserves the right to charge on c.c. at 1/- per cubic foot.
33 lbs. ←	222	→ 3d. per lb.	
25 lbs. ←	333	→ 4d. per lb.	

GROUND TRANSPORT is provided by the Company at Glasgow and Campbeltown, also at Isle of Man, but in this instance seats must be reserved for which booking fee is charged—Ramsey 3d. and Douglas 1/-. At Islay cars at preferred rates.

THIS TIMETABLE IS SUBJECT TO ALTERATION WITHOUT NOTICE

CONDITIONS OF CARRIAGE
Tickets are issued subject to "Conditions of Carriage" displayed at Company's offices, extracts of which appear on passenger tickets.

"It was at this meeting that I first became aware of the difference in financial stability of the Western Isles services - whereas Highland Airways had been making ends meet and were beginning to show a profit, Northern and Scottish had been in the 'red' for a long time. Their traffic density did not appear as great as ours but their operating mileage was much longer. Further, they were using a more expensive operating type of aircraft then we were (the Spartan Cruisers) and all this added up to a not too rosy picture.

"It was at this juncture that I submitted to the new Board that our accounts should be kept separately and shown separately at each Board Meeting."

This was agreed to by the directors, and in future years it was often the case where the Northern Section's profits helped to subsidise the loss in the Southern Section, and more than cover it to still give an overall combined profit !

Mr Bradbury confided in Ted Fresson after the meeting (back at their hotel at Rothesay where the two families spent the weekend together) that Wing Cmdr. Measures had been appointed basically in order to co-ordinate the Railway Air Services with the new Scottish Airways operations, and see that there was no overlapping or other divergencies in them.

Linking-up; wrong way around !
In mid-September 1937 Ted Fresson records that he and his family were on the way south for a holiday, and staying overnight at Perth. Before they motored on , next day he called up William Cumming, George Nicholson's company secretary of the Southern Section in Renfrew. Ted was planning the start next spring (1938) of his long anticipated idea of joining up Inverness by air with Glasgow, something that had been close to his heart for three years. During the conversation with William, Ted learned that Wing Cmdr Measures, in talking with George Nicholson recently had decided on the operation of the service - by originating the aircraft from Renfrew - not Inverness !

Ted asked how on earth could that decision have been made without talking to him? For he had always planned to originate the flight at Kirkwall in the early morning, call at Wick and Inverness and get the passengers to Glasgow for a day's business there, returning in the evening. When he learned that Measures had authorised it he nearly blew his top, and got onto Measures straight away in London.

The decision was taken to re-examine the whole method of operating the route at the next Board Meeting, and when this took place, it was decided that George's Section would operate the service in 1938 for the first year, and that in 1939 Ted could reverse it from the North, and a comparison of traffic would show which way was 'best'!

From here on, Measures and Co. said they would make sure that Ted Fresson was invited down to Renfrew to attend all meetings which involved policy of Scottish Airways Ltd as a whole, or operations that impinged on both Sections.

Ted, however, was often heavily engaged in flying services himself, and being in the North, it was easy to forget to invite him down to Renfrew. A new Operations Director of Scottish Airways was appointed in Renfrew, and became a constant source of worry to Ted - so much so that the latter invited him up to Inverness one day ' to clear the air'. They sat on the edge of the airfield at Longman, and talked it out. Ted insisted orders should not be given without his consent, and that unless it stopped, he would make a major issue of the fact at the next Board Meeting.

Opposite page: A second edition of NSA's 1937 Summer Timetable, effective from July 1st, was issued to coincide with Scottish Airways Ltd combined network commencing. (John Stroud Collection)

He repeated that it was incongruous for the loss-making Southern unit to be always dictating to the profitable North, what to do! Matters apparently became less strained after this, and more co-operative!

Hankins to Kirkwall; Stornoway progress
In the autumn of 1937 Capt. John Hankins (who had joined George's NSA in March 1936) was transferred from the Renfrew base, up to Kirkwall in Orkney, to become resident pilot there for Ted Fresson. He was also to operate the Air Ambulance service in the Orkney Islands, and he superceded Fresson's earlier and legendary pilot there, 'Johnny' Rae.

Although Glyn-Roberts was still inhibiting Scottish Airways starting a Glasgow - Stornoway service, Ted Fresson had managed after several years trying, to finally get things moving with the building of a land aerodrome there. He had flown over from Inverness on November 19th 1937, and had signed an Agreement with the Stornoway Trustees, to construct a four runway aerodrome on part of the Melbost Golf Course there. He obtained a long lease for Scottish Airways, on condition they footed most of the bill for construction. There were protection clauses built in, however, in case the long lease was broken.

So on December 2nd 1937 Ted flew an L.M.S. Co. surveyor over to Stornoway from Inverness, to mark out the Golf Course for levelling into the four strips. In January 1938 he took a party of L.M.S. surveyors over again and stayed with them several days, outlining the four runways. While they were there, Ted came to a novel conclusion - why waste a lot of money flattening a huge circular area of the Links? Why not just level the four strips, each about 150ft wide, and not bother with the land in between ? It would save thousands of pounds altogether - as they found when they costed it out. Ted then had to get his Scottish Airways' Board to accept the idea - which they did, and also received Air Ministry permission. As it turned out, it proved a blueprint for a new type of aerodrome, with grass runways - not an open area of grass alone. Future RAF and RN airfields would follow the example - and grass strips would eventually become tarmac or concrete strips.

Miscellaneous events in 1937
Apart from the routine line-flying in 1937, David Barclay, the Chief Pilot of the Southern Section, carried out a protracted aerial survey of the Newcastle-on-Tyne, York, Doncaster and Tollerton areas of Yorkshire in May - July this year, making many flights in the Dragon II G-ACMO fitted with the necessary aerial cameras. He usually took one of the senior engineers with him on the flights, such as T. Richardson or even Bill Mann himself (the Chief Engineer).

While flying the Western Isles service, David's log book records the many variations to the basic multi-stop route that he could fly, day by day, as 'on demand' calls were inserted. Thus during one 7-day period in June 1937, he operated:

1. Renfrew - Islay - Barra - South Uist -North Uist - Benbecula - North Uist - Skye - Renfrew (an 8 - stop service in one day taking 4hrs 45mins flying, and a nightmare for passenger reservations !)
2. Renfrew - Skye - North Uist - Benbecula - North Uist - South Uist - Barra - Renfrew.
3. Renfrew - Barra - South Uist - Harris - North Uist - Skye - Renfrew.
4. Renfrew - Skye - North Uist - Harris - North Uist - South Uist - Barra - Renfrew.
5. Renfrew - Barra - South Uist - North Uist - Skye - Renfrew.

All these particular flights were on the Spartan Cruiser II, G-ACSM, and on July 31st David flew Mr W. Elliot, the Secretary

NSA's Spartan Cruiser III G-ACYK, after it ploughed into the 1,711 ft high Hill of Stake, east of Largs in Ayrshire on January 14th 1938 in bad visibility. There were no injuries, but the aircraft was abandoned where it lay. (John Stroud Collection). The hulk remained at the location until removed in July 1973 to East Fortune Museum by a Sea King of 819 Naval Air Squadron as the cutting insert shows.

of State for Scotland, around the Western Isles in 'CSM, flying for a total of 4hr 10mins in all. Two more aerial surveys came up for David on 'CMO in August - to Donibristle and Leuchars.

Use of Radio

Since October 26th 1935, when David had inaugurated the use of Radio by the pilots on a flight to Islay in Dragon G-ACNH, communications had become much more sophisticated, and of a routine nature. Thus the carrying of a 'W.T.O.' (Wireless Telegraphy Officer) had started on December 17th 1935 when David had carried out a Skye/SouthUist trip in Dragon G-ACFG, and since then the recruitment of W.T.O.s had increased, and one was now carried on every Western Isles service.

The first W.T.O. in NSA had been F.R. Hughes - recruited

The Marconi Type A.D.49/50 Transmitter/Receiver radio set (operated by a wind-driven generator on top of the Port wing) is shown in a DH Dragon Rapide. Capt. E.E. Fresson is flying, with his R.adio Officer sitting in the forward right hand seat.
The notice on the forward bulkhead, partly obscured by the R.O's arm states that 'Passengers are requested to keep their seats when approaching the aerodrome and landing'! (Leslie Serjeant)

early in 1936 - who had been the only W/O (as they were later called) for some months. Hughes flew mostly with David Barclay, and had been with David when they made the first scheduled landing on Harris in 'CSM on June 2nd 1936. On May 25th 1937, when he was with David on a Western Isles service, during the stop at North Uist he had a bad accident which put him out of action until July 17th.

Early on January 15th 1938 David Barclay was 'scrambled' urgently to look for their Spartan Cruiser III, G-ACYK, which had suffered an unfortunate crash the previous evening in low cloud and bad visibility over the high ground behind Largs. Still flying in the colours (blue and silver) of Northern & Scottish Airways Ltd. it had miraculously pancaked onto the top of the 1,711ft high Hill of Stake in a horizontal attitude, on a piece of soft heathery ground. But in doing so it had bent its centre-engine's metal propeller, and broken the wooden outers, but leaving an intact fuselage (showing how strongly the Spartans were constructed, and owing much to the all-metal design). The occupants had already been rescued and had all survived with bruising, and David flew out at first light from Renfrew in Dragon 'CMO to locate the crash site. (In the event, only the engines and removable equipment were salvaged, and the Spartan's fuselage and wings were left there, until in July 1973, over 35 years afterwards, an RN Sea King helicopter airlifted the fuselage for placing into the Royal Scottish Museum's 'Museum of Flight' at East Fortune near Edinburgh.

Immediately after returning from his aerial survey of the wreck, and noting the damage done to it from a series of low fly-pasts, David was sent off again in 'CMO, this time with a spare wheel for the Cruiser II G-ACYL (which David would otherwise have been flying that day), which had punctured a tyre landing at North Uist on the morning schedule. (Punctured tyres were a fairly rare event even in those days, but David had had one notable such occurrence in the Spartan Cruiser II, G-ACZM on January 9th 1936. Landing on the beach at Northbay (Barra), he had punctured one of the mainwheels of the Cruiser on a sharp rock. This had necessitated staying all day while another wheel was flown in and helping to jack up the aircraft to put the new one on. But such events had their compensations - David was invited for lunch to the nearby cottage of Sir Compton MacKenzie, the

Name Change! Some time after August 12th 1937, a ground engineer at Renfrew paints the new combined airline's name on the nose of a DH Dragon Rapide. In the foreground are two important figures in the story of NSA - Left is the airline's first, and later Chief Radio Officer F. R. Hughes. On the right is the Operations Director, W.D.T. ("Bill") Gairdner. (DH/British Aerospace)

famous writer, and was 'very well looked after' into the bargain ! (Sir Compton was well-known for the strength of his welcome, his cook's seafood dishes, and his own choice of single malts). In the evening he had managed to fly out the Cruiser to North Uist and thence, next day back to Renfrew.

Change of Name

Although some of George's aircraft were still flying around in early 1938 with the old company name of 'Northern and Scottish Airways Ltd' on them, this changed from April 1st 1938 with the start of the new financial year, and the name 'Scottish Airways Ltd' was adopted everywhere after this date. Meanwhile the old company ('Northern and Scottish Airways Ltd') which was now, of course, a major shareholder in 'Scottish Airways Ltd' had its name changed officially back to 'Northern Airways Ltd' on September 6th 1937 to avoid any accounting confusion with Scottish Airways Ltd. During the period between September

1937 and April 1st 1938, pilot's log-books and company paperwork was still stamped up with the old *"Northern and Scottish Airways Ltd'* name in the interests of economy, but the words *'and Scottish'* were deleted with a pen!

Winter 1937-38 Timetables

During the first winter as the newly operating 'Scottish Airways' (or 'Western Isles Airways' for the Hebridean services), the routes were severely chopped back, and operated at reduced frequency. In the attempt to reduce empty leg flying on the Western Isles, Skye was taken out of the multi-stop route and given a terminator service to itself. The Western Isles route then operated outbound on Monday, Wednesday and Friday, returning on Tuesday, Thursday and Saturday, with the aircraft and crew overnighting at Sollas, North Uist. The new hangar there took care of the aircraft, and the Lochmaddy Hotel and 'Mine Host' A.F. Martin (who also sold the air tickets and arranged transport and check-in) looked after the pilot and W.O.! A local engineer also now had to be employed at Sollas by Scottish Airways.

There was no service to the Isle of Man any more, and the Campbeltown - Islay service operated daily except Sunday to both points (not triangular). The fares - incredibly - were no different to those used in the previous two years.

David Barclay's log-book gives a good example of the Western Isles run, in January 1938. On Wednesday January 5th he flew outbound in the Cruiser II G-ACSM along the route: Renfrew - Islay - Barra - South Uist - North Uist - Stornoway - North Uist, then overnighted at Sollas. On the next morning he returned: North Uist - Benbecula - North Uist - South Uist - Barra - Renfrew. And on Monday January 17th he flew out again in Cruiser II 'CZM this time: Renfrew - North Uist - Harris - North Uist, returning next day: North Uist - South Uist - Barra - Benbecula - North Uist - Barra - Renfrew ! There were obviously a great many combinations of service that could be achieved - and were so - if passengers were available at the different points of call. Certainly no-one in those islands ever had cause to think they were isolated or cut-off from the mainland, since George Nicholson had started the routes in 1935. For this, if nothing else, he will be remembered.

NORTHERN AND SCOTTISH AIRWAYS
(NORTHERN AIRWAYS LIMITED)
TIME-TABLE—Operative from 4th October, 1937, until further notice.

GLASGOW—CAMPBELTOWN—ISLAY.
Daily except Sundays.

WEST BOUND.

			a.m.
GLASGOW	{ Grosvenor Restaurant	dep.	9.00
	{ RENFREW AIRPORT	dep.	9.45
CAMPBELTOWN	{ KINTYRE AIRPORT	arr.	10.30
	{ White Hart Hotel	arr.	10.45
	{ White Hart Hotel	dep.	10.15
	{ KINTYRE AIRPORT	dep.	10.35
ISLAY	{ GLENEGEDALE AIRPORT	arr.	11.00
	{ + Bowmore	arr.	—
	{ + Port Ellen	arr.	—

EAST BOUND.

			p.m.
ISLAY	{ + Bowmore	dep.	—
	{ + Port Ellen	dep.	—
	{ GLENEGEDALE AIRPORT	dep.	12.25
CAMPBELTOWN	{ KINTYRE AIRPORT	arr.	12.50
	{ White Hart Hotel	arr.	1.06
	{ White Hart Hotel	dep.	12.35
	{ KINTYRE AIRPORT	dep.	12.55
GLASGOW	{ RENFREW AIRPORT	arr.	1.40
	{ Grosvenor Restaurant	arr.	2.10

+ Cars can be hired at preferred rates: FREE BAGGAGE ALLOWANCE—25 LBS.

GLASGOW—BARRA—SOUTH UIST—NORTH UIST.

NORTH BOUND.
MONDAY, WEDNESDAY, FRIDAY.

			a.m.
GLASGOW	{ Grosvenor Restaurant	dep.	9.00
	{ RENFREW AIRPORT	dep.	9.40
BARRA	{ NORTH BAY	arr.	11.30
	{ NORTH BAY	dep.	11.40
SOUTH UIST	{ ASKERNISH AIRPORT	arr.	11.50
	{ ASKERNISH AIRPORT	dep.	12.00
			p.m.
x NORTH UIST	SOLLAS AIRPORT	arr.	12.30

SOUTH BOUND.
TUESDAY, THURSDAY, SATURDAY.

			a.m.
x NORTH UIST	SOLLAS AIRPORT	dep.	10.40
SOUTH UIST	{ ASKERNISH AIRPORT	arr.	11.10
	{ ASKERNISH AIRPORT	dep.	11.20
BARRA	{ NORTH BAY	arr.	11.30
	{ NORTH BAY	dep.	11.40
			p.m.
GLASGOW	{ RENFREW AIRPORT	arr.	1.30
	{ Grosvenor Restaurant	arr.	2.10

SKYE: Particulars on Application.

x HARRIS and BENBECULA—Connections available on demand (under charter conditions) in conjunction with regular Northbound and Southbound Services, subject to tide and weather.

FREE BAGGAGE ALLOWANCE—25 LBS.

THE COMPANY DOES NOT PROVIDE ROAD TRANSPORT IN THE OUTER HEBRIDES. PASSENGERS CAN MAKE ARRANGEMENTS FOR CARS WITH LOCAL AGENTS. (See List overleaf).

The last NSA timetable under its own name was for Winter 1937-38, showing an abbreviated Western Isles service. (John Stroud Collection)

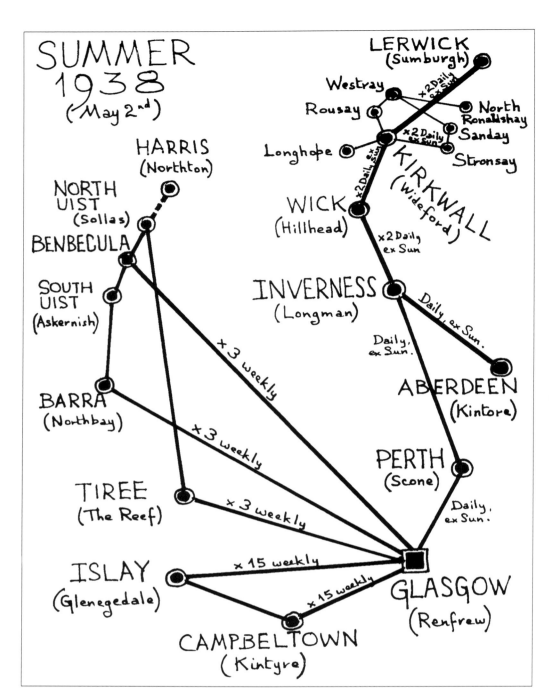

SUMMER
1938
(May 2nd)

LERWICK
(Sumburgh)

Westray

Rousay

North
Ronaldshay

Sanday

×2 Daily
ex Sun

Longhope

Stronsay

×2 Daily
ex Sun

KIRKWALL
(Wideford)

HARRIS
(Northton)

×2 Daily ex Sun

NORTH
UIST
(Sollas)

BENBECULA

WICK
(Hillhead)

×2 Daily
ex Sun

SOUTH
UIST
(Askernish)

INVERNESS
(Longman)

Daily, ex Sun.

Daily,
ex Sun.

×3 weekly

ABERDEEN
(Kintore)

BARRA
(Northbay)

×3 weekly

TIREE
(The Reef)

×3 weekly

PERTH
(Scone)

Daily,
ex Sun.

ISLAY
(Glenegedale)

×15 weekly

×15 weekly

GLASGOW
(Renfrew)

CAMPBELTOWN
(Kintyre)

*The combined Scottish
Airways' route network for
Summer 1938 - its first fully
integrated season - showing
the link-up between Glasgow
and Inverness, and the Orkney
inter-island service (Author)*

*An ambulance patient is
disembarked at Renfrew from
Scottish Airways' Spartan Cruiser
III G-ADEL.
(Eric Starling)*

CHAPTER 10

Network Development

Since George Nicholson had founded Northern and Scottish Airways at Renfrew, he had lived with his wife and son and daughter at "The Red House" Milliken Park, a few miles west of Paisley on the road to Largs and Saltcoats. It was not a long drive from there to his office at Renfrew, and George, like Ted Fresson in Inverness, liked to be 'on the job' most of the time, working away in his office with William Cumming the Company Secretary, and Bill Gairdner the Air Superintendent, close by down the corridor. And there were always the superb services of the Scottish Flying Club's headquarters, its spacious lounge and good food, in which to entertain visitors. They could even be put up for the night in the Club.

Through the winter of 1937-38, while Ted Fresson was organising the surveying of his intended grass aerodrome on the Melbost Golf Links at Stornoway, that other intrepid aviator at Renfrew, Mr Glyn-Roberts, was still announcing that his West of Scotland Air Services was going to open a seaplane service, by now a *"three times weekly flight between Greenock, Tobermory, Portree and Stornoway within the next month or two ....."* In fact he went across to visit Stornoway harbour on September 9th 1937 with two Air Ministry officials.

But by the end of March 1938 still there was no sign at all of a Glasgow - Stornoway service, and patience began to run short in certain places. So much so that Malcolm Macmillan, Labour M.P. for Inverness, Ross, Cromarty and the Western Isles, asked a question in the House of Commons on March 16th 1938: *"Why is there still no landing ground at Stornoway, and when is an air service thither likely to commence ?"*

To which the Under Secretary of State for Air, Lt Col. A.J. Muirhead, said that progress had been held up by the cost of one site, but others were being examined.

To this, Mr Macmillan replied that : *"Every rock among the Western Isles seems to have a air connection, - except this important island !"*

Lt. Col Muirhead said that all technical assistance was being given by the Air Ministry, but in accordance with the policy of the Government, no financial help could be given for aerodromes.

Glasgow - Inverness link-up
And so we come to the single most important step the new combine would make in order to join together the two networks and be able to wield considerably more influence in Scotland in general, and the Highlands in particular.

It was not until April 20th 1938 that any major official announcement was made about the formation of Scottish Airways Ltd, and the objectives behind its creation. The Aberdeen *Press and Journal* published a major piece about the new company and for the first time mentioned a date for the intended link-up of both halves, with a new Glasgow (Renfrew) - Perth (Scone) - Inverness (Longman) service. In its April 21st issue it stated:

"TWO NEW ROUTES:
GLASGOW-PERTH-INVERNESS LINK
Speed - up in Air Services.
Big Developments in Scotland.
Inter-availability with Rail and Steamships.
Bookings Possible at any Railway Station.

Scottish air services speeded-up; new routes introduced; bookings for air, rail, and sea travel possible at any railway station in the country.

These are the principal new features in Scottish air travel, revealed last night with the announcement of the formation of Scottish Airways, Ltd.

This new company will operate the services now

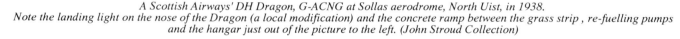

A Scottish Airways' DH Dragon, G-ACNG at Sollas aerodrome, North Uist, in 1938.
Note the landing light on the nose of the Dragon (a local modification) and the concrete ramp between the grass strip , re-fuelling pumps and the hangar just out of the picture to the left. (John Stroud Collection)

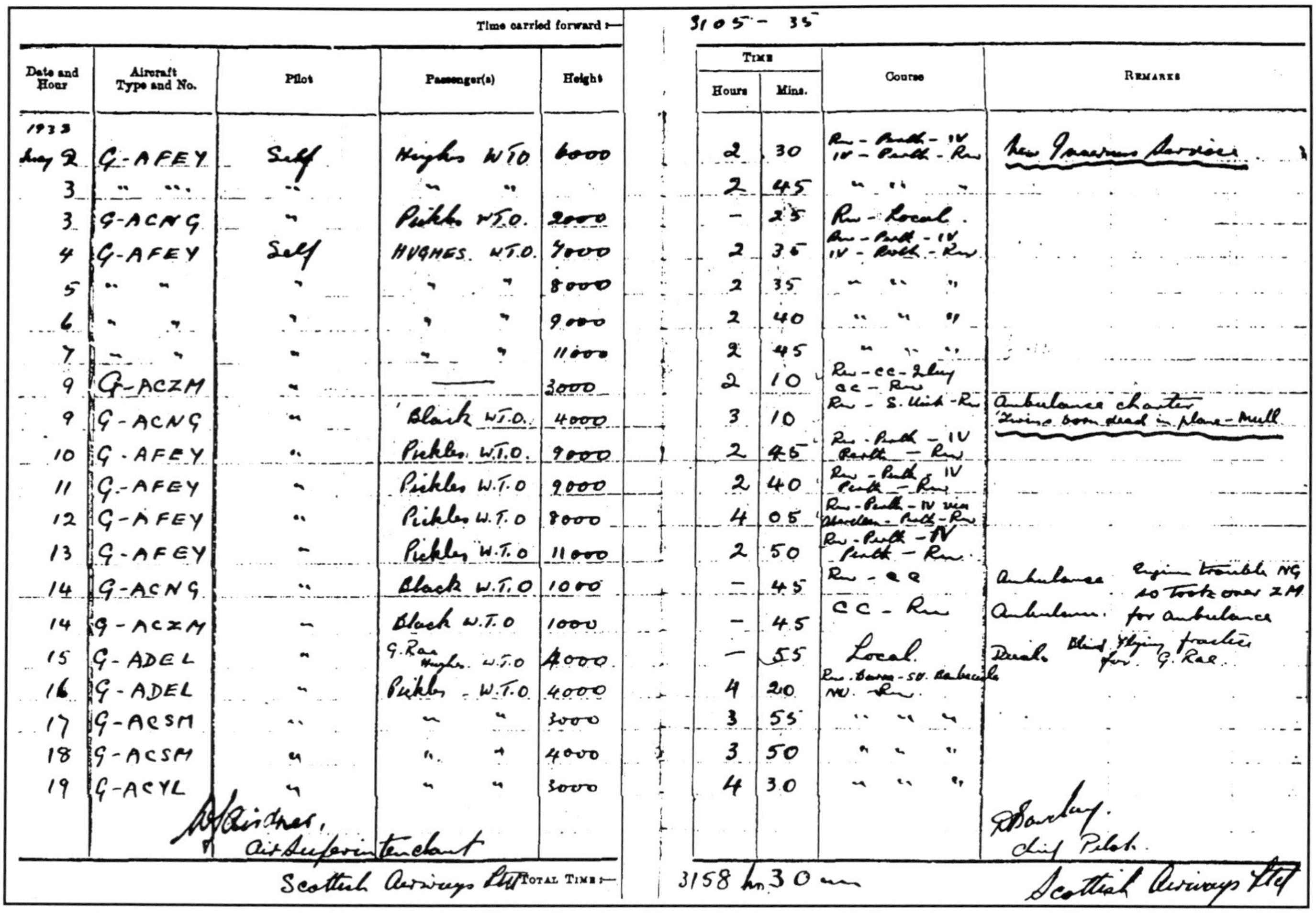

Date and Hour	Aircraft Type and No.	Pilot	Passenger(s)	Height	Time Hours	Time Mins.	Course	Remarks
				Time carried forward	3105	35		
1938 May 2	G-AFEY	Self	Hughes W.T.O.	6000	2	30	Rw - Perth - IV / IV - Perth - Rw	New Inverness Service
3	" "	"	" "		2	45	" " "	
3	G-ACNG	"	Pickles W.T.O.	2000	–	25	Rw - Local.	
4	G-AFEY	Self	HUGHES W.T.O.	7000	2	35	Rw - Perth - IV / IV - Perth - Rw	
5	" "	"	" "	8000	2	35	" " "	
6	" "	"	" "	9000	2	40	" " "	
7	" "	"	" "	11000	2	45	" " "	
9	G-ACZM	"	——	3000	2	10	Rw - CC - Islay / CC - Rw	
9	G-ACNG	"	Black W.T.O.	4000	3	10	Rw - S. Uist - Rw	Ambulance charter "Twins born dead in plane - Mull"
10	G-AFEY	"	Pickles W.T.O.	9000	2	45	Rw - Perth - IV / Perth - Rw	
11	G-AFEY	"	Pickles W.T.O	9000	2	40	Rw - Perth - IV / Perth - Rw	
12	G-AFEY	"	Pickles W.T.O	8000	4	05	Rw - Perth - IV via Aberdeen - Perth - Rw	
13	G-AFEY	"	Pickles W.T.O	11000	2	50	Rw - Perth - IV / Perth - Rw	
14	G-ACNG	"	Black W.T.O	1000	–	45	Rw - CC	Ambulance. Engine trouble NG so took over ZM
14	G-ACZM	"	Black W.T.O	1000	–	45	CC - Rw	Ambulance. for ambulance
15	G-ADEL	"	G. Rae Hughes W.T.O	4000	–	55	Local	Dual. Blind flying practice for G. Rae.
16	G-ADEL	"	Pickles W.T.O.	4000	4	20	Rw. Barra - SU. Benbecula NU. - Rw.	
17	G-ACSM	"	" "	3000	3	55	" " "	
18	G-ACSM	"	" "	4000	3	50	" " "	
19	G-ACYL	"	" "	3000	4	30	" " "	
				Total Time	3158 hrs	30 mins		

[signature], Air Superintendent, Scottish Airways Ltd

D. Barclay, Chief Pilot. Scottish Airways Ltd

A page from David Barclay's log, with the entry for May 2nd 1938 showing the inaugural flight from Renfrew to Perth and Inverness. The ambulance charter on May 9th and "Blind Flying Practice" for Gilbert Rae on the 15th are also interesting. (Mrs Sheila Harper)

undertaken by the two principal air transport concerns in Scotland - Northern and Scottish Airways Ltd. and Highland Airways Ltd. By the linking up of services, which will operate as from May 2, passengers will be able to travel by air from the Shetlands as far south as the Channel Islands.

Glasgow to Inverness - 85 minutes

Perhaps nothing will appeal to travellers more than the fact that they can now walk into any railway station in Scotland, make their reservations, and have the facilities of inter-availability of tickets by air, rail, and sea.

The whole scheme is an important step in the co-ordination of air services, and in the economic development of air travel in Scotland.

"The first real concrete answer to the report of the Maybury Committee," was how an official of the new Scottish company last night put it.

New routes

Two new routes to be introduced with the coming into operation of Scottish Airways, Ltd., are Glasgow-Tiree and Glasgow-Perth-Inverness. They embrace a route mileage of approximately 2,500 miles - a weekly average of 12,500 miles.

The new services promise to be a boon to travellers to the north of Scotland and to the Western Isles and the Hebrides.

The journey from Renfrew Airport (headquarters of the new company) to Barra will be done in ninety minutes; to Inverness in eighty-five minutes; and to Wick in two hours twenty minutes. From Barra to South Uist will take exactly ten minutes.

Lerwick can be reached from Perth in little more than three hours, and Kirkwall in just over two hours. Aberdeen to Inverness takes only forty-five minutes, and Wick ninety minutes.

Economic Development

All these routes are being linked up by a chain, which, it is believed, will secure the economic development of air transport throughout Scotland.

This striking development in Scottish air travel has been made possible through unification of ownership, in which are concerned British Airways Ltd.; David MacBrayne, Ltd.; and the L.M.S.

The inclusion of sea and rail interests, will, of course, facilitate the correlation of steamship, rail, road, and air services. The services hitherto operated by Northern and Scottish Airways from Glasgow to the Western Isles and the Hebrides will be taken over by an affiliated company called Western Isles Airways, Ltd."

In *The Aeroplane* magazine for April 27th, a piece by the Editor, C.G. Grey, tried to unravel the bewildering series of mergers and take-overs that had been taking place:

MIXTURE AS BEFORE

Scottish transport aviation has been much reorganized on the commercial side by the merging of Northern and Scottish Airways Ltd. and Highland Airways Ltd into another group of companies. The services themselves will not be visibly affected, except by increases already announced .

Scottish Airways Ltd. will now operate those services hitherto run by Highland Airways Ltd. from Aberdeen. Inverness and Northern Scotland to the Orkneys and Shetlands: also the services recently announced by Northern and Scottish Airways Ltd. from Glasgow to Perth and Inverness.

Western Isles Airways Ltd. is an affiliated company formed to take over the Northern and Scottish Airways routes from Glasgow to the Western Isles and the Hebrides.

Both companies are owned by British Airways Ltd., David MacBrayne Ltd., and the London Midland and Scottish Railway Company.

And so the mixing goes on. Mr. E. E. Fresson started Highland Airways, and the Inverness - Orkney service, on May 8, l933. A year later he was awarded a contract to carry on that service all first-class mails without surcharge; the first such service in the British Empire, where a certain noise has been made of late about similar but later arrangements.

The services kept astonishing regularity, and were extended from time to time.

In 1935 competition arose from United Airways Ltd., a company formed by Whitehall Securities which embraced Mr. Thurgood's Jersey Airways. Shortly afterwards a merger was arranged. The result was still Highland Airways, managed by Mr. Fresson, but largely owned by the interests which later became British Airways. This was one of the first of the almost inextricable minglings which are still proceeding and have reached a point at which relationships between companies require a genealogical expert to explain.

Northern and Scottish Airways Ltd. was formed in 1934 by Mr. George Nicholson. For practical purposes it took up the routes discontinued by Mr. John Sword just before. Either then or soon after the same interests became concerned in it as in United Airways, so an affiliation was quickly reached between N. and S. and Highland Airways, although their routes did not then meet.

British Airways was formed in 1935 from Hillman's, Spartan and United, and came into control of N. and S. and Highland.

In 1937 British Airways disposed of the N. and S. lines South of the Border to Railway Air Services Ltd.

By the reorganization now announced, and explained in the opening paragraphs hereof, the remaining lines of N. and S., and those of Highland Airways, also come under railway influence."

On April 15th 1938, George Nicholson took delivery of a brand new De Havilland DH 89A Dragon Rapide, (G-AFEY) to start the new Inverness link and David Barclay was given some 25 minutes dual instruction on the new Mk II Rapide (fitted with flaps) by Bill Gairdner, the Operations Manager of the Southern Section - but still acting as the local De Havilland sales agent for the Brian Lewis concern.

David Barclay then flew it on the Campbeltown run on the 16th on its first service trip, and on April 19th he flew the first route - proving trip over the new link Renfrew - Perth - Inverness in 'FEY, carrying Radio Officer W ('Bill') Black and making the roundtrip in 3hrs 15mins.

On April 22nd Wing Cmdr. Measures and some Air Ministry officials had come up to Renfrew and David took them on a tour of the Western Isles aerodromes - Tiree (to which they were starting a schedule in a few days time), Barra, South Uist, Benbecula, Stornoway, North Uist and back. (At Stornoway they were still using the shore at Melbost, pending the Golf Course work being finished).

Then on April 26th David flew the party up to Perth in the Spartan Cruiser III G-ADEL for the official opening lunch to presage the start of the Renfrew - Perth - Inverness link. As *The Aeroplane* magazine for May 4th stated:

THE CREW DISEMBARK

The crew disembark from the Scottish Airways' Spartan Cruiser II G-ACSM at Renfrew after a flight from the Hebrides. Note the Captain climbing out of the flight-deck roof!
(John Stroud Collection)

Passengers disembark from a Cruiser II at Renfrew, assisted by a member of Scottish Airways' ground staff.
A schoolgirl waits for the rest of the party, possibly on her way to Boarding School.
(John Stroud Collection)

THE PASSENGERS ALIGHT

"THE NEW SCOTTISH LINK

A new service by Scottish Airways Ltd., between Glasgow, Perth and Inverness, was opened officially on April 26. A Spartan Cruiser and a Dragon Rapide took a party of guests as far as Perth, where an official lunch was held.

Among those present were the Marquess of Douglas and Clydesdale, Sir John Sutherland, Lord Provost Nimmo of Perth, Provost Michie of Renfrew, Bailie A Murray of Glasgow, Bailie Mrs. Mann of Glasgow, Capt. E. E. Fresson and Mr George Nicholson, both of Scottish Airways Ltd.

At the lunch Provost Michie made his startling announcement of the imminent closing of Renfrew Airport, the principal terminus of the new service."

The 'startling announcement' will be referred to later. The Rapide was probably flown across by Bill Gairdner, carrying the remaining guests in 'FEY.

The service proper then opened on May 2nd, and David Barclay flew G-AFEY across to Perth, where he picked up Capt Fresson as well as some passengers, and let Ted Fresson fly it up to Inverness (at first in a clear blue sky, then overcast later on). David disembarked at Inverness at around 10.15, and waited there while one of Fresson's pilots took it on up to Wick, Kirkwall and Shetland, and brought it back into Inverness again at about

14.50. Then he flew it back to Glasgow, taking 2hrs 30mins for the roundtrip this time. His W.O. was F.R. Hughes on the first few trips, then Pickles later on (they were both very experienced). The actual published time-table for the service was:

08.30	dep.	GLASGOW (Renfrew)	arr.	16.45
09.05	arr.	PERTH	dep.	16.10
09.15	dep.	(Scone)	arr.	16.00
10.15	arr.	INVERNESS (Longman)	dep.	15.00
10.30	dep.	INVERNESS	arr.	14.50
11.10	arr.	WICK	dep.	14.10
11.15	dep.	(Hillhead)	arr.	14.05
11.35	arr.	KIRKWALL	dep.	13.45
11.50	dep.	(Wideford)	arr.	13.30
12.35	arr.	LERWICK (Sumburgh)	dep.	12.45

The service was flown daily, except Sundays, the fares being:

An illustration that was originally used in the Sales Brochure for the De Havilland Dragon Rapide, G-AFEY is seen from Spartan Cruiser G-ADEL, approaching the old Perth bridge and the North Inch Park of the city of Perth on April 26th 1938.
On board the Rapide are invited guests attending the official launch lunch of Scottish Airways' Glasgow - Perth - Inverness service.

SECTOR		FARES	
		Single	**Return**
Glasgow	- Perth	£1. 5s. 0d.	£2. 5s. 0d.
	- Inverness	£2. 10s. 0d.	£4. 5s. 0d.
	- Wick	£4. 5s. 0d.	£7. 5s. 0d.
	- Kirkwall	£5. 0s. 0d.	£8. 15s. 0d.
	- Lerwick	£6. 0s. 0d.	£10. 0s. 0d.
Perth	- Inverness	£1. 15s. 0d.	£3. 0s. 0d.
	- Wick	£3.10s. 0d.	£6. 0s. 0d.
	- Kirkwall	£4. 5s. 0d.	£7.10s. 0d.
	- Lerwick	£5. 15s. 0d.	£10. 0s. 0d.
Inverness	- Wick	£1. 15s. 0d.	£3.0s. 0d.
	- Kirkwall	£2. 10s. 0d.	£4. 10s. 0d.
	- Lerwick	£4. 0s. 0d.	£7. 0s. 0d.
Wick	- Kirkwall	£1. 0s. 0d.	£1. 15s. 0d.
	- Lerwick	£3. 0s. 0d.	£5. 10s. 0d.
Kirkwall	- Lerwick	£2. 10s. 0d.	£4. 10s. 0d.

A close-up of the special landing light fitted to the nose of Scottish Airways' DH Dragons, seen here on an aircraft at the Barra airstrip. (John Stroud Collection)

David Barclay flew the southern sectors for the first two weeks of May, then went back to the tricky Western Isles routes, leaving another pilot to carry on the daily Perth/Inverness. During the second half of May, though, some unusual occurrences came to Ted Fresson's notice at Inverness. He was alerted one morning to the fact that the Renfrew plane had arrived completely iced-up, and practically fell into the aerodrome. It could not proceed to Shetland like that, and so a substitute aircraft was put on, for the northern link.

A few days later it happened again, and this time Ted Fresson went to talk to the pilot. The latter said he understood that the Managing Director at Renfrew had told the Operations Manager to suggest to the pilots that they always try to fly above the clouds on the Perth - Inverness sector, so as not to subject the passengers to the roughness and 'frightening experience' of flying in the clouds. But to do this the pilot had to often climb above 10,000 ft or more, and on some days it was impossible to get high enough to get above them at all. It was on these latter such days that in trying to get high enough, the aircraft got badly iced-up, whereas staying at a lower level - even though still in cloud - such would not have occurred.

Ted said that this dangerous process must stop immediately - as they could not afford any fatal accidents - but all that Renfrew said was that the pilots had been told to return to Perth if things got too bad. So knowing that the matter could be resolved without that necessity, Ted had a word in the ear of all the 'Southern' pilots that flew up to Inverness. He told them that he had evolved the

'Dog Leg' route for that sector to avoid icing, and they flew two separate courses to Perth - one as far as the Drumochter Pass and then a change of bearing to the second one. They could fly no higher than 5,000 ft all the way, and if necessary in cloud, but there would be no icing up.

The Southern pilots gave it a try, and hence-forward they always adopted Ted's system, born of hard-earned experience. Nothing was mentioned at management level at Renfrew and the pilots just ignored the previous instructions !

Tiree, the Western Isles and the Isle of Man
Getting back to the rest of the Summer 1938 time-table for Scottish Airways, the other innovations included a three times daily Renfrew - Islay service, two calling at Campbeltown en route (morning and evening), with a mid-day non-stop service Renfrew - Islay on Monday, Wednesday and Friday. A new Renfrew - Tiree (The Reef) service operated on Monday, Wednesday and Friday, and gave steamer connections onwards to Barra and South Uist. And there was a daily (except Sunday) service to the Western Isles, routeing outwards: Renfrew - Benbecula (Balivanich) - North Uist (Sollas), and back via Benbecula, South Uist. and Barra to Renfrew on Days (1) (3) and

Pilots at Ease!
Waiting in the sunny entrance to one of the hangars at Renfrew to 'scramble' on duty are Capt. Jock Young (right) and R.O. Andrew Ruthven (left). (Alison Mills)

Reflections in the sands - Scottish Airways' DH Rapide G-AFRK during a sunny morning on the beach at Barra. It was this salty environment that caused severe corrosion, especially on the all-metal Spartan Crusiers. (John Stroud Collection)

(5); and on Days (2) (4) and (6) flying out via Barra, South Uist and Benbecula to North Uist and back via Tiree (on demand) direct to Renfrew. (Connections could also be made to/from Harris on demand).

From June 1st to September 10th there was a three times daily Glasgow - I.O.M. service (including weekends) operated from the I.O.M./Ronaldsway Aerodrome) by Isle of Man Air Services Ltd (equally owned by the LMS /Railway, I.O.M. Steam Packet Co. and Olley Air Service since the RAS withdrew in September 1937). But there were occasions when Scottish Airways Southern Section provided its own aircraft at times to keep the service going in 1938. Interestingly, the I.O.M. Air Services' 1938 Summer timetable actually included a following years' (1939) time-table and booking reservation form!

As for Ted Fresson's Northern Section time-table, all part of the group now, his schedules showed two flights daily between Inverness and all points up to Shetland - one being the Renfrew plane and the other being the Sumburgh night-stop aircraft, which flew down to Inverness and across to Aberdeen (Kintore) before turning around there and flying back. Shetlanders could now leave Sumburgh at 0845 and spend from 1040 to 1330 in Inverness before returning the same day; or Glaswegians could spend from 10.15 to 15.00 in Inverness. And Ted Fresson's Orkney inter-island service had its own time-table each day, operating from Kirkwall (Wideford) to North Ronaldsay, Westray, Stronsay, Sanday, Longhope and Rousay.

A little matter of Renfrew

We have seen the reference to the 'startling announcement' made by Provost Michie of Renfrew at the inaugural luncheon in Perth of the new Glasgow- Inverness service. It was indeed startling, as *The Aeroplane* magazine explained in its May 4th 1938 issue :

"THE RENFREW RACKET

Major D.K. Michie, Provost of the Royal Burgh of Renfrew loaded his discourse with the highest of explosive at Perth on April 26. In celebrating the opening of Scottish Airways' service between Glasgow, Perth and Inverness he made an announcement which will leave at least one end of that service flapping loose at its Lowland end.

Because of "the procrastination and discourtesy of the Civil Aviation Department of the Air Ministry", he said, Renfrew Airport would close down on May 15.

The principal tenant of Renfrew Airport is the Scottish Flying Club, to which the closing of the place would be a disaster. Now that air transport in Scotland is becoming really significant the Club may no longer be the main consideration but for most of ten years it has represented all that was soundest in Scottish Aviation. Besides that the club has been run on excellent business lines and has grown opulent and a benefit to society.

The Club's lease as tenant and manager of Renfrew Airport for the Corporation expires on May 15. The parties have been talking of renewal, and terms, since last September.

For some years Renfrew has grown more and more important as an airport; that is, as a port of call for commercial aeroplanes. For example, if Renfrew be closed on May 15, 26 daily services will be stopped.

The Council therefore began last September to consult the Air Ministry about an official traffic control. The Air Ministry stated its requirements and asked for a plan. Three weeks later a letter suggested a meeting on this urgent matter.

The meeting was held in November and the main features agreed upon. The new plan was sent to the Air Ministry on Dec. 8 and acknowledged, much to the indignation of the Council, by a postcard. This was, no doubt, the usual printed card intimating arrival and the bestowal of attention.

From time to time the Town Clerk wrote for instructions to proceed with the Control Tower and other decorations, or for some reply. Eventually an appointment was made by telephone for another visit by an Air Ministry representative, but this was later cancelled by telegram and letter. After that, until March 22, the Air Ministry did not write.

The Town Clerk was less idle. He wrote that the Town Council would extend the aerodrome and put up the buildings demanded by the Air Ministry if some guarantee were given that Renfrew would be recognized as the aerodrome for the South-West of Scotland. If not they felt that further spending of the ratepayers' money was not justified.

The Royal Burgh has spent about £11,000 on improvements and lost about £300 to £500 per year since they set up as aerodrome owners,

Provost Michie protests that the Council are most anxious to have an airport at Renfrew and encourage Civil Aviation, but at a price. Reasonable ratepayers will not go on subsidising what ought to be a National Service.

The last remark opens a totally different line. Provost Michie must not say such things if he wants to sustain the role of the keen aviationist driven to frenzy by Government slights. Everybody knows that Government Departments move slowly, and many aver that the Air Ministry is slower than most, but that is no reason for killing about two-thirds of Scottish Aviation with one brick.

The Council may take up either of two attitudes: (a) that they want to encourage civil aviation in Scotland by a good airport at Renfrew but cannot get the Air Ministry to take action; and (b) that they are tired of losing money on the airport and want to sell it for an housing estate. But the two will not mix.

The first cause could be served better by renewing the Club's lease for a short term only, holding up all work which involved higher rates and generally standing pat on the *status quo* with loud protests of injured innocence. A large and motley body of opinion would get busy at once and probably have effect. The Scottish Flying Club do not particularly want to be stabbed in the back, nor the air line companies to be cut off at the roots. Scottish Airways has its main base and all its workshops at Renfrew.

They would all support the Royal Burgh in almost any sort of protest which did not involve sawing off the branches on which they sit.

If, on the other hand, Renfrew is tired of the airport and want council-houses instead, combined with the glory of martyrs in the cause of Aviation, they might conceivably do as they are doing. But their crowns are likely to look dishevelled before the matter is forgotten.

In the meantime the squabble has been adjourned by the Air Ministry which telegraphed to the Scottish Club on April 28 saying that it would renew Renfrew's licence for two years."

This however, was not the end of the affair, as *The Aeroplane* for the following week, May 11th, shows:

"RENFREW CONTINUED-OR DISCOUNTINUED

An affair such as that of Renfrew was not to be missed by Mr. Robert Perkins, M.P., and others. He asked the Under-Secretary of State for Air on May 3 whether he was aware of the impending shut-down, brought on by the procrastination and discourtesy of the Air Ministry.

He also asked whether he knew that such shutting-down would stop valuable ambulance services to the Western Isles; and there was also the Glasgow Exhibition. He wanted a reassuring statement.

Scottish Airways Ltd		
Aircraft Fleet - Summer 1938		
1.	Spartan Cruiser II	G-ACSM
2.	Spartan Cruiser II	G-ACYL
3.	Spartan Cruiser II	G-ACZM
4.	Spartan Cruiser III	G-ADEL
5.	De Havilland DH 84 Dragon II	G-ACNG
6.	De Havilland DH 84 Dragon I	G-ACIT*
7.	De Havilland DH 84 Dragon II	G-ADCT*
8.	De Havilland DH 89A Dragon Rapide	G-AFEY
9.	De Havilland DH 89 Dragon Rapide	G-ADAJ*
10.	De Havilland DH 89A Dragon Rapide	G-AEWL*

* Aircraft based, and used by Northern Section, at Inverness, etc. Rest are based, and used by Southern Section at Renfrew.

Lt.-Col. A. J. Muirhead was unable to give one. He admitted the delay in correspondence but refused to consider his Department responsible for the Renfrew Town Council's decision.

The assurance which they demanded, that Renfrew would continue to be recognized as the civil aerodrome for the South West of Scotland, could not be given because Renfrew, as the Council well knew, was not first-class and could not be substantially improved.

The Air Ministry had offered to recognize Renfrew in the sense demanded for two years, but the Renfrew Council had telegraphed their refusal to accept that offer.

Further questions by Messrs Maxton and Ganacher neither added nor elicited any more information.

The situation is undeniably a poser for the best administrative and diplomatic brains.

The Renfrew Town Council are asking for an aerodrome to be recognised permanently which has some notorious disadvantages of size, surface and surroundings. Real improvements would be so expensive as to be impracticable

As arguments on its side the Council quotes its efforts and expenditure in the past, the lack of another site, and finally, by way of shock tactics, the crippling of Civil Aviation in South-West Scotland if Renfrew shuts down on May 15.

On the other side the Air Ministry is, by implication, asking the Council to go on spending money on a lost

Renfrew from the air in the 1930's - an aerial picture taken looking across the hangar and office area towards the north-west, with the River Clyde and shipyards at the top left.

A poor quality, but interesting photograph, for it shows the three aircraft types in the Scottish Airways fleet (L to R) DH84 Dragon, DH89A Dragon Rapide and Spartan Cruiser (in this case, G-ADEL, a Mk.III)

cause. When its representatives advised new buildings and control tower they did so without knowing that Renfrew was not a permanency; an example of the finger in this pie not knowing what the finger in the next pie doeth. Naturally the Air Ministry, and most others, would like the Royal Burgh to go on carrying the baby till someone else was ready, but they have no arguments, which would have much effect on a Scotsman.

Renfrew was first taken over on compulsory lease during the war 1914-1918, and was afterwards handed back with the buildings thrown in, and a cash sum in lieu of reinstating the ground in agricultural condition. This was in 1933 after the Scottish Flying Club had already been the tenants of the Air Ministry there for five years.

Since then the Council have spent money on it and sustained an annual loss as an investment for the future. Doubts about the soundness of the investment began to arise some time ago, when successive designs of civil aeroplanes produced complaints of the aerodromes smallness or roughness or approaches. It has been used successfully by Mew Gulls and Comets, but regular air transport in all weathers needs plenty of room.

Abbotsinch, a mile or so away across the canal westwards, is much larger and smoother, and has very good approaches. It can also be expanded. It is the home of an Auxiliary Squadron, although civil and Service operations have worked well at Castle Bromwich and elsewhere.

Something of this sort may be in the official mind, but for the present the needs of the R.A.F. are paramount and may include Abbotsinch. But there is not nearly enough accommodation there for the civil operations based at Renfrew. The suggested two years might solve both these problems but the Renfrew Council are allowing two weeks."

More developments followed rapidly as noted in *The Aeroplane* for May 25th 1938:-

"RENFREW REPRIEVED

Renfrew is to remain an airport for at least three years after all. The ultimatum of the Renfrew Town Council has had the effect of getting an undertaking out of the Air Ministry to recognise it for three years as the main airport of South-west Scotland.

This was made known in the House of Commons on May 10 in answer to Mr. Neil Maclean (Soc. Govan). Lt. Col. A. J. Muirhead, Under-Secretary of State for Air, said that recognition for the five years could not be guaranteed as asked because of Renfrew's disabilities in size, surroundings and surface. The undertaking for three years had been given together with arrangements for the use of Abbotsinch by civil aeroplanes when Renfrew was too affected by bad weather.

On May 10 Mr. A. H. Wilson, Assistant Director of Civil Aviation, and Mr. F. W. Hancock, of the Operations Department, Air Ministry, flew to Renfrew and met representatives of the local interests. Major D. K. Michie, Provost of Renfrew, and Mr. Robertson, Town Clerk, were there for the Royal Burgh; Mr. G. F. Luke and Lt. Col. M'William represented the Scottish Flying Club, and Mr. George Nicholson, of Scottish Airways Ltd., represented the operators.

After an hour of " most cordial deliberations " the decision was announced.

The decision to shut down is cancelled on the following terms:—
1. Renfrew is to be the recognised airport for South-west Scotland for three years from May 15, 1938.
2. It is to be licensed as the aerodrome of the Scottish Flying Club for five years from May 15, 1938.

The famous Orkney-based pilot, John Philip Rae, seen standing beside the DH Dragon G-ADCT 'Orcadian' at Wideford aerodrome, Kirkwall. (John Rae)

A rare air-to-air photograph of the Northern Section's DH Dragon G-ACET flying across Scapa Flow, Orkney. This Dragon is currently (1995) under restoration to flying condition. (John Rae)

3. Abbotsinch Aerodrome is to be available as a stand-by when Renfrew is not suitable for any reason.

4. The Air Ministry is to decide as soon as possible about the permanent aerodrome for South-west Scotland.

5. Traffic control organisation is to be provided as soon as possible by the Air Ministry.

Mr. Nicholson, for the operators, said he was quite satisfied. His company had prepared to cancel all its services, but now had time to make future plans and go on with services and developments.

Mr. Luke, for the Scottish Flying Club, was also delighted with the outcome, and remarked that if agreement had not been reached there was still plenty of ammunition in the bag with which to press for a settlement.

He also points out that a three-year guarantee is not enough to justify the Renfrew Council in spending enough to make Renfrew first-class. The Air Ministry do not think such a thing is possible, but even the minimum requirements are costly enough .

The owners of Renfrew claim that if 90 acres and the road on the North side of the aerodrome be brought in, which would take three years besides much money, Renfrew would then have runways of 1,400 yds. and 950 yds. at right angles. Only Croydon, Lympne and Speke can offer any more.

If this work is to be done the Air Ministry decision for the future, after the three years, must come quickly.

The use of Abbotsinch as a regular civil aerodrome has drawbacks. Although No. 259 Sqdn., R.A.F., are to be moved from it, the Auxiliary Air Force Squadron, No. 602, is to be doubled. Also the Blackburn works at Dumbarton are to use that aerodrome for the assembly and testing of machines which they bring down the river on barges.

On the other hand, the Air Ministry has bought more land adjacent to Abbotsinch and can enlarge it, as far as ground accommodation is concerned. Congestion in the air would not be reduced."

After which, the last word appeared in the House of Commons on May 18th:

"RENFREW'S OUTLOOK

Renfrew Aerodrome provided our new Secretary of State for Air, Sir Kingsley Wood, on May 18, with his first question and answer in the House of Commons in his new job. The Marquess of Clydesdale and Mr. Maclean both asked the Secretary of State for Air whether there was anything more to be said about Renfrew.

Sir Kingsley Wood said that arrangements had been made by the Town Council that Renfrew should continue to be recognised as the civil aerodrome for South West Scotland for three years and that the licence of the aerodrome should, subject to its being suitably maintained, be renewed for five years for the Scottish Aero Club. And air traffic control was to be established by the Air Ministry as soon as possible. Sir Kingsley added that the Air Ministry would continue to explore the possibility of finding an alternative civil aerodrome for this area, and in the meantime the R.A.F. aerodrome at Abbotsinch would be available as a stand-by when conditions are too bad for aircraft at Renfrew. If at the end of three years a better aerodrome were not available the question of extending the recognition of Renfrew would be considered. So there the matter stands at present."

Not so smooth...

All transitions in merged companies can be difficult of course, and this was no more true than of Ted Fresson's position as General Manager of a highly profitable Northern section of the new Scottish Airways, when compared with the loss-making Southern section around which the Headquarters and overall controlling staff members were based.

Ted therefore felt he had to underline some of the original intentions once more, and wrote a letter to this effect dated 30th May 1938 to Mr W.D. L. Roberts, their own Chairman (and Vice-Chairman of British Airways Ltd):

"Dear Mr Roberts

Further to my brief note of yesterday. I have been meaning to write to you ever since my return from Town in order to confirm the points discussed during the hour or more you were kind enough to give me Tuesday morning.

Briefly, the object of my conversation was to point out to you that the principals outlined in your letter addressed to me on the 10th July 1937 are not being adhered to. In this letter you stated that:-

'It is the intention that the M.D. of Northern & Scottish Airways shall become the manager of the Western Section and shall be co-opted as a member of the Board of Scottish Airways and Western Isles Airways; and similarly, the M.D. of Highland Airways shall be the manager of the Northern Section and be co-opted as a member of the Board of Scottish Airways and Western Isles Airways'.

It would appear to me that as matters are moving at present the Renfrew management will eventually obtain control of both the Western Isles and Northern Section, which would automatically make the Inverness organisation redundant. This will either jeopardise my position or subordinate me to the Renfrew management who are both my juniors in years and experience. In support of this contention I refer you to the penultimate para. in Wing Commander Measures' operational

Ted Fresson (left) points something out on the map to Capt. Charles Bernard ("Tug") Wilson, beside Dragon G-ADCT at Inverness. (E.E.Fresson)

programme ending 30th Sept. 1938 wherein it is stated:

'While the administration salaries at Renfrew may appear to be high it must be borne in mind over the past few months very considerable additional work has been involved as a result of the merger. This staff will require to be retained to provide for the additional administrative work which will be brought about by the inclusion of Highland Airways in the merger.'

The signs are not wanting that this absorption is slowly taking place. Our economies are being taken from us, my wishes and recommendations are invariably thrown out in favour of the Renfrew point of view, and as far as I can see it is proposed to take over our Publicity, Traffic and Operational management. The Glasgow - Perth - Inverness route which I have been working on for the past three years and for which I was anxious to join forces with the L.M.S. in order to avoid competition, has been taken away from me and is being run by the Renfrew management as a separate route and with a separate machine and separate pilot. It is improperly advertised and is bound to be uneconomical by nature of its separation from the Northern Section. I am not aware that the Renfrew management ever gave a moment's thought to this route prior to the amalgamation. This section is just tacked on to the Inverness - Shetland service instead of being an integral part of it, when one aircraft could build up an economical number of hours during the year.

While you were away in Africa, Wing. Cmdr. Measures' report referred to above was discussed at a Board meeting held in London during January or February. Capt. Balfour took exception to Highland Airways being saddled with additional staff expense from Renfrew. He argued, the same as I do, why saddle the Northern Section with such extra expense when they are a self contained unit and working far more economically.

I wish to submit to you and the Directors of British Airways that the policy outlined in your letter dated 10th June 1937 should be adhered to and thus avoid mixing the Northern Section up with the proposed huge financial loss of £30,000 odd per annum.

With the Glasgow - Perth - Inverness section made integral with my present service to Shetland, I am of the opinion that it is possible to develop a self supporting service and with a bit of luck regarding mail contracts to eventually show a profit. Already we have the Inverness - Kirkwall section paying its way and as soon as the Shetland - Kirkwall section and Glasgow - Inverness section have been consolidated, you will see the colour of the picture is not too bad. I fail to see any such promise for the Western Isles section unless drastic modifications are made to the routes operated, and it would appear to me that it is most desirable to keep the two sections separated for comparison purposes, instead of jumbling the lot together. For my point of view it is essential as my past work and future is wrapped up in the ultimate success of the Northern Section. You will no doubt appreciate that I have given five of the best years of my life in trying to achieve this end. The fact that I have never asked the new Board for a penny seems to indicate some measure of such.

I would like you to show this letter to Major McCrindle and I hope to hear that you will find yourselves in agreement with my suggestions and that I may rely on your support to induce the Board to carry them through.

I am writing to you separately regarding my qualifications for administration.

Yours sincerely
(signed)
E.E. Fresson."

To which Roberts replied in a letter dated 9th June 1938:
"Dear Fresson
As regards to additional information you send down about yourself and notes confirming the points you told me about verbally, I am leaving these with Major McCrindle.

Scottish Airways' Spartan Cruiser II G-ACZM on a brief stop at Benbecula's Balivanich aerodrome, being piloted by Capt. Henry Vallance. (Henry Vallance)

IN

SUMMER...

My suggestion, if I may make one, is to mark time and continue with your endeavours to make the business in your area a success.

For the moment I can say no more.

Mr Gerard d'Erlanger will act as alternate Director whilst I am away and you will find him very alert to the question of efficiency.

I leave Southampton on Saturday. As you know, Major McCrindle is appreciative of the troubles and difficulties which arise immediately after an amalgamation of this sort and is always willing to do what he can to help straighten them out.
Yours sincerely
(signed)
W.D.L. Roberts

PS
I have had a talk with Measures and understand that he was up in Inverness at the end of last week.

I think you will find that Measures will be making certain alterations. I feel confident that you will do your utmost to fit in with these."

There the matter rested for the time being, except that Ted dropped a line to Major McCrindle in London to make sure his remarks were on record and especially passed to Gerard d'Erlanger, the new alternate director:

"June 30th 1938
Dear McCrindle
Prior to Mr. Roberts departure abroad, he wrote me on the 9th inst. tendering some advice regarding matters I had discussed with him in London relative to the amalgamation. I gather you have a copy of this letter.

The second para states:-

'My suggestion, if I may make one, is to mark time and continue with your endeavours to make the business in your area a success.'

As you know, the whole of my endeavours for the past five years have been based on these lines, but it must be understood that I am now controlled by an expensive and somewhat cumbersome system. While I can do my best to increase passenger traffic and see that the service runs as regularly as possible, I am afraid the figures in future for the Northern Section are not going to compare as favourably in relation to income and disbursements, as they have done in the past.

With Renfrew having been appointed by the Board as G.H.Q. a considerable amount of work is being duplicated and in some cases triplicated. This is a wasteful expense and I cannot control it.

Of course, as long as I am connected with the new Company, my whole endeavours will be for its betterment, but I am sure you will understand that I could only be responsible for a policy in which my approval and

...OR

WINTER

consent has been obtained. This is not the case at the moment.

For my future protection, it is necessary for me to put these observations on record. Would you please convey these remarks to Mr. Gerard d'Erlanger, whom Mr. Roberts mentioned in his letter, as becoming the alternate Director in his absence.

Your sincerely

(signed)

E.E. Fresson."

Ted Fresson, it must be remembered had come up the hard way, having been a barnstorming pilot and one who had formed and run his own joy-riding company - just like Sir Alan Cobham in his day. For those who had learned how to control expenditure and keep flying costs to a minimum, it was doubly hard to have others with more grandiose ideas take over your business and be seen to be wasting money!

A sad ambulance trip

David Barclay, already the uncrowned king of the Scottish Air Ambulance flights (numerically speaking) had a less fortunate such occasion on May 9th 1938.

A full account of all his ambulance flights since joining Northern & Scottish Airways in Spring 1935 will be found in Appendix 3, but this occasion merited a mention even in *'The Aeroplane'* magazine for May 25th 1938:

"AIR AMBULANCES

From different parts two very different stories of service to the sick by air transport came to hand recently.

Early in May the Imperial Airways flying boat *Circe* brought into Southampton a Scottish Master Mariner, Capt. Jones Smith, on a stretcher. He had fallen ill at Karachi and was sent home from his ship by air for an operation. He spent the nights at Basra and Brindisi in the respective hotels with other passengers, but still on a stretcher. Flight Clerk H. S. Bingham and Steward J. Bryden attended him on the journey according to doctors instructions.

He was taken by motor-ambulance to a London hospital.

The other incident ended less happily. Capn. David Barclay of Western Isles Airways Ltd., answered an urgent call and left from Renfrew with a radio-operator in a DH Dragon for South Uist on May 9. He took on board a Mrs McLean, her husband and Nurse Govan, and started back.

During the journey Nurse Govan sent Mr McLean up forward with the crew and officiated single-handed at the birth of twins to Mrs McLean. The infants did not live. According to doctors the emergency was such, in fact, that their survival was not hoped for. Mrs McLean was taken to a Glasgow hospital alive, but seriously ill."

David had taken the Dragon G-ACNG, with Black as his W. O.

and made the round trip to Askernish and back in 3hrs 10 mins, but sadly, as he recorded in his log-book: "Twins - born dead in plane - (over) Mull". (shown in log illustrated on page 54).

Indicative of the periodicy with which these alerts occurred, is the fact that David's previous call-out to this had been on April 20th - to Skye in G-ACNG, and his next one was to Campbeltown on 'CNG again on May 14th, but on this occasion when he arrived at Kintyre aerodrome he was having problems with one of 'CNG's engines and switched aircraft there to Spartan Cruiser II G-ACZM to bring in the patient.

It was not often, in fact, that births ever occurred on the air ambulance, and an even rarer occasion that the babies were born dead. David was to get his share of happier circumstances later in his career however, although Capt. Eric Starling (who succeeded him after retirement as BEA's Air Ambulance pilot) always hoped for, but never did quite manage a birth on the flight!

A trip round the Isles.

Railway Air Services' Summer 1938 time-table included a twice daily London - Belfast service, via Birmingham, Manchester (Ringway now, which had just superceded Barton), Liverpool and the Isle of Man. Connections to/from Scottish Airways' flights at Renfrew could thus be made by either changing planes at the Isle of Man, or at Belfast. RAS ran three flights daily between Belfast and Renfrew, and Isle of Man Air Services ran the IOM - Renfrew services.

In *The Aeroplane* magazine for July 6th 1938, a pilot and a writer of considerable skills, F. D. Bradbrooke had been commissioned to sample George Nicholson's Western Isles run and describe it in the magazine. He had flown up to Renfrew himself, and flew back again the same day, but his description of flying with David Barclay is so vivid, that it is reproduced here for the sampling. The piece was, incidentally, entitled *'Air Road to the Isles'* and it was this exact title that Capt. Ernest Edmund Fresson, OBE, himself used for his autobiography (published after his death in 1963). Bradbrooke's piece therefore has a little place in history:

"Renfrew was busy at that hour of a drizzly Summer morning. D.H.86s and Rapides of Railway Air Services and North-Eastern Airways were being run up alongside Spartan Cruisers of the Scottish Airways' service to the Western Isles.

Some time before the latter were ready to start, the bus arrived with passengers, and also with Mr. George Nicholson, Director of Scottish Airways and General Manager of the Southern Section, and Miss L. B. McDougall, Publicity Manager. They managed to compress a deal of Scottish hospitality into a few minutes and a lunch basket, which I was to take with me. It spoke volumes for Northern appetites and the Cruiser's capacity for overload.

The Spartan Cruiser has disappeared from the South in these days, and even the Gipsy Majors mutter musically in Gaelic. I learned that when biplanes are used to the Hebrides, the islanders regard them as foreign interlopers,

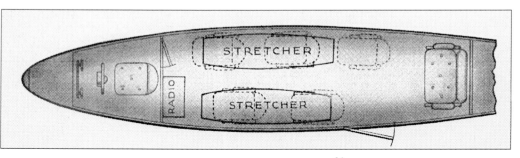

How the patients travelled. The layout of the ambulance aircraft, with space for two stretchers taking up room normally occupied by five seats (shown in dotted lines). There is also room for two additional travellers, presumably one being a medical attendent on the rear bench seat.

Ted Fresson's Shetland-based pilot, Capt. John Veasey (right) talks to Highland Airways Ltd Director and Company Secretary, William Hamilton at Sumburgh. (E.E. Fresson)

but the sturdy old monoplanes are quite familiar to these folk, many of whom have never seen a train.

In spite of being clean and well maintained, the fleet has the well-used look of four years' hard service. This is no Flying Pullman affair, but a bus route with a time-saving factor of seven or eight to one. A digest of passenger lists and freight manifests would be an eye-opener to many critics and enthusiasts alike of air transport.

Rods and guns figure large in the baggage at certain seasons, which is the luxury side. The company's rules say that animals must be crated, but perforce this clause has been changed in favour of dogs, and hints on canine diet before flying are given to sportsmen and shepherds.

Invalids are frequent, apart altogether from the emergency service with special ambulance machines. Capn. David Barclay, Chief Pilot, took us off and flew along the Clyde under low cloud. The bumps were severe but we did not go up through at first. There are quite high mountains about, and, although a blind climb to a safe height would generally be successful, Scottish Airways allow for the possible failure of an altimeter, a compass, a blind flying instrument or a motor.

We therefore buzzed and heaved by Greenock, Gourock, Dunoon and Rothesay, across the Isle and Kyles of Bute, before turning North into Loch Fyne. The ceiling lifted slightly here, and as we got to Lochgilphead, Capn. Barclay took us above the clouds, and for an hour we saw nothing but sunshine on white masses.

When I at last identified the islands of Coll and Tiree below, after mistaking them for the Hebrides. I began to realise what a wind there was. It came from slightly South of West at about 50 m.p.h.,—according to calculation from the foam streaks on the sea. Anyway, the 40-mile crossing to Barra contained more depression, and we were properly bounced while flying under it. At Barra we approached a wide, yellow beach, to leeward of a ridge which made itself felt in the gusts. Barclay's landing was a work of art, and nearly full throttle was needed to taxi against the wind to where the car waited. The airport hut at Barra is slightly farther along the coast, so the car had been brought to the machine.

A decentish house nearby was alleged by a fellow-passenger to belong to Mr. Compton Mackenzie, the novelist.

We dropped one passenger, an elderly lady, and took on two men. The crew crept into the car to fill in forms and sign manifests, etc. The Spartan rocked and the gale squealed audibly over the cabin, although the motors were still running.

By now we were fairly late, but the wind would now be on the quarter. We rose into a tempest of turbulence over the isthmus and swung Northward up the line of the Isles.

The geological backbone of the Hebrides is the mountain ridge on the East side. The slope Westward is gradual and cut up by innumerable lochs and pools. The fields are divided by stone walls, which, with the cattle, give domestic flavour of a wild, bleak sort. I found the utter treelessness uninviting .

We were making 140 m.p.h. now, and passed over the aerodrome at South Uist, as we had nobody to land or pick up. Benbecula has a grass aerodrome, with a frenzied windsock and a tiny hut where the local agent receives passengers and handles his papers. Here we left our two men passengers.

I asked Nurse Campbell if she lived in North Uist, which was the only place left. She said she did, and was coming back from her sixth trip to Glasgow by air with patients. She seemed to look forward to the seventh.

In former days, before these new-fangled life-savers, the islanders had the fatalistic outlook of all remote dwellers. If they died for lack of special medical care, that was merely a manifestation of Providence. Now the aeroplane is a manifestation of Providence, and is accepted as calmly.

I asked whether prospective mothers presumed on it,

Five mechanics swarm all over a Scottish Airways' Spartan Cruiser III undergoing maintenance in a hangar at Renfrew Airport. (Henry Vallance)

as pilot friends from Canada and Australia tell me is the tendency. Instead of moving out to civilisation by canoe, sleigh, wagon or camel some months before the baby arrives, they wait till the last day or so and take the 'plane. Nurse Campbell thought it was not quite as bad as that. Only real emergencies were taken to Glasgow.

Sollas Airport is impressive, because of its large concrete floored hangar and petrol pumps. Like all the rest, it has been prepared entirely by Scottish Airways, and a week later was licensed for public use by an Air Ministry Notice of June 27.

Once more the Spartan sloped towards the whipping grass and did a step dance at 0 m.p.h. while considering whether and when to sit down. Looking from the cabin window down the length of the wing one could see at the tip a pile of knuckles suddenly agglomerate. The ground-crew were seeing that we stayed down.

Capn. Barclay taxied right into the hangar, which was panting and drumming in the gale, and the Gipsy Majors coughed to a stop. After 12 engine-hours already that day, and as much more to come, I imagined the shocked astonishment which any one of them would cause if it did not run perfectly.

I learned that Sollas is commonly windswept, although the weather until recently had been gorgeous. The indigenes were solidly nonchalant. While Sassenachs may be bundled to leeward, grabbing their chattels wildly until brought up by something solid, such as a rock or a native, the islanders stand calmly unmoved. Even their clothes and beards, if any, flicker gently by contrast with foreign growths.

The Spartan was fuelled and oiled while the crew supervised and lunched. There are good offices and waiting rooms in the shed, and Sollas has a radio station with direction finding equipment.

A full passenger list was already waiting for the return trip. Among others, Sir Simon Campbell-Orde, Laird of North Uist, and Lady Campbell-Orde were going back to the South; an elderly lady was going to Glasgow by air for the first time, and a little crippled girl was carried aboard and made comfortable.

We taxied out, festooned with hangers-on, --the Mee-toos of Aviation serve an important purpose hereabouts, -- and left the ground about as soon as released. David Barclay had told me he intended to fly down the West side

of the Islands, even with a sacrifice of time, to avoid the violent bumps to leeward of them. The clouds were still too thick to go up and over with proper safety.

This was a Tuesday, wherefore the intermediate calls had been made on the outward trip, and the homeward run was non-stop. The on-demand call at Tiree was not needed. On alternate days the procedure is reversed.

Over Mull and Jura we gained height steadily, and when a gap in the clouds showed Loch Fyne we were about 6,000 ft. While coming gently down towards the Renfrew I noted that the gale had spread so far.

Capn. T. H. ("Jock") Wilson had got back from his trip to Campbeltown and Islay some hours ago, and Mr. George Nicholson had come with him. The latter had been on business to the former, which is the old aerodrome established some years ago by Mr. John Sword on the Isthmus of Kintyre midway between Campbeltown and Machrihanish.

He was quite close about it. but I fancy there will be news from thereabouts soon, and another big new aerodrome.— Mr. McQuisten has been asking questions in Parliament.

On Islay the landing ground of Port Ellen is on the shores of Laggan Bay, and a fair stretch of turf with the usual tiny reception hut.

This service of Scottish Airways among the Western Isles differs from most others, in Europe at least, by being a definite utility, and by having to find its own aerodromes.

Miss L. B. McDougall, the alert manager of the company's publicity, gave a vivid picture of just what this means. Anyone who has flown over the Islands, even on a dull day can see the difficulty of picking out a fairly level area. After finding the spot comes the preparation, and casual labour as understood on the mainland does not exist. The expense of taking men over by boat or air is prohibitive, so each aerodrome job has to be the subject of tactful negotiation with the islanders. They will not bind themselves, and cannot be persuaded by mere money, so good relations must be established and maintained till the job is done.

As mentioned before, they have no qualms about using the air line, whatever they may have thought about it at first. In fact. after a prisoner had been brought by air for trial at Glasgow a minor outbreak of crime was feared.

A busy office!

Scottish Airways' Sales Office at MacRae & Dick's garage, Inverness. Capt John Hankins (far left) talks to Miss Jean MacDonald (Sales Executive), Mrs "Tug" Wilson, and Traffic Superintendent, "Sandy" Cumming. (E.E. Fresson)

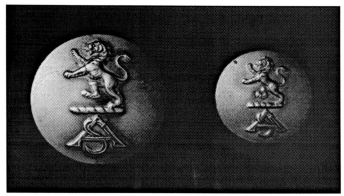

Scottish Airways' coat and sleeve buttons specially designed for their new uniform in 1938. (Eric Starling)

The ambulance service is highly organised. When a call comes, by telephone, telegram or radio, the Traffic Manager advises the Air Superintendent, Mr. W. D. T. Gairdner, the Chief Pilot, Capn. David Barclay, and the Chief Engineer Mr. W. Mann. Incidentally, Bill Gairdner, who is a director also holds a "B" Licence and takes either regular services or ambulance specials when necessity arises.

The Chief Pilot gets a weather report, and locates the destination, and reports to the Superintendent. The Chief Engineer details ground engineers, who bring out the machine and run it up.

The Traffic Office then informs Radio Control, which holds all traffic untl the ambulance is away. The radio rules are comprehensive, and Renfrew is kept informed of progress. The choice of landing place is left to the pilot, as calls often come from remote fields. As soon as the ambulance takes off on the return trip, usually with a nurse, and sometimes a doctor and/or relatives besides the patient, the signal is sent through, and a motor ambulance is summoned to Renfrew.

One of these errands of mercy brought the publicity squad a crushing disappointment recently. An emergency call from two different islands to fetch three maternity cases and an accident in one day promised a good news story, and the outline was got ready for the filling-in of names when the machine landed.

The passenger list, seized from the pilot, showed the names prefixed by Mrs., Miss, Miss and Miss respectively. And Mrs was the accident case. The affair was considerately kept from the Scottish papers.

Now that Highland Airways and Scottish Airways have joined there are two distinct sections, and the Northern portion is a separate story. It includes Inverness, Aberdeen, the Orkneys and the Shetlands, and is still looked after by Capt. E. E. Fresson, Director and General Manager for that section. Its whole history is that of his pioneer work, and a mere timetable does not describe it.

Scottish Airways, as a whole, operates 12,500 miles per week over routes which total 2,500 miles. They have three D.H. Dragons, three Rapides and four Spartan Cruisers, a flying staff of eight pilots and five radio operators

The Chairman of Scottish Airways Ltd. is Mr. W. D. Roberts, of British Airways, who hold a large interest. The Managing Director is Wing. Cmdr. A. H. Measures, of Railway Air Services and among other directors, besides those mentioned, is Major T. R. McCrindle, also of British Airways."

Sometimes the R.A.S. links into Renfrew had to be cancelled for technical reasons, etc, and often George Nicholson's airline would be asked to supply a replacement plane - to operate in the reverse direction of course. Thus David Barclay operated a Renfrew - Newtownards (Belfast) - Renfrew service in Cruiser III G-ADEL on June 7th 1938 and a Renfrew - I.O.M. (Ronaldsway) - Prestwick (diverted for weather) on June 23rd in the Cruiser II G-ACZM, followed by two more Isle of Man

A Spartan Cruiser III of Scottish Airways is given its routine inspection at Renfrew before starting the daily schedule. Cruisers had a very distinctive stalk-like undercarriage that was covered on the Mk.III with light alloy 'trousers'. (John Stroud Collection)

RAILWAY AIR SERVICES
GLASGOW—BELFAST—LONDON and INTERMEDIATELY

Daily except Sunday.

								Read Down		Read Up
								a.m.		**p.m.**
LONDON	Airway Terminus	...	...	...	...	...	dep.	8.45	arr.	12.45
	CROYDON AIRPORT	...	...	...	...	...	dep.	9.30	arr.	12.00
★BIRMINGHAM	CASTLE BROMWICH AIRPORT (on request)						arr.	10.20	dep.	11.10
	Snow Hill Station	...	...	...	...	...	arr.	10.50	dep.	10.35
	New Street Station	...	...	...	...	...	arr.	10.55	dep.	10.30
	New Street Station	...	...	...	...	...	dep.	9.45	arr.	11.40
	Snow Hill Station	...	...	...	...	...	dep.	9.50	arr.	11.35
	CASTLE BROMWICH AIRPORT (on request)						dep.	10.25	arr.	11.05
★STOKE-ON-TRENT	★★ MEIR AERODROME (on request)		...	...			arr.	10.40	dep.	10.50
	MEIR AERODROME (on request)		...	...			dep.	10.45	arr.	10.45
LIVERPOOL	SPEKE AIRPORT	...	...	...	...	...	arr.	11.05	dep.	10.20
	Adelphi Hotel	...	...	...	...	...	arr.	11.30	dep.	10.00
	Lime Street Station	...	...	...	...	...	arr.	11.35	dep.	9.55
	Lime Street Station	...	...	...	...	...	dep.	10.45	arr.	10.50
	Adelphi Hotel	...	...	...	...	...	dep.	10.50	arr.	10.45
	SPEKE AIRPORT	...	...	...	...	...	dep.	11.20	arr.	10.15
MANCHESTER	RINGWAY AIRPORT	...	arr.					11B30	dep.	10B00
								p.m.		
	Midland Hotel	...	...				arr.	12.05	dep.	9.20
	Victoria Station	...	...				arr.	12.10	dep.	9.15
	Piccadilly Omnibus Station						arr.	12.15	dep.	9.10
	London Road Station	...					arr.	12.20	dep.	9.05
								a.m.		
MANCHESTER	London Road Station	...					dep.	9.55	arr.	11.25
	Piccadilly Omnibus Station						dep.	10.00	arr.	11.20
	Victoria Station	...					dep.	10.05	arr.	11.15
	Midland Hotel	...	...				dep.	10.10	arr.	11.10
	RINGWAY AIRPORT	...					dep.	10B50	arr.	10B35
								p.m.		
BELFAST	HARBOUR AIRPORT	...	...	...			arr.	12.35	dep.	9.00
	11 Donegall Place	...	...				arr.	12.50	dep.	8.40
	Midland Hotel, York Road Station						arr.	1.00	dep.	8.30
	Midland Hotel, York Road Station						dep.	12.10	arr.	9.10
	11 Donegall Place	...	...				dep.	12.20	arr.	9.00
	HARBOUR AIRPORT	...	...	...			dep.	12.45	arr.	8.45
GLASGOW	RENFREW AIRPORT	...	...				arr.	1A40	dep.	7A50
	Central Station	...	...	...			arr.	2.10	dep.	7.15
										a.m.

★—The service will call at Birmingham (Castle Bromwich) and Stoke-on-Trent (Meir Aerodrome) for the conveyance of passengers to and from Glasgow, Belfast and London on not less than 6 hours' notice being given to any R.A.S. Booking Office.

★★—Taxis are available at Stoke-on-Trent Station; also at Meir Aerodrome on notice being given at the time of booking. (Fare 5/- in either direction).

A—At Belfast, passengers to and from Glasgow change aeroplanes.

B—By Isle of Man Air Services Ltd., passengers change at Liverpool.

Full information as to the Continental Services from Croydon can be obtained at R.A.S. Booking Offices.

SCOTLAND and NORTHERN IRELAND

			Read Down				Read Up			
							N S All Season	Sept. 12 to Oct. 22	Oct. 23 to Feb. 25	From Feb. 26
			N S	**D**			**N S S**	**D**	**D**	**D**
			a.m.	**a.m.**			**p.m.**	**p.m.**	**p.m.**	**p.m.**
GLASGOW	Central Station (by road) ...	dep.	7.15	9.00	arr.		2.10	5.10	4.15	5.30
	RENFREW AIRPORT ...	dep.	7.50	9.35	arr.		1.40	4.40	3.45	5.00
BELFAST	HARBOUR AIRPORT	arr.	8.45	10.30	dep.		12.45	3.45	2.50	4.05
	11 Donegall Place (by road)	arr.	9.00	10.45	dep.		12.20	3.30	2.35	3.50
	Midland Hotel, York Rd. Station (by road)	arr.	9.10	10.55	dep.		12.10	3.20	2.25	3.40

D—Daily, Sundays included. N S—Not Sundays.

For Conditions of Carriage of Railway Air Services Ltd. see that Company's separate time table. Those conditions are, however, identical with Scottish Airways' conditions on page 14 hereof.

CHILDREN—Same as for Scottish Airways Ltd.—See page 2.

BAGGAGE—Each passenger is allowed 25 lbs. of personal baggage free of charge. No free baggage is allowed to children travelling at reduced fares or travelling free. Baggage in excess of the free allowance—Air Freight rates. (Minimum charge not made.)

Through booked passengers to and from the Continent are allowed 15 Kgs. (33 lbs.) baggage free.

The connections to Scottish Airways' flights provided by Railway Air Services at Glasgow are listed here for the 1938-39 season. (John Stroud Collection)

services on July 16th and 18th, etc, etc.

On July 19th David operated two Isle of Man services, but this time landed at Hall Caine, Ramsey (one of the last times George Nicholson's airline used the aerodrome before it was closed for good). More I.O.M. trips followed, but all to Ronaldsway, and some in the Rapide.

On the Northern link, although David normally flew their Rapide G-AFEY only as far as Inverness, and 'slipped' there to pick up the southbound flight when it returned later from Shetland, on June 18th he actually flew it as far as Kirkwall and back (a 4hr 35mins trip). And he topped this on July 7th, 8th and 9th when he flew it all the way to Sumburgh and back - 10 stops

taking a time of 6hrs 05 mins, 6 hrs 55 mins and 6hrs 20 mins respectively! (They must have been short of pilots at the time).

David also took the opportunity - at Ted Fresson's bidding - to travel to Orkney and sample the inter-island routes there on occasions, flying the Dragon G-ADCT to the outer islands.

Towards the end of the summer season in 1938, David Barclay tried out a new landing field on Arran, this time landing the Dragon G-ACNG on the Golf Course at Brodick, on the east side of the island. He flew some more I.O.M. services to Ronaldsway (on behalf of R.A.S.) and then carried a party of Air Ministry officials on a grand tour of all the landing grounds again

One of Scotland's greatest pioneer airline pilots -
Capt. Henry Vallance is seen here in his Scottish Airways' uniform.
(Henry Vallance)

During its first 12 months of operating as Scottish Airways - up to August 15th 1938 - the new combined company had carried 13,207 passengers, and the aircraft had flown a total of 1,082,316 passenger miles.

Winter 1938/39

The first winter schedules for the combined and newly linked-up Scottish Airways began on October 3rd 1938. Reduced frequency was the main effect as usual, with the Campbeltown/Islay service dropping to a daily (except Sunday) rota, and the Western Isles dropping to a Monday and Friday outbound via all the stops (and a non-stop inbound); and a Tuesday and Saturday outbound non-stop to North Uist (Sollas), (and inbound via all points). (The points in the schedule were: Tiree, Barra, South Uist, Benbecula and North Uist).

To the North, there was no Glasgow - Perth - Inverness link for the winter, but Inverness - Wick - Kirkwall operated daily, except Sunday; and a Kirkwall - Sumburgh link only operated on Tuesday, Wednesday, Thursday and Saturday. Services between Kirkwall and the outer islands were on demand on Monday, Wednesday and Saturday (to Longhope, Westray, Sanday, Stronsay and North Ronaldsay). And, as usual, the R.A.S. were running twice daily connections into Glasgow from Belfast, connecting with the London - Belfast services.

Renfrew waterlogged

The weather in October and November was diabolical at Glasgow, and Renfrew aerodrome rapidly became a sea of mud. As *The Aeroplane* for November 30th 1938 noted:

"BANG GOES MANY SAXPENCES

Scottish Airways Ltd have been flying full loads to and from the Western Isles lately, and Renfrew has become too soggy for them. The old flood trouble has been fought stoutly by the Renfrew Flying Club and Renfrew Town Council and their drains have kept the water away, but traffic overtook them. Aeroplanes became so heavy and so many that the wet ground churned up.

For safety the company moved operations to the RAF station at Abbotsinch for a few days. They did so reluctantly, for expenses are much heavier there. The have told the Renfrew authorities that the move is costly, and that something should be done to keep Renfrew serviceable.

Glasgow is important, and must become more so, in the air-line network, so all of this is just foolish. If the city cannot provide an airport it ought to guard the companies which serve it against such losses as this."

(this seemed to be a popular excursion for the men in bowler hats from London). He took them in Spartan Cruiser II 'CSM to Barra, South Uist, Benbecula and North Uist, and then in 'CYL to Tiree and Skye (he had engine trouble leaving Tiree and had to take them back there for lunch while he sorted it out).

Capt. John Annesley Hankins, whom George Nicholson had transferred to Ted Fresson up in Orkney since Autumn 1937, also distinguished himself in September 1938, when he made a dramatic early morning dash from Sumburgh in Shetland, taking a Glasgow man to the bedside of his dying mother. John left Sumburgh at 04.30 and arrived at Inverness at 06.10, where he transferred the man, Mr Hislop to Capt. Bernard Wilson's aircraft. The latter left immediately to fly Mr Hislop to Glasgow, where he arrived at 07.30. John Hankins returned to Sumburgh and flew the mid-day southbound service back to Inverness and Aberdeen!

The DH Dragon Rapide G-AFRK shown in Scottish Airways' silver and cobalt blue livery at Renfrew. Note the Control Tower on top of the Scottish Flying Club office block. (John Stroud Collection)

Capt Donald Prentice joined Scottish Airways in 1939, left later for war service, and rejoined the company in 1945. (Henry Vallance)

MORE
PILOTS

Capt. Iain Ramsey joined Scottish Airways in 1939, but left for war service. (Henry Vallance)

In fact David Barclay was regularly flying out of and into Abbotsinch between November 17th and December 16th, often positioning empty between Renfrew and Abbotsinch, and loading/unloading at the RAF airfield. The problem also reared its head again between January 10th and 18th in the New Year (1939).

Army Co-operation

Starting on February 20th 1939, David Barclay began an increasing amount of Army Co-operation flying around the Glasgow area. These were usually night flights for the benefit of Army Ack-Ack gun batteries and searchlights in readiness for the war all knew by then was bound to come before too long.

These contracts were lucrative, and came in the hours that scheduled flying would not normally be required. But they did give the pilots extra hours to have to work, on top of their daylight duties.

New Pilots for Summer 1939

Finally, towards the end of the winter period 1938-1939, David Barclay took on some more new pilots for the planned Summer 1939 schedules.

Thus, Henry Vallance arrived on March 1st 1939, together with Donald Prentice, followed by B.T.O' Reilly on March 12th, and George Geffs and Capt. Workam on March 24th. Henry Vallance already had as much experience of flying in Scotland as David - and would stay with Scottish Airways now (having just transferred from Allied Airways at Dyce) until 1946, becoming one of the top Scottish pioneer pilots of all time, and outliving most of them. With Ted Fresson himself, Eric Starling and David Barclay, Henry was in a class of his own.

And so the airline geared itself for starting the 1939 summer season, the last in peacetime for several years, and now encompassed in a mass of new licensing regulations resulting from the Maybury Committee recommendations.

A fine picture of Ted Fresson's favourite DH Dragon Rapide in the Northern Section, G-ADAJ, seen here at Wideford aerodrome, Kirkwall. (John Rae)

CHAPTER 11

Licensing Decisions, and Airfields

On June 23rd 1938 an Order in Council under the 1936 Air Navigation Act provided for the licensing of all scheduled air services in the UK, to become effective from November 1st. As a result of this, and following the Maybury Committee's recommendations, the Air Transport Licensing Authority was set up to deal with all the licence applications, and if necessary hold special hearings to determine the winners of competitive applications.

George Nicholson and Ted Fresson therefore had to apply for temporary licences for their network, and these were issued as follows:

Licence No.	Routes	Issued to	Effective from
P9	Between Inverness and and Shetland, via Wick and Kirkwall.	Scottish Airways	21/10/38
P16	Between Kirkwall and Longhope, Westray, North Ronaldsay, Sanday, Stronsay and Wick.	Scottish Airways	21/10/38
PA5	Between Glasgow (Renfrew) or Abbotsinch and North Uist, via Tiree, Barra, South Uist and Benbecula.	Western Isles Airways Ltd.	12/12/38
PA6	Between Glasgow (Renfrew) or Abbotsinch and Islay via Campbeltown, or direct.	Western Isles Airways Ltd.	12/12/38

These licences were however, only issued in the knowledge that the A.T.L.A. had called for a hearing to be held in Edinburgh from January 16th - 19th 1939, where all airlines wanting to fly services to and within Scotland would have to put forward a good case as to why they should be licensed for such.

George Nicholson's Southern Section faced no competition as it turned out, but Ted Fresson's Northern Section faced a great deal, from his long-time adversary in Aberdeen, Eric Gandar Dower and his Allied Airways.

Ted had been the first to start up a scheduled service from Aberdeen (to Wick and Kirkwall), and had also been the first to fly a commercial charter from the fields at Dyce - having them suitably flattened for the purpose. But his adversary there, Eric Gandar Dower, had subsequently bought the fields at Dyce and made them into an aerodrome, and as the owner, had been able to stop Ted using them any more.

Ted had been forced to operate from Seaton Links at first, on the front at Aberdeen's north shore, then later from Kintore, an aerodrome he had paid to construct near Inverurie. As long as Gandar Dower had kept radio out of Dyce, he had been able to keep Ted out too (the condition of the Air Ministry installing radio was that the aerodrome must then be open to all comers). And he had done just this - though by 1939 Gandar Dower's own

Allied Airways operations were often very irregular in bad weather, because of the lack of radio aids at Dyce.

In the event, although Ted had started the UK's first internal Air Mail service from Inverness to Kirkwall on May 29th 1934, and had regarded the award of the Aberdeen to Shetland mail contract as eventually rightly his too, when he had commenced Aberdeen - Sumburgh flights he was underbid by Gandar Dower at a ridiculously non-profit making figure, and so had lost the contract to Allied Airways.

Now, with the first full-blooded Licensing Authority Hearing for all these routes, to establish their operation for good, Ted's Northern Section had therefore applied for the right to operate:
1. Aberdeen - Shetland, with intermediate landings at Wick and Kirkwall (Thurso to be substituted for Wick, if built).
2. Glasgow - Inverness, via Perth.
3. Aberdeen - Stornoway, via Inverness.
4. Kirkwall - Longhope, Westray, N. Ronaldsay, Sanday, Stronsay, Wick and/or Thurso.

But his competitor, Allied Airways in Aberdeen, had applied for:
1. Aberdeen - Thurso
2. Thurso - Kirkwall, via South Ronaldsay.
3. Thurso - Stromness (via S. Ronaldsay).
4. Kirkwall - Shetland
5. Stromness - Sumburgh
4. Thurso - Inverness - Aberdeen
5. Aberdeen - Shetland (direct).

In the event, once the Hearing started, it was Ted Fresson who had to go into bat strongly for Scottish Airways, as George Nicholson was ill in any case, and could not attend, and indeed it was only the routes flown by Ted's Northern Section where conflict arose.

One of the best summaries of the three-day Hearing was published in *The Aeroplane* for February 1st 1939:

"Applications for licences by Scottish air transport companies were heard by the Licensing Authority, under Mr. Trustram Eve in Edinburgh on January 16-19.

The application of Scottish Airways Ltd for services in Northern Scotland, the Orkneys and Shetland Islands was opened by the reading of a memorandum from Mr. George Nicholson, Director and General Manager of the Company. He was unfortunately unable to attend because of illness. The memorandum gave the history of the company's foundation and its later merging with Highland Airways in conjunction with the L.M.S. Railway

Scottish Airways specialised in transporting its passengers between city centre and aerodrome - on the left is one of its luxury Coaches, and right, a large Limousine for passenger use. (Henry Vallance)

A series of Press comments about Scottish Airways - taken from its 1939 network brochure. (Henry Vallance)

Company and the shipping firm of David MacBrayne Ltd. Of the 20 aerodromes to which it operated in Scotland and the islands, all but three had been developed by the company or its predecessors.

A memorandum by Capt. E. E. Fresson, founder of Highland Airways and now a director and Northern Manager for Scottish Airways Ltd., said that no passenger had been killed or seriously injured in five and a half years of operation. Mail contracts between Inverness, Wick, and Kirkwall had been retained since 1934 (the first British "all-up" air mails), and the company had valuable experience and connections.

Mr. Woodward, for Scottish Airways, referred to the unsettled state of affairs in relation to aerodromes in Scotland, and said that in the licence the place rather than the aerodrome should be named, so that if more than one aerodrome were available the company could choose.

This last recommendation touched upon a bone of contention between Scottish Airways and Allied Airways (Gandar Dower) Ltd., who were objecting to the application. Scottish Airways would evidently like to use Thurso instead of Wick for the jumping-off place for the service to the Northern Islands. Although these are different towns, and not alternative aerodromes for the same town, they have been drawn into the bitter competition between these two companies.

Mr. Trustram Eve, Chairman of the Authority, asked why Scottish Airways wished to use the Allied Airways aerodrome at Thurso instead of their own at Wick. Mr. Woodward replied that holiday traffic predominated and the fact that Thurso is "wet" and Wick is "dry" might have some bearing on it.

Mr. Woodward also submitted that the company should be free to cancel services if there were no mail or pre-booked traffic, and to change its time-tables seasonally.

Mr. Trustram Eve said there ought to be some easy arrangement whereby other operators could be warned when timetables were to be changed. A suggestion had been made that the Authority should get out a set of rules for changes in timetables as between Winter and Summer.

Mr. Woodward thought his company would approve. He then took up the objection of Allied Airways to operation by Scottish Airways to and from Thurso. He contested the claim of Allied Airways to monopoly there. Further, Scottish Airways did not admit that Allied Airways were justified in seeking a monopoly by means of protective fares on the Shetland - Aberdeen service, or preventing connection with his company's Aberdeen - Stornoway service.

Mr. Eric Blain spoke for Allied Airways (Gandar Dower) Ltd. He mentioned the large sums spent by the company on Dyce Aerodrome, Aberdeen, and said his company had always been willing to throw it open to other operators not in direct opposition. They were still willing to do so if Scottish Airways and Allied Airways got licences on different routes. Allied Airways had no objection to Scottish Airways getting the Aberdeen - Inverness - Stornoway (Orkney) service but wanted the direct Aberdeen - Shetland service as applied for.

In support of this claim Mr. Blain said they had operated from Aberdeen to Shetland for two Winters as well as Summers, and they held the Shetland mail contract. He suggested that the Stornoway - Aberdeen machine which stops at Inverness should connect with any machine which the Authority might license from Thurso to Inverness.

Wing Cmdr. A. H. Measures, Managing Director of Scottish Airways, who gave evidence for the company on the second day, created a sensation by sweeping criticisms of Renfrew Airport and the suggestion that Abbotsinch Aerodrome (R.A.F.) should be made the focal point of commercial flying in Scotland.

The Chairman asked whether the Glasgow military authorities had been approached, to which Wing Cmdr. Measures said he thought they had, but not by his company.

The Chairman felt that this representation should be reported to the Air Ministry at once.

Baillie James H. Moar, of Stromness (Orkney), gave evidence as an independent witness in favour of present services.

Capt. E. E. Fresson said in his evidence that a direct service between Aberdeen and Shetland by any other company was unnecessary.

He was cross-examined for Allied Airways by Mr. Blain and upheld his company's right to meet competition by adjustment of landing fees, etc. He did not think the time

THE AIR TRANSPORT LICENSING AUTHORITY

THE AIR NAVIGATION ACTS 1920 AND 1936

The Air Navigation (Licensing of Public Transport) Order, 1938

LICENCES GRANTED

Name and address of applicant.	Serial No(s).	Licence No.	Publication.	Route.	Validity.	Date of issue.	Remarks.
Western Airways Ltd., 17, Manchester Square, London, W.1.	25	7	Aeroplane, 19.10.38 Flight, 20.10.38	Weston-super-Mare and Cardiff	1.1.39 to 31.12.45	12.7.39	—
Do.	27, 63, 75, 77.	17	Aeroplane, 19.10.38 23.11.38 8.2.39 Flight, 20.10.38 24.11.38 9.2.39	Swansea, Barnstaple, Newquay and Penzance	1.5.39 to 30.4.42	12.7.39	The applications each covered portions only of the service now licensed and were for 7-year licences, whereas a 3-year licence has been granted.
Do.	28, 76.	18	Aeroplane, 19.10.38 8.2.39 Flight, 20.10.38 9.2.39	Weston-super-Mare, Bristol, Birmingham and Manchester.	1.5.39 to 30.4.40	12.7.39	The applications were for 7-year licences. A single licence expiring on the 30th April, 1940, has been granted.
Do.	26, 27, 77.	19	Aeroplane, 19.10.38 8.2.39 Flight, 20.10.38 9.2.39	Cardiff and Swansea.	1.1.39 to 31.12.43	12.7.39	The applications each covered the service now authorised but extended over a longer route. A 5-year licence has been granted but the applications were for 7-year licences.
Do.	26, 27, 77.	20	Aeroplane, 19.10.38 8.2.39 Flight, 20.10.38 9.2.39	Bristol and Cardiff	1.5.39 to 30.4.42	12.7.39	The applications covered the service now authorised, inter alia. A single licence for 3 years has been granted upon applications for 7-year licences.
Allied Airways (Gandar Dower) Ltd., Aberdeen Airport, Dyce, Scotland.	49, 50.	6	Aeroplane, 26.10.38 Flight, 27.10.38	Aberdeen, Wick, Thurso and Kirkwall	1.1.39 to 31.12.43	13.7.39	The two applications combined covered the route authorised by the licence. A licence for 5 years has been granted upon applications for 7-year licences.
Do.	51.	21	Aeroplane, 26.10.38 Flight, 27.10.38	Thurso, South Ronaldsay and Stromness	1.1.39 to 31.12.45	13.7.39	—
Do.	50.	22	Aeroplane, 26.10.38 Flight, 27.10.38	Thurso, South Ronaldsay and Kirkwall	1.4.39 to 31.3.41	13.7.39	A licence for 2 years has been granted upon an application for a 7-year licence.
Do.	55.	23	Aeroplane, 2.11.38 Flight, 3.11.38	Aberdeen and Shetland	1.5.39 to 30.4.41	13.7.39	A licence for 2 years has been granted upon an application for a 7-year licence.
Do.	52.	24	Aeroplane, 2.11.38 Flight, 3.11.38	Kirkwall and Shetland	1.1.39 to 31.12.40	13.7.39	A 2-year licence has been granted upon an application for a 7-year licence.

The next four pages show the new air licences officially granted to UK scheduled airlines in 1938. Theses had to be advertised in the aviation press - as shown here.

Name and address of applicant.	Serial No(s).	Licence No.	Publication.	Route.	Validity.	Date of issue.	Remarks.
British-American Air Services Ltd., Heston Airport, Middlesex.	48.	12	*Aeroplane*, 26.10.38 *Flight*, 27.10.38	Between Heston and various racing centres, direct or with intermediate landings at Lambourn and/or Newmarket	1.4.39 to 31.3.42	15.7.39	—
Guernsey Airways Ltd., 6, New Street, Guernsey, C.I.	58.	15	*Aeroplane*, 23.11.38 *Flight*, 24.11.38	Guernsey and Southampton	1.5.39 to 30.4.41	21.7.39	A licence for 2 years has been granted upon an application for a 7-year licence.
Do.	59.	33	*Aeroplane*, 23.11.38 *Flight*, 24.11.38	Guernsey and Brighton	1.5.39 to 30.4.41	21.7.39	A licence for 2 years has been granted upon an application for a 7-year licence.
Do.	56.	34	*Aeroplane*, 23.11.38 *Flight*, 24.11.38	Guernsey and Exeter	1.5.39 to 30.4.41	21.7.39	A licence for 2 years has been granted upon an application for a 7-year licence.
Do.	57.	35	*Aeroplane*, 23.11.38 *Flight*, 24.11.38	London, Portsmouth, Southampton and Guernsey	1.5.39 to 30.4.41	21.7.39	A licence for 2 years has been granted upon an application for a 7-year licence.
Jersey Airways Ltd., Airways House, 1, Mulcaster Street, St. Helier, Jersey, C.I.	31.	3	*Aeroplane*, 26.10.38 *Flight*, 27.10.38	Southampton and Jersey	1.1.39 to 31.12.45	21.7.39	—
Do.	34.	30	*Aeroplane*, 26.10.38 *Flight*, 27.10.38	Jersey and Brighton	1.5.39 to 30.4.41	21.7.39	A licence for 2 years has been granted upon an application for a 7-year licence.
Do.	33.	31	*Aeroplane*, 26.10.38 *Flight*, 27.10.38	Jersey and Exeter	1.5.39 to 30.4.41	21.7.39	A licence for 2 years has been granted upon an application for a 7-year licence.
Do.	32.	32	*Aeroplane*, 26.10.38 *Flight*, 27.10.38	London, Portsmouth, Southampton and Jersey	1.1.39 to 31.12.45	21.7.39	—
North Eastern Airways Ltd., Airport of London, Croydon, Surrey.	87.	2	*Aeroplane*, 8.3.39 *Flight*, 9.3.39	London, Newcastle-on-Tyne, Grangemouth, Perth and Aberdeen	17.4.39 to 31.10.39	14.7.39	A licence expiring on the 31st October of this year has been granted upon an application for a 2-year licence.
Olley Air Service Ltd., 88, Kingsway, London, W.C.2.	80.	14	*Aeroplane*, 15.2.39 *Flight*, 16.2.39	London and Newmarket (direct or with intermediate landings at Lambourn); and London and Doncaster, direct or with intermediate landings at Lambourn and/or Newmarket	1.4.39 to 31.3.42	19.7.39	—
Scottish Airways Ltd., Airport for Glasgow, Renfrew, Scotland.	12.	5	*Aeroplane*, 19.10.38 *Flight*, 20.10.38	Inverness, Wick, Thurso and Kirkwall	1.1.39 to 31.12.43	13.7.39	The application was for a licence authorising services between Inverness and Shetland for a period of 7 years. The licence granted does not authorise services beyond Kirkwall and is limited to 5 years.

The Air Transport Licensing Authority—*continued.*

Name and address of applicant.	Serial No(s).	Licence No.	Publication.	Route.	Validity.	Date of issue.	Remarks.
Scottish Airways Ltd., Airport for Glasgow, Renfrew, Scotland.	14.	25	*Aeroplane,* 19.10.38 *Flight,* 20.10.38	Glasgow, Perth and Inverness	1.4.39 to 31.3.40	13.7.39	A licence for 1 year has been granted upon an application for a 7-year licence.
Do.	12.	26	*Aeroplane,* 19.10.38 *Flight,* 20.10.38	Kirkwall and Shetland	1.1.39 to 31.12.40	13.7.39	The application was for a licence for the entire route between Inverness and Shetland for a period of 7 years. The licence granted is for a period of 2 years and is limited to the Kirkwall-Shetland section of the route.
Do.	24.	27	*Aeroplane,* 19.10.38 *Flight,* 20.10.38	Kirkwall, Sanday, Stronsay, West-ray, Longhope and North Ronaldsay	1.1.39 to 31.12.45	13.7.39	—
Do.	24.	28	*Aeroplane,* 19.10.38 *Flight,* 20.10.38	Kirkwall and Wick	1.1.39 to 31.12.45	13.7.39	The application covered, in addition to the route now licensed, that licensed under Licence No. 27 above.
Do.	24.	29	*Aeroplane,* 19.10.38 *Flight,* 20.10.38	Thurso, Longhope and Kirkwall	1.4.39 to 31.3.41	13.7.39	The application covered, in addition to the route now licensed, those licensed under Licences Nos. 27 and 28 above. The application was for a 7-year licence, but the licence granted in respect of this part of the route is for 2 years only.
Western Isles Airways Ltd., Airport for Glasgow, Renfrew, Scotland.	9.	8	*Aeroplane,* 19.10.38 *Flight,* 20.10.38	Glasgow, Campbel-town and Islay	1.1.39 to 31.12.45	21.7.39	—
Do.	10.	41	*Aeroplane,* 19.10.38 *Flight,* 20.10.38	Glasgow, Tiree, Barra, South Uist, Benbecula and North Uist	1.1.39 to 31.12.45	21.7.39	—
Great Western and Southern Air Lines Ltd., 88, Kingsway, London, W.C.2.	70.	9	*Aeroplane,* 11.1.39 *Flight,* 12.1.39	Brighton, Ryde (Isle of Wight), Southampton, Bristol, Birmingham, Manchester and Liverpool	1.5.39 to 30.4.44	26.7.39	The intermediate landing places applied for at Cheltenham and Cardiff have been disallowed. A licence for 5 years has been granted upon an application for a 7-year licence.
Do.	72.	42	*Aeroplane,* 11.1.39 *Flight,* 12.1.39	Heston, Croydon and Ryde (Isle of Wight)	1.5.39 to 30.4.46	26.7.39	—
Do.	71, 89.	43	*Aeroplane,* 11.1.39 15.3.39 *Flight,* 12.1.39 16.3.39	Brighton, Ryde (Isle of Wight), Bournemouth and Bristol	1.5.39 to 30.4.44	26.7.39	A single licence for 5 years has been granted upon the two applications which cover the same route or parts thereof. Application No. 71 was for a 7-year licence and application No. 89 for a 5-year licence. The extension of the route from Bristol to Cardiff is disallowed in this licence but is dealt with in licence No. 44.

Name and address of applicant.	Serial No(s).	Licence No.	Publication.	Route.	Validity.	Date of issue.	Remarks.
Great Western and Southern Air Lines Ltd., 88, Kingsway, London, W.C.2.	71.	44	*Aeroplane*, 11.1.39 *Flight*, 12.1.39	Bristol and Cardiff	1.5.39 to 30.9.39	26.7.39	The remainder of the route for which application was made is covered by licence No. 43. This licence only authorises operation of services on the Bristol-Cardiff section of the route until the 30th September, 1939.
Do.	73.	45	*Aeroplane*, 11.1.39 *Flight*, 12.1.39	Bristol, Exeter, Plymouth and Penzance	1.5.39 to 30.4.44	26.7.39	—
Do.	88.	46	*Aeroplane*, 15.3.39 *Flight*, 16.3.39	Penzance and the Isles of Scilly	8.5.39 to 7.5.46	26.7.39	—
Railway Air Services Ltd., Airways House, London, S.W.1.	7, 8.	1	*Aeroplane*, 19.10.38 *Flight*, 20.10.38	London, Birmingham, Manchester Liverpool, the Isle of Man, Belfast and Glasgow	1.1.39 to 31.10.39	27.7.39	A single licence has been issued to cover the services applied for in both applications. 7-year licences were applied for but a single licence expiring on the 31st October, 1939, has been granted.
Do.	7, 95.	36	*Aeroplane*, 19.10.38 22.3.39 *Flight*, 20.10.38 23.3.39	London, Manchester, Liverpool and Glasgow	1.1.39 to 31.10.39	27.7.39	A single licence to expire on the 31st October, 1939, has been granted upon both applications, one of which was for a 7-year licence and the other for a licence to expire on the 16th September, 1939.
Do.	69.	37	*Aeroplane*, 21.12.38 *Flight*, 22.12.38	London and Birmingham, London and Manchester and London and Liverpool	1.4.39 to 31.3.40	27.7.39	The application requested authorisation (during a period of 7 years) for services between London and 41 different destinations, to be operated direct or with intermediate landings at Newmarket and/or Lambourn during the period of Race Meetings, Trade Conventions, Agricultural Shows, Motor Races, Regattas, Golf Tournaments, Music Festivals and the like. The licence granted is for a period of 12 months from the 1st April, 1939, and is limited as appears in this notice. It is further limited to the periods of horse-race meetings at Birmingham, Manchester and Liverpool respectively.

By Order of the Air Transport
Licensing Authority

DENIS CAPEL-DUNN,

Secretary.

ripe to make tickets inter-available between the two companies.

Mr. R. Le Mesurier, for North-Eastern Airways Ltd., suggested that a machine should leave London early in the morning and give ample time to connect with the aeroplane for Orkney and Shetland on the same day, either at Perth or Inverness.

On the third day of the sitting Mr. Trustram Eve said that the Authority agreed with Scottish Airways thus far; that Civil Aviation North to Inverness and Aberdeen, inclusive, should ideally be operated under a single control, subject to safeguards of the public interest. He did not think, though, that Scottish Airways had made good their case to have a monopoly in this area, or to exclude Allied Airways. The Authority thought that the evidence was in favour of licences to Scottish Airways and Allied Airways for services respectively from Inverness and from Aberdeen, each to be exclusive.

Such licences might be affected by the requirements of the Post Office, and the Chairman invited both applicants to suggest how to get the views of the Postmaster-General on the matter.

These views of the Authority were based upon the evidence and the existing situation. He invited suggestions about the period for which the licences should be granted. He also asked each side to produce a map of what they would do if they had a monopoly. In the afternoon the maps were examined and the only difference between them was the direct route Aberdeen Shetland proposed by Allied Airways.

Mr. John E. P. Robertson, Town Clerk of Stromness, said emphatically that the burgh of Stromness did not want to lose its air services. (Stromness is the aerodrome established by Allied Airways for the Orkneys, to avoid using Kirkwall, where Scottish Airways was already entrenched.) He also said they wanted to go to Thurso rather than Wick and that the fares as charged were quite suitable. As for Shetland, the burghers of Stromness were not really interested. They went North every year to the county football match.

Provost William M. Brims, of Thurso, said that his Municipality could not provide an aerodrome. They had so informed the Air Ministry. But he admitted that the present air service was a great boon to the community of Thurso. Mr. Woodward, for Scottish Airways, asked whether Provost Brims remembered Highland Airways having made an offer to make good any loss on a municipal aerodrome? The Provost could not remember

that. In reply to the Chairman, the witness said Thurso wanted a service to the Orkneys, either Kirkwall or Stromness. They would like both, and Kirkwall was the more important.

Councillor William B. Leslie, of Zetland, said his County Council very much wanted a direct service to Aberdeen. It would shorten the present route by something like 100 miles, and if that brought lower fares business would be much better. On the fourth and last day the Chairman had a telegram from Wick Town Council asking that decision should be deferred until the Royal Burgh of Wick could be heard. Evidently the news had gone through that Wick might be deserted for the moister atmosphere of Thurso if Scottish Airways got the chance of opening shop in the latter.

Capt. E. E. Fresson, of Scottish Airways, and Mr. E. L. Gandar Dower, of Allied Airways, were asked their views on the provisional summing-up of the Authority. No decision had been or would be made until all applications had been heard. The Chairman said he did not suggest that either company should get the whole of the traffic on the Orkney and Shetland route, but was very ready to make representations to the Postmaster-General to get the situation improved.

Mr. Gandar Dower thought that some sort of co-ordination was possible between Orkney and Shetland. Capt. Fresson said that there was not enough traffic for both. Mr. Le Mesurier, for North-Eastern Airways, again put forward the proposal for a Shetland-Croydon service in two tentative forms. The first was drawn up on the basis of machines as now used, and the second foresaw the substitution between Croydon and Edinburgh of new fast aeroplanes. He suggested certain timetables as a basis for discussion. Counsel for Scottish Airways and Allied Airways then replied to the Chairman's request for their views. Apparently the two parties had met to see whether the perfect solution of single control were possible. They had failed in that, but concurred generally with the findings of the Authority. Both companies suggested a three-year licence for the various routes except Allied Airways, which asked for a two-year licence on the direct route to Shetland. Mr. Trustram Eve explained that the enquiry stood adjourned, but not closed.

Unusually, therefore, before the Hearing ended, the Commissioners had suggested the solutions and put them before the two main parties, but subject to the Post Office view on mail contracts continuing, and the Commissioners' final verdicts.

A D.H. Dragon of Scottish Airways prepares to taxi out from the passenger hut at Benbecula's Balivanich aerodrome. Note the nose landing light on the aircraft.

Above: The Orkney County Council Air Ambulance arrangements as advertised to local doctors in October 1934. (Richard Fresson)

Right: Scottish Airways' map of their 1938 route network. (Henry Vallance)

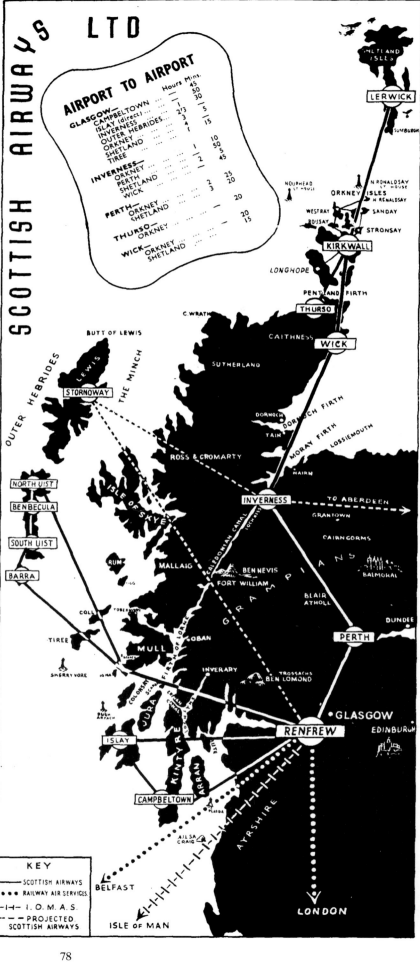

These came ultimately on February 12th 1939, and were published next day in the *Press and Journal* newspaper as follows:

"IMPORTANT DECISIONS BY NEW LICENSING AUTHORITY
EFFORT TO END WASTEFUL COMPETITION
Wireless Facilities Urged
For Dyce As " Open " Aerodrome

The future of the air services which radiate from Aberdeen and Inverness to the North of Scotland and the Northern Isles has been provisionally decided by the Air Transport Licensing Authority, which have now issued their findings on the evidence heard at a four-day inquiry in Edinburgh.

In outline the Authority have decided that Scottish Airways, who at present operate from Inverness to the North, shall continue to do so;

That Allied Airways shall operate as at present from Aberdeen to Thurso and Orkney;

That the two companies shall share the Orkney Shetland service;

That Allied Airways shall operate the Aberdeen Shetland direct service (a new service);

That Scottish Airways shall operate the Aberdeen Inverness-Stornoway service (also new); and

That the two companies shall share the Thurso Kirkwall service.

An important condition is that the Stornoway service of Scottish Airways will have its eastern terminal point at Dyce and that it will not carry through passengers via Inverness to the Orkneys.

The decisions also lay down provisions with regard to co-operation between the companies in the use of their respective aerodromes in the north.

Regulating Competition

Commenting on the need for an early issue of its decision the authority say "the summer programmes are already late, and upon the decision now to be given may depend the operation of an important through route to London."

The authority have decided that a case has not been made out by Scottish Airways to exclude Allied Airways from the area north of Aberdeen and Inverness.

The authority will not upon the present applications, authorise any service to the Orkneys or Shetlands by Scottish Airways from either Dyce or Kintore. They also will not upon the present applications authorise any such services by Allied Airways from Inverness.

"The present position", they state, "is unsatisfactory, and is leading to wasteful competition. The main object of the services is to carry passengers and mail between the mainland and the islands, and unless the competition is regulated, one of the most promising districts in the United Kingdom for civil aviation will undoubtedly remain unprofitable to both operators. In the view of the authority the best method will be to grant licences for the present to each operator to the exclusion of the other, from his present base, for services to the Orkneys and Shetlands."

Open 'Drome at Dyce

"Before issuing licences to Allied Airways the Authority will ask for an undertaking that Dyce will be opened for use to all operators and that the company will use its best endeavours to obtain the installation of wireless facilities at Dyce as soon as possible.

"The Authority will only grant licences for Kirkwall at Wideford and will ask for undertakings from Scottish Airways that Wideford will remain available to Allied Airways during the currency of the licence at reasonable landing fees to be approved by the Authority. The Authority will ask for a similar undertaking in the case of Sumburgh (Shetland).

"For the summer services of 1939," it is announced, "The Authority propose to fix schedules from the mainland to Kirkwall and Sumburgh, which will entitle each company to operate a similar number of journeys per week - one per day for each company to Kirkwall and three per week for each company from Kirkwall to Sumburgh. The Authority will not be prepared at present to license more than one service per day in each direction between Kirkwall and Sumburgh."

This proposal involves the sub-contracting of the mails.

Experimental Services

"The Authority are prepared to grant a licence to Allied Airways to operate an experimental service direct from Aberdeen to Sumburgh, and are also prepared to grant a licence to Scottish Airways to operate an experimental service from Aberdeen (Dyce) to Stornoway with an intermediate landing at Inverness.

"Upon this latter service Scottish Airways will not be entitled to carry through passengers via Inverness to the Orkneys and schedules will be so arranged to avoid connection.

"Whether these routes will obtain licences for regular services will be considered after the result in relation to frequencies has been studied," it is added.

"Both companies have developed "ferry" services across the Pentland Firth. The results for each company are satisfactory and the services are useful to the public. The Authority are of the opinion that these services should be encouraged to the full, and the only regulation necessary is to see that each company operates approximately half the service.

"The principal traffic across the Pentland Firth is between Thurso and Kirkwall. In recent times all this traffic has been carried by Allied Airways. The opening of Thurso aerodrome to Scottish Airways and the granting of a licence to that company for ferry traffic will in the view of the Authority prove a financial advantage to Scottish Airways. The Authority has taken this factor into account in their distribution of licences."

Basic Assumptions

The periods for which the licences are issued vary from two years for the experimental services, and those in which the schemes of co-operation are suggested to seven years for the services from Inverness and Aberdeen to the North of Scotland and Orkney.

Details are given of the suggested frequencies of the services and other licences including the optional and the round-the-islands services, and the decisions are summarised on the following assumptions:

"The interavailability of Thurso, Wick, Wideford and Sumburgh aerodromes to both companies throughout the licences; the continuance of the carriage of mail from Aberdeen and Inverness respectively to the Shetlands and Orkneys; that steps be taken to obtain a public use licence and wireless facilities at Dyce aerodrome; and that both companies are prepared to collaborate in working the services between the Orkneys and Shetlands and the local services between Kirkwall

LICENSED AIR SERVICES OPERATING AT AUGUST 1939				
COMPANY	ROUTE	LICENCE NO.	PERIOD	REMARKS
Allied Airways (Gandar Dower) Ltd.	Thurso - South Ronaldshay - Stromness	21	7 years	subsidised
	Aberdeen - Wick - Thurso - Kirkwall	6	5 years	subsidised
	Thurso - South Ronaldshay - Kirkwall	22	2 years	subsidised
	Aberdeen - Shetland	23	2 years	subsidised
	Kirkwall - Shetland	24	2 years	subsidised
British American Air Services Ltd.	Heston and various racing centres (Intermediate landings at Lambourn and/or Newmarket)	12	3 years	un-subsidised
Great Western and Southern Air Lines Ltd.	Heston - Croydon and Ryde	42	7 years	subsidised
	Penzance - Scilly Isles	46	7 years	subsidised
	Brighton - Ryde - Southampton - Bristol - Birmingham - Manchester and Liverpool	9	5 years	
	Brighton - Ryde - Bournemouth - Bristol	43	5 years	subsidised
	Bristol - Exeter - Plymouth - Penzance	45	5 years	subsidised
	Bristol - Cardiff	44	less than 1 year	subsidised
Guernsey Airways Ltd.	Guernsey - Southampton	15	2 years	subsidised
	Guernsey - Brighton	33	2 years	subsidised
	Guernsey - Exeter	34	2 years	subsidised
	London - Portsmouth - Southampton - Guernsey	35	2 years	subsidised - did not operate to Portsmouth
Isle of Man Air Services.	Isle of Man - Blackpool - Liverpool - Manchester	10	7 years	subsidised
	Isle of Man - Glasgow	49	5 years	
	Isle of Man - Belfast	48	3 years	
	Isle of Man - Carlisle	47	2 years	
Jersey Airways Ltd.	London - Portsmouth - Southampton - Jersey	32	7 years	subsidised - did not operate to Portsmouth
	Southampton - Jersey	3	7 years	subsidised
	Jersey - Brighton	30	2 years	subsidised
	Jersey - Exeter	31	2 years	subsidised
Lundy & Atlantic Coast Air Lines Ltd	Barnstaple - Lundy Isle	11	7 years	subsidised
North Eastern Airways Ltd.	London - Newcastle - Grangemouth - Perth - Aberdeen	2	less than 1 year	subsidised
Porthsmouth, Southsea and Isle of Wight Aviation Ltd.	Portsmouth - Ryde	4	7 years	subsidised
	Bournemouth - Southampton - Ryde	40	5 years	subsidised (Bournmouth - Ryde only)
	Southampton - Ryde	39	5 years	subsidised did not operate to Southampton.
	Portsmouth - Lea	38	2 years	subsidised
Olley Air Services Ltd.	London - Newmarket/London - Doncaster	14	3 years	un- subsidised - Race Meetings.
Railway Air Services Ltd.	London - Birmingham - Manchester - Liverpool - Isle of Man - Belfast - Glasgow	1	less than 1 year	subsidised
	London - Manchester - Liverpool - Glasgow	36	less than 1 year	subsidised
	London - Birmingham - Manchester - Liverpool	37	1 year	subsidised
Scottish Airways Ltd.	Kirkwall - Sanday - Stronsay - Westray - Longhope - North Ronaldshay.	27	7 years	subsidised
	Kirkwall - Wick	28	7 years	subsidised
	Inverness -Wick - Thurso - Kirkwall	5	5 years	subsidised - did not call at Thurso
	Kirkwall - Shetland	26	2 years	subsidised
	Thurso - Longhope - Kirkwall	29	2 years	subsidised
	Glasgow - Perth - Inverness	25	1 year	subsidised
Western Airways Ltd.	Weston - Cardiff	7	7 years	subsidised
	Cardiff - Swansea	19	5 years	subsidised
	Swansea - Barnstaple - Newquay - Penzance	17	3 years	subsidised
	Bristol - Cardiff	20	3 years	subsidised
	Weston - Bristol - Birmingham - Manchester	18	1 year	subsidised
Western Isles Airways Ltd	Glasgow - Campletown - Islay	8	7 years	subsidised
	Glasgow - Tiree - Barra - South Uist - Benbecula -North Uist	41	7 years	subsidised

A complete list of the newly licensed UK domestic route operators, as at August 1939, showing details of their routes and the validity of the licences. (Author)

and Thurso.
"If these assumptions are unfounded and either applicant is unable to give to the Authority the necessary undertakings, the Authority will reconsider the matter and issue other decisions. The detailed decisions now given are to be treated as provisional until the necessary undertakings are received."

On March 8th *The Aeroplane* magazine reported the results of the Hearing as regards the licences sought by George Nicholson's Section for the western service:

"WITHOUT OBJECTION

Applications for three licences by Western Isles Airways Ltd. were granted by the Air Transport Licensing Authority at the end of February. The Enquiry was held privately in Edinburgh on Jan. 18.

In accordance with the principle of granting a seven-year licence where pioneering rights existed, the service from Glasgow to Campbeltown and Islay was authorised for this period, and also the service to the Western Isles from Glasgow, calling at Tiree, Barra, Benbecula and North Uist.

The first of these will run twice daily in each direction by way of Campbeltown to Islay, and once direct both ways on Mondays, Fridays and Saturdays. Extra services are optional. The coordination with Railway Air Services and North Eastern Airways at Glasgow is to be as close as possible.

This route was opened by Northern and Scottish Airways, the predecessor company of Scottish Airways Ltd. on December 1 st 1934, and has been regularly operated ever since.

The Western Isles service is to be run at least once daily to and from Glasgow, and besides the specified stops, South Uist may be used as an intermediate landing. Again co-ordination is recommended with other air lines at Glasgow.

The island service was begun in 1935 and has been operated regularly. Reliability has been very good in all weathers.

A two-year licence for an experimental service between Glasgow, North Uist and Stornoway was also granted in order to test the demand, but this is conditional on a licensed aerodrome in Stornoway."

Subsidies

Another recommendation form the Maybury Committee bore fruit in December 1938 - a White Paper was published giving details of the subsidies that the Government were now going to give to domestic airlines. There was a sum of £100,000 to be allocated in any one year, and this was divided between the various airlines, including Scottish Airways Ltd and Western Isles Airways Ltd., and the nine others concerned. They all came into effect for the first time on January 1st 1939.

Airports and new routes

When Scottish Airways was formed, amongst its objectives had been opening new stations at Oban, Stornoway, and Thurso. Oban never was opened, no suitable aerodrome there being discovered or constructed. Stornoway was now at last under construction (as we have seen) but Thurso remained an enigma. Gandar Dower had been operating his Allied Airways services out of a field at Claredon, just east of Thurso on the Castletown road, but this did not meet Ted Fresson's nor the Air Ministry's strict requirements for a first class civil aerodrome, and had only been given a temporary licence. In any case Gandar Dower prevented Scottish Airways from using it - to avoid any competition.

Although Thurso had more tourists than Wick and was the jumping off point for sea traffic (through its port of Scrabster) to Orkney, and was also a 'wet' town (unlike the 'dry' Wick) - the

Town Council never seized its opportunity to build a municipal aerodrome to steal the business from Wick (which it undoubtedly would have done).

By the end of 1938 the Air Ministry had approved the land at Dixonfield Farm to become a municipal aerodrome - land owned by Sir Archibald Sinclair, Bart., who was willing to accept a low price for the Farm, which the local Thurso business interests and Scottish Airways contributions would have made into a profitable enterprise. But a decision was never made, and no new aerodrome was built at Thurso, leaving Wick (as it was expanded in WW 11 by the RAF) to be the only large civil aerodrome in the area today.

At Kirkwall, Fresson had always used Wideford for his airfield some 200 ft up on top of the rolling hills just south of Kirkwall town, but liable to be lost in the mist or low cloud on bad weather days - whereas Hatston, down to the west of the town at sea - level on the coast road, could be in the clear. His original choice had been Hatston Farm there, but in 1933 he had been unable to obtain permission to use it by the owners - who had had business interests which they had feared could have been affected by an airline !

As the War loomed in 1938, however, the Admiralty sent up a team to look for a Naval Air Station site, and Ted not only pointed out the site to them but drew up the line of the four runways to be laid down. The aerodrome was eventually finished with a new style of tarmac runways laid over the surface to avoid becoming boggy in winter (another idea of Ted's). And Scottish Airways came to an arrangement with the Admiralty that the airline would use and manage the airfield in Peacetime.

Unfortunately, War intervened, but Ted managed to obtain permission to use Hatston for a time, under it first C.O. When the C.O. changed later on (in Summer 1940) the agreement ended, and so Scottish had to start using two other new RAF/RN aerodromes in the West of the mainland - RAF Skeabrae and RNAS Twatt, up to the time RAF Grimsetter was built and opened, (close to Wideford) in December 1941 (and is still in use today as the civil airport).

Summer Schedule 1939

After all the new licensing conditions, the Summer 1939 schedules had to be somewhat revised from what they might otherwise have been.

Thus, Fresson was allowed to start a Kirkwall - Glasgow service from the Northern end - as promised previously when the two companies had combined their operations. But George Nicholson mounted a Glasgow - Sumburgh roundtrip as before, with the difference that the Kirkwall - Sumburgh sector could only be flown on Monday, Wednesday and Thursday (on Tuesday, Friday and Saturday it was mounted by Allied Airways

Details of the address at which reservations could be made in 1939 for Scottish Airways' flights. (Henry Vallance)

RESERVATIONS • Scottish Airways Limited

HEAD OFFICES:

| RENFREW - - | AIRPORT FOR GLASGOW | ★ INVERNESS - Academy Street, (Struthers Lane) |

Tel.: Renfrew 230/233 (24 Hour Service). Grams: "Scotairway, Renfrew." "Air Ambulance, Renfrew." Tel.: Inverness 1000. Grams: "Scotairway, Inverness."

Glasgow Terminal: The Grosvenor Restaurant, 74 Gordon Street. Tel.: Central 3132.

SEATS SHOULD BE BOOKED IN ADVANCE FOR FORWARD AND RETURN JOURNEYS.

RESERVATIONS MAY BE MADE AT SCOTTISH AIRWAYS' HEAD OFFICES AS ABOVE; AT BOOKING OFFICES AS UNDER, ALL AIRPORTS, RAILWAY STATIONS AND TRAVEL AGENCIES.

GLASGOW—
Central Station.
    Tel.: Douglas 2900 (Ext. 91).
44 Robertson St. Tel.: Central 9955.
153 Hope Street. Tel.: Central 5214.
EDINBURGH—
Princes Street Station. Tel.: 23276.
Waverley Station. Tel.: 23081.
2 Castle Street. Tel.: 32205.
ABERDEEN—Mackay Bros. & Co., Ltd.,
35a Union Street. . Tel.: 825.
LONDON—
Terminal House, 52 Grosvenor Gardens, S.W.1. Tel.: Sloane 0091.
London House, New London Street, E.C.3. Tel.: Royal 4545.
Euston House, Seymour Street, N.W.1. Tel.: Euston 1234 (Ext. 640).

BARRA—John Macpherson, Post Office, North Bay.
BENBECULA—Donald MacGillivray, Muir of Aird.
CAMPBELTOWN—James MacGeachy, Union Street. Tel.: C'town 2384/3.
HARRIS—
J. MacCallum, Rodel Hotel, Leverburgh.
D. Macdonald, Tweed Merchant, Tarbert.

ISLAY—Scottish Airways Ltd., Glenegedale. Tel.: Port Ellen 22.
KIRKWALL—9 Broad St. Tel.: 159.
LERWICK—
Ganson Bros. Ltd. (Garage). Tel.: 11.
W. K. Conochie, Ltd., 74 Commercial Street. Tel.: 67.
NORTH UIST—A. F. Martin, Lochmaddy Hotel.
Victoria Station Enquiry Office] Tel.: Waterloo 5100.
Waterloo Station Enquiry Office]
Paddington Station Booking Office. Tel.: Paddington 7000 (Ext. 2237).
Airway Terminus, Victoria Station, S.W.1. Tel.: Victoria 2323.

PERTH—The Manager, Perth Airport.
    Tel.: Scone 212.
Perth Station. Tel.: Perth 794
SOUTH UIST—F. S. Mackenzie, Lochboisdale Hotel.
THURSO—James Wilson, Royal Hotel.
    Tel.: 29.
TIREE—Colin McPhail, Crossapol House.
WICK—Alex. Robertson & Sons, Bridge Street. Tel.: 41.

81

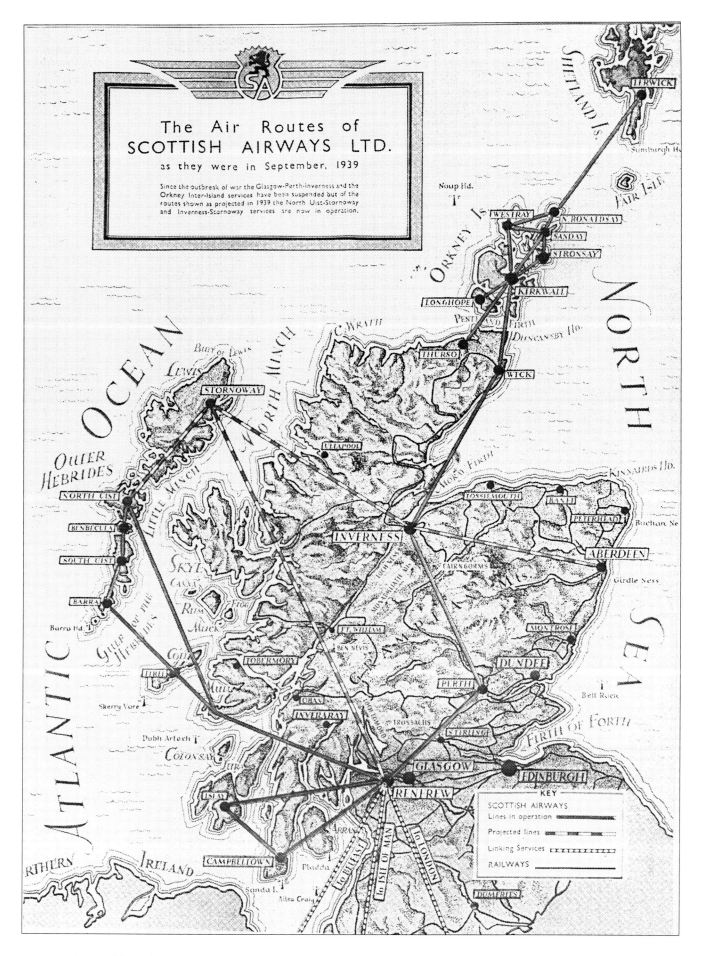

The Air Routes of
SCOTTISH AIRWAYS LTD.
as they were in September, 1939

Since the outbreak of war the Glasgow-Perth-Inverness and the
Orkney Inter-Island services have been suspended but of the
routes shown as projected in 1939 the North Uist-Stornoway
and Inverness-Stornoway services are now in operation.

KEY

SCOTTISH AIRWAYS
Lines in operation
Projected lines
Linking Services
RAILWAYS

A map of Scottish Airways' route network as at the start of World War Two in September 1939. (John Stroud Collection)

on their Aberdeen run).

Scottish Airways' flights left Kirkwall daily (except Sunday) at 06.30, calling at Wick (only on demand), Inverness and Perth and arriving at Renfrew at 09.10. Then the aircraft returned from Glasgow at 15.30 arriving Kirkwall at 18.25. The reciprocal service left Glasgow at 08.30 daily (except Sunday), flying via Perth, Inverness and Wick to Kirkwall (arriving 11.35) and on to Sumburgh on the days indicated (arriving at 12.30). Return from Sumburgh was at 12.45 via all the stops to arrive Renfrew at 16.40.

A Thurso (Claredon) - Kirkwall (Wideford) service was to operate daily (except Sunday), from May 15th to September 30th, and with a second daily service from July 17th to September 16th - this used the Allied Airways' field for this summer -the one and only time Fresson ever operated there. The Orkney inter-island service was to operate on Monday, Wednesday and Saturday up to June 17th, then daily (except Sunday) to September 30th. Flights departed from Wideford at 12.00 (25mins after the arrival from Glasgow and Inverness, etc) and called at Longhope, Westray, Sanday, Stronsay, and North Ronaldsay (if there was any traffic to pick-up/put-down), returning to Kirkwall by the 13.50 departure for Inverness and Glasgow, etc.

An interesting snippet appeared in the Orkney newspaper one day this summer:

"ORKNEY-IRELAND-ISLE OF MAN FLYING SERVICES

Few people in Orkney appear to know that the airliner that sets out southwards from Kirkwall at 6.30 each morning now serves a much longer route than the Kirkwall- Glasgow stretch announced by Scottish Airways Ltd. when that service was opened several weeks ago.

The liner and its crew -a pilot and a wireless operator - go from Kirkwall to Inverness, Perth, Glasgow, Belfast and the Isle of Man, returning immediately back along the same route. The machine returned to Kirkwall twelve hours after having set out, that is, at 6.30 in the evemng.

Five radio operators, all Renfrew Aerodrome men, serve on this route, taking it in turns to spend a night in Kirkwall, and in turns to a week-end here.

Three of the pilots operating this particular service are well known in Orkney -Captain J. Annesley Hankins, Captain Vallance and Captain C.B. Wilson.

Captain Hankins lives in Kirkwall, Captain Vallance in Finstown and Captain Wilson in Inverness, although the last-named is quartered in Glasgow occasionally for a week at a time."

As for George's network at Renfrew, the Campbeltown Islay services ran twice daily, with a third non-stop Renfrew Islay service in the early afternoon on Monday, Friday and Saturday from June 30th.

The Western Isles' services ran a different course on Monday, Wednesday and Friday, to those on Tuesday, Thursday and Saturday. On the first days mentioned, the aircraft routed: Renfrew - Tiree - Benbecula - North Uist (Sollas), and returned North Uist -Benbecula - Barra - Renfrew. On the alternate days it flew: Renfrew -Tiree - Barra - Benbecula - North Uist; and North Uist - Tiree - Glasgow.

The stop at South Uist (Askernish) was dropped from the programme from this season henceforth, passengers being asked to use Benbecula in future. Harris was again included -but only as an 'on demand' stop and Stornoway aerodrome was not yet completed for them to use. The Tiree call was also 'on request' and with 12 hours notice (the usual in these cases).

At Glasgow, R.A.S. provided connections to/from their London services (calling at Belfast or the Isle of Man, Liverpool, Manchester and Birmingham), and at Perth, North Eastern Airways provided connections to Newcastle-on-Tyne. There were also the usual summer services between Glasgow and the Isle of Man by I.O.M.A.S. (twice daily, with up to three flights on Saturdays). This Summer was to prove the high point of Scottish Airways operation just prior to WW II breaking out on September 3rd 1939, and compared with 1938 (and obviously due to the new licensing regime and a closer look at costings) the fares on many Northern sectors were reduced by Scottish Airways. Hence the following newspaper report on May 6th 1939 when the timetable was announced:

"SCOTTISH AIRWAYS
New Services and Fare Reductions

Details of new services and fare reductions are included in the summer schedules just issued by Scottish Airways Ltd. There will be a new service between Thurso and Orkney (Kirkwall) with a flying time of 20 minutes, and a daily frequency (Sunday excepted) in each direction until July 16. Thereafter it will operate twice daily. Another addition is the service between Orkney (Kirkwall) and Glasgow, via Wick, Inverness and Perth, covered daily in each direction (Sunday excepted) in 2 hours 50 minutes. This service is scheduled to allow passengers six hours in Glasgow; departing Kirkwall at 6.30 a.m., it stops at Wick and Inverness.

Certain fare reductions on the Glasgow -Shetland section have been made as follows: Glasgow -Orkney, reduced by 10s. single and 15s. return: Glasgow Shetland 10s. and 15s.; Glasgow -Wick 5s. and 10s.; Orkney - Shetland 5s. and 10s.; Orkney -Perth 5s. and 10s.; Shetland -Perth 10s. and 25s.; Shetland -Wick 5s. and 10s.; Perth -Wick 5s. and 10s.

Timings have been scheduled to establish connections at Renfrew between London, Belfast, the Isle of Man, and Scottish Airways' routes over the West and North of Scotland. The following through connections have also been arranged :

London to Orkney, via Glasgow, Perth, Inverness and Wick; flying time 6 hours 25 minutes. From London to Glasgow by Railway Air Services, with a 90 minute luncheon stop at Renfrew.

Belfast to Orkney, via Glasgow, Perth, Inverness and Wick; flying time 4 hours. From Belfast to Glasgow by Railway Air Services, with a 90 minute luncheon stop at Renfrew.

Orkney to London via Wick Inverness, Perth and thence by North Eastern Airways; flying time 6 hours 20 minutes.

Orkney to Newcastle, via Wick, Inverness, and Perth thence by North Eastern Airways; 4 hours 25 minutes.

The schedules also show greater frequency on established routes."

So David Barclay opened the Summer 1939 schedules by flying the first service up to Inverness and Sumburgh and back on May 15th, using the Renfrew Rapide G-AFEY and Hughes as the R.O. He took 7 hours 25 minutes for the return trip that day, flying 10 sectors altogether.

The calm before the storm
As Allied Airways had now had its activities at Dyce curbed, so as to dovetail with and complement Scottish Airways' operations, and because of the fact that each company had to run alternate days on the Kirkwall -Sumburgh sector, there was a

SCOTTISH AIRWAYS LTD
Aircraft Fleet - Summer 1939

1	Spartan Cruiser II	G-ACYL
2	De Havilland DH84 Dragon II	G-ACNG
3	Spartan Cruiser II	G-ACSM
4	Spartan Cruiser II	G-ACZM
5	Spartan Cruiser III	G-ADEL
6	De Havilland DH89A Dragon Rapide	G-AFEY
7	De Havilland DH89A Dragon Rapide	G-AEOV
8	De Havilland DH89A Dragon Rapide	G-AFFF
9	De Havilland DH89A Dragon Rapide	G-AFRK
10	De Havilland DH84 Dragon I	G-ACIT*
11	De Havilland DH84 Dragon II	G-ADCT*
12	De Havilland DH89 Dragon Rapide	G-ADAJ*
13	De Havilland DH89A Dragon Rapide	G-AEWL*

* Aircraft based in Northern Section, at Inverness.

good measure of harmony now between the companies -and staff, particularly pilots -and often one company would find an aircraft to fill in for the other (when the latter's went 'technical' somewhere, etc.) On one occasion in late summer, Henry Vallance, now flying for Ted Fresson's Northern Section (but previously having been with Allied Airways at Dyce from 1935 to 1938), was flying the normal schedule from Kirkwall to Inverness on the evening of August 21st 1939. He took Fresson's Dragon Rapide G-ADAJ, and set off from Wideford for Longman. But mist and fog was closing in over the entire Northern area and Henry had to divert to Aberdeen, as the *Press and Journal* for August 22nd reported:

"AIR LINER FORCED DOWN AT CULTS

An aeroplane roaring round the housetops of Cults last night blanketed from view by thick fog which fell suddenly on the North-east, brought people running to the streets with storm lamps fearing an air crash.

Suddenly through a rift in the fog belt a silver air liner glided down to make a perfect landing on a field close by the River Dee on the farm of Easter Ardoe.

The machine, an eight-seater twin-engined Rapide liner of Scottish Airways carrying six passengers and a crew of two left Kirkwall early in the evening.

When it arrived over Aberdeen the pilot, Captain Henry Vallance, found the airport fogbound.

CIRCLED OVER DISTRICT

He made a wide circle over the district, having diverted from Inverness, where his wireless operator, Mr MacCill, had reported fog was rapidly closing in, making a landing there impossible.

In the course of his circuit Captain Vallance sighted a break in the low "ceiling" and, after circling the field twice glided down to a normal landing.

Captain Vallance taxied back to where he had landed, near the south end of the Shakkin' Briggie, where his passengers disembarked.

FINE PIECE OF AIRMANSHIP

It was a fine piece of airmanship on the part of Captain Vallance, a young pilot who figured in a thrilling errand of mercy to the north isles of Shetland about two years ago. (the Esha Lighthouse trip - see *'Flying against the Elements'* by the same author).

Answering an SOS from a lighthouse keeper, he landed on a narrow strip of ground near the rugged sea shore and flew the invalid keeper to Edinburgh. "

In fact, there was no one better qualified than Henry for landing

in a large flat field around Dyce, as he knew the area like the back of his hand . But few other pilots would have found a safe landing that evening, and the real culprit was the lack of radio aids at Dyce, for Gandar Dower still had not installed the equipment (or rather - succeeded in asking the Air Ministry for it to be installed, after all his previous procrastinations. And he did not succeed in this before WW II broke out!)

Henry had left Wideford at 18.55 and he got down safely at 20.45 just 1hr 50 mins. after leaving Orkney, and having circled Aberdeen for some time. The fog had been very thick to the north side of the city (around Dyce), and of course, flying now for Fresson's airline, Henry no longer had the air-to-ground set up that Allied Airways had used to find Dyce (the ground crew listened on a radio for the sound of the aircraft - then shouted "motors overhead" and the pilot chopped the throttles, executed a diving turn, and came over Dyce at the right height to suddenly see the grass). So he had flown up the River Dee to the South side of the City, under the fog, and landed in a large field beside the South Deeside Road, opposite Cults, and on Easter Ardoe farm on the south bank of the river. In fact, coming at this stage just before the war with Germany, there was quite a scare locally - as rumours abounded that a 'German aircraft' was trying to land spies! There was a large cattle pond in the middle of the field, and Henry just managed to avoid this by swerving the Rapide around it. The Rapide was undamaged and Henry flew it to Inverness next day, and on the schedule down to Glasgow that afternoon.

Capt Henry Vallance and his Radio Officer Hugh Black, seen here sharing a joke at Renfrew. (Henry Vallance)

SCOTTISH AIRWAYS LIMITED

SERVICE 742

GLASGOW — TIREE — BARRA — SOUTH UIST — BENBECULA — NORTH UIST

NORTHBOUND

			M a.m.	T a.m.
GLASGOW	The Grosvenor Restaurant, Gordon Street / RENFREW AIRPORT ...	dep.	9.00 / 9.40	9.00 / 9.40
★TIREE	THE REEF AIRPORT ...	arr. / dep.	10.55 / 11.00	10.55 / 11.00
BARRA	NORTHBAY AIRPORT ...	arr. / dep.	11.40 / 11.45	— / —
★☆SOUTH UIST	ASKERNISH AIRPORT ...	arr.	11.55	—
BENBECULA	BALIVANICH AIRPORT	arr. / dep.	12.30 / 12.35	11.40 / 11.45
NORTH UIST	SOLLAS AIRPORT ...	arr.	12.45	11.55

SOUTHBOUND

			M p.m.	T p.m.
NORTH UIST	SOLLAS AIRPORT ...	dep.	12.45	—
BENBECULA	BALIVANICH AIRPORT	arr. / dep.	12.55 / 1.00	1.35
★☆SOUTH UIST	ASKERNISH AIRPORT ...	arr. / dep.	1.40 / 1.50	—
BARRA	NORTHBAY AIRPORT	arr. / dep.	— / —	2.15 / 2.20
★TIREE	THE REEF AIRPORT ...	arr. / dep.	3.30	3.15
GLASGOW	RENFREW AIRPORT ... / The Grosvenor Restaurant, Gordon Street	arr. / dep.	3.30 / 4.00	3.15 / 4.00

M—MONDAY, WEDNESDAY and FRIDAY. T—TUESDAY, THURSDAY and SATURDAY.

★ On request and subject to 12 hours' notice being given.
★☆ Passengers to and from South Uist will be set down or picked up at Benbecula.
GROUND TRANSPORT—See page 3 (para. 17). Harris—Particulars on application.
FARES, EXCESS BAGGAGE AND FREIGHT RATES—See pages 6 and 7.

SCOTLAND—ISLE OF MAN

Operated by Isle of Man Air Services Ltd., Isle of Man Airport, Derbyhaven, I.O.M.
Summer Time Table (1939) 26th May to 17th September, inclusive.

GLASGOW AND ISLE OF MAN

Daily (including Sunday) except where indicated otherwise.

			S a.m.	★M a.m.	S p.m.	★M p.m.	S p.m.
GLASGOW	Central Station, Glasgow / RENFREW AIRPORT ...	dep.	9.00 / 9.50	11.00 / 11.35	12.00 / 12.30	4.30 / 5.00	4.45 / 5.15
ISLE OF MAN RONALDSWAY AIRPORT ...		arr.	10.55	12.40	1.35	6.05	6.20

			★M a.m.	S a.m.	S p.m.	★M p.m.	S p.m.
ISLE OF MAN RONALDSWAY AIRPORT ...		dep.	10.20	11.25	2.10	4.00	6.45
GLASGOW	RENFREW AIRPORT ... / Central Station, Glasgow	arr.	11.23 / 1.15	12.30 / 1.15	3.15 / 3.40	5.05 / 5.35	7.50 / 8.30

★M—Daily including Sunday until 30th June, thereafter Saturdays excepted.
S—Commences as from 1st July. Saturdays only.
ROAD TRANSPORT—Isle of Man Airport (Derbyhaven)—Isle of Man Road Service buses provide services between the Airport and all points on the Island. Glasgow Airport (Renfrew)—Coach or car service provided by the Company between Airport and Central Station, Glasgow.
AIR CONNECTIONS—Available at Renfrew, as per Scottish Airways' schedules, for Perth, Inverness, Wick, Orkney, Campbeltown and Islay.
BAGGAGE—Same as Scottish Airways Ltd.—See page 7.
FARES—See pages 6 and 7.

LUGGAGE IN ADVANCE
INTER-AVAILABILITY OF TICKETS } See Isle of Man Air Services' separate Time Table.
CONDITIONS OF CARRIAGE
FREIGHT
CHILDREN

SCOTTISH AIRWAYS LTD
GO BY AIR
GLASGOW · RENFREW · PERTH · INVERNESS · THURSO · KIRKWALL · CAMPBELTOWN · ISLAY · TIREE · BARRA · BENBECULA · NORTH UIST · LONDON · BELFAST · ISLE OF MAN
SUMMER TIME TABLE 1939
MAY to 30TH SEPTEMBER

Scottish Airways' timetable - Summer 1939

The cover is a typical design for the period, with Scottish Airways' slogan 'Go by Air' and their destinations predominant. Right: The schedules to the Western Isles, and the connections to the Isle of Man and Glasgow. Over Page: The schedules to the Inner Hebrides and the new Thurso - Kirkwall route, along with the details of fares, cargo rates, train and other airline connections.
(John Stroud Collection)

In order to place these apparently low fares into perspective, the reader may care to convert the fares into 1995 values for interest. One Shilling (1/-) in this timetable is worth £1.36 in 1995. Therefore the return London - Inverness fare, quoted at 250/- is now equivalent to £340.00!

SCOTTISH AIRWAYS LIMITED

SCALE OF FARES, EXCESS BAGGAGE AND FREIGHT RATES.

	Single	Return	Excess Baggage and Freight per lb.
BARRA to—			
Benbecula ...	25/-	—	4d.
North Uist ...	35/-	65/-	
BELFAST to—			
Glasgow (R) ...	40/-	65/-	3d.
Inverness ...	90/-	150/-	7d.
Kirkwall ...	130/-	225/-	9d.
Perth ...	65/-	110/-	5d.
BENBECULA to—			
Glasgow ...	80/-	150/-	4d.
North Uist ...	20/-	—	
CAMPBELTOWN to—			
Islay ...	15/-	30/-	2½d.
GLASGOW to—			
Barra ...	80/-	150/-	4d.
Benbecula ...	80/-	150/-	4d.
Belfast (R) ...	40/-	65/-	3d.
Birmingham (R) ...	80/-	150/-	7d.
Campbeltown ...	25/-	45/-	4d.
Inverness ...	50/-	85/-	4d.
Islay ...	35/-	45/-	2½d.
★ Isle of Man (i) ...	40/-	75/-	4d.
Kirkwall ...	90/-	160/-	8d.
Lerwick ...	110/-	185/-	8d.
Liverpool (R) ...	65/-	110/-	4d.
London (R) ...	120/-	190/-	10d.
Manchester (R) ...	67/6	115/-	4d.
North Uist ...	80/-	150/-	4d.
Perth ...	25/-	45/-	2d.
South Uist ...	80/-	150/-	4d.
Tiree ...	52/6	95/-	3d.
Wick ...	80/-	135/-	5d.
INVERNESS to—			
Glasgow ...	50/-	90/-	4d.
Kirkwall ...	80/-	140/-	4d.
Lerwick ...	35/-	60/-	4d.
Perth ...	35/-	60/-	4d.
Wick ...	35/-	60/-	4d.
ISLAY to—			
Campbeltown ...	15/-	—	4d.
ISLE OF MAN to—			
Campbeltown ...	65/-	120/-	4d.
★ Glasgow (i) ...	40/-	75/-	4d.
Inverness ...	90/-	160/-	7d.
Islay ...	75/-	225/-	9d.
Kirkwall ...	190/-		5d.
Lerwick ...			
Perth ...	65/-	120/-	4d.
Wick ...	120/-	210/-	
KIRKWALL to—			
Inverness ...	50/-	90/-	4d.
Lerwick ...	45/-	—	2d.
Longhope ...	10/-	—	
North Ronaldsay ...	15/6	—	
Perth ...	80/-	140/-	
Sanday ...	10/-	—	
Stronsay ...	10/-	—	
Thurso ...	20/-	35/-	
Westray ...	12/6	—	
LERWICK to—			
Inverness ...	80/-	140/-	4d.
Perth ...	105/-	175/-	
Wick ...	55/-	100/-	
LONDON to—			
Campbeltown ...	145/-	235/-	11½d.
Glasgow (R) ...	120/-	190/-	10d.
Kirkwall ...	180/-	250/-	✕
Lerwick ...	155/-	255/-	11½d.
North Uist ...	210/-	340/-	14d.
Wick ...	195/-	310/-	✕
NORTH UIST to—			
Barra ...	25/-	—	} 4d.
Benbecula ...	20/-	—	

SCOTTISH AIRWAYS LIMITED

SCALE OF FARES, EXCESS BAGGAGE AND FREIGHT RATES—Continued.

	Single	Return	Excess Baggage and Freight per lb.
PERTH to—			
Inverness ...	35/-	60/-	3d.
Kirkwall ...	90/-	140/-	8d.
Lerwick ...	105/-	175/-	8d.
Wick ...	65/-	110/-	4d.
THURSO to—			
Kirkwall ...	20/-	35/-	3d.
WICK to—			
Kirkwall ...	20/-	35/-	3d.
Lerwick ...	55/-	100/-	4d.

★ Special Mid-week Return Fare 65/—Available Outwards Tuesday, Wednesday or Thursday; return any Tuesday, Wednesday or Thursday within One Month. Passengers may travel other days within Three Months on payment of difference between mid-week and Ordinary Return fares. 25 lbs. of Free Baggage allowed per each Adult Passenger.

R—Railway Air Services.   i—Isle of Man Air Services.   ✕—Particulars on application.

FREIGHT

Freight accepted for transport on all services (at Owner's Risk) at the rates per lb. shown. Minimum charge is 2/- and the Company reserves the right to charge on c.c. at 1/- per cubic foot. Further particulars on application.

DOGS

By arrangement dogs, accompanied are permitted in certain circumstances to travel uncrated, and owners are invited to give full particulars when making reservations. Other livestock—See General Information, para. 10.

BAGGAGE

Each adult passenger is allowed 25 lbs. personal baggage free of charge. No free baggage is allowed to children travelling at reduced fares or travelling free. Baggage over this weight may be carried subject to accommodation being available and is charged for at the rates per lb. shown.

GROUND TRANSPORT

See General Information (para. 17).

AIR CONNECTIONS

Air Connections to and from London, Birmingham, Manchester, Liverpool, Belfast and The Isle of Man with Scottish Airways' routes can be made at Renfrew.

RAIL CONNECTIONS

Service No. 741.—Westbound and Eastbound AIR Service connect with London and Edinburgh Trains as per L.M.S. and L.N.E.R. schedules.

Service No. 742.—Northbound and Southbound AIR Services connect with London and Edinburgh Trains as per L.M.S. and L.N.E.R. schedules.

Service No. 743.—Northbound and Southbound AIR Services connect with Trains as per L.M.S. and L.N.E.R. schedules. Passengers travelling by rail from London to Inverness are advised to travel by the first portion of the evening trains from Euston or King's Cross.

SCOTTISH AIRWAYS LIMITED

Effective from 29th May to 30th September, 1939 (inclusive).

SERVICE 741

GLASGOW—CAMPBELTOWN—ISLAY

WESTBOUND

		D a.m.	W p.m.	D★ p.m.
GLASGOW { The Grosvenor Restaurant, Gordon Street	dep.	9.00	1.40	4.30
RENFREW AIRPORT ...	dep.	9.45	2.30	5.10
CAMPBELTOWN { Kintyre Airport ...	arr.	10.30	—	5.55
{ Argyll Arms Hotel ...	arr.	10.50	—	6.15
{ Argyll Arms Hotel ...	dep.	10.15	—	5.40
{ KINTYRE AIRPORT ...	dep.	10.40	—	6.05
ISLAY GLENEGEDALE AIRPORT ...	arr.	11.05	3.20	6.30

EASTBOUND

		D a.m.	W p.m.	D★ p.m.
ISLAY GLENEGEDALE AIRPORT ...	dep.	11.25	4.00	6.40
CAMPBELTOWN { KINTYRE AIRPORT ...	arr.	11.50	—	7.05
{ Argyll Arms Hotel ...	arr.	12.15	—	7.25
{ Argyll Arms Hotel ...	dep.	11.35	—	6.50
{ KINTYRE AIRPORT ...	dep.	12.00	—	7.15
GLASGOW { RENFREW AIRPORT ...	arr.	12.45	4.50	8.00
{ The Grosvenor Restaurant, Gordon Street	arr.	1.15	5.35	8.30

D—DAILY EXCEPT SUNDAY.
W—MONDAY, FRIDAY and SATURDAY ONLY from 30th June.
★—SERVICE OPERATES One Hour earlier from 4th September.

GROUND TRANSPORT—See page 3 (para. 17).
FARES, EXCESS BAGGAGE AND FREIGHT RATES—See pages 6 and 7.

SCOTTISH AIRWAYS LIMITED

SERVICE 744

THURSO—ORKNEY

Daily except Sunday.

		A a.m.	B p.m.
THURSO { Royal Hotel	dep.	9.10	4.40
{ THURSO AIRPORT ...	dep.	9.30	5.00
KIRKWALL { WIDEFORD AIRPORT ...	arr.	9.50	5.20
{ Kirkwall Hotel	arr.	10.10	5.40

		a.m.	p.m.
KIRKWALL { Kirkwall Hotel	dep.	8.40	4.10
{ WIDEFORD AIRPORT FOR	dep.	9.00	4.30
THURSO { THURSO AIRPORT ...	arr.	9.20	4.50
{ Royal Hotel	arr.	9.40	5.10

A—15th May to 30th September, 1939, inclusive.
B—17th July to 16th September, 1939, inclusive.

ORKNEY ISLANDS SERVICE (KIRKWALL—NORTH ISLES)

Service 745   Mondays, Wednesdays and Saturdays until 17th June.
Daily except Sundays from 19th June until 30th September.

		a.m.
KIRKWALL { WIDEFORD AIRPORT	dep.	11.20
{ Kirkwall Hotel	dep.	12.00

FOR
LONGHOPE, WESTRAY, SANDAY, STRONSAY and NORTH RONALDSAY.

Service returns to Wideford Airport to connect with departure at 1.50 p.m. for Inverness and the South.

GROUND TRANSPORT—See page 3 (para. 17). FARES, EXCESS BAGGAGE, FREIGHT RATES—See pages 6-7.

Another of George Nicholson's pilots who had likewise gone North to fly for Fresson's Section in Orkney was John Annesley Hankins, and he celebrated his marriage in Kirkwall on Saturday March 4th 1939 to Miss Sheelah Daphne Annesley (from the same original branch of an Irish family). John himself had been born in New Zealand, and his wife born in Rhodesia, and they had met on Islay when John was flying for Northern and Scottish Airways two years previously.

A film on the Air Ambulance service

The Scottish Air Ambulance Service, founded by John Sword in 1933 and later taken over by George Nicholson and Ted Fresson (both eventually being combined as Scottish Airways) was expanding so quickly and had already become so well-known publicly, that a documentary film was produced about the service in the Winter of 1938-39.

As *The Aeroplane* magazine for February 22nd 1939 wrote:

"A SCOTTISH AIRWAYS FILM

Ambulance flying is going on steadily in almost all parts of the World where there are great distances or physical obstacles in the way of surface travel. It gets little more notice than regular air transport. This is because the successive "mercy" flights, as some will insist on calling them, seldom have much of variety or sensation, not because this branch of flying is one of the outstanding items to the credit of Aviation nowadays.

Air ambulance work is too common for comment in many of the Dominions and wilder portions of the Empire, but in Great Britain it is almost confined to the Islands on the North and West Scotland.

Scottish Airways Ltd., who have a special organisation at Renfrew for ambulance purposes, have co-operated with Pathé Pictorial Ltd in a short film which has just been released.

This brief record shows the receipt of an emergency call at Renfrew and the start of a Spartan Cruiser Mark II (three 130 h.p. Gipsy Majors) with a crew of three and a nurse. The audience are given glimpses of the forbidding scenery over which many of these flights are made, and the Hebridean setting at the other end is authentic.

This interesting little film is on view since Feb. 18 at the Eros News Theatre, Piccadilly, and the News Theatres at Waterloo and Victoria Stations. Its Scottish showings began in Glasgow on Feb. 6. and will go throughout the whole of Scotland by filtering down through the various divisions of the cinema world between now and July 10. The list is unfortunately too long to give entire, but the film ought to be looked for and seen. "

A group of Ted Fresson's engineers at Inverness in front of the D.H. Dragon G-ACIT.

They are, left to right: Bert Farminer, George Griffiths O.B.E, Archie MacDonald (top), Theo Goulden (bottom), Brian Watt, M.B.E. and Capt. Adam Smith. (Brian Watt, M.B.E.)

Capt. Adams' apparel is of interest, for apart from the heavy flying boots, he has a distinctly 'non uniform' scarf tucked inside his greatcoat to ward off the winter chills of flying in the North!

Right: An advertisement in Scottish Airways' brochure for some of the other services provided by Macrae & Dick - apart from being a founder shareholder and supporter in Ted Fresson's Highland Airways (later Scottish Airways) . (Henry Vallance)

Below: Another advert from the Scottish Airways' brochure - this time for Ted Fresson's original travel agent and airport coach operator in Shetland - Ganson Brothers. (Henry Vallance)

Above: Scottish Airways' Spartan Cruiser G-ACYK is seen flying over Glasgow University.

Left: Seen standing outside the offices of Scottish Airways are (left to right) Bill Cumming, Capt. David Barclay, George Nicholson and Bill Mann.

Below: Flight Crew and handlers pause while loading the mail onto Spartan Cruiser II G-ACSM at Sollas.
More bags await collection on the steps in the foreground.
(John Stroud Collection).

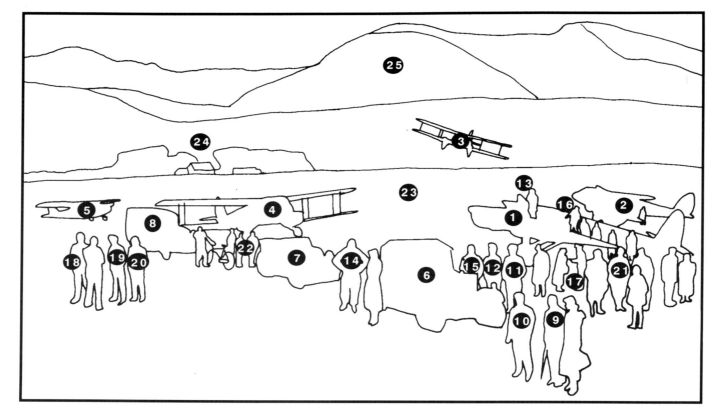

"Wings over the Glens"

Glen Brittle aerodrome, Skye, in the shadow of the Cuillin Hills, on a typical busy day in Summer 1937. Aircraft, passengers and crew of Northern and Scottish Airways (NSA) gather there on their way between Glasgow and other aerodromes in the Western Isles.

Key to the painting

The Aircraft:
1. A Spartan Cruiser II, G-ACSM, with its distinctive three engines, stalky undercarriage and metal fuselage.
2. One of NSA's De Havilland DH89 Dragon Rapides, G-ADDF, acquired from British Airways' pool of aircraft.
3. Another Dragon Rapide acquired from the same pool, G-ADAH, makes a low pass over Glen Brittle.
4. One of NSA's DH 84 Dragon IIs, G-ACMO, also transferred from British Airways for the airline to use.
5. This De Havilland DH85 Leopard Moth, G-ACUO, was used by NSA for ambulance work.

The Vehicles:
6. At the head of the line of vehicles is the little Humber 8 motor car owned by the Glen Brittle aerodrome manager, Ewen MacRae. He later had a large cylindrical petrol tank fitted on top of the car's boot from which he refuelled the aircraft.
7. The 1936 open top Morris 8 Tourer belongs to the friends meeting one of the passengers.
8. The van belongs to the local butcher, B. M. Steele, and was a regular visitor to the houses close to the aerodrome.

The Personalities and scenery:
9. George Nicholson, founder of "Northern and Scottish Airways Ltd" (and before that, "Northern Airways"), who later ably guided the Renfrew-based operation of Scottish Airways Ltd through the period 1937 - 1947.
10. Capt. David Barclay, MBE, M.St.J, the Chief Pilot of NSA and later Scottish Airways Ltd. from 1935 to 1947, including the entire war period. He flew more ambulance flights during his lifetime than anyone else.
11. Capt. Henry Vallance, pioneer Scottish pilot, who flew for Scottish Airways Ltd throughout the entire war period, based mostly in Inverness.
12. Capt. "Bill" Baillie, MVO, OBE, who also flew for Scottish Airways Ltd throughout World War Two.

13. Capt. John Annesley Hankins AFC, who joined NSA in 1936 and stayed with the airline until 1947, except for war service in the RAF (1940-1944). He is suitably dressed to fly the Leopard Moth.
14. Capt "Jock" Young, who joined NSA in 1936 and served throughout World War Two, leaving in 1946.
15. William ("Bill") Cumming joined NSA as Company Secretary in 1936, serving until after nationalisation in 1947. He was always George Nicholson's right-hand man, and shared responsibility for the airline's successes.
16. Chief Radio Officer F. R. Hughes, NSA's first Wireless Telegraphy Officer (W.T.O.) - later changed to Radio Officer (R.O.) - who joined in 1936.
17. Radio Officer Hugh Black, who joined NSA in 1937 and stayed on with BEA after 1947, retiring back to Shetland.
18. Ewen MacRae, the Glen Brittle Aerodrome Manager, who lived in Glen Brittle House and drove the Humber 8 car.
19. Senior Traffic Officer John Swann, NSA's first Traffic Manager, who joined NSA in 1936 and continued until after nationalisation in 1947, serving BEA thereafter.
20. William ("Bill") Mann, the Chief Engineer of NSA, who joined the airline in 1935 and served in that capacity until it was nationalised in 1947. With his hand-picked team of engineers and apprentices, he maintained and overhauled the airline's ever-increasing fleet of aircraft types - from DH Dragons to Douglas DC-3s.
21. Some joining passengers, attired in warm 'Highland' clothing, and awaiting boarding the aircraft for their next destination.
22. Local fishermen and schoolboys were frequent interested bystanders at the airfields served by NSA - being the earliest form of 'Aeroplane Spotters'!
23. The rectangular grass aerodrome at Glen Brittle was located on flat fields at the foot of the glen, by the sea-shore (lower left of picture).
24. Gen Brittle House, where the Aerodrome Manager, Ewen MacRae and his brother and parents lived. Refeshments and the use of a telephone were available here.
25. The south-west ridges of the famous Cuillin Hills of Skye.

CHAPTER 12

Sold off to the L. M. S.

As the Summer of 1939 passed slowly by, David Barclay carried out some aerial photography of the Western Isles and it's landing strips from the air, for the publicity department of Imperial Airways Ltd. He also made another landing on Colonsay on June 9th, to search for an ideal airstrip there.

On August 1st 1939, David flew out a party of top Air Ministry officials and two Civil Aviation officers (Hildred and Stallybrass) to check the final condition of Stornoway's new grass airfield, so Ted Fresson could open an Inverness - Stornoway service on September 1st. David landed on the tidal basin sands there, and stayed overnight, returning to Glasgow next day. Everything seemed to be almost finished with the aerodrome between the golf bunkers, and it promised to bring a long overdue and very necessary boon to the islanders of Lewis and Harris.

During these summer months, another significant development in British Civil Aviation occurred, which also affected Scottish Airways. As the year 1938 had dawned, another Report had landed on Air Ministry and Government desks about the future of civil aviation in Britain, this time presented by the Cadnam Committee. It produced a series of recommendations to ensure that the U.K. developed its overseas aviation network to best advantage. These included the view that the U.K. airlines should fly to many more European cities, and that Imperial Airways should concentrate on longer - haul routes to the far flung Empire, while British Airways should expand into Europe in a big way.

During 1938 and 1939 British Airways (the parent company of both Northern and Scottish Airways Ltd and Highland Airways Ltd - and thus of Scottish Airways too) took the Cadnam Committee to heart, and expanded its services to Europe, as well as starting to survey routes to West Africa and South America. There was no doubt it had increasingly aggressive tendencies in overseas aviation - to Imperial Airway's alarm.

From April 16th 1939 British Airways merged its London - Paris service with that of Imperial Airways, and they operated jointly between Croydon and Le Bourget. On April 17th B.A. began services to Brussels, Frankfurt and Budapest from Heston, and to Stockholm, Berlin and Warsaw also. Then on June 12th a Bill was introduced into the House of Commons by Sir Kingsley Wood, providing for the merger of British Airways with Imperial Airways into a new British Overseas Airways Corporation (or B.O.A.C.) It had its second reading on July 10th,

and received Royal Assent on August 4th, and then on November 24th 1939 B.O.A.C. was finally established with its chairman being Sir John Reith, and Deputy Chairman the Hon. Clive Pearson (of Whitehall Securities and British Airways). (By March 6th 1940 the Hon. Clive Pearson had moved up to become Chairman of B.O.A.C.).

One of the provisos, however, of such a large merger affecting all the overseas interests of British Civil Aviation was that British Airways Ltd must sell off its domestic airline interests to others.

The scheme in detail

The scheme was disclosed in a letter to both George Nicholson and Ted Fresson on June 7th 1939, when Horace Davey, the Solicitor acting for British Airways, sent the details to all the shareholders of the original two companies, Northern and Scottish Airways Ltd (now Northern Airways Ltd) and Highland Airways Ltd, to explain what was to happen.

The letter sent to Ted Fresson and the other five shareholders of Highland Airways read as follows (taken from the copy sent to Mr. T. L. Adam of the North of Scotland & Orkney & Shetland Steam Navigation Co. Ltd):-

"This letter is also sent to:
Robert Donald Esq.
The Secretary, Messrs Macrae & Dick Ltd
Col. J. J. Robertson
Robert Wotherspoon Esq.

T. L. Adam Esq   7th June 1939
42 Regent Quay
Aberdeen

Dear Sir,
    I am the solicitor for British Airways Limited and am writing to you in the absence from his office of Mr Roberts who unfortunately has been suffering from influenza and will probably not be returning until the end of this week.

    As you are aware the Government are proposing to form a new Corporation for the purposes of acquiring the undertakings of Imperial Airways Limited and British Airways Limited with the exception in the case of British Airways, of its interest in internal air services. This last

Airport Ground Staff (left) - one of the well-trained team of local farmers at Westray airstrip, Orkney Isles, waiting to dash out from the shelter of stone walls and hold on to Ted Fresson's aircraft in high winds. Airport Dog (right) - the Wideford 'hound' that was trained to clear sheep off the landing strip prior to aircraft arrival. (Brian Watt, MBE)

SCOTTISH AIRWAYS LTD.

Organisation - 1939

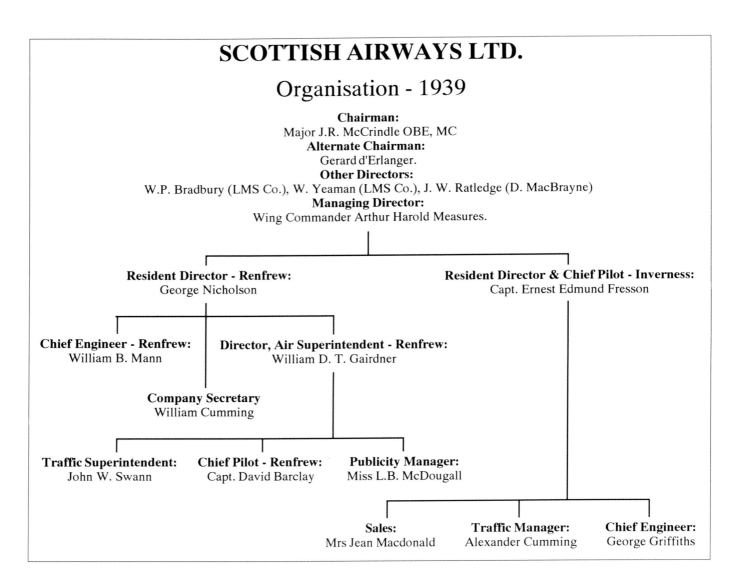

Chairman:
Major J.R. McCrindle OBE, MC
Alternate Chairman:
Gerard d'Erlanger.
Other Directors:
W.P. Bradbury (LMS Co.), W. Yeaman (LMS Co.), J. W. Ratledge (D. MacBrayne)
Managing Director:
Wing Commander Arthur Harold Measures.

Resident Director - Renfrew:
George Nicholson

Resident Director & Chief Pilot - Inverness:
Capt. Ernest Edmund Fresson

Chief Engineer - Renfrew:
William B. Mann

Director, Air Superintendent - Renfrew:
William D. T. Gairdner

Company Secretary
William Cumming

Traffic Superintendent:
John W. Swann

Chief Pilot - Renfrew:
Capt. David Barclay

Publicity Manager:
Miss L.B. McDougall

Sales:
Mrs Jean Macdonald

Traffic Manager:
Alexander Cumming

Chief Engineer:
George Griffiths

mentioned interest consists of that Company's holdings in Highland Airways Limited and Northern Airways Limited which two companies hold shares in Scottish Airways Limited. One of the terms of the sale to the new Government Corporation is that British Airways shall be wound up and as a consequence the directors of British Airways have decided to endeavour to dispose of their indirect interest in Scottish Airways.

Mr Gerard d'Erlanger, on behalf of British Airways, had been in negotiation with Lord Stamp representing the L.M. & S. Railway Company and Messrs. David McBrayne Limited, which two companies, as you know, are the holders of the shares in Scottish Airways other than those owned by Highland Airways and Northern Airways and are, under the provision of the Articles of Association of Scottish Airways, the parties to whom shares in that company must be first offered. As a result of such negotiations Lord Stamp has offered to acquire British Airways' interest in Scottish Airways shares at 11/- per share.

You will remember that Highland Airways hold 14,485 "A" ordinary shares of £1 each in Scottish Airways and Northern Airways hold 25,515 "A" ordinary shares. The issued capital of Highland Airways is £16,000 of which British Airways hold £11,150 leaving other parties holding £4,850. The British Airways holding in Highland Airways is through United Airways.

One of the terms of the arrangement between Mr

d'Erlanger and Lord Stamp is that the shareholders in Highland Airways, other than British Airways, should be entitled either (1) to call upon the L.M. & S. Railway Company to purchase their interest in Scottish Airways on the same terms as those offered to British Airways, namely 11/- per Scottish Airways share, or (2) to retain their present holdings as they stand. If they decide to retain their present holding a request by them to increase such holdings at a cost of 11/- per share will be favourably considered.

Perhaps you will be good enough to consider these proposals which have been conveyed to the shareholders of Highland Airways other than British Airways. If it be desired, the Secretary of Highland Airways will make the necessary arrangements to hold an informal meeting of such shareholders to discuss the above mentioned offer. Captain Fresson has kindly agreed to place himself at your disposal to give you any further information which you may require before the informal meeting. Should you desire to avail yourself of this opportunity, would you please communicate direct with Captain Fresson.

I ought to say that if the transaction with the L.M. & S. Railway Company takes place by a sale by Highland Airways to the L.M. & S. Railway Company of shares in Scottish Airways, there will be payable in addition to the stamp duties on the transfers of such shares, which will be borne by the L.M. & S. Railway, a few hundred pounds of stamp duty which were saved under a certain Act of

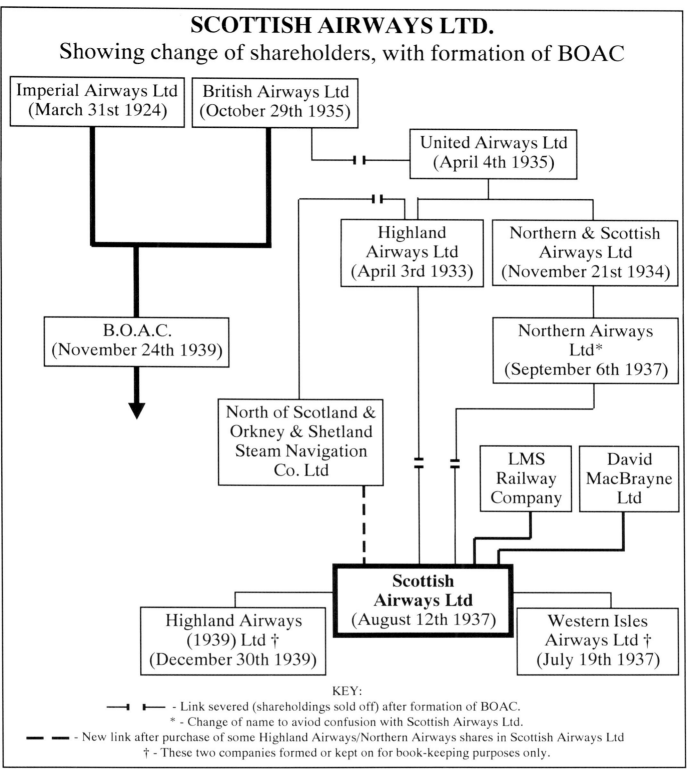

SCOTTISH AIRWAYS LTD.
Showing change of shareholders, with formation of BOAC

Imperial Airways Ltd
(March 31st 1924)

British Airways Ltd
(October 29th 1935)

United Airways Ltd
(April 4th 1935)

Highland
Airways Ltd
(April 3rd 1933)

Northern & Scottish
Airways Ltd
(November 21st 1934)

B.O.A.C.
(November 24th 1939)

Northern Airways
Ltd*
(September 6th 1937)

North of Scotland &
Orkney & Shetland
Steam Navigation
Co. Ltd

LMS
Railway
Company

David
MacBrayne
Ltd

**Scottish
Airways Ltd**
(August 12th 1937)

Highland Airways
(1939) Ltd †
(December 30th 1939)

Western Isles
Airways Ltd †
(July 19th 1937)

KEY:
- Link severed (shareholdings sold off) after formation of BOAC.
* - Change of name to aviod confusion with Scottish Airways Ltd.
- New link after purchase of some Highland Airways/Northern Airways shares in Scottish Airways Ltd
† - These two companies formed or kept on for book-keeping purposes only.

Parliament when Scottish Airways was formed, the reason for the payment of the further duties being that the sale will take place within two years from the date of such formation. The method that will be required to be adopted to avoid payment of such further stamp duty will be for the L.M.S. Railway Company to acquire shares in Highland Airways, in which case they would be asked to pay something slightly in excess of 11/- per Scottish Airways share, because of the assets held by Highland Airways in addition to their shareholding in Scottish Airways.

As a part of the deal between British Airways and L.M. & S. Railway Company an existing arrangement whereby British Airways would participate in the subscription for any additional capital issued by Scottish Airways would be cancelled.
Yours faithfully
(Signed) Horace Davey"

In addition, Horace Davey sent a note to Fresson (and presumably George too) to say he had sent details of the scheme to The North of Scotland & Orkney & Shetland Steam Navigation Co. Ltd., as it appeared that they were interested with the LMS Railway, in buying up some of the British Airways' stake in Scotland Airways.

Ted Fresson's reply to the letter is shown here:

"H. Davey Esq.,   13th June 1939
47 Parliament Street,
Westminster. S.W.1.

Dear Mr Davey,
    Thank you for your letter of 7th June, in which you were good enough to enclose copy letter addressed to the North of Scotland & Orkney & Shetland Steam Navigation Co. Ltd., and also a copy of your letter to the other five shareholders of Highland Airways Limited.
Yours faithfully
for E.E. Fresson"

These arrangements were finally concluded by April 1st 1940, when B.O.A.C. officially took over the operations of both Imperial Airways and British Airways, although both had worked together in practice since September 1939 and the outbreak of War. So, the 50 per cent share of Scottish Airways Ltd. that was owned by Northern Airways and Highland Airways together (40,000 "A" Shares of £1 each) was now taken over by the LMS Railway Co. and by the North of Scotland & Orkney & Shetland Steam Navigation Co. Ltd. (who were also shareholders in Highland Airways Ltd). The control of Scottish Airways Ltd. thus passed to LMS Railway Co., David MacBrayne Ltd., and the North of Scotland & Orkney & Shetland Steam Navigation Co Ltd., and remained with these three shareholders for the rest of its existence.

The smaller individual shareholders in Northern Airways Ltd., and Highland Airways Ltd. also now all sold their shares to the LMS Railway Co, with the exception of The North of Scotland & Orkney & Shetland Steam Navigation Co Ltd., a shareholder in Highland Airways Ltd., which in effect retained its holding, and added to it by purchasing more shares at the set rate of 11s. 0d. per £1 share from the LMS Railway Co.

In all, therefore, Northern Airways received a total of 11s. 0d per share for its 25,515 'A' shares in Scottish Airways Ltd, or a sum of £14,033. 5s. 0d., and Highland Airways received a sum of £7,966 15s. 0d. (14,485 shares @ 11s. 0d). Control of Scottish Airways Ltd was thus relinquished by British Airways' subsidiary, United Airways, for a total sum of £22,000. In Northern Airways case, where United Airways owned some 33,248 of its 38,000 issued shares, this meant that United Airways only collected £12,278, and in Highland's case, where United Airways owned some 11,150 of the 16,000 issued shares this gave it a sum of £5,552. So ultimately, United only received £17,830 less any Stamp Duties required, and British Airways Ltd., the ultimate parent company, only received an amount proportionate to its share of capital in United Airways Ltd. The names British Airways and Imperial Airways had to be dropped, now, as they were merged together into the new Government - formed (and financed) Corporation - British Overseas Airways Corporation, or B.O.A.C. for short.

The three ultimate shareholders in Scottish Airways Ltd had thus gained control at bargain prices, and as they were all concerned with either rail or steamship travel in the Highlands and Islands of Scotland, had also acquired a perfect operating partner in the shape of the air services. It was probably one of the best deals in the history of British civil aviation!

Finally, apart from Scottish Airways Ltd., another company incorporated on December 30th 1939 - Highland Airways (1939) Limited - and the subsidiary of Scottish Airways - Western Isles Airways Ltd - both survived for accountancy purposes right up to the date in the 1970s when B.E.A. merged with B.O.A.C. to form (the second) British Airways Ltd.

Loading the mail at Renfrew aboard Scottish Airways' DH Dragon Rapide G-AFEY for the journey north.

CHAPTER 13

Wartime Operations

As the end of August 1939 approached it was fairly obvious that War with Germany was likely to be declared at almost any minute, and the Nation began to gear itself up accordingly. In fact a slow but inexorable build-up for War had been in progress for almost three years now - hence the attention by the Air Ministry and Admiralty in new airfields in Scotland over the last two years.

An immediate effect of the imminent presence of War was noticeable at Stornoway. Ted Fresson saw the new grass aerodrome there completed and ready for use in August 1939, and he made the only two landings there - on August 25th for an Ambulance flight and on the 29th for a Government charter. Then, before a schedule could be started, the Air Ministry sequestered the entire aerodrome and Golf Links, and a lot of extra ground, and ploughed up the whole area to make a much larger wartime aerodrome there!

Cessation/re-starting services

The Scottish Airways' network operated as usual up to the day War was declared by Great Britain on Germany - September 3rd 1939. At the beginning of the season a number of newer aircraft - D.H. 89A Dragon Rapides - had been acquired from the British Airways group pool: G-AEOV on May 1st 1939, G-AFFF on May 26th and G-AFRK on July 19th. The first of these ('EOV) was in fact the original prototype Dragon Rapide to be fitted with wing flaps and the last ('FRK) had been used by Isle of Man Air Services until transferred.

Just prior to the outbreak of War the Air Ministry told Scottish Airways to close their radio station at Sollas (North Uist), which they did on September 1st. And on the 3rd, the Air Navigation (Restriction in Time of War) Order, 1939 was promulgated, under which all civil aviation movements ceased unless authorised in writing by the Secretary of State for Air. As *The Aeroplane* magazine reported in its issue of September 21st 1939.

"RESTRICTION IN TIME OF WAR

As already announced, the Air Navigation (Restriction in Time of War) Order, 1939, came into effect on September 3rd 1939.

This order applies to every aircraft in or over the United Kingdom or its territorial waters.

The principal provision is that no aircraft shall fly except without a permit in writing issued by the Secretary of State for Air. The terms of such a permit must be strictly observed.

Map of Stornoway aerodrome, as developed during and after WWII, with the area marked where Ted Fresson had a grass aerodrome laid out in 1939. (Author)

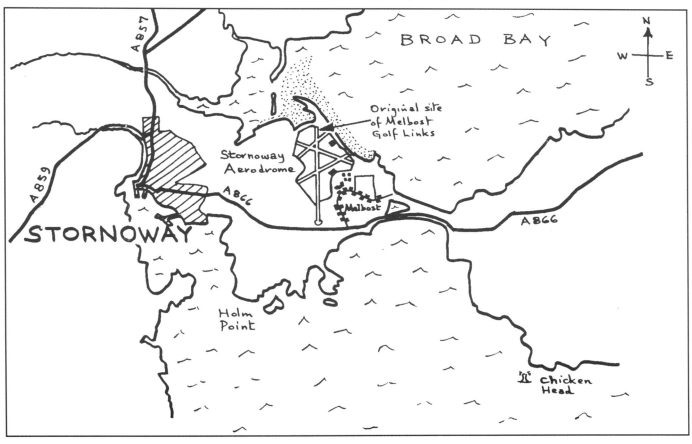

Aircraft which have permits must comply generally with certain provisions except in so far as their permit absolves them.

The prohibited area, which embraces most of the Eastern part of the United Kingdom, has already been described, and a map is published herewith which gives also other prohibited areas and prescribed corridors for machines entering or leaving the United Kingom.

No machine may fly between the hours of sunset and sunrise, and any which does so will be deemed to be flying over a prohibited area and be subject to the prescribed penalties.

The most important of the results which may accrue from the flying in a prohibited manner or over a prohibited area is that His Majesty's Naval, Military or Air Forces may lawfully fire at or into such an aircraft. In other words, anyone who attempts to fly without a permit or in a manner not covered by his permit will be shot down.

In the likely contingency of machines straying in bad weather, or finding themselves in prohibited

The prohibited areas for civil flying as laid down at the outbreak of WWII (to the east of the line shown).

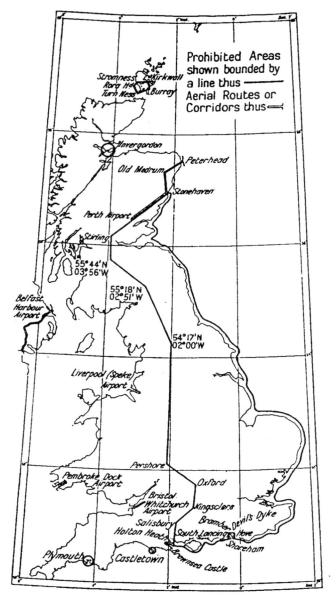

Prohibited Areas shown bounded by a line thus ———
Aerial Routes or Corridors thus ⟞

<table>
<tr><th colspan="2">SCOTTISH AIRWAYS
Traffic Totals
(August 1st 1937 - August 31st 1939)</th></tr>
<tr><td>Passengers Carried</td><td>30,168</td></tr>
<tr><td>Cargo (lbs)</td><td>219,764</td></tr>
<tr><td>Mail (lbs)</td><td>402,069</td></tr>
<tr><td>Revenue Passenger miles</td><td>2,510,714</td></tr>
<tr><td>Aircraft miles</td><td>1,257,722</td></tr>
<tr><td>(incl Army Co-Op a/c miles:</td><td>131,613)</td></tr>
</table>

circumstances by error, they are directed to fly away at once from the prohibited area and not to descend over it unless forced to. Such aircraft must also give the usual signals of distress while correcting the error."

At the moment of stoppage of operations on September 3rd, Scottish Airways Ltd combined fleet of 13 aircraft were flying up to 30,000 miles per week, and using 18 aerodromes around Scotland of which 14 had been developed by the company at its own expense (the other 4 being provided by Local Authority or other sources).

From September 3rd, therefore, all Scottish Airways' flights were temporarily suspended, and the airlines, airports, equipment and personnel were all placed at the Ministry's disposal. The Air Ministry also withdrew all radio facilities along the routes.

In the North, Ted Fresson was asked to operate some charters for the Navy and Air Ministry up to Orkney and Thurso, which he flew on September 4th, 7th, and 8th in the DH Rapide G-ADAJ. In the South, David Barclay flew a group of Air Ministry officials on September 6th on an aerial inspection of Renfrew aerodrome, using the Spartan Cruiser II G-ACYL.

The North and West of Scotland was rather remote from hostilities at that moment and suspension of service was causing hardship in many places, so urgent representation from George Nicholson and Co. in Renfrew soon elicited the Air Ministry's permission to re-start flights on September 11th. David Barclay immediately flew a Renfrew - Tiree - Benbecula - North Uist - Barra - Skye - Renfrew round trip in the Cruiser II G-ACSM with Bradley as his R.O. Next day (September 12th) he flew to Skye and back; on the 13th he flew an ambulance flight from Barra, followed by flying to Tiree on the 14th; then on the 15th he flew down South in the Rapide G-AFRK via Carlisle and Liverpool to Duxford, returning next day after meeting Ministry officials there. Finally, on the 19th David resumed normal daily services on Renfrew - Campbeltown - Islay and return.

The ambulance flight was flown in the Cruiser II 'CSM, and David returned from Barra with two crew, Nurse Govan and the patient, Miss Christine McKeggan. This was Scottish Airways' first call out in wartime.

Ted Fresson in Inverness, unfortunately, had not been told about the resumption of services on September 11th and only discovered this next day when he rang Renfrew! He then immediately re-started the normal Inverness - Kirkwall services on September 12th.

From September 1st, the airlines all began to operate under overall direction from the Air Ministry in the shape of an organisation called the National Air Communications (or N.A.C.). This loosely managed their affairs until May 1940, when it was replaced by the Associated Airways' Joint Committee (A.A.J.C.). Until then, however, the NAC existed at Exeter Airport under Wing Cmdr. Measures from the RAS, and

SCOTTISH AIRWAYS

Pre-War Statistics 1937-1939

	1937*	1938	1939	TOTAL
1. Passengers carried:				
Scottish Airways Ltd	3,629	7,250	8,881	19,760
Western Isles Airways Ltd	2,815	5,957	4,536	13,308
Total:	6,444	13,207	13,417	33,068
2. Passenger Load Factor (%)				
Scottish Airways Ltd	53.7	40.9	56.2	-
Western Isles Airways Ltd	48.8	48.4	56.2	-
3. Cargo carried (lbs x 000)				
Scottish Airways Ltd	20.4	46.0	78.5	144.9
Western Isles Airways Ltd	25.0	54.3	31.1	110.4
Total:	45.4	100.3	109.6	255.3
4. Mail carried (lbs x 000)				
Scottish Airways Ltd	78.5	178.1	245.2	501.8
Western Isles Airways Ltd	-	-	9.3	9.3
Total:	78.5	178.1	254.5	511.1
5 Aircraft Miles flown (x 000)				
Scottish Airways Ltd	118.4	308.4	541.0	967.8
Western Isles Airways Ltd	106.4	212.7	168.2	487.3
Total:	224.8	521.1	709.2	1,455.1

* - From August 1st to December 31st. 1937

the fleet of RAS and part of the fleets of British Airways and Imperial Airways were flown there and combined under his control.

On September 1st, Scottish Airways' newly - joined Captain "Bill" Baillie was told by NAC to fly the DH Dragon II G-ACNG down to Harwell, and from there, during the next 14 days Bill flew to French airfields and back almost daily, carrying Service Personnel and Equipment in both directions. They were called "S.P. & E." flights, in fact.

Thus Bill flew in turn to Rheims (four consecutive days), then from Shoreham he flew to Auberive and Rheims, then to Poix, and finally back to Renfrew in the Rapide G-AFEY (which one of the other pilots had flown to Harwell) on September 14th. Bill remembers that at Harwell they were billeted overnight at the C.O.'s empty house (he had just been posted away). But at Shoreham, they went into Brighton and stayed at the Grand Hotel with everything laid on (and charged it all to expenses afterwards)!

Henry Vallance took Fresson's Dragon I G-ACIT down to Harwell on September 2nd and found the airfield crowded with all kinds of aircraft, from DH Fox Moths to a Handley Page HP 42. There was a shortage of maps so Henry was told to look at another pilot's map, to see how to get to Rheims, in Eastern France, and then memorise it and fly there himself !

While the pilots were all being briefed, their aircraft were taken into hangars, one by one, and some ground staff with buckets of camouflage dope, and brushes, poured the paint all over the tops of the wings and fuselage and brushed the dope along the sides and underneath in a very crude, very hasty manner! They were walking on the top of the fabric - covered wings and tails - heedless of the normal rules never to stand on these parts ! He flew to the same French airfields for several days before returning 'CIT to Renfrew and then taking the Rapide G-AFRK down to Harwell on September 5th.

The reason for changing aircraft was to get more power! Henry had been to Bristol aerodrome to load up with soldiers and ammunition for France. Trying to take off in G-ACIT, he had only just cleared the hedge at the far end of the field. And even then, he only just cleared the South Downs - he couldn't even get up to the 1000 ft level at which they were supposed to cross the Channel! He then piloted 'FRK to Rheims, etc, and returned it to Renfrew on September 14th. Henry remembers arriving in Rheims and seeing a collection of very ancient looking French aircraft there. There was no fuel to put in their tanks, so while they waited overnight for it, they went into town and had a great time for some hours !

Back home, Henry took the Spartan Cruiser II G-ACYL on September 15th and re-commenced flying the Campbeltown - Islay service again, with R.O. Bradley.

Bill Baillie however, was sent off back to France again, flying 'FRK and shuttling back and forth across the Channel until November 14th doing valiant work for the Army and RAF during this time.

The other pilots, in the North and South Sections, were also sent onto the S.P. & E. flights at times during that Autumn, or called up for RAF service. David Barclay operated a special charter on September 26th from Renfrew, picked up a Captain and Commander from the US Navy at Donibristle RN aerodrome and flew them up to see the new Hatston RN aerodrome in Orkney and back.

New Air Mail Service; Lifeboat search
On October 2nd 1939, David Barclay inaugurated a new Air Mail contract to carry mails between Renfrew and Campbeltown. He took RO Black and operated the Cruiser II G-ACYL on this flight, which also included Islay on the service. (In the North, Ted Fresson had recently inaugurated the first 'all-in' air mail service (parcels included) between Kirkwall and N.

RECORD OF FLIGHTS.

Date	Aircraft Type	Markings	Engines Type	H.P.	From	To	Time of Departure Hrs.	Mins.	Time of Arrival Hrs.	Mins.	Time in Air Hrs.	Mins.	Pilot	Remarks
						Brought forward					2149			
2-9-39	AW 14	G·ACIT	Gipsy Major	260²	Hanwell	Rheims	14	30		55	3	35	self	S P & E
3-9-39	"		"	"	Rheims	Hanwell	09	10	12	10	3	"		Service personnel & equipment
	"		"	"	Hanwell	Rheims	14	15	17	10	2	55		
	"		"	"	Rheims	Shorham	17	50	19	55	2	05		
4-9-39	"		"	"	Shorham	Hanwell	08	30	09	20	–	20		
	"		"	"	Hanwell	Rheims	12	10	14	55	2	45		
	"		"	"	Rheims	Hanwell	15	55	18	00	3	05		
5-9-39	"		"	"	Hanwell	Liverpool	10	50	12	10	1	20		Ferry
						Carried forward					2168	25		

RECORD OF FLIGHTS.

Date	Aircraft Type	Markings	Engines Type	H.P.	From	To	Time of Departure Hrs.	Mins.	Time of Arrival Hrs.	Mins.	Time in Air Hrs.	Mins.	Pilot	Remarks
						Brought forward					2018	45		
14.10.39	D.H.89	G·AFRK	Gipsy Vi	200	Dieppe	Yyal	12	15	13	50		35	self	National Air Comm
					Dieppe	Amiens	16	00	15	35		35		
					Amiens	Arras	15	40	16	00		20		
					Arras	Amiens	16	05	16	35		30		
					Amiens	Arras	09	00	09	20		20		
					Arras	Coulommiers	09	30	10	45	1	15		
					Coulommiers	Arras	16	30	17	50	1	00		
16.10.39					Arras	Amiens	17	35	18	00		25		
						Carried forward					2023	45		

Two examples of the kind of Service, Personnel and Equipment (SPE) flights to France flown at the start of World War Two by Henry Vallance (above) and Bill Baillie (below).

Ronaldsay on July 31st 1939). Then David took the Spartan Cruiser III G-ADEL down to Liverpool on October 6th 1939 and stayed at Speke until December 12th flying local Army Co-operation flights of 2 to 2 1/4 hours duration each time, to help tune up the local air defences around Lancashire and Cheshire.

After this, he returned to Renfrew and as the New Year arrived David was mostly on the Campbeltown run. (He even flew a service to Campbeltown and Islay on Christmas day.). The link between Renfrew and Inverness had not been re-started after September 3rd, and would not again be during the hostilities. So when David had to position the Rapide G-AFRK back to Inverness on January 11th he flew it empty from Prestwick (where it had been landed due to bad weather over a period of several days at Renfrew). The fog had been very bad and unpredictable in its clearing, and during this time the Spartan Cruiser II G-ACZM had been badly damaged at Renfrew on January 9th and was consequently written off and never flew again.

Up in the North, David then took a turn at flying the Inverness - Kirkwall - Sumburgh service for several days, before returning to Glasgow and the Campbeltown run again on the Cruiser II G-ACYL.

Henry Vallance for his part, had been back to France again in October and had then flown the Campbeltown/Islay service almost continuously until December 18th, when he managed to get posted back to Inverness on a permanent basis. On November 25th however, he was en route to Islay from Campbeltown on his usual run, when he heard via his Radio Officer Black, that a merchant ship, the *M.V. Sliedrecht* had been torpedoed somewhere to the south of the Western Isles and one of the lifeboats with some of the crew on board was missing in the area.

The weather was bad, with gales and rainstorms, but once Henry had landed at Islay, he took off again and spent 1hr 40 mins searching the seas between Islay and South Uist. It was growing dark, and Henry couldn't see any sign of a lifeboat or flotsam, and finally he had to land at Sollas (North Uist) for the night.

Next day Henry set off again from Sollas and searched in difficult conditions for 2hrs 25mins this time, before landing at Islay, and picking up the Renfrew schedule again. Henry never found any trace of the lifeboat, unfortunately, but on arrival back at Renfrew sent a detailed report of his search to the vessel's owners, Messrs Van Ommeron Ltd. The owners were very grateful for Henry's efforts, and sent a message to NAC HQ in Bristol to that effect. And NAC HQ sent a duly appreciative message to Henry at Renfrew.

Bill Baillie, meanwhile, had been back to France in October and was kept flying across the Channel by the NAC until December, finally returning to Renfrew on December 7th and - like the others - to the Campbeltown/ Islay schedule. But he too was transferred up to Inverness early in January 1940, and went onto the Inverness - Orkney - Shetland service. Ted Fresson thus had two excellent pilots with him in the North, Henry Vallance and Bill Baillie, both of whom had worked for Allied Airways at Dyce, and knew the Northern Isles like the back of their hands. One of the other Northern pilots however, wrote off the DH Rapide G-AFEY while landing at Wideford on March 18th 1940 - luckily without serious injuries to anyone.

A nasty accident

David Barclay found himself flying the Campbeltown - Islay service regularly during April 1940, but also had a pleasant experience on April 11th when he was asked to air-test an Avro 638 Club Cadet, G-ACHP, for Airwork Ltd (who had used it in their pilot training school since it was built in June 1933). He gave it two flights of 20 and 10 minutes duration and cleared it for use again (after having its C of A renewed).

On the 2nd of the month, he had been saddened to have to hand over three of the Renfrew aircraft to a 'Requisitioning Officer' of the RAF. The latter arrived at Renfrew overnight and David had to give him a 15 minute test flight in the Spartan Cruiser II G-ACSM and the Cruiser III G-ADEL, before the RAF removed them for their use elsewhere. The Cruiser II G-ACYL was test-flown by another pilot (probably Bill Gairdner) and also removed. (The DH Rapide G-AEOV had already been removed back on January 10th).

On April 18th he flew the Rapide, G-AFRK, on the Renfrew - Campbeltown - Islay run, and next day April 19th he took the DH Dragon, G-ACNG, with Gray as his R.O. and flew it across to Edinburgh (Turnhouse) picked up some Admiralty, Army, and Air Ministry officials, and flew them up to Hatston RNAS Station at Kirkwall. On the final approach to Hatston, in difficult weather conditions a sudden downdraught hit David as he crossed the boundary of the aerodrome and the Dragon crashed

North Ronaldsay, July 31st 1939 - the day Ted Fresson flew the inaugural inter-island Air Mail service between Kirkwall and North Ronaldsay. Ted, (left, in flying suit) can be seen standing by the sacks of mail and parcels that were carried and some of the welcoming islanders. (Richard Fresson)

```
COPY                              N.A.C. Headquarters,
                                       BRISTOL

Hq.ref.394/DOSI/CBC               30th November, 1939.
```

Gentlemen,
     With reference to the search by your aircraft, G-ACSM on November 25th and 26th for a missing lifeboat and crew from the torpedoed vessel MV Sliedrecht, I am directed to express the Air Ministry's appreciation of the fine performance of your pilot, Mr. H. Vallance, in carrying out the search under very difficult weather conditions while flying over dangerous waters.
     A copy of your pilot's report, teleprinter ref. RW.24P 26/11, was sent to the owners of the lost vessel, Messrs. Van Ommeron Ltd, on November 27th, after having been telephoned to them on November 26th. They also expressed their appreciation of the endeavours made.

I am, Gentlemen,
      Your obedient Servant,

(Signed) Chas. Gardner.

for Director of Operational Services and Intelligence.

(Below) a complimentary Souvenir, and (Right) a Postal Cover of the inauguaral Air Mail Service from Glasgow to Campbeltown on October 2nd 1939. (Dr. J Forbes)

```
          -SOUVENIR-
  INAUGURAL AIR MAIL SERVICE
   -GLASGOW/CAMPBELTOWN-
      2nd October 1939
   With Compliments


   SCOTTISH AIRWAYS LTD.,
     AIRPORT FOR GLASGOW,
          RENFREW.
```

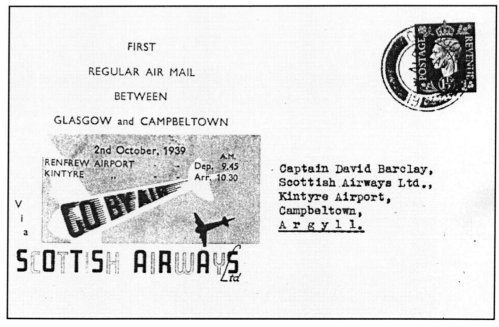

```
          FIRST
      REGULAR AIR MAIL
         BETWEEN
  GLASGOW and CAMPBELTOWN

                2nd October, 1939
   RENFREW AIRPORT      Dep. 9.45
   KINTYRE              Arr. 10.30
   GO BY AIR
   SCOTTISH AIRWAYS Ltd
```

Captain David Barclay,
Scottish Airways Ltd.,
Kintyre Airport,
Campbeltown,
A r g y l l.

The page in David Barclay's log-book recording his near fatal crash at Hatston, Orkney on April 19th 1940 ,when his D.H. Dragon G-ACNG was written off in a downdraught. (Mrs Sheila Harper)

heavily into the grass area before reaching the tarmac strip, wrecking the front of the cockpit. There were no serious injuries amongst the passengers, or to Gray, the Radio Operator, but David was badly hurt, breaking his pelvis and suffering other fractures and bruising in the somersaulting aircraft. He was taken to hospital in Kirkwall, and it was February 18th 1941 - 10 months afterwards, before he flew again, having in the meantime been flown back to Glasgow, and eventually recuperating at his home in Bishopton.

The net result of his accident was to move Bill Baillie back the next day from his Inverness base, to take over at Renfrew, and fly the daily Campbeltown/Islay runs (no service was yet being flown to the other Western Isles).

A.A.J.C. takes over

On May 5th 1940 the Government set up the Associated Airways' Joint Committee (or AAJC) to oversee the running of the necessary defined domestic air routes for the rest of the War. This committee had Sir Harold Hartley (of Railway Air Services) as its Chairman, and John Elliot, J.W.S. Comber, H.G.N. Read, J.S. Wills, K.W.C. Grand (all of various other British domestic airlines) and J.W. Ratledge (of Scottish Airways) as other committee members.

It set up an HQ at Liverpool's Speke Airport, and its main functions were to act as a 'go-between' between the Air Ministry on the one hand and all the continuing airline operators on the other; to negotiate and come to agreements on behalf of the operators, distribute subsidies fairly, establish a central pool of aircraft and spares at Speke, and set up a repair depot there plus anything else considered of vital necessity.

So from May 6th 1940, the Air Ministry paid out subsidies to the airline companies in this scheme, on the basis of a third of fixed costs (described in the Estimates made by the companies to the Ministry on March 12th 1940), plus 4d per capacity ton-mile flown on approved routes. (Later on, these calculations had to be revised as traffic fell substantially below forecast, and rates varied).

Scottish Airways was one of seven airlines to be part of the AAJC with RAS, IOMAS, etc., (Jersey and Guernsey Airways were not part of the committee, and Allied Airways at Aberdeen had a completely separate agreement with the Air Ministry).

Re-opening Western Isles services

The decision was taken in May 1940, to re-open services to the Western Isles, not only to carry Government and Service personnel to and from the aerodromes out there, etc, but also to carry Forces Mail to those stationed on the islands.

The service was planned (as part of the new summer schedules) to start on May 14th 1940 to those points previously served, and on May 15th a new Glasgow - North Uist -

Stornoway service (operating on Mondays, Wednesdays, and Fridays) was to be inaugurated, to the newly enlarged RAF aerodrome being built there.

Since the beginning of May, the Renfrew - Campbeltown - Islay service had been flown on a daily (except Sunday) basis, Bill Ballie doing most of the flying.

On Tuesday May 14th Bill started flying to the old Western Isles aerodromes again, and he left Renfrew at 0945 to fly Renfrew - Tiree - Barra - Benbecula - North Uist, arriving Sollas at 12.25. He left Sollas at 13.10 and flew back the same way, arriving Renfrew at 15.20 for a roundtrip time of 3hrs 50 mins. He used the DH Rapide G-AFRK for this re-start of Hebridean services.

Next day, May 15th Bill flew two complete roundtrips on the Renfrew-Campbeltown - Islay service, but he did not inaugurate the advertised Renfrew - Sollas - Stornoway service.

On Thursday May 16th Bill flew the Renfrew - Tiree - Barra - Benbecula - North Uist service again but on Friday May 17th all domestic services in the UK were suddenly cancelled by the Air Ministry, and all airlines ordered to RAF stations to stand by for evacuating troops from Dunkirk. The order was cancelled on the same evening.

Saturday May 18th therefore saw Bill Baillie operate two round-trips to Campbeltown and Islay, and finally on Monday May 20th Bill operated the first Renfrew - Sollas (North Uist) - Stornoway - Sollas - Renfrew service, landing on the newly enlarged RAF aerodrome which included the four original strips on the Melbost Golf Links that had been prepared for Ted Fresson to use in 1939.

Next day, Tuesday May 21st, Bill flew two services to Campbeltown/Islay, but the Air Ministry suddenly stopped all flights again on May 22nd and ordered all pilots and aircraft down South, (first to Croydon then to Heston) to be prepared to evacuate the troops from France. The pilots from Renfrew and Inverness, including Bill Baillie and Henry Vallance, sat at Heston until May 31st, but were not used as an air armada (to complement the seaborne armada) as they were deemed too vulnerable to German fighters. (No doubt had the seaborne

---

ASSOCIATED AIRWAYS' JOINT COMMITTEE
In association with
Air Commerce Ltd, Great Western and Southern Airlines Ltd, Isle of Man Air Services Ltd, Olley Air Service Ltd, Railway Air Services Ltd, Scottish Airways Ltd, West Coast Air Services Ltd and Western Isles Airways Ltd
Members of the Committee:
John Elliot *(Chairman)*, E.N.Biggs, G.Morton, J.W. Ratledge, H. G.N. Read.
Manager: Wing Cdr. A.H. Measures, CBE, M.I.Tech.E.
Secretary: W.C. Gaskin.
Address: Terminal Building, Liverpool Airport, Liverpool, 19.
T. Garston 1871-3. T.A.: Aircomity, Liverpool.

armada not been effective, then they would have been sent into the air).

Returning once more to Renfrew on June 1st, Bill Baillie flew a Renfrew - Tiree - Barra - Benbecula - North Uist service again on Tuesday June 4th, then a repeat performance on Saturday June 8th, two Campbeltown/Islays on Monday June 10th, and a Renfrew - Tiree - Sollas (North Uist) - Stornoway - Tiree - Renfrew on Wednesday June 12th (believed to be only the third flight to Stornoway, due to all the disruptions).

On Friday June 14th the Air Ministry once more ordered all aircraft South, cancelling the services from June 15th onwards. (Services in the North from Inverness were not affected). Bill was left in Glasgow, as the Acting Chief Pilot (and only one) there.

By this time, the only aircraft left operating with Scottish Airways were DH Dragon Rapides G-AFFF, G-AFRK, and G-AFOI (Southern Section), and DH Dragon G-ACIT, and DH Dragon Rapides G-ADAJ, G-AERN and G-AEWL (Northern Section). Of these, all but the Dragon 'CIT were flown down south to Heston, etc, and were there put onto evacuation flights from aerodromes in western France (such as Bordeaux).

Scottish Airways Southern Section services were thus suspended between June 14th and 26th, but 'FFF and 'FRK were returned in time for Bill Baillie to restart services on June 20th to Campbeltown/Islay, after a 10 minute test flight on 'FFF to see that it was still in one piece! (Northern Section flights were kept going between Inverness and Sumburgh by the Dragon 'CIT).

The third Rapide, 'FOI was returned eventually by July 12th - a little later than had been expected! This was due to a slight mishap and a lot of guts. The Rapide had left Bordeaux with a full load of escaping Forces personnel, right under the eyes of the Germans, but some poor quality engine oil that had been used to

Capt. David Barclay (centre) with John Swann (left) - the Traffic Manager - and Andrew Ruthven (right) - the Radio Officer - beside a Scottish Airways Dragon Rapide. Note the obscured main cabin windows - in the interests of wartime security - so that the passengers could not see over where they were flying! (Richard Fresson)

SCOTTISH AIRWAYS LTD
Aircraft Fleet - June 1st 1940
SOUTHERN SECTION:

De Havilland DH89A Dragon Rapide	G-AFFF
De Havilland DH89A Dragon Rapide	G-AFRK
De Havilland DH89A Dragon Rapide	G-AFOI

Recently impressed into RAF service:
Spartan Cruiser II G-ACYL (April 2nd 1940) as X9431
Spartan Cruiser II G-ACSM (April 2nd 1940) as X9433
Spartan Cruiser III G-ADEL (April 2nd 1940) as X9432
De Havilland D89A Rapide G-AEOV (Jan 10th 1940) as W6456

Recently crashed or written off:
Spartan Cruiser II G-ACZM. Damaged beyond repair at Renfrew January 9th 1940.
De Havilland DH89A Rapide G-AFEY. Crashed at Kirkwall (Wideford) March 18th 1940.
De Havilland DH84 Dragon II G-ACNG. Crashed at Hatston April 19th 1940.

NORTHERN SECTION:

De Havilland DH84 Dragon I	G-ACIT
De Havilland DH89 Dragon Rapide	G-ADAJ
De Havilland DH89A Dragon Rapide	G-AERN
De Havilland DH89A Dragon Rapide	G-AEWL

Recently crashed or written off:
De Havilland DH84 Dragon II G-ADCT. Crashed at Inverness (Longman) December 14th 1939 and written off by February 1940.

---

top up the Gipsy VIs there gave some alarming engine trouble on the flight back over the Bay of Biscay. The pilot put 'FOI down at an almost deserted Jersey Airport on the way, and the crew discovered one of Jersey Airways' four - engined DH 86s in the maintenance hangar. Working all night the pilot, radio officer and flight engineer (they were fortunate to be carrying) managed to take out the Rapide's sick engine and replace it with one off the DH 86! They took off next morning just ahead of the Germans and made the South of England safely! And 'FOI after a full check by the new AAJC maintenance unit at Speke, returned to the fold at Renfrew in July.

Airfield development
We have read about the Air Ministry's take-over and sudden expansion of Stornoway aerodrome, and the Admiralty's construction of Hatston at Kirkwall. But the Government had requisitioned most of Scottish Airways' aerodromes including Sumburgh, Campbeltown, Islay, Tiree and Benbecula, and the local authority run aerodromes at Inverness (Longman), Perth (Scone), and Renfrew (Glasgow).

In addition to expanding all these, the Air Ministry also began construction of a large aerodrome at Wick - adjacent to the fields at Hillhead Farm used by Fresson - and one near Kirkwall and just East of Fresson's hill-top site at Wideford.

Eventually, as the war years went by, Wick had hard runways laid down, as did Dalcross (a new RAF aerodrome built some 6 miles East of Inverness) and Machrihanish (at Campbeltown), Port Ellen (at Islay), Balivanich (at Benbecula), and finally Sumburgh (Shetland). Inverness (Longman) remained a grass 'drome as did Wideford (Kirkwall) - but in Orkney, Ted Fresson used RAF Grimsetter and its hard runways, as soon as it was built.

"Scottish Airways Carry On"
A very large full colour wartime poster that humorously shows
a Scottish Airways' Rapide flying serenely under a dog-fight
between a Spitfire and a German aircraft that is being flown by a
caricature of Hermann Goering, head of the Luftwaffe.
The poster has been photographically copied, hence the vertical
distortion. (Eric Starling)

Renfrew for its part, had two hard runways constructed in 1943 but from the start of the War became important as a collection point for warplanes to be crated up and shipped from Glasgow Docks to all War zones; and later, for aircraft to arrive at the Docks from the USA and Canada, to be uncrated at Renfrew and flown to RAF Squadrons.

Winter 1940/41 Timetable

Because of increasing demand for the flights, although it had been planned initially to operate just three times weekly to North Uist and Stornoway, and once daily to Campbeltown and Islay, by the time the Winter Season started from September 23rd 1940, both these services were given a 100 % increase in flights.

Thus the Northbound Western Isles services consisted of Renfrew - Tiree - Barra (on demand) - Benbecula - North Uist - Stornoway on Mondays, Wednesdays, and Fridays; and Renfrew - North Uist - Stornoway on Tuesdays, Thursdays and Saturdays. Southbound they operated the reverse routes, the long one on Tuesdays, Thursdays and Saturdays, and the shorter one on Mondays, Wednesdays and Fridays.

Campbeltown and Islay had two services daily in each direction, except on Sundays.

In the North, Inverness - Kirkwall - Sumburgh and return operated on Monday, Wednesday, Thursday and Saturday, while there was also a mid-day Inverness - Kirkwall service daily (except Sunday), and an Inverness - Wick - Kirkwall afternoon flight daily except Sunday. The Northern Section needed two pilots based in Inverness, and one in Kirkwall, with their respective aircraft. Although the mid-day Kirkwall - inter - island service was no longer flown, cover was needed locally for ambulance or charter work, etc.

The Southern Section needed one pilot for the Campbeltown run and two pilots for the Stornoway runs, and their respective aircraft.

Badge for the R.O.s

George Nicholson was always available to see his staff, especially if they had useful ideas to pass on to him. Andrew Ruthven, the Radio Officer who joined Scottish Airways in November 1940, soon had a point he wanted to discuss with George - the question of an insignia to wear on their uniforms to denote being an 'R.O.'.

The timetable of the new Glasgow - Stornoway services, which
began on Monday 20th May 1940, after several false starts.
(John Stroud Collection)

SCOTTISH AIRWAYS LTD.

TRI-WEEKLY
AIR SERVICES
BETWEEN
STORNOWAY AND GLASGOW
via North Uist

TIME TABLE
Mondays, Wednesdays & Fridays
from 15th May, 1940

STORNOWAY—NORTH UIST—GLASGOW						Southbound
STORNOWAY	County Hotel ...	...	...	...	...	Dep. 12.45 p.m.
	Stornoway Airport	...	...	...	...	Dep. 1.05
NORTH UIST	Sollas Airport	...	...	...	...	Arr. 1.45
	Sollas Airport	...	...	...	...	Dep. 2.00
GLASGOW	Renfrew Airport ...	...	...	...	...	Arr. 3.50
	Grosvenor Restaurant, 74 Gordon Street	...	...		...	Arr. 4.30

GLASGOW—NORTH UIST—STORNOWAY						Northbound
GLASGOW	Grosvenor Restaurant, 74 Gordon Street	...	...		...	Dep. 8.30 a.m.
	Renfrew Airport ...	...	...	...	...	Dep. 9.40
NORTH UIST	Sollas Airport	...	...	...	...	Arr. 11.30
	Sollas Airport	...	...	...	...	Dep. 11.40
STORNOWAY	Stornoway Airport	...	...	...	...	Arr. 12.20 p.m.
	County Hotel ...	...	...	...	...	Arr. 12.35

FARES, EXCESS BAGGAGE and FREIGHT RATES				Excess Baggage and Freight
		Single	Return	Per lb.
STORNOWAY GLASGOW ...	...	110 -	200 -	6d.
STORNOWAY NORTH UIST	...	30 -	50 -	4d.
NORTH UIST GLASGOW ...	...	90 -	170 -	4d.

ROAD TRANSPORT
Passengers are conveyed free of charge between The County Hotel, Stornoway and Stornoway Airport, also between Renfrew Airport and The Grosvenor Restaurant, Gordon Street, Glasgow.

CONDITIONS OF CARRIAGE
The conditions under which passengers, baggage and goods are carried by SCOTTISH AIRWAYS LTD., are displayed at the Airports served by the Company and can be inspected at the advertised Booking Offices. While the Company will endeavour to maintain the schedules as far as possible **ALL SERVICES ARE SUBJECT TO ALTERATION OR CANCELLATION WITHOUT NOTICE.**

TRAVEL PERMITS
Passengers are requested to make themselves aware of the conditions governing regulations regarding Travel Permits, Prohibited Articles, etc.

BOOKINGS, ETC.
Particulars on application to :—
NORMAN MACIVER, MARITIME BUILDINGS, STORNOWAY.
Telephone : Stornoway 12

SCOTTISH AIRWAYS LIMITED, Airport for Glasgow, Renfrew.
Telephone: Renfrew 2231 Telegrams: Scotairway, Renfrew; Air Ambulance, Renfrew.
AND PRINCIPAL TRAVEL AGENTS

GO BY AIR AND SAVE 12¼ HOURS TRAVEL TIME!

A portrait of Andrew Ruthven, Radio Officer at Renfrew, showing the 'half wing' emblem he personally designed for Scottish Airways' R.O.'s (Andrew Ruthven).

Up to this stage although the early R.O.s (or W.T.O.s - as they were called at first) had worn the dark navy blue uniform that the pilots used, whilst they sported the gold cuff rings to denote seniority they had not had any form of brevet on their breast pocket (where the pilot's 'wings' were displayed).

So Andrew talked to George about the idea of a 'half-wing' on their uniforms designed in a suitable manner, and George told Andrew to prepare a design for him. This he promptly did, and was told to go to the uniform shop in Glasgow - 'Paisleys' - and get a sample prepared. Soon Andrew showed this to George and David Barclay, and the design was approved and adopted henceforth as the R.O.s 'half-wing' badge (see picture).

Barclay back
By now George Nicholson and his family had moved home from Milliken Park out to an imposing house called "Wemba" at Prestwick (Tel. Prestwick 7626), where he lived for the rest of his career in Aviation. The weather was much better in this beautiful part of Ayrshire and George distanced himself from the fogs and smogs of the Clyde Valley - which became particularly prevalent during the War, with all factories working flat out and their chimneys belching incessant smoke.

Bad weather was evident during the Winter of 1940/41 too, and Prestwick had often to be used as a diversion. Bill Baillie had been transferred up to Inverness again in August 1940, and remained up there now until November 1943.

In February 1941, however, David Barclay was fit enough to start work again at Renfrew. He was given a dual instruction test in an RAF Tiger Moth (X5107) at Renfrew on February 18th, lasting all of 25 minutes followed by 1hr 15mins flying and landing practice on the Rapide G-AFRK with Capt. Jock Young supervising, and he was promptly given a licence renewal for flying again.

On February 22nd 1941 David went down to Liverpool (Speke) and 'air-tested' a replacement DH 89 Dragon Rapide, G-ACPP, for their much used G-AFFF which had just been sent back to Liverpool for a C of A renewal. He flew it back to Renfrew by means of operating an RAS schedule from Liverpool to Belfast (Sydenham), and from Sydenham to Renfrew the same day, and then it went into use alongside the later model Rapides G-AFOI and G-AFRK.

On March 4th, David had to collect another old Rapide from Liverpool, G-ACYR, and with his R.O. Garside, flew a party of Air Ministry officials up via Prestwick and Barra to Stornoway. Here they made a succession of approaches over a 4-day period, calibrating the wireless aids for the new RAF aerodrome, finally returning to Renfrew with them on March 7th.

Aircraft changes
David resumed line flying on March 7th on the Campbeltown - Islay run, and on the next day, the 8th, he flew an air ambulance service from Campbeltown. He was back in harness again, and it felt good!

At the beginning of the 1941 Summer Schedule David managed to get rid of the old Rapide 'CPP, and exchanged it with a later model, G-AERZ (which Ted Fresson had been using in Inverness until G-ADAJ had been overhauled). Now, 'ERZ was sent down to Renfrew on May 15th, and David immediately started a twice daily Campbeltown- Islay service on it.

On June 26th David had to receive the old Rapide G-ACPP back, as G-AERZ was now sent to Liverpool for routine maintenance. But on August 18th the old favourite G-AFFF arrived back after its C of A overhaul, and soon after, David sent 'CPP South again!

On September 7th David went to Dumfries to collect an ex-RAF Rapide, X7387 which was to be registered as G-AGDG for the Inverness fleet. Four days later another ex-RAF Rapide arrived at Renfrew (X7388) and David flew this up to Inverness to be registered as G-AGDH for Ted Fresson's fleet (it did not, however, stay very long in the North, being sent back to Renfrew on October 13th 1941). Here, David Barclay flew it on the Campbeltown run until November 25th, when he flew it up to Stornoway. He had a difficult landing there, in the teeth of a developing gale and whilst the Rapide was on the ground during the turnaround the wind increased to a 95 mph gale, and a violent gust struck it, tipping it over and wrecking it beyond repair. This was despite the usual efforts of the ground team to hold onto the aircraft, and lash the tail to the back of a lorry! Fortunately there were no injuries to any of the passengers or crew.

For the whole of 1941, David Barclay tried to keep to the shorter Renfrew - Campbeltown - Islay service, letting the other Renfrew pilot fly the longer route to the Western Isles, in order to help him recover from his injuries gradually. His hip still hurt with pressure on the rudder pedals, and the longer flight up to Stornoway was just more than he really wanted at that stage. He had a limp in any case, - something he had to put up with for the rest of his life now.

Contraband Whisky
The Radio Operator, Andrew Ruthven, remembers one trip he made to Barra and the Hebrides just after the famous wreck of the S.S. *Politician* in the area. He and Jock Young flew out with George Nicholson, Bill Cumming and Bill Mann to talk to their Traffic Manager on Barra, and some of the islanders (one of

whom was Sir Compton Mackenzie, who subsequently wrote the book on the incident - *'Whisky Galore')*.

While they were in the Traffic Manager's cottage George asked 'Coddy' (as they called him) "So where's all this whisky then, that has got washed up on the shore? Can you find us a bottle apiece?" The 'Coddy' denied all knowledge of it, but no-one believed him, and George told him he wanted to take some home and expected him to find some!

The Coddy disappeared, and a little later they saw him carrying a garden spade into the distance. After some time he re-appeared, put the spade away and proudly dusted off three bottles, which he passed over to George and Co! They little suspected the rarity value of those bottles in years to come!

Wartime schedules - 1941 to 1944

From 1942 through the rest of the war years there was little change to the schedules. There was no connection between the Southern and Northern Sections by air through this period, and Ted Fresson in the North often used to drive down halfway to Glasgow, if a meeting was necessary with George Nicholson and William Cumming. George would drive his colleagues up from Glasgow on the road to Glencoe and Ft. William, and the two groups of men would meet over a business lunch at the Bridge of Orchy Hotel. Quite often Fresson's wife, Gwen, would ask Henry Vallance's wife, Dorothy, to go along for the day too. This saved time - and particularly, wartime petrol! And no doubt the drive gave them all a pleasant day out through some of the Highlands' finest scenery (though Ted Fresson, no doubt would have preferred to fly to any business venue. For to him, using an aeroplane was as natural as riding a bicycle to go anywhere. And being such a legendary pilot, had made Ted Fresson into the best airline manager, engineer, and even aircraft designer of his generation).

The 1941 Summer timetable, effective May 1st, consisted of a twice daily Campbeltown/Islay round-trip leaving Glasgow at 09.30 and 16.30 and arriving back at 12.15 and 19.00, and a single daily (except Sunday) Glasgow - Tiree - Barra (on demand) - Benbecula - North Uist - Stornoway service, returning the same way and leaving Glasgow at 09.40, and Stornoway at 13.25 (15mins after arriving). The Northern Section operated three flights daily (except Sunday): One departing Inverness at 09.30 and arriving Kirkwall at 10.30; one leaving Inverness at 10.30, calling at Kirkwall and arriving at Sumburgh at 12.40; and the last leaving Inverness at 12.00, arriving at Kirkwall at 13.05. (None of the three services called at Wick any longer). Flights arrived back at Inverness at 12.10, 15.10 and 14.55.

The services were given Numbers (like bus-routes) and Service No. 1 was the Inverness - North route; No. 2 was the Kirkwall - Orkney Outer Islands (suspended for the War); No 3 was the Campbeltown/ Islay run from Glasgow; and No. 4 and 5 the Western Isles routes (No. 4 being multi-stop, and No. 5 being the one-stop to Stornoway).

From September 22nd 1941, the 1941-2 Winter schedule was little changed over the previous summer with the exception that the daily Western Isles service dropped to Monday, Wednesday, and Friday north, and Tuesday, Thursday, Saturday south, during the period November 10th - February 21st only.

In summer 1943, Service 1 went to a four times daily (except Sunday) frequency between Inverness and the North Isles (one routeing non-stop to Sumburgh; one via Kirkwall; and two flights terminating at Kirkwall). Again no stops were made at Wick, and this schedule continued through Winter 1943-44. The Campbeltown/Islay ran twice daily (except Sunday) as usual, and on through the Winter as well, and the Western Isles operated daily, Summer and Winter, with the difference between November 8th 1943 and February 19th 1944 being that flights on Tue. Thurs. and Sat. operated Renfrew - Tiree - Stornoway, cutting out Benbecula and North Uist northbound; and in reverse cut out those points southbound on Mon. Wed. and Fri.

For Summer 1944 Service No. 1 remained at the four flights a day northbound out of Inverness. Service No. 2 was now a brand new route long-awaited by Ted Fresson and finally now established on May 24th 1944 - a three times weekly Inverness - Stornoway service (operating on Mon. Wed. Fri.). Service No. 3 was the Renfrew - Campbeltown route flown twice daily but with Islay (Service No. 4) now split off and having a separate daily non-stop flight from Glasgow. To the Hebrides (Service No. 5) the flights operated just as they had done the previous winter (daily, with stops omitted on certain days in each direction).

SCOTTISH AIRWAYS LIMITED

Summer Time Table—effective 1st May, 1941, until further notice

SERVICE 1

INVERNESS—KIRKWALL—SHETLAND
Daily except Sundays

NORTHBOUND

		a.m.	a.m.	a.m.
INVERNESS	Academy St. (Struthers Lane)	dep. 8.45	dep. 9.30	dep. 11.15
	Airport	dep. 9.30	dep. 10.30	dep. 12.0
WICK	Airport			
	Station Hotel			
	Airport			p.m.
KIRKWALL	Airport	arr. 10.40	arr. 11.35	arr. 1.5
	9 Broad Street	arr. 10.55	arr. 11.50	arr. 1.20
	9 Broad Street		arr. 11.10	
	Airport		arr. 11.55	
SHETLAND	Airport		arr. 12.40p	
	Queen's and Grand Hotels, Lerwick		arr. 1.50	

SOUTHBOUND

		a.m.	p.m.	p.m.
SHETLAND	Queen's and Grand Hotels, Lerwick	dep. 11.15		
	Airport			
KIRKWALL	Airport		dep. 1.0	
	9 Broad Street			
	Airport		arr. 1.45 / dep. 2.0	
WICK	9 Broad Street	dep. 10.15	dep. 1.20	dep. 1.5
	Airport	dep. 11.00	dep. 2.5	dep. 1.50
	Station Hotel			
	Airport			
INVERNESS	Airport	arr. 12.10	arr. 3.10	arr. 2.55
	Academy Street (Struthers Lane)	arr. 12.20	arr. 3.20	arr. 3.5

SERVICE 3

GLASGOW—CAMPBELTOWN—ISLAY
Daily except Sundays

WESTBOUND

		a.m.	p.m.
GLASGOW	Grosvenor Restaurant	dep. 8.45	dep. 3.45
	Renfrew Airport	dep. 9.30	dep. 4.30
CAMPBELTOWN	Kintyre Airport	arr. 10.5	arr. 5.5
	Argyll Arms Hotel	dep. 10.15	dep. 4.45
	Argyll Arms Hotel	dep. 9.45	dep. 5.15
	Kintyre Airport	dep. 10.15	dep. 5.15
ISLAY	Glenegedale Airport	arr. 10.35	arr. 5.35

EASTBOUND

		a.m.	p.m.
ISLAY	Glenegedale Airport	dep. 11.10	dep. 5.55
CAMPBELTOWN	Kintyre Airport	arr. 11.30	arr. 6.15
	Argyll Arms Hotel	dep. 11.40	dep. 6.25
	Argyll Arms Hotel	dep. 11.10	dep. 5.55
	Kintyre Airport	dep. 11.40	dep. 6.25
GLASGOW	Renfrew Airport	arr. 12.15 p.m.	arr. 7.0
	Grosvenor Restaurant	arr. 12.45	arr. 7.45

SERVICES 4/5

GLASGOW—TIREE—BENBECULA—NORTH UIST—STORNOWAY
Daily except Sundays

NORTHBOUND

		a.m.
GLASGOW	Grosvenor Restaurant	dep. 8.45
	Renfrew Airport	dep. 9.40
TIREE	Reef Airport	arr. 10.40
	Reef Airport	dep. 10.50
BARRA*		
BENBECULA	Balivanich Airport	arr. 11.35 p.m.
	Balivanich Airport	dep. 11.45
NORTH UIST	Sollas Airport	arr. 11.55
STORNOWAY	Sollas Airport	arr. 12.15 p.m.
	Stornoway Airport	arr. 12.55
	Maritime Buildings	arr. 1.10

SOUTHBOUND

		p.m.
STORNOWAY	Maritime Buildings	dep. 1.25
	Stornoway Airport	dep. 1.45
NORTH UIST	Sollas Airport	arr. 2.15
	Sollas Airport	dep. 2.25
BENBECULA	Balivanich Airport	arr. 2.45
	Balivanich Airport	dep. 2.55
BARRA*	Reef Airport	dep. 3.5
BARRA*	Reef Airport	arr. 3.50
TIREE	Reef Airport	dep. 4.0
GLASGOW	Renfrew Airport	arr. 5.0
	Grosvenor Restaurant	arr. 5.35

NOTES

1. Under present conditions Booking Arrangements for Service I should be made direct with Inverness Office—Academy Street (Struthers Lane), Inverness.

Telephone: Inverness 1666.   Telegrams: Scotairway, Inverness.

2. Owing to the exigencies of war, the Train from London and the South, scheduled to arrive in Inverness at 9.57 a.m., does not always afford a connection with the scheduled Northbound Air Service departure from the Company's town terminal at 11.15 a.m. Failure to take up reservations necessitates the forfeiture of the Air fare unless 24 hours' notice of cancellation is given. Passengers from the South are therefore advised to reach Inverness the previous evening in order to ensure making connection with the Northbound Air Service on which their reservations have been made.

SERVICE 2   KIRKWALL—NORTH ISLES—SUSPENDED

ALL SERVICES SUBJECT TO ALTERATION OR CANCELLATION WITHOUT NOTICE

FARES, EXCESS BAGGAGE & FREIGHT RATES

	Single	Return	Excess Baggage and Freight per lb.
INVERNESS to—			
Wick	30/6	46/-	3d.
Kirkwall	55/-	99/-	4d.
Lerwick	80/-	114/-	6d.
WICK to—			
Kirkwall	30/-	48/-	2d.
Lerwick	77/-	143/-	4d.
KIRKWALL to—			
Lerwick	55/-	99/-	4d.
GLASGOW to—			
Campbeltown	27/6	49/6	2½d.
Islay	38/6	71/6	2½d.
Tiree	60/-	105/-	3d.
Barra	90/-	170/-	4d.
Benbecula	90/-	170/-	4d.
North Uist	90/-	170/-	4d.
Stornoway	90/-	170/-	4d.
CAMPBELTOWN to—			
Islay	16/6	33/-	2½d.
TIREE to—			
Barra	27/6	55/-	4d.
Benbecula	55/-	110/-	4d.
North Uist	55/-	110/-	4d.
Stornoway	80/-	160/-	4d.
BARRA to—			
Benbecula	27/6	55/-	4d.
North Uist	27/6	55/-	4d.
BENBECULA to—			
North Uist	22/-	44/-	4d.
Stornoway	52/-	94/-	4d.
NORTH UIST to—			
Stornoway	30/-	50/-	4d.

Freight Rates.—Note minimum charge is 2/- per package.

The conditions under which the carriage of passengers and baggage is undertaken are shown on pages 2 and 3 and are also displayed at Scottish Airways' Booking Offices or at Airports.

* Barra—Tide and weather permitting, service calls on request, and subject to 24 hours' notice being given.

A wartime snapshot of Capt. John Young (left), standing in front of Scottish Airways' D.H. Dragon Rapide G-AFOI in its hastily arranged and applied early camouflage scheme. Interestingly, both civil and military markings have been applied - RAF roundels on the underside of the mainplanes and on the fuselage, with the registration letters left in a 'box'. (Alison Mills)

Inverness - Stornoway inaugural

One of the passengers on that inaugural flight from Inverness to Stornoway was the Editor of *The Stornoway Gazette,* James Shaw Grant. James worked for 30 years on the newspaper, being Editor for the best part of this time, and he developed a great interest in air communications with the Western Isles during the Second World War.

He had first come into contact with Ted Fresson in 1934 when the latter visited Stornoway at the start of his quest to begin a scheduled service from Inverness.

James remembers that there was a lot of politics surrounding the scheme by Fresson to open an airstrip. Ted Fresson earmarked the Melbost Golf Links as the only decent place to have a flat landing strip, but found it was very difficult to get the required permission from the crofting community in the villages on either side, as they had cattle grazing on the fields. A small number of radically-minded (but well-educated) men, James remembers, held up the chance of opening an airstrip at an early date because of their campaigning "that such an air service would do nothing for the people of the island or its business community". For the most part however, the business community was anxious to have the flights laid on, and it was galling for them to see the delaying actions of these radicals.

Fresson eventually had many friends amongst the Provost and Seniors of the town who backed the scheme for an airport, including David Tolmie. David became a close friend of Ted Fresson, and had been manager of one of the largest banana plantations in Jamaica in his youth, but in the recession of the 1920s he lost his job and returned to Lewis to go into the Tweed trade.

James remembers Fresson's wartime service from Inverness and George Nicholson's longer established service from Glasgow had to share RAF Stornoway with squadrons of RAF Flying Fortresses and droves of US-built fighter and bomber aircraft that lobbed into Stornoway en-route from the USA and Canada to Southern England and Europe (by then).

But above all, he states, the coming of the scheduled air services between Glasgow or Inverness and Stornoway during the war completely revolutionised and transformed life in the

isles. Islanders who had never seen or travelled in a railway train took to the air like ducks to water! In those days in the 1940s, the Local Authority Headquarters controlling affairs in Lewis was in Dingwall (Ross & Cromarty), while that for Harris was Inverness (Inverness-shire), and the new air service from May 1944 brought instant benefits in travel between Council HQ's.

When the earlier Glasgow - Stornoway link started at the beginning of WWII, James remembers that he was the only journalist in the Western Isles producing a newspaper.

James came across George Nicholson in Glasgow, when that air service first began, because the Scottish Press Censor was located in the city and James, as Editor, had to fly there frequently to obtain clearance for articles in his newspaper. The Stornoway Gazette was actually printed in Dingwall, and James found his letters from the Western Isles were being heavily edited by the Censor in Inverness (the regional censorship headquarters covering the Hebrides and the North of Scotland) before they even reached the newspaper's printers, thus cutting out a lot of his articles. But many of these had already appeared in *The Times* of London, and so James had to travel to Glasgow on occasion to sort things out with the Head Censor!

Schedules 1944 - 1945

From October 2nd 1944 the 1944/45 Winter schedule showed little difference on Service 1 except that the non-stop Inverness - Sumburgh service was down to a Tue. Thurs. Sat. operation only. Inverness - Stornoway continued at a Mon. Wed. Fri. frequency. Renfrew - Campbeltown and Islay still operated as separate routes now, the first at twice daily, the latter at daily frequency;

Opposite Page: The 1941 Summer time-table issued by Scottish Airways, with the wartime booking arrangements. Time-tables in World War Two were not advertised, and generally kept only in the airline's offices. (John Stroud Collection)

SCOTTISH AIRWAYS LTD	
Aircraft Fleet - Summer 1941	
Southern Section:	
De Havilland DH89A Dragon Rapide	G-AFRK
De Havilland DH89A Dragon Rapide	G-AFOI
De Havilland DH89 Dragon Rapide	G-ACPP
De Havilland DH89A Dragon Rapide	G-AERZ
Northern Section:	
De Havilland DH84 Dragon I	G-ACIT
De Havilland DH89 Dragon Rapide	G-ADAJ
De Havilland DH89A Dragon Rapide	G-AERN
De Havilland DH89A Dragon Rapide	G-AEWL

SCOTTISH AIRWAYS LTD
Aircraft Fleet - Summer 1942

Southern Section:

De Havilland DH89A Dragon Rapide	G-AFRK
De Havilland DH89A Dragon Rapide	G-AFOI
De Havilland DH89A Dragon Rapide	G-ACPP
De Havilland DH89A Dragon Rapide	G-AGED

Northern Section:

De Havilland DH84 Dragon I	G-ACIT
De Havilland DH89 Dragon Rapide	G-ADAJ
De Havilland DH89A Dragon Rapide	G-AERN
De Havilland DH89A Dragon Rapide	G-AEWL
De Havilland DH89A Dragon Rapide	G-AGDG

and the Hebrides service ran on unchanged from Summer.

Finally, the 1945 Summer time-table was effective a month earlier than normal - from April 9th this time - but all the Inverness routes showed no change from Winter 1944/45, nor did the Campbeltown or Islay services. It was only on the Service No. 5 to the Hebrides, where a combination now of three different routeings gave a total of nine flights weekly each way (up from six). Thus three flights per week ran Renfrew - Tiree - Stornoway; three routed Renfrew - Tiree - Benbecula - North Uist - Stornoway; and three, Renfrew - Stornoway direct, and vice versa.

During these War years 1941-45, it can be seen from the frequency / capacity allocated to each destination that there must have been a dramatic increase in traffic between Renfrew and Stornoway, Campbeltown and Tiree and between Inverness and Sumburgh - not surprising however, in view of the amount of RAF and RN operations taking place in those areas and from the aerodromes themselves. The difference between the schedules offered in Summer 1941, and Summer 1945 can be illustrated thus :

Weekly Seats offered:*		1941 Summer	1945 Summer	Increase/ Decrease
Renfrew	- Campbeltown	42	84	(+100%)
	- Islay	42	42	-
	- Tiree	10.5	15.75	(+50%)
	- Benbecula	10.5	5.25	(-50%)
	- North Uist	10.5	5.25	(-50%)
	- Stornoway	10.5	36.75	(+250%)
Inverness	- Kirkwall	105	105	-
	- Sumburgh	21	42	(+100%)
	- Stornoway	-	21	-

* On the basis of each Rapide = 7 passenger seats, and capacity allocated equally between intermediate points.

Other wartime activities

On September 25th 1941 David Barclay checked out a new pilot for the Renfrew services - Capt. J Kennedy - on the Rapide G-AFOI and cleared him to begin operating the Hebrides service. And in November and December, David began to fly the Herbridean route again himself - probably because he was now getting over the pain of his hip injury, and also because Winter weather made it vital that only the most experienced pilots flew those services - and he was, after all, the Chief Pilot!

In the four days, December 26th, 27th, 29th and 30th for instance, David flew a total of 22 sectors to and from Stornoway (including flying 7 sectors alone on December 30th)!

The Rapide wrecked in the gale at Stornoway (G-AGDH) had been replaced on November 29th by another from the AAJC pool - G-ACYR. And the old G-ACPP rejoined the Renfrew fleet again on January 2nd 1942 while G-AFOI was away on maintenance.

January 1942 saw bad weather conditions at Renfrew again - coupled with the construction work there to put down hard runways, and from January 20th to February 10th inclusive all Scottish Airways' flights had to use Prestwick as their passenger terminal.

Up to the end of the 1941-42 Winter schedules the Renfrew fleet consisted of the Rapides G-ACPP, G-ACYR and G-AFRK, but on April 25th 1942 they received a brand new DH 89A Dragon Rapide straight from the makers, G-AGED, and promptly returned G-ACYR to the AAJC pool at Liverpool for overhaul. The Renfrew fleet for Summer 1942 thus now consisted of G-ACPP, 'FRK, 'FOI, and 'GED.

On August 9th 1942 David Barclay took the Home Secretary out to Barra in G-AFOI, landing at Northbay on the tide-washed sands, and on the return trip (empty) he flew over Coll, and landed on a flat site there which he decided he could use in future if an air ambulance flight was necessary. (Before he had left Renfrew, he had spent an hour with Capt. Clark, trying out landings on the four-engined DH 86B (G-AENR) of RAS which had brought the Home Secretary up to Glasgow).

An additional service which was operated from Renfrew starting from July 7th 1942, was the Renfrew - Belfast (Sydenham) route. David Barclay himself flew many of these Monday, Wednesday, Friday services, which were being operated again on behalf of RAS, and these flights continued on through the Winter of 1942-43.

At the end of the Summer David flew the Rapide 'CPP back to Liverpool on September 17th and brought back G-AERZ which had been overhauled there, to use in the Renfrew fleet.

ENSA Charters, etc

David Barclay flew a special charter for ENSA on November 15th 1942, taking a party of music-hall artists to Stornoway, Sollas, and Islay on a day-long round-trip to entertain the troops and RAF personnel. This was the beginning of a tremendous war-time effort, flying ENSA charters to all parts of Scottish Airways' network which eventually totalled over 150 flights altogether during the 1940-45 period. Artists such as Vera Lynn, Anne Shelton, etc, were transported to concerts at the remote Forces' camps, and not one flight failed to get through even under the most unfavourable weather conditions. Numerous expressions of appreciation were received from the serving personnel who appreciated the special effort made by all concerned for their entertainment.

SCOTTISH AIRWAYS LTD
Aircraft Fleet - Summer 1943

Southern Section:

De Havilland DH89A Dragon Rapide	G-AFFF
De Havilland DH89A Dragon Rapide	G-AFOI
De Havilland DH89A Dragon Rapide	G-AERZ
De Havilland DH89A Dragon Rapide	G-AGEE[1]
De Havilland DH89A Dragon Rapide	G-AFRK[2]
De Havilland DH89A Dragon Rapide	G-AGIF[3]

Northern Section:

De Havilland DH84 Dragon I	G-ACIT
De Havilland DH89 Dragon Rapide	G-ADAJ
De Havilland DH89A Dragon Rapide	G-AERN
De Havilland DH89A Dragon Rapide	G-AEWL
De Havilland DH89A Dragon Rapide	G-AGDG
De Havilland DH89A Dragon Rapide	G-AGIC[4]

[1] - Was sent back for overhaul at beginning of July.
[2] - Returned to replace 'GEE on July 7th.
[3] - Received on June 19th.
[4] - Arrived end of August .

SCOTTISH AIRWAYS LIMITED

Time Table — effective 4th October, 1943, until further notice

SERVICE 1

INVERNESS—KIRKWALL—SHETLAND

Daily except Sundays

NORTHBOUND

		a.m.	a.m.	a.m.	a.m.
INVERNESS	Academy St. (Struthers Lane)	dep. 8.45	dep. 9.00	dep. 9.00	dep. 11.30
	Airport	dep. 9.30	dep. 10.00	dep. 10.10	p.m. dep. 12.30
WICK		—	—	—	—
KIRKWALL	Airport	arr. 10.40	arr. 11.10	—	arr. 1.40
	7 Broad Street	arr. 10.55	arr. 11.20	—	arr. 2.15
	7 Broad Street	—	dep. 10.00	—	—
	Airport	—	dep. 11.25	—	—
SHETLAND	Airport	—	p.m. arr. 12.10	arr. 12.00	—
	Queen's and Grand Hotels, Lerwick	—	arr. 1.20	arr. 1.20	—

SOUTHBOUND

SHETLAND	Queen's and Grand Hotels, Lerwick	—	dep. 10.30	dep. 10.30	—
	Airport	—	p.m. dep. 1.0	p.m. dep. 1.10	—
KIRKWALL	Airport	—	arr. 1.45	—	—
	7 Broad Street	—	arr. 2.15	—	—
	7 Broad Street	a.m. dep. 10.00	dep. 1.0	—	p.m. dep. 1.00
	Airport	dep. 11.00	dep. 2.5	—	dep. 2.00
WICK		—	—	—	—
INVERNESS	Airport	p.m. arr. 12.10	arr. 3.15	arr. 3.00	arr. 3.10
	Academy St. (Struthers Lane)	arr. 12.20	arr. 3.20	arr. 3.20	arr. 3.20

NOTES

1. Under present conditions Booking Arrangements for Service 1 should be made direct with Inverness Office—Academy Street (Struthers Lane), Inverness.

   Telephone: Inverness 728.   Telegrams: Scotairway, Inverness.

2. Owing to the exigencies of war, the Train from London and the South, scheduled to arrive in Inverness at 9.52 a.m., does not always afford a connection with the scheduled Northbound Air Service departure from the Company's town terminal at 11.30 a.m. Failure to take up reservations necessitated the forfeiture of the Air fare unless 24 hours notice of cancellation is given. Passengers from the South are therefore advised to leave Euston the previous day on the 1 p.m. train which reaches Inverness approximately 5.45 a.m. in order to ensure making connection with the Northbound Air Service on which their reservations have been made.

3. At Inverness and Kirkwall, Military Control Formalities, Weighing, etc., are carried out at the Company's Town Office. All passengers, therefore, must report at Inverness (Struthers Lane) and at Kirkwall (Broad Street) not later than the advertised Road Departure Time. ON NO ACCOUNT SHOULD THEY PROCEED TO THE AIRPORT DIRECT.

SERVICE 2

KIRKWALL—NORTH ISLES—SUSPENDED

SERVICE 3

GLASGOW—CAMPBELTOWN—ISLAY

Daily except Sundays

WESTBOUND

			a.m.	p.m.
GLASGOW	Grosvenor Restaurant		dep. 9.00	dep. 1.00
	Renfrew Airport		dep. 9.45	dep. 1.45
CAMPBELTOWN	Airport		arr. 10.20	arr. 2.20
	Royal Hotel		arr. 10.35	arr. 2.35
	Royal Hotel		dep. 9.50	dep. 1.50
	Airport		dep. 10.35	dep. 2.35
ISLAY✱	Glenegedale Airport		arr. 10.55	arr. 2.55

EASTBOUND

			a.m.	p.m.
ISLAY✱	Glenegedale Airport		dep. 11.10	dep. 3.10
CAMPBELTOWN	Airport		arr. 11.30	arr. 3.30
	Royal Hotel		arr. 11.45	arr. 3.45
	Royal Hotel		dep. 11.00	dep. 3.00
	Airport		dep. 11.40	dep. 3.40
GLASGOW	Airport		p.m. arr. 12.15	arr. 4.15
	Grosvenor Restaurant		arr. 12.45	arr. 4.45

SERVICES 4/5

GLASGOW—TIREE—BENBECULA—NORTH UIST—STORNOWAY

NORTHBOUND

		A Daily Except Sundays	B Mons., Weds., & Fris.	B Tues., Thurs. & Sats.
		a.m.	a.m.	a.m.
GLASGOW	Grosvenor Restaurant	dep. 9.00	dep. 9.00	dep. 9.00
	Renfrew Airport	dep. 9.45	dep. 9.45	dep. 9.45
TIREE✱	Reef Airport	arr. 10.45	arr. 10.45	dep. 10.45
	Reef Airport	dep. 10.55	dep. 10.55	dep. 10.55
BENBECULA✱	Balivanich Airport	arr. 11.40	arr. 11.40	—
	Balivanich Airport	dep. 11.50	dep. 11.50	—
NORTH UIST✱	Sollas Airport	arr. 12.00	arr. 12.00	—
	Sollas Airport	p.m. dep. 12.15	p.m. dep. 12.15	p.m.
STORNOWAY	Airport	arr. 12.55	arr. 12.55	arr. 12.15
	Maritime Buildings	arr. 1.20	arr. 1.20	arr. 12.35

SOUTHBOUND

STORNOWAY	Maritime Buildings	dep. 1.0	dep. 12.50	dep. 12.15
	Airport	dep. 1.30	dep. 1.20	dep. 12.40
NORTH UIST✱	Sollas Airport	arr. 2.20	—	arr. 1.30
	Sollas Airport	dep. 2.35	—	dep. 1.45
BENBECULA✱	Balivanich Airport	arr. 2.45	—	arr. 1.55
	Balivanich Airport	dep. 2.55	—	dep. 2.05
TIREE✱	Reef Airport	arr. 3.40	arr. 2.50	arr. 2.50
	Reef Airport	dep. 3.50	dep. 3.00	dep. 3.00
GLASGOW	Renfrew Airport	arr. 4.50	arr. 4.00	arr. 4.00
	Grosvenor Restaurant	arr. 5.30	arr. 4.45	arr. 4.45

NOTES

✱ Passengers must arrive at these Airports at least 15 minutes prior to advertised departure time to enable weighing and other formalities to be completed.

A. Service operates 4th October, to 6th November, 1943, and from 21st February, 1944.

B. Service operates 8th November, 1943, to 19th February, 1944.

ALL SERVICES SUBJECT TO ALTERATION OR CANCELLATION WITHOUT NOTICE

Wartime exigencies - The 'Notes' in this 1943-44 winter time-table shows the conditions affecting passenger travel in Scotland at this time. (John Stroud Collection)

Something else the Forces appreciated was the special mail delivery that was set up during the war. Called the RAF Mail Service, Scottish Airways in conjunction with the Post Office set up a regular, fast delivery of Forces Mail between Renfrew and Islay, Tiree, Benbecula, North Uist and Stornoway (there was a GPO Air Mail service operating to Campbeltown). Large quantities of mail were carried - as was also the case with the Northern Section in Inverness, who operated the system to Kirkwall and Sumburgh. And once again many Service C.O.s commented upon the extremely high level of regularity in the air mail deliveries.

There were many other charters carried out for special purposes, for all sorts of Government Departments, including the Air Ministry. Admiralty, War Office, Ministries of Supply, Information, Aircraft Production, etc, and the Dept. of Health for Scotland.

George Nicholson's Southern Section also participated in the production of several documentary films produced under the auspices of the Ministry of Information and other Government Departments.

By mid 1944, only five of the pilots employed by Scottish Airways at the outbreak of the War were still flying with the airline - Ted Fresson himself, Henry Vallance and Bill Baillie in the North, and David Barclay and Jock Young at Renfrew. As William Cumming, the airline's Secretary based at Renfrew stated:

"As will be appreciated, very heavy demands have fallen on these remaining five pilots, as is indicated by the fact that each of them have flown over 1000 hours per year since the War began.

"Tribute should also be paid to the Radio Officers and to the depleted staff of Ground Engineers, who have maintained the limited number of aircraft made available to the Company with such efficiency that at no time has it been necessary to cancel a scheduled flight by reason of aircraft being unserviceable !"

More mishaps.

Their old Rapide G-AFFF re-joined the Scottish Airways' fleet at Renfrew again on December 10th 1942, giving a boosted fleet of five Rapides through the winter ('FFF, 'FOI, 'FRK, 'ERZ and 'GED). The weather was bad again at the beginning of January

1943, and David Barclay had to use Prestwick, or divert there frequently. On January 2nd for instance, he had to divert to Prestwick on one engine (the starboard motor had packed up) after a flight from the Isle of Man in G-AFRK. He also had to divert there with a 'dead' starboard engine in G-AGED on January 6th, flying from Stornoway and Tiree. And twice on January 4th David was forced to divert to Prestwick while awaiting to get in to a fog-bound Renfrew - but being held up by RAF aircraft trying to get down in front of him.

One of the other pilots at Renfrew (Bob Pepper), however, crashed on the aerodrome there on February 2nd 1943, writing off Rapide G-AGED, and so the AAJC organised the delivery of a replacement, G-AGEE to Renfrew by February 5th.

Only ten days later, David Barclay flew G-AFRK down to Prestwick (due to the weather at Renfrew) to pick up passengers for Tiree, but a gale was blowing out in the Hebrides, and once again during the turnaround, G-AFRK was damaged by buffeting and flying debris, necessitating remaining overnight while the Chief Engineer and others were flown out from Renfrew to effect repairs.

Using RAF Abbotsinch

Their use of Prestwick had increased so much during January - March 1943 (not just through weather, but because of the finishing off of the new hard runways) that on March 25th David Barclay took the Traffic Manager from Renfrew, John Swann, and the Chief Engineer Bill Mann across to RAF Abbotsinch to examine the facilities there with a view to using that aerodrome for a time. Next day, March 26th David Barclay originated the Western Isles and Tiree services from Abbotsinch and started flying the scheduled services from the RAF aerodrome. Occasionally, Prestwick was used also, but for the most part Abbotsinch became the traffic origination/destination point for Scottish Airways flights at Glasgow, through until May 22nd 1943 - a period of two months.

By then the summer schedules had started with the Isle of Man service being operated additionally for RAS (sometimes three times daily by the Renfrew pilots - particularly on Tuesdays or Saturdays). Rapide 'FRK came back from overhaul on July 7th, replacing 'GEE and David brought up an ex-RAF Rapide (X7349) from Dumfries to Renfrew on May 18th which Ted Fresson took up to Inverness as a fleet replacement in the North (registered for its C of A as G-AGIC).

July 19th saw David air test a replacement Rapide for Renfrew, G-AGIF which promptly went into service there. This aircraft had been previously used by the RAF at Macmerry aerodrome, Edinburgh, by various RAF units.

Capt. B. T. O'Reilly arrived back at Renfrew on July 27th 1943 and David checked him out on the Isle of Man service that day on 'FFF. Taking over the Isle of Man services meant the

---

SCOTTISH AIRWAYS LTD
Aircraft Fleet - Summer 1944
Southern Section:

De Havilland DH89A Dragon Rapide	G-AFFF
De Havilland DH89A Dragon Rapide	G-AFOI
De Havilland DH89A Dragon Rapide	G-AGIF
De Havilland DH89A Dragon Rapide	G-AGJF

Northern Section:

De Havilland DH84 Dragon I	G-ACIT
De Havilland DH89A Dragon Rapide	G-AEWL
De Havilland DH89A Dragon Rapide	G-AGDG
De Havilland DH89A Dragon Rapide	G-AGIC
De Havilland DH89A Dragon Rapide	G-AGJG

SCOTTISH AIRWAYS LTD
Airfield Codes used in World War Two
The following codes were used by most pilots in their log-books during World War Two, representing the aerodromes to which they flew:

Southern Section (Renfrew):

RW	Glasgow (Renfrew)
CC or ST	Campbeltown (The Strath)
IY	Islay
IH	Barra (North Bay)
IU	Benbecula (Balivanich)
SM	North Uist (Sollas)
SV	Stornoway
TG	Tiree
HA	Harris (Northton)
AD	Aberdeen (Dyce)
PT	Perth (Scone)
DB	Donibristle
JE	Abbotsinch
JW	Prestwick
JT	Belfast (Sydenham or Harbour)
LV	Liverpool (Speke)
CY	Croydon
GZ	Guernsey
JY	Jersey
NL	Northolt
OM	Isle of Man (Ronaldsway)
DW	Dublin

Northern Section (Inverness):

IV	Inverness (Longman)
WK or WP	Wick (Hillhead)
OY	Kirkwall (Wideford)
OY/H or HAT	Kirkwall (Hatston)
OY/G	Kirkwall (Grimsetter)
OY/S or SB	Orkney (Skeabrae)
SJ	Sumburgh
STY	Stronsay
SDY	Sanday
NR	North Ronaldsay
W	Westray
LH	Longhope
TP	Thurso (Claredon)
CT	Castletown
SV	Stornoway

Renfrew base now needed five aircraft and at least that number of pilots to operate in summertime.

Amongst the different charters that Scottish flew out of Renfrew were a trickle of so-called 'funeral charters' to places in the Western Isles, carrying the coffin as well as relatives of the deceased, to be laid to rest in his local burial ground. David flew one such charter to Barra in 'FRK on September 26th 1943.

Yet another ex-RAF DH89A Rapide, was collected by David Barclay from Dumfries on October 10th 1943 - X7326 - which he flew back to Renfrew for conversion to a civil machine, registered G-AGJF. It was air-tested by David (as 'GJF) on October 29th at Renfrew, and then put into service through the winter of 1943-44, together with G-AGIF (easily confused), G-AFOI and G-AFRK.

The end of the war

January and February 1944 were notable for their gales, one of them catching out David Barclay at Tiree one afternoon and leading to him having to picket the aircraft down, find a hotel for the passengers, and stay overnight until it subsided the next day. February 11th saw 'FRK back again off maintenance and 'FOI went south to be overhauled. David also had another starboard engine failure (on 'GIF this time) between Tiree and Benbecula

---

Catching the Orkney 'bus to market!
Local flower growers and egg farmers line up in North Ronaldsay at the end of World War Two to take the
Scottish Airways DH Dragon Rapide G-AGJG to Kirkwall.
This aircraft is currently (1995) under restoration to pristine condition with David and Mark Miller at Duxford .(John Stroud Collection)

on February 21st, and after landing gingerly at Benbecula, he had to wait all day while a new engine was flown out from Renfrew and fitted. Then he flew 'GIF back at 1800 in the dark, qualifying for 1hr 40 mins 'night flying' for a change!

May 24th saw 'FOI back again for the summer 1944 schedules, while 'FRK went down for maintenance, returning in August once more to switch with 'GIF. An old colleague dropped into Renfrew on August 20th 1944 to see the Scottish Airways' staff, and in particular George Nicholson and David Barclay. It was their pre-war Captain John Annesley Hankins, now a Squadron Leader in the RAF in charge of a Dakota Squadron with an Air Force Cross awarded in the 1943 New Year's Honours. John took David up in his military Dakota and gave him an hour's dual and landing practice!

October 25th 1944 saw G-AGIF back from maintenance being air-tested at Renfrew by David, and this time G-AGJF went south for overhaul. Another pilot arrived on secondment at the end of November - Capt W. H. Morton - to help give the hard-worked stalwarts at Renfrew some well deserved leave over Christmas.

Punctures were rare, but slightly less so now hard runways had been put down on many of the aerodromes, although Rapides could still (and did) land on the grass areas of the larger ones, including Renfrew. David suffered one at Ronaldsway (IOM) on December 13th 1944 and had to stay overnight while 'FFF was repaired, and made ready to fly back next morning by the local ground engineer of RAS subsidiary, IOMAS.

The Rapide G-AGJF came back off maintenance on January 16th 1945 and 'FFF went off for attention in its place. Then on February 19th 1945, David air-tested another newly converted Dragon Rapide (ex-RAF NR681) now registered G-AGLP,

which Scottish Airways had prepared at Renfrew for use by Railway Air Services, to whom it was now delivered for a special purpose as we shall see later. And some weeks later, on March 4th 1945, David collected yet another newly-converted Rapide from Liverpool, G-AGLE (ex-RAF NR685) and brought it back to Renfrew to add to the Scottish fleet there for the summer 1945 schedules.

New Glasgow -London service.

With the end of the war obviously in sight now, George Nicholson & Co were planning new services to get back on track to their pre-war expansion ideas. On March 7th 1945 David Barclay flew George and their Chief Engineer, Bill Mann, around the Western Isles on a survey of the aerodromes, paying particular attention to Prestwick, Stornoway and North Uist (Sollas). They called at Prestwick in both directions, to assess the potential of post-war scheduled services operating from this fine large airfield.

SCOTTISH AIRWAYS	
Traffic Statistics	
(August 1st 1937 - December 31st 1944)	
Aircraft miles	5,472,526
Passenger miles	17,862,154
Cargo (lbs)*	1,224,682
Mail (lbs)	4,207,851
* Including excess baggage	

An historic, if somewhat dark photograph showing the inauguration of the Inverness - Stornoway service that finally took place on May 24th 1944. Ted Fresson was the pilot and is seen here with an Inverness Councillor (left) Provost A. Mackenzie OBE of Stornoway (second left) and Provost Hugh Mackenzie, MBE of Inverness (right). (Richard Fresson)

Rapide 'FFF arrived back off maintenance on March 28th and 'FOI went into the hangars in its place. Then, on March 30th, David and his R.O. 'Paddy' O'Gorman, with Bill Mann on board made some full-load take-offs from Renfrew in the new Rapide they had recently prepared for RAS - G-AGLP - flying it around for an hour to check its fuel consumption, etc. The purpose was soon to be made clear, for on April 9th Scottish Airways began to operate a Glasgow - London service on behalf of the parent company, Railway Air Services. The other new Dragon Rapide G-AGLE was used for the inaugural, and David Barclay took off from Renfrew at 09.05, called at Prestwick to meet the Trans-Atlantic services of Trans-Canada Airlines (now Air Canada), took off again at 09.40, called at Liverpool (Speke) and arrived at London (Croydon) at 13.45 (after 3 hrs 55 mins total flying time).

Next day, David flew 'GLE back the same way, leaving Croydon at 14.00, and arriving back at Renfrew at 1810. He had taken the Chief R.O. with him, Jimmy Mitchell, who went on to fly quite a few of the schedules, which from April 11th for the R.O.s (but not the pilots) consisted of a round-trip on each weekday departing Renfrew at 09.05 arriving Croydon 13.20; departing Croydon 14.00 and arriving back at Renfrew at 18.10. (The pilots always overnighted at Croydon).

The next time David flew the service was on April 27th. Some days before this, a cross-over aircraft pattern had been introduced, with both aircraft departing at 14.00 from Croydon and Prestwick, in opposite directions. This Friday, David left Renfrew at 13.25 in G-AGLP, Prestwick at 14.00 and after calling at Speke, arrived at Croydon for the night. Next day, Saturday April 28th, he left Croydon at 14.05 in 'GLP and arrived back at Renfrew at 18.45 - not calling at Prestwick at all this time (as there was no TCA transatlantic flight connection on the Saturday).

The Rapide G-AGLE was not always used on the Croydon run, and it was frequently scheduled on the other routes.

Thursday May 3rd saw David operating to Croydon again, and back on Friday the 4th (still keeping the same timings and still calling at Prestwick and Liverpool each way).

On Sunday May 6th David operated 'GLE on a Renfrew - Liverpool - Andover and return routeing, carrying a load of service personnel; and on May 9th and 10th he took 'GLE down again on the full Croydon schedule. On Tuesday May 15th however, he flew the first non-stop Renfrew - Croydon service on G-AGLP, in a time of 3 hrs 50 mins, and flew back on Wednesday the 16th non-stop, too. From here the service ran in non-stop cross-over fashion both ways, on weekdays only, cutting out both Prestwick and Liverpool. Times eventually came down to around 3 hrs 15 mins - 3 hrs 35 mins, without even a 'tech stop' for fuel at Speke.

As a matter of interest, David Barclay's non-stop Glasgow - London flight on May 15th 1945 probably represented the first such scheduled service since John Sword's Midland & Scottish Air Ferries' last such flight on July 4th 1934, when Miss Winifred Drinkwater had flown the DH83 Fox Moth G-ACBZ from Renfrew to Romford *and back* in the one day on the airlines' advertised scheduled service! (She had taken 8 hrs 30 mins for the round trip. David Barclay took 8 hrs 10 mins, but spread over two days!)

Liberation of the Channel Isles

Shortly after the end of the war in Europe, in July 1945, a Scottish Airways' crew was involved in the re-starting of mainland air services to Jersey and Guernsey. Jersey Airways had already begun Croydon - Guernsey - Jersey services on June 21st, using RAS aircraft, but now came the start of RAS' own scheduled service to the islands. After flying the Renfrew - Croydon service, the Scottish crews began to be scheduled on the re-

Circling over Renfrew - the Scottish Airways' D.H. Dragon Rapide G-AFOI seen from a sister Rapide at the end of World War Two.
(John Stroud Collection)

started Croydon - Guernsey - Jersey service, overnighting in Jersey and returning next day Jersey - Guernsey - Croydon and then Croydon - Renfrew.

The first such flight was on July 7th to the Channel Islands, and John Annesley Hankins was the Captain, with Andrew Ruthven as his R.O., both having originated in Renfrew that morning and flying Rapide G-AGLR down to Croydon and G-AGLP on to Jersey. Next day (July 8th) they returned in 'GLP to Croydon and took 'GLR back to Renfrew.

Peak capacity - Summer 1945

This summer of 1945 there were 9 flights a week on the Western Isles service - split into three different routeings. The Rapide fleet at Renfrew was now up to six and flying was carefully planned on each aircraft for maximum efficiency. Thus David could fly three different routes in one day, e.g: Renfrew to each of Campbeltown, Islay and the Isle of Man and return (total = 8hrs flying). The Western Isles routeing took between 4 and 4 3/4 flying hours for the round-trip, with flight variations between each (Renfrew - Tiree - Stornoway; Renfrew - Tiree - Benbecula - North Uist - Stornoway; and Renfrew - Stornoway direct). These services, for want of better description were now just referred to in the pilot's log books as "Hebs" (for Hebrides).

Up in the Northern Section at Inverness frequency hit its peak on Inverness - Kirkwall/Sumburgh, with no less than three flights daily being operated to Kirkwall (departures. from Inverness at 09.30, 10.00 and 12.30) and up to two daily on Inverness - Sumburgh (deps at 10.00 and 10.10 - the latter on Tue, Thurs, and Sat, - from Inverness and non-stop to Shetland). Inverness - Stornoway continued at a three times weekly service,

on Mon, Wed, Fri, only (most of the traffic with the Hebrides was on the Glasgow axis).

Another new Rapide, G-AGLR was operated by David Barclay on the Croydon run on June 8th, being one of the trio recently taken over from the RAF (with 'GLE and GLP) to operate the London run, and fitted with a closed-off new compartment (pilot and R.O.) and toilet, and only five passenger seats as a consequence.

The veteran Rapide 'FOI re-appeared from maintenance on July 6th, and 'ERN was added to the fleet again on August 31st, 'FRK disappearing again for overhaul.

Wartime efforts rewarded.

The Southern Section had experienced no close aerial encounters with German aircraft throughout the War, although at times enemy aircraft had been reported to be in the vicinity of Scottish Airways' flights. The Northern Section had experienced some close calls, however, and Ted Fresson and Henry Vallance between them had been chased or machine-gunned in the air or on the ground (See *"Rivals in the North"* by the same Author.)

David Barclay, the Chief Pilot of Scottish Airways, was appointed an M.B.E. early in 1944 - a richly deserved award for all his wartime efforts, despite his bad crash at Hatston - and as most people thought, not nearly a good enough recognition for what he had achieved. Ted Fresson, founder, and still Chief Pilot (through the war years) of Highland Airways in Inverness, received the O.B.E. in July 1943 for his amazing work with the Northern Section both on the ground and in the air. Henry Vallance in the North, received the King's Commendation for

111

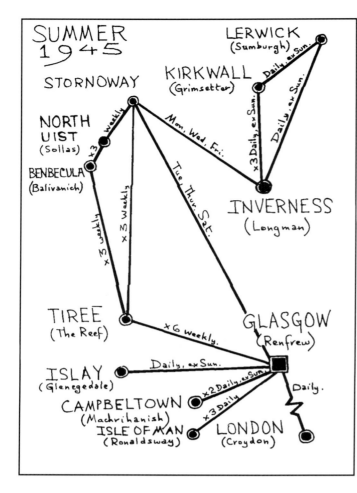

Above: *The Scottish Airways' route network in Summer 1945, before the Glasgow - Inverness link-up. (Author)*

Below: *An impressive wartime line-up at Renfrew - five D.H. Dragon Rapides of Scottish Airways shown before the start of the day's operations in late 1944. The two machines on the left are G-AFOI and G-AFRK; the other three are probably G-AFFF, 'GIF and 'GJF. (John Stroud Collection)*

Valuable Services in the Air in August 1945, and several ex-Scottish Airways' pilots were decorated in RAF or B.O.A.C. service during the war.

Wartime traffic results

The War in Europe came to an end on May 8th and the War in the Pacific finished on August 15th, 1945. Figures released by Scottish Airways in June 1944 showed that during the period September 1939 to April 1944, Air Ambulance aircraft of Scottish Airways flew over 50,000 miles, and brought some 300 patients to the Mainland for urgent medical or surgical treatment.

A total of over 100,000 passengers had been carried by Scottish Airways during this time, without serious mishap, and a regularity of 98% was maintained throughout that entire 1939-45 period!

In fact Scottish Airways as a whole (combined with its Western Isles Airways subsidiary) in the years 1940-1945 carried 136,186 passengers (36.7% of all passengers carried by the LMS group of airlines or subsidiaries including Railway Air Services, Isle of Man Air Services, West Coast Air Services, G.W. & S. Air Lines, Scottish Airways and Western Isles Airways; but excluding Allied Airways in Aberdeen.) It also carried 1,292,400 lbs of air cargo (61.7%); 4,319,800 lbs of Mail (67.5%), and flew 4,636,500 Aircraft miles (47.9%), - a very creditable effort!

Revenue passenger miles in 1945 alone totalled 2,321,600, and the revenue passenger load-factors during the War had been quite astonishing - viz:

	Passenger Load Factor (%)	
Year	Scottish Airways	Western Isles Airways
1940	80.4	52.3
1941	88.7	75.4
1942	92.6	74.0
1943	89.8	75.0
1944	89.4	79.5
1945	86.5	79.7

Of course, there had been a demand for passenger travel during the War years by the Services and various Government Departments that might not be expected to continue now in Peacetime, but the high load factors led the airlines to believe even bigger aircraft could be used in future, now things were returning to normal.

SCOTTISH AIRWAYS
Wartime Passengers Carried.

	Scottish Airways	Western Isles Airways	TOTAL	All other RAS and associated airlines*	GRAND TOTAL	Scottish Airways %
1940	9,832	5,427	15,259	16,787	32,046	47.6
1941	11,754	10,369	22,123	30,129	52,252	42.3
1942	11,495	10,926	22,421	36,765	59,186	37.9
1943	11,619	10,548	22,167	43,310	65,477	33.9
1944	12,395	12,248	24,643	42,089	66,732	36.9
1945	14,443	15,130	29,573	65,395	94,968	31.1
TOTAL	**71,538**	**64,648**	**136,186**	**234,475**	**370,661**	**36.7**

* Includes Railway Air Services, Isle of Man Air Services, West Coast Air Services and GW&S Air Lines.

SCOTTISH AIRWAYS
Wartime Cargo Carried. (lbs x 000)

	Scottish Airways	Western Isles Airways	TOTAL	All other RAS and associated airlines*	GRAND TOTAL	Scottish Airways %
1940	89.6	30.6	120.2	54.1	174.3	69.0
1941	106.0	66.9	172.9	91.5	264.4	65.4
1942	113.4	84.2	197.6	97.2	294.8	67.0
1943	120.5	116.3	236.8	120.6	357.4	66.3
1944	134.2	103.9	238.1	139.5	377.6	63.1
1945	198.3	128.5	326.8	301.0	627.8	52.1
TOTAL	**762.0**	**539.4**	**1,292.4**	**803.9**	**2,096.3**	**61.7**

* Includes Railway Air Services, Isle of Man Air Services, West Coast Air Services and GW&S Air Lines.

SCOTTISH AIRWAYS
Wartime Mail Carried. (lbs x 000)

	Scottish Airways	Western Isles Airways	TOTAL	All other RAS and associated airlines*	GRAND TOTAL	Scottish Airways %
1940	554.7	29.9	584.6	227.5	812.1	72.0
1941	630.7	52.2	682.9	333.9	1,016.8	67.2
1942	758.5	74.7	833.2	385.7	1,218.9	68.4
1943	701.1	105.7	806.8	373.1	1,179.9	68.4
1944	672.9	126.6	799.5	395.6	1,195.1	66.9
1945	499.6	113.2	612.8	367.8	980.6	62.5
TOTAL	**3,817.5**	**502.3**	**4,319.8**	**2,083.6**	**6,403.4**	**67.5**

* Includes Railway Air Services, Isle of Man Air Services, West Coast Air Services and GW&S Air Lines.

SCOTTISH AIRWAYS
Wartime Aircraft Miles Flown (x 000)

	Scottish Airways	Western Isles Airways	TOTAL	All other RAS and associated airlines*	GRAND TOTAL	Scottish Airways %
1940	390.4	193.2	583.6	379.5	963.1	60.6
1941	400.6	309.5	710.1	607.2	1,317.3	53.9
1942	419.3	330.4	749.7	726.4	1,476.1	50.8
1943	433.6	337.8	771.4	806.1	1,577.5	48.9
1944	479.7	351.2	830.9	802.3	1,633.2	50.9
1945	503.8	487.0	990.8	1,728.1	2,718.9	36.4
TOTAL	**2,627.4**	**2,009.1**	**4,636.5**	**5,049.6**	**9,686.1**	**47.9**

* Includes Railway Air Services, Isle of Man Air Services, West Coast Air Services and GW&S Air Lines.

These tables give Scottish Airways' and Western Isles Airways' principal traffic statistics recorded in the six years of World War Two, and compare their totals with the rest of the Railway Air Companies combined. (BEA archives)

113

DETAILS OF ANNUAL AIRCRAFT MILAGES OPERATED BY RAILWAY AIR SERVICES
AND ASSOCIATED AIR COMPANIES IN WHICH RAILWAY COMPANIES ARE FINANCIALLY INTERESTED.
(period is to 31st December unless otherwise stated)

Year	RAILWAY AIR SERVICES		Scottish Airways	Western Isles Airways	Isle of Man Air Services (Year to 31/3)*	Jersey Airways	Guernsey Airways	West Coast Air Services (Year to 31/3)*	GW&S Air Lines (Year to 31/3)*	TOTAL
	LMS Railway	GW&S Railway								
1934	111,891 (a)	98,966	-	-	-	-	-	-	-	210,857
1935	459,709	196,263	-	-	-	-	-	-	-	655,972
1936	774,741	130,556	-	-	-	-	-	-	-	905,297
1937	851,832	152,364	118,356 (b)	106,398 (b)	147,315 (c)	682,621	-	-	-	2,058,886
1938	468,160	102,000	308,369	212,684	618,342	614,844	-	-	-	2,324,399
1939	397,875	-	540,990	168,219	313,157	482,415	112,240	-	260,009 (d)	2,274,905
1940	115,114	-	390,398	193,165	225,560	No Ops	No Ops	-	38,898	963,135
1941	215,248	-	400,618	309,532	255,520	No Ops	No Ops	121,472	14,868	1,317,258
1942	324,153	-	419,278	330,353	243,144	No Ops	No Ops	121,272	37,944	1,476,144
1943	430,480	-	433,629	337,774	232,880	No Ops	No Ops	98,761	43,976	1,577,500
1944	394,322	-	479,656	351,216	264,264	No Ops	No Ops	96,712	47,016	1,633,186
1945	1,151,897	-	503,837	486,947	283,731	Restarted June 1945	Restarted June 1945	217,910	74,592	2,718,914

a - from 20.8.34 to 31.12.34.   b - from 1.8.37 to 31.12.37.   c - from 26.9.37 to 31.3.38.   d - from 5.12.38 to 31.3.40.   * - Year following

---

NUMBER OF PASSENGERS CARRIED (and Passenger Load Factor)

Year	RAS LMS/GW&S Railways	Scottish Airways	Western Isles Airways	Isle of Man Air Services (Year to 31/3)*	Channel Island Airways (b)	West Coast Air Services (Year to 31/3)*	GW&S Air Lines (Year to 31/3)*	TOTAL
1934	2,237 (12.60%)	-	-	-	-	-	-	2,237
1935	13,293 (35.50%)	-	-	-	-	-	-	13,293
1936	22,076 (42.00%)	-	-	-	-	-	-	22,076
1937	25,523 (39.10%)	3,629 (53.70%)	2,815 (48.80%)	3,925 (63.34%)	32,411 -	-	-	68,303
1938	7,082 (43.50%)	7,250 (40.89%)	5,957 (48.40%)	21,279 (56.52%)	33,875 (74.00%)	-	-	75,443
1939	5,313 (39.00%)	8,881 (56.20%)	4,536 (56.20%)	12,185 (52.75%)	33,072 (65.00%)	-	12,898 (a) -	76,885
1940	4,271 (57.23%)	9,832 (80.40%)	5,427 (52.30%)	9,264 (92.07%)	Ops ceased	-	3,252 (46.00%)	32,046
1941	11,843 (84.98%)	11,754 (88.70%)	10,369 (75.40%)	12,052 (91.83%)	-	4,859 (81.00%)	1,375 (51.00%)	52,252
1942	16,043 (85.66%)	11,495 (92.60%)	10,926 (74.00%)	11,664 (93.24%)	-	5,189 (83.00%)	3,869 (64.00%)	59,186
1943	20,094 (82.47%)	11,619 (89.80%)	10,548 (75.00%)	12,147 (97.40%)	-	5,030 (77.00%)	6,039 (73.00%)	65,477
1944	17,117 (87.45%)	12,395 (89.40%)	12,248 (79.50%)	14,567 (95.92%)	-	3,812 (64.00%)	6,593 -	66,732
1945	29,716 (76.00%)	14,443 (86.50%)	15,130 (79.70%)	16,172 (94.94%)	restarted 6/45	7,201 -	12,306 -	94,968

a- from 5.12.38 to 31/3/40   b- Jersey Airways (plus Guernsey Airways 11,088 passengers for 1939 only).   * - Year Following.

ANNUAL FREIGHT CARRIED (expressed in lbs)

Year	RAS LMS/GW&S Railways	Scottish Airways	Western Isles Airways	Isle of Man Air Services (Year to 31/3)*	Jersey Airways	Guernsey Airways	West Coast Air Services (Year to 31/3)*	GW&S Air Lines (Year to 31/3)*	TOTAL
1934	6,000	-	-	-	-	-	-	-	6,000
1935	167,498	-	-	-	-	-	-	-	167,498
1936	39,862	-	-	-	-	-	-	-	39,862
1937	117,934	20,389	25,007	67,461	959,063	-	-	-	1,189,854
1938	48,459	46,040	54,267	153,965	1,002,515	-	-	-	1,305,246
1939	50,049	78,479	31,113	58,259	1,181,081	-	-	52,930	1,698,623
1940	13,727	89,638	30,588	24,533	Ops ceased	Ops ceased	-	15,779	174,265
1941	40,661	105,990	66,893	29,438	-	-	15,770	5,640	264,392
1942	45,186	113,394	84,146	23,706	-	-	15,105	13,258	294,795
1943	62,067	120,511	116,288	23,119	-	-	16,012	19,361	357,358
1944	74,660	134,189	103,906	32,267	-	-	14,597	17,928	377,547
1945	128,647	198,262	128,467	71,760	restarted 6/45	restarted 6/45	27,432	73,257	627,825

ANNUAL MAIL CARRIED (expressed in lbs)

Year	RAS LMS/GW&S Railways	Scottish Airways	Western Isles Airways	Isle of Man Air Services (Year to 31/3)*	Jersey Airways	Guernsey Airways	West Coast Air Services (Year to 31/3)*	GW&S Air Lines (Year to 31/3)*	TOTAL
1934	5,625	-	-	-	-	-	-	-	5,625
1935	21,631	-	-	-	-	-	-	-	21,631
1936	385,027	-	-	-	-	-	-	-	385,027
1937	454,926	78,522	-	158,755	131,719	-	-	-	823,922
1938	490,917	178,080	-	324,252	197,527	-	-	-	1,190,776
1939	309,406	245,146	9,264	202,274	173,431	42,104	-	-	981,625
1940	-	554,701	29,894	227,456	Ops ceased	Ops ceased	-	-	812,051
1941	16,661	630,648	52,193	317,289	-	-	-	-	1,016,791
1942	64,110	758,451	74,706	321,580	-	-	-	-	1,218,847
1943	45,300	701,050	105,686	327,823	-	-	-	-	1,179,859
1944	50,717	672,872	126,638	344,867	-	-	-	-	1,195,094
1945	51,082	499,565	113,195	316,719	restarted 6/45	restarted 6/45	-	-	980,561

These tables give the official traffic figures for Scottish Airways for each year from their inception in 1937, up to the end of 1945.
(BEA Archives)

CHAPTER 14

Paving the way for Nationalisation

In March 1945 the Government produced a White Paper on the future of civil air transport in Britain, once the War was finished. It had been in course of preparation for some time under the direction of the Minister of Civil Aviation, Viscount Swinton, and outlined Government policy on future Rail, Sea and Air Travel co-ordination.

In the Paper, it was stated that those Companies controlled by the Railway Companies would be responsible for the operation of all internal air lines in Britain.

Debate began at once in the newspapers, in Parliament, etc; and the LMS Railway Co moved its plans for post-war flying into top gear. The newspapers underlined the White Paper's proposal that 'day and night flying in fast passenger planes with the latest safety and all-weather devices are envisaged...' A large expansion in the network operated by Scottish Airways and its associated companies was forecast.

Unfortunately, there had been a number of smaller air companies which had not become part of the Railway Air Services' group, and these included Eric Gandar Dower's Allied Airways in Aberdeen. He amongst others was rightfully incensed about the threat of his existing Aberdeen - Orkney/Shetland services disappearing into his big rival. Indeed, he began to argue for new rights to fly to Glasgow, Edinburgh and London; as well as from Aberdeen and Newcastle to points all over Scandinavia - building on services tried out by him just prior to World War Two breaking out.

Scottish Airways, on the other hand, wanted its old pioneering Aberdeen - Wick - Kirkwall - Sumburgh route back (taken away by the Licensing Authority early in 1939), and so in the Northern Section of Scottish Airways, much lobbying went on with the Orkney and Shetland Island Councils, to regain the Aberdeen route.

Adviser appointed

Back in the summer of 1944, R.A.S. had taken on a Dennis Handover, recently Traffic Manager of Imperial Airways (and later B.O.A.C.), to be responsible for preparing plans for the company's Post-War development.

Handover had visited George Nicholson in Renfrew on September 29th 1944, to see the operation there and discuss future developments. David Barclay flew Dennis Handover, together with Wing Cmdr Arthur Measures (who was showing him around the Group), and Bill Mann and Bill Gairdner on a sight-seeing trip in G-AFOI to Islay, North Uist, Stornoway and Inverness, dropping the passengers there and returning empty to Renfrew.

In Inverness, Dennis Handover and Measures & Co discussed Ted Fresson's future plans and ideas until leaving him on October 4th by train, after flying up to Kirkwall (Grimsetter) that morning with Ted at the controls of Rapide G-ADAJ to give Dennis a taste of bad weather flying up the East Coast/Latheron routeing.

Back at the RAS HQ in London, Dennis Handover and his team worked on the Group Plan for Post-War development, and in October 1944 had presented this to Viscount Swinton's department as RAS' idea for expanding British Civil Aviation after the War ended.

RAS had itself proposed a stunning plan to operate the bulk of British domestic and short haul European services (leaving B.O.A.C. - at that time the only other Government backed organisation - to range wider afield).

Moreover, the Railways would:

i) Operate free of subsidy, providing all competing European airlines were not allowed to claim any subsidy.

ii) Form a new airline company with a capital of £5M to operate the network.

iii) Seek partnerships from other airline, and shipping companies operating in the area.

iv) Offer ticket inter-availability on land, sea and air routes.

v) Buy British aircraft if possible and available.

The RAS plan envisaged flying 20 million miles a year from the start, and opening routes in four stages - all domestic flights to start with, followed by three phases of opening European services.

Scottish Airways' D.H. Dragon Rapide G-AFFF about to depart from Renfrew towards the end of WWII, when it was deemed safe to fly aircraft without camouflage. Behind the aircraft are the Scottish Flying Club's offices and the Airport Control Tower.

Interestingly, the Rapide bears the "Railway Air Services" titling on the nose, as it was part of the AAJC pool of aircraft.

(John Stroud Collection)

The domestic routes envisaged, that would involve Scottish Airways organization, were:

Prestwick - London
Glasgow - Manchester - London *
Aberdeen - Edinburgh - Newcastle - Hull - London
Glasgow - Belfast *
Glasgow - Perth - Inverness - Wick - Kirkwall - Sumburgh**
Kirkwall - Thurso **
Orkney Inter-Island services**
Inverness - Kirkwall - Sumburgh*
Aberdeen - Inverness - Stornoway**
Glasgow - Campbeltown - Islay*
Glasgow - Tiree - South Uist - Benbecula - North Uist - Stornoway*
Glasgow - Isle of Man *

and the European routes included:

London - Glasgow - Stornoway - Iceland.

The Glasgow - Stornoway sector was already being flown of course, as were those above marked (*). Those marked (**) had been operated up to the War, or been authorised in the 1939 Licensing round.

Award to Vallance; thanks all round.

On July 26th 1945 a shock General Election result overthrew the wartime coalition Government in Britain led by Sir Winston Churchill, and formally installed a Labour Government. The Air Minister was soon announced to be Lord Winster.

A new chairman was now elected to Scottish Airways Board - Sir Steven Bilsland - and George Nicholson and Ted Fresson (who were each 'Regional Director' and 'General Manager' of the different Sections - Southern and Northern) went down to attend a Board Meeting held in the Glasgow offices of Coastline Shipping Co., and David MacBrayne Ltd. They were told that the post-war plans of Scottish Airways would continue to be promoted.

On Saturday September 8th 1945, the new chairman travelled up to Inverness for a very special banquet, principally to congratulate Capt Henry Vallance on the award of the Kings' Commendation for Valuable Services in the Air, and to thank everybody in Scottish Airways - not least the Northern Section,

for their herculean efforts during the war years. The local *Highland News* reported:

"Highland Airways Pioneers
Scottish Chief's Tribute
Honouring Captain Vallance.

Sir Steven Bilsland, chairman of Scottish Airways, Ltd., presided at a banquet given in Inverness' Caledonian Hotel on Saturday night in honour of Captain Henry Vallance, their Chief Pilot for the Northern Section, in appreciation of the distinction recently conferred on him by His Majesty the King, whose commendation he received in appreciation of his work in maintaining lines of communication in Great Britain.

The occasion afforded Sir Steven Bilsland the opportunity of referring to the foundation work of Mr Robert Wotherspoon and Mr R.Donald, in connection with the establishment of Highland Airways, and also to the inspiring leadership of Captain Fresson in the greater development of that service.

Sir Steven also thanked all associated with the Northern air link for their grand teamwork during the war period. As to the future, he referred to the "very considerable development plans" which his company have evolved, and which await Government consideration before being put in operation. In the development of Scotland, the Highland Counties, he added, would also figure.

Sprigs of white heather were among the table decorations. and on the wall, above the principal table, there was a symbolic reminder of " S. A.'s" (Scottish Airway's) big part in civil aviation.

The gathering consisted of—Sir Steven and Lady Bilsland; Mr Cumming. Secretary of Scottish Airways, Ltd.; Captain and Mrs Vallance; Mr and Mrs Robert Wotherspoon; Mr and Mrs Donald; Mrs Fresson; Colonel Hamilton and Mrs Hamilton; Miss H Barron; Capt. Hayes, Capt. Fresson, Capt. O'Reilly, Capt. MacFarlane, Wing Commander Ralph (all of Scottish Airways); Radio-Officers—Stewart, MacAulay. Crisp and

One of Scottish Airways' great pioneer pilots - Capt. Henry Vallance - who flew throughout WWII with the airline.
(Henry Vallance)

Emerson; Chief Engineer Griffiths and Mrs Griffiths; Mrs O'Reilly, Mrs Hayes, Mrs MacFarlane; Administrative Staff—Mrs McManus and Mrs Chisholm.

Highland Airways Pioneers

Sir Steven Bilsland, after extending a very hearty welcome to the guests said he had particular pleasure in welcoming the ladies of the party. It was a great pleasure to him that this was the first duty he had to perform since the had the honour of being made Chairman of Scottish Airways Ltd. This was a kind of family gathering in relation to an important section of Scottish Airways Ltd. men who had given such distinguished service during the war, and of the pioneers of an important air area - he referred to Mr Donald and Mr Wotherspoon. He was

particularly happy to welcome Col. Hamilton. who had just returned from Italy, after distinguished service there. But they were met particularly to honour a gallant and distinguished pilot of Scottish Airways Ltd.- Capt. Vallance -on whom His Majesty the King had recently conferred the special distinction of his commendation for wartime services. Sir Steven said he wished also to take that opportunity of paying sincere tribute to the pilots, ground staff and also the administrative staff, under the splendid leadership of Capt Fresson, who had maintained that vital service of airways during the six years of war.

Sir Steven had before him a letter from the Minister of Civil Aviation conveying to all of them the appreciation of His Majesty's Government, and a copy of which would be given to each member of the staff.

Guest of the Evening

Proceeding to pay tribute to the guest of the evening, Sir Steven said it was certainly with great pride and pleasure that all of them received the news of the distinction which the King had conferred on Capt. Vallance - an honour which not only reflected great credit on him personally but one that had brought honour to the Company. Capt. Vallance had had very considerable experience as a pilot; he began in 1936, and had nearly 8000 hours flying experience. He joined Scottish in 1938, and now had had over 6000 flying hours' experience with the company. He had built up a fine reputation during that period. Many stories could be told about him, and one very important thing was this - he had a record of regularity almost amounting to 100 per cent.

"That," added Sir Steven, amid applause, "is a remarkable feat when one considers the climatic conditions in these Northern latitudes."

In the early days of the war Capt. Vallance was sent off at very short notice - he hadn't had time to pack his bag—to pilot aircraft to France, bringing munitions etc. He then returned to the service of Scottish Airways, and one of his early experiences was that he encountered a Junker machine in the air, but which he had skillfully 'out-manoeuvred', bringing his full complement of passengers safely to Inverness.

On another occasion Capt. Vallance was sent out at the special request of the Air Ministry to the Hebrides, in order to look after the crew of a merchant ship who had taken to their boats in rough and boisterous seas. There was another occasion, when on an emergency ambulance trip, he had to land on an extreme part of Shetland - the edge of a steep cliff.

These were some of the experiences which had won for Capt Vallance a very high reputation as a pilot, and in the course of his work he had given outstanding service to the Company.

Capt. Fresson's Leadership

"I want to say a word about that team which has done so well under the inspiring and able leadership of Capt. Fresson, all through the war. All of you can take credit for the splendid reputation which has been built up and also for the high standard of efficiency which has been maintained. Scottish Airways in this area have supplied a key service, and very much has depended on the regularity of that service, carrying passengers of first importance and also dealing with matters which all had an extremely important bearing on the war effort. We are very proud of the reputation which has been built up by all of you. You have been maintaining that reputation magnificently throughout the war; the service, notwithstanding difficult climatic conditions, has gone on like clockwork!"

Sir Steven, after reading the letter of appreciation on behalf of the Government, said it was a tribute that had been well earned, and in which all could share - pilots, ground staff and administrative staff.

Future Plans.

Their war job was ending and their peace time job beginning. Very considerable plans were being developed by Scottish Airways which must await various decisions on the part of the Government before they could be put into operation They were anxious to provide the best possible services on the widest scale as early as might be possible to do so. He was a firm believer in the importance of their line assisting in bringing the natural resources and produce of the Highlands to market as speedily and cheaply as possible.

All of them were fully confident of the great importance of air lines in the development of the tourist industry, in which, he hoped, Scottish Airways would have a large share after the war,

"I can assure you that Scottish Airways will do everything possible to promote the development of Scotland and not least that of the Highland Counties. We have a fine team on which to build; this gives us every encouragement, and augurs well for the future.

"To-night we have an outstanding member of that team in Capt. Vallance, to whom we offer our sincere congratulations on the special commendation he has received from His Majesty the King."

Sir Steven Bilsland then asked the company to drink to the health of Capt Vallance. This was done, and before the acknowledgement, the company sang "For he's a jolly good fellow."

Capt. Vallance, in reply, said he had been overwhelmed. If, however, he had maintained a very high percentage of regularity in the Company's service, he felt that considerable credit for that - certainly a great share of it - was due to the radio and engineering staffs. He therefore felt that the honour that had been conferred upon him by H.M. the King embraced the whole Company, and he would like to take that opportunity of thanking all his colleagues for their contribution towards the work which had earned for him this award.

Early Days of Highland Airways.

Sir Steven Bilsland at this stage called upon Mr Donald who, he remarked, had been chairman of Highland Airways in the early days, and one of those who had helped to build up the fine reputation in which Scottish Airways were sharing to-day. Mr Donald was one to whom they owed a great deal as a pioneer of air-lines in Scotland.

In lighter mood Mr Donald recalled the early days and he pointed out that they were not without anxiety - of Highland Airways. His first recollection of civil aviation consisted in flying No. 1 Highland Airways at the Longman, Inverness. Among the highlights of that venture was the contract for the conveyance of His Majesty's mail. In spite of what would now be regarded as a somewhat primitive type of machine they were able to run 95 per cent regularity (and 98 per cent during the

ENSA Concert Tour - members of the Glasgow String Orchestra about to leave Inverness for Stornoway on September 28th 1945 in three Scottish Airways DH Rapides to entertain the troops. (Richard Fresson)

A late acquisition by Scottish Airways, the DH Dragon Rapide G-AGOJ is seen at Renfrew at the end of 1945.
(John Stroud Collection)

summer months) - a very remarkable feat. It made him very proud indeed to hear that Scottish Airways had been able to maintain the regularity which was established by Captain Fresson in the early days of Highland Airways.

In those days, went on Mr Donald, the thing that had impressed most was the very high sense of duty of their pilots, from Captain Fresson and his team; nothing stood in their way of maintaining a regular service. There never was engine failure, and for this they had to thank Mr Griffiths and his ground staff. He (Mr Donald) was certainly proud of his early association with Highland Airways.

Captain Fresson's thanks.

Sir Steven, before calling on Captain Fresson to address the gathering, said they had a fine leader in that gentleman, and he should like to pay tribute to the splendid service that Captain Fresson had given since the beginning of air lines in the North, as well as during the war.

Captain Fresson acknowledged the practical aid provided by Mr Donald and Mr Wotherspoon in ensuring the advent of Highland Airways. Since the war broke out the Northern wing of Scottish Airways had conveyed 2,000 tons of mail for H.M. Forces in Orkney and Shetland, and this had been done with an extraordinary degree of regularity. The job had been well done.

Captain Fresson expressed thanks on behalf of the gathering to all those who had worked so hard for their pleasure that night. They all joined in the congratulations to their friend Captain Vallance whose commendation by the King had been so well earned, he was a very excellent pilot.

Mr Donald and Mr Wotherspoon had been Directors of the Company that had paved the way for Scottish Airways, and he (Captain Fresson) was indebted to these gentlemen for all they had done during the inception of the movement.

Tribute to Sir Steven

Mr Wotherspoon proposed a cordial vote of thanks to Scottish Airways, Ltd., for the provision of a magnificent dinner. On behalf of the gathering he could assure Sir Steven Bilsland and his co-directors of their great appreciation, and they were specially glad to welcome Sir Steven and for presiding at the function. Sir Steven had told them that that was his first appearance since he had been elected chairman of the Board; they sincerely hoped it was but the fore runner of very many visits in their midst. Scottish Airways were singularly fortunate in having as their chairman such a fine advocate of Scottish affairs as Sir Steven Bilsland whose dynamic personality revealed itself wherever he went. He created an enthusiasm that was remarkable and everyone connected with Scottish Airways, from the most junior member of the ground staff, would find it a pleasure to serve under him. Whatever Sir Steven recommended, enthusiasm prevailed and became infectious. To him and his co-directors the gathering recorded their best thanks.

Acknowledging, Sir Steven said it had been a great pleasure to preside at a function in honour of their good friend Captain.Vallance.

"I feel greatly honoured in occupying the position I hold, and I have the interests of every one of you very much at heart," concluded Sir Steven, amid applause.

Labour Government's ideas

But on November 1st 1945 came the bolt from the blue - the Labour Party, victorious since the General Election, issued its intended Civil Aviation policies in Parliament prior to making

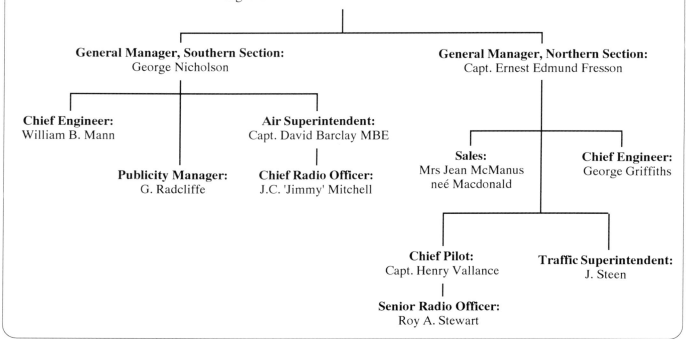

SCOTTISH AIRWAYS LTD.

Organisation - 1945

Chairman:
Sir Steven Bilsland Bt. MC, DL
Directors:
J.W. Ratledge, T.L. Adam, W. P. Bradbury, E. E. Fresson OBE, H.T. Leith,
G. N. Nicholson, Maj. M Speir MC, W. Yeaman, Wing Commander A. H. Measures CBE.
Managing Director
Wing Commander Arthur Harold Measures CBE.

General Manager, Southern Section:
George Nicholson

General Manager, Northern Section:
Capt. Ernest Edmund Fresson

Chief Engineer:
William B. Mann

Air Superintendent:
Capt. David Barclay MBE

Publicity Manager:
G. Radcliffe

Chief Radio Officer:
J.C. 'Jimmy' Mitchell

Sales:
Mrs Jean McManus
neé Macdonald

Chief Engineer:
George Griffiths

Chief Pilot:
Capt. Henry Vallance

Traffic Superintendent:
J. Steen

Senior Radio Officer:
Roy A. Stewart

them into a White Paper. Lord Winster announced that:

"The State will operate all British air transport services, own all airports used for scheduled services, and provide all radio meteorological and air traffic services. Railway and shipping companies will have no financial share in three State-owned Corporations that are to be formed. It is hoped, however, that they will co-operate with the new organisation.

"The three new Corporations will be the British Overseas Airways Corporation (BOAC) operating Commonwealth, North American and Far Eastern services; another for Internal and European routes; and a third for South American Services. Others may be added.

"Prestwick will be designated an international airport.

"The Brabazon Committee will be retained, and existing flying companies will be free to continue only until the new organisation is established.

"Private flying and gliding clubs will not be affected. The ban on private flying will go as from January 1st 1946."

Lord Winster went on to say that all Corporations or Subsidiaries would be financed solely out of Public Funds, and he would take powers to appoint their Boards and to determine such appointments if he ever thought that necessary.

Until the necessary legislation had been made, B.O.A.C. (already in operation since 1940, of course) would continue to be

responsible for all external routes, Lord Winster affirmed. And he said that he would request B.O.A.C. to inaugurate European and S. American routes and operate them - until the other Corporations could be formed.

Next day the newspapers were full of comment about the Labour Government's ideas, and one leader stated:

"DEAD HAND ON AVIATION

Two schemes of nationalisation were announced by the Government last night. One will strangle all enterprise in the development of civil aviation. The other, commented on in more detail in the following leader note, is dangerous to national security.

In some respects the civil flying scheme repeats the broad lines of the Swinton scheme approved by the late Coalition. There will be three 'chosen instruments' with assigned routes of operation. But whereas the Swinton scheme did seek to make use of the experience and knowledge of pre-war and present air operators, and held out to them the inducement of financial rewards for enterprise, the Government proposals jettison the experience and kill the incentive to development.

The North of Scotland and the islands, which are appreciative of the enterprise of the operators who serve them and are looking for still further advantages, will note that their familiar services are to disappear. They will have to take what some large organisation, whose interests will be many, thinks is good enough for them.

In passing, it may be remarked that the terms to be offered to dispossessed operators are infamous. They are to be given only the value of their physical assets, and nothing for goodwill: They have run financial risks to build up that goodwill, but the Socialist Government proposes to step into their businesses and rob them of the fruits of their enterprise.

Cheers greeted the announcement that Prestwick was to be designated an international airport. That is so far satisfactory. Is it to be used as well as designated? No answer to that is found in the statement, which is vague and commits the Government to very little.

"Certain internal services" are to be operated from Prestwick. There is nothing in that; we expect as much for Aberdeen, Inverness, Orkney, Shetland, Lewis, and a dozen other places in Scotland. What matters very much is overseas services. On this, it will be seen, Ministers said nothing at all definite. Unless there is a big and active aviation centre in Scotland, the country will not be able to share in all the benefits, industrial as well as travel, of this great new form of transport.

Scotland was prepared, through private enterprise, to enter overseas and home fields, with Prestwick as the base. That hope is killed by Government policy. The Scottish nation's destiny in the air will be in the power of a handful of bureaucrats in the Ministry of Civil Aviation, which has, until lately kicked and buffeted into realisation, shown itself insensitive to Scotland's needs."

Sir Steven Bilsland told *The Glasgow Herald:*

The Company and its predecessors have been operating Air Services in Scotland from its principal bases at Inverness and Renfrew since 1933 and 1934 respectively and during this time its senior officials (the majority of them have had upwards of 10 years continuous experience) have acquired a considerable knowledge of and experience in day to day problems of aircraft operation.

During the War Years alone from September 1939 to September 1945 the Company's aircraft have flown some 5 million miles and carried upwards of 200,000 fare-paying passengers in addition to considerable quantities of mail and freight, all without injury to passengers.

It may be pointed out that following upon the suspension of all Internal Air Lines on the outbreak of War when the Aircraft and Crews were urgently required for Communication Duties in connection with the transfer of the B.E.F. to France, Scottish Airways was the first Company to resume Regular Air Services and as early as 11th September 1939 the Renfrew - Campbeltown - Islay Route was recommenced, followed the next day by the Inverness - Wick - Kirkwall Service, later extended to Shetland.

With the exception of the Service between Aberdeen - Orkney and Shetland operated by Allied Airways (Gandar Dower) Ltd. these were the only services operating within the United Kingdom until May 1940 when Railway Air Services and its Associated Companies recommenced operations on the Liverpool/Belfast, Liverpool/Dublin, Liverpool/Isle of Man, Glasgow/Belfast and Lands End/Scilly Routes.

The tendency in the Press is to accuse Scottish Operators of lack of initiative and to infer that during the War Years the interests of Scotland so far as Aviation is concerned have been neglected. It is admitted that the resources of Aircraft and personnel made available to Scottish Airways has not enabled them to convey anything like the number of passengers desiring to travel by Air but this complaint may equally be applied to Surface Travel. It is pertinent to point out that during the War Years from September 1939 Scottish Airways has operated over 50% of the total aircraft mileage operated by all Internal Air Lines in the U.K. and has carried over 50% of the total Passengers which having regard to the relative population of Scotland and England is felt to be a not unfavourable proportion. (These figures have been over exaggerated in this report - Ed.).

A further point worthy of note is that in each of the years 1940 to 1945 the annual aircraft mileage operated by the Company has shown a consistent increase and that the Company's aircraft are now operating an Aircraft Mileage at the rate of approximately 1 1/2 million miles per annum and during the three months ended 30th September the monthly passenger carryings averaged between 4/4,500 per month.

There seems a general lack of appreciation of the difficulties with which Internal Air Line Operators have

Inverness line-up - the four 'Northern Section' D.H. Dragon Rapides in use in late 1944 seen in front of their hangars on the Longman aerodrome. The aircraft closest to the camera is G-AGIC. (John Stroud Collection)

Another picture of the islanders from North Ronaldsay climbing aboard the Scottish Airways D.H. Rapide G-AGJG at the end of WWII to take their produce to Kirkwall market. (DH/BAe)

had to contend in the U.K, competing as they were with fast and comfortable Railway Services and the fact that the distances between major centres of population are not great. Until the War, Aerodromes were relatively few and it was only a few enlightened local authorities who saw fit to give any encouragement to Operators who were unsubsidised until the moderate subsidy was received from the Government early in 1939. On the outbreak of War, Scottish Airways were operating to 19 Aerodromes and Landing Grounds in Scotland, 15 of which had been developed at their own expense and of these 15, 7 have now been enlarged and extended by the Government into first class Aerodromes with concrete or tar macadam runways. But for the earlier development work of Scottish Airways in the Western Isles, Orkney and Shetland, the defence of the Western Approaches would have been much more difficult following upon the Fall of France."

Scottish Airways had many friends in the North, and in London, who rallied around now to protest and lobby on its behalf against the proposed Nationalisation. The Labour Government also proposed to nationalise the Railway companies as well (into 'British Railways') so the future of the airlines in an independent role would have meant a complex severing of their organisations from their previous Railway masters - but the RAS Group plan had envisaged taking up all the internal routes again and opening many more all across Europe, without subsidy. The country could have had a large independent and profitable airline - perhaps. But only if it had been managed by people like George Nicholson and Ted Fresson. What it was about to get was something very different, run by people who had not been through the furnace of tough, day-to-day profit-making scheduled airlines and were used only to Service - style administration and waste - and grandiose ideas.

George Nicholson did his share of lobbying in Glasgow but Ted Fresson up in Inverness took up the cudgels in a bigger - and much more Public - way. By now, he and his longtime competitor in Aberdeen, Eric Gandar Dower (owner of Allied Airways Ltd) were acting together to fight the prospect of nationalisation. Gandar Dower himself had just been elected

M.P. for Caithness and Sutherland, and had a brother, Alan Vincent Gandar Dower, who was already an MP. Between the two of them they could muster some Tory support in the House against the Labour Government.

Thus, Eric Gandar Dower had made a speech in October in the House, saying:

"The subject before this House is one which I have very much at heart. I think it is usual to make known one's interest in any particular industry and therefore I must confess that I have been operating an air line for eleven years. But I approach the subject as a Member of this House and as a lover of the whole wonderful idea of shortening communications throughout the world and persuading people to travel in comfort and safety about the globe. This indeed is not a party matter. If only I could persuade the House that the development of civil aviation is beyond all party politics.

"It is a heritage which this country cannot stand to throw away because of any bickering between sides in this House. I sat in the Public Gallery and listened to Debate after Debate on civil aviation before I had the honour to become a Member of this House and I always went away with grievous disappointment that politics had interfered with it.

"I plead that the Government will interfere as little as possible with the development of civil aviation. It should be given its own head. The Government should interfere only if there are signs of unreliability, profiteering or unfair employment of staff. I hope that the delay which the Government have shown on the production of their policy is due to the fact that they are studying the various excellent reports submitted to the late Minister of Civil Aviation by knowledgeable bodies.

"I would ask the Minister who had undertaken the responsible task of organising the future of air transport to limit his responsibilities as far as possible to safety, to the conditions under which staff are employed and to the restoration of the Air Transport Licensing Authority .

"Aviation possesses one unique quality. No one who has anything to do with it ever wishes to give it up."

Ted Fresson, meanwhile, after hearing the Labour Party's intention on November 1st, made an appointment to see Lord Winster himself, on behalf of Scottish Airways. After that meeting Ted said:

"He assured me that insofar as Scottish Airways were concerned, they would remain as a Scottish Division under the State Corporation to be formed for the operation of the British and European air routes, and he again told me my position would be secure in view of the valuable services Scottish Airways had provided throughout the war. He requested me to do all I could to bring about successful transition from war time to peace time operations. I left him, thinking that perhaps after all, State Control could be made to work, but I failed to take into account the scheming and jockeying for power which eventually reared its ugly head and the type of individual who would hold control against which there would be no appeal.

"Not so long after my interview with Lord Winster, he resigned his appointment as Air Minister and he was replaced by an individual who was not so appreciative of the work performed by our company!"

Two weeks later, Ted received a letter from Sir Steven Bilsland that said:

"I had a meeting in London last week with Sir Harold Hartley to discuss the situation created by the Minister's speech on 1st November.

"The position is that we will continue to operate our services until the new organisation has been formed. Furthermore, it is important that we should not relax our efforts in any way to develop and advertise our services and to ask for any additional aircraft that are needed to meet public demand. The Director General of Civil Aviation told Sir Harold, that he would welcome any suggestions from us as to new routes.

"With regard to capital expenditure, it has been arranged that any new aircraft for which we have not already paid be hired, and the terms of hire are to be negotiated.

"With regard to other schemes of urgent development involving capital expenditure, Sir Harold has asked me to put them up to him without delay, so that they may be discussed at the Ministry.

"We will be discussing the whole position at our meeting on 30th November, (namely Scottish Airways' Board Meeting)."

In fact, apart from discussion at that Board Meeting, there was little else that could be done - except to go on lobbying the Government.

Ted continued to do most of the lobbying for himself and George Nicholson - both men now distinctly feeling that their combined Scottish Airways company set up and existing through the fruits of their very hard-earned expertise was being left out in the cold, and forgotten by the big guns that were duelling it out in London and Westminster. In fact they felt they were really becoming very much a side-show.

Ted then made a speech at an Aberdeen Rotarian lunch on January 8th 1946, which was reported next day in the *Press & Journal*:

"Captain E.E. Fresson, pioneer of Civil Aviation in Scotland wants a petition asking the Scottish Secretary to intercede for a separate Division to operate airways in Scotland within the framework of the Corporation proposed for European and internal routes. Now is the time for such a move by municipalities, Chambers of Commerce and other business organisations, he told the Aberdeen Rotary Club yesterday. Suggesting the present Companies should be the basis of such an Organisation, he remarked that other claims in this direction savoured of; "You've grown the plums and we are now going to eat them". Others who claimed the right for themselves had never to his knowledge, run an air service in Scotland. They had had the same opportunities as the pioneers of 1933-39, but had not seized them.

Captain Fresson got a resounding "Hear, hear", from his Rotarian audience when he declared that Government Policy should develop along the lines of a Scottish Division within the greater Corporation, rather than absorb the present organisations into a Corporation with its headquarters in London, and with no special interest in or knowledge of, Scottish needs.

Advocating that Scottish Airways and Allied

Photographed at Inverness towards the end of the war, Scottish Airways' Rapide G-AGIC clearly shows the wartime camouflage scheme and registration letters underlined in red, white and blue.

An evocative picture of Scottish Airways' DH Dragon Rapide G-AGJF on the beach airstrip at Barra's North Bay, just below the high water mark. (John Stroud Collection)

Airways should be the backbone of such an Organisation, he pointed out that they had pioneered, maintained and developed a large network of routes over the past thirteen years. They had plans and facilities for considerably enlarging their post-war operations. They held mail contracts. They had an experienced and specialised staff who knew every rock in Scotland. What had been achieved, he emphasised, has been done successfully by individual effort which gave a man drive to work twenty four hours a day, if necessary. It gave him a pull, over any organisation swamped in some big undertaking."

Scottish Airways, and in particular the Northern Section, received considerable support from all quarters for this plea - from Provosts of all the towns served, to businesses and chambers of commerce. Gandar Dower continued his attacking speeches in the House, saying:

"I feel sure that the pioneers of air transport have never felt so downcast as at this moment. The Government policy as set out in this White Paper is the last of a line of bitter disappointments. Commercial air transport has proved to be an industry wrecked by circumstances outside its control. It suffered at its birth by becoming a stepchild of the Secretary of State for Air. It was put out to nurse under directors often chosen for their lack of nuisance value. It was many years before those directors were dignified by the name of "Director-General," and further time lapsed before the position was considered worthy of knighthood. Placing air transport under a Minister chiefly interested in the Royal Air Force was comparable to employing the Admiralty to develop a healthy mercantile marine. Between 1934 and 1939 air transport was held back by

preparations for war, and during six years of war there has been no chance of natural development. Finally, when it could enjoy its first opportunity the Government suggest that the pent-up energy of the individual should be thrown away and the dead hand of public ownership substituted!

"British air transport, as we have heard on all sides, is too young for such treatment. The Government are stealing a child from the nursery. Whatever may be thought of nationalisation, the Government would be incapable of running anything but a well-established industry. I think it is admitted by all of us that British air transport is vital to the prosperity of the nation. It is also essential to the Empire, which will lean towards those countries which can provide the quickest and the best facilities for contact and trade. I believe that if Parliament had left British civil aviation alone, greater progress would have resulted. Instead, it has been organised and re-organised, it has had this Paper and that, and Commission after Commission reporting on its welfare. There has been no continuity of policy, and its leading personnel, I can truly say, have often been driven to despair."

And Eric advocated:

"We cannot do better than adopt and improve on the American system. It has 19 prosperous airlines providing air transport at five cents per passenger mile and operating without subsidy. It has three companies flying the Atlantic at the same time. While we talk, they succeed. Why? Because America leaves air transport to businessmen."

Scottish Airways' Rapide G-AGLE taxying out at Renfrew after World War Two .(John Stroud Collection)

He went on:

"Scotland has every claim to control its own Air Transport by a separate Corporation or by a powerful subsidiary to the proposed British European unit. Scotland wishes to operate her own domestic and international airlines. Scotland can point out that long before England was air-minded, she was pioneering air routes which have proved uniformly successful. They have operated throughout the war when few, if any, internal airlines have run in England. For years, passengers, who have never seen a railway train, have been flying on the Scottish airlines.

"I should like to pay tribute to pioneers such as Mr John Sword, who opened the routes from Glasgow to Campbeltown and Islay, to Captain Fresson, who formed Highland Airways and connected the Orkneys to the mainland, obtaining the first air mail contract in Great Britain, and Mr George Nicholson who took over the Glasgow services and extended them to additional Western Islands. I would also draw attention to those air-minded steamship companies Messrs. MacBraynes and the North of Scotland, Orkney and Shetland, which have assisted in developing Scottish air transport."

1945-46 Winter Schedules

The airline had to continue operating as usual during all this political decision making that was going on, of course, and so the 1945-46 Winter schedules commenced on October 8th 1945.

From this date the use of Sollas Aerodrome on North Uist was discontinued for all time - the state of the grass fields there was not at all good (rather like Thurso's Claredon aerodrome which Ted Fresson thought extremely poor). Wick had not yet been reinstated, but the Western Isles' services stayed at nine weekly, with the direct services to Stornoway from Renfrew now on Monday, Wednesday and Friday, doubling up on a Renfrew - Tiree - Stornoway service on the same days (both flights left Renfrew at 09.00). On the alternate days the 09.00 departure from Renfrew operated via Tiree and Benbecula to Stornoway.

The airline's new town terminal was Central Station - no longer the "Grosvenor" restaurant in Gordon Street (quaint as this idea had been!). The rest of the services continued much as they had in Summer 1945 and Scottish Airways continued to operate the Renfrew - Croydon and Renfrew - Belfast services on behalf of Railway Air Services.

Fares to London were £9 single, and £14. 10s. 0d. return, and to Belfast £2. 10s. 0d. single, £4. return.

Trials with Avro XIX aircraft

On January 20th 1945, Railway Air Services had taken delivery via the AAJC of a new Avro 652A Anson Mk XIX feeder liner, G-AGNI, for a short-term lease to see if the type was worth buying in quantity. Eventually starting later in the year, a series of orders were placed with A. V. Roe & Co for a final total of 14 Avro XIXs in all. This Anson was in fact a Mk XII, MG159, built for the RAF but converted to represent a nine-seat feeder liner to conform to the Brabazon Committee's XIX Feeder-liner specification. While at Liverpool on February 17th 1945, Capt Bill Baillie of Scottish Airways practised some lightweight landings on it to give George Nicholson a report on its suitability for eventual use.

The first production Avro XIX Series 1 to be built by Avros, G-AGPG, was flown up to Renfrew on September 24th 1945, where David Barclay was given a conversion course on it by Capt. John Michie, one of David's pilots in Scottish Airways who had himself been earlier shown how to fly the Avro XIX by the maker's test-pilots. David eventually flew it for 9 hours 15 minutes altogether up to October 9th, and was then checked out on 'GPG as fully converted to the larger metal aircraft. Bill Baillie flew it too, on September 28th and October 8th, making more 'lightly-loaded' landings on it on the former date and some 'heavily-loaded' landings on the latter occasion.

In October, the Southern Section fleet now consisted of Rapides G-AFFF, 'FOI, 'GIF, 'GJF, 'GLE, 'ERN, 'GLR, and a newcomer G-AGOJ which arrived on October 17th 1945. G-AFRK was also back in action by December 22nd and another Rapide, G-AGUR joined the fleet on January 12th 1946. Rapide 'GOJ had come from De Havilland's repair base at Witney after being converted from an RAF machine (NR774), and 'GUR was converted by the Brush Co. from ex-RAF NR846, both being registered first with Scottish Airways.

SCOTTISH AIRWAYS LTD.

SUMMER TIME TABLE 1946

Effective 15th April, 1946, until further notice

E.T. 14

FARES, EXCESS BAGGAGE & FREIGHT RATES

	Single	Return	Excess Baggage and Freight per lb.
GLASGOW to—			
Campbeltown	27/6	49/6	2½d.
Islay	38/6	71/6	3d.
Tiree	60/-	105/-	4d.
Barra	90/-	170/-	5d.
Benbecula	90/-	170/-	5d.
North Uist	90/-	170/-	5d.
Stornoway	90/-	170/-	6d.
Inverness	50/-	85/-	4d.
Wick	85/-	150/-	5d.
Kirkwall	95/-	170/-	6d.
Lerwick	120/-	210/-	8d.
TIREE to—			
Benbecula	55/-	110/-	4d.
North Uist	55/-	110/-	4d.
Stornoway	80/-	160/-	5d.
BARRA to—			
Benbecula	27/6	55/-	4d.
BENBECULA to—			
North Uist	22/-	44/-	4d.
Stornoway	52/-	94/-	4d.
NORTH UIST to—			
Stornoway	30/-	50/-	4d.
INVERNESS to—			
Wick	38/6	66/-	3d.
Kirkwall	55/-	99/-	4d.
Lerwick	88/-	154/-	6d.
Stornoway	50/-	90/-	4d.
WICK to—			
Kirkwall	30/-	60/-	2d.
Lerwick	77/-	143/-	4d.
KIRKWALL to—			
Lerwick	55/-	99/-	4d.

Freight Rates.—Minimum charge 2/- per package.

CHILDREN

Children under 3 years of age accompanied by an adult and not occupying a seat are carried free ; three years of age and under seven, and younger children occupying a seat, half-fare ; seven years and under fourteen, two-thirds fare ; fourteen years of age and over, adult fare.

H.M. AND ALLIED FORCES AND MEMBERS OF THE MERCHANT NAVY

H.M. Forces and Members of Allied Forces are allowed a fare rebate of 10 per cent. if travelling in uniform or on presentation of a certificate establishing membership. Members of the Merchant Navy are also allowed a similar concession on production of their Mercantile Marine Identity Card. Such bookings require to be effected directly with the Company at one of its offices or at any Railway Station or Office.

NOTES TO SERVICE 5

*BARRA—Subject to tide and weather.
A—Passengers from Barra to Glasgow change at Benbecula.
B—10 a.m. southbound service ex Stornoway calls at Benbecula on request with passengers for Barra only. No Benbecula bookings by this service.
*NORTH UIST—Service suspended until further notice.

The front cover (left) and rear cover of Scottish Airways' last time-table in its illustrious career - the summer of 1946.
(John Stroud Collection)

Summer 1946 - Avro XIXs and Dakotas

The Summer 1946 schedule was introduced from April 15th and for this last 'Swan song' that Scottish Airways would enjoy, the Campbeltown schedule went to a three times daily again (except Sunday), Islay went to twice daily, non-stop; and the Hebrides network went up to (a) Renfrew - Stornoway (non-stop) daily except Sunday at 09.30, and additionally on Mon., Wed., and Fri., at 13.15 out of Glasgow; (b) Renfrew - Tiree - Benbecula - Barra (subject to tide and weather) - Benbecula (again) - Stornoway; (c) Renfrew - Tiree, on Tue., Thur., and Sat. only.

The Glasgow - Inverness link was re-introduced again (daily except Sunday),but omitting the call at Perth, continuing up to Kirkwall and Sumburgh; there were non-stop daily (except Sunday) services from Inverness to Kirkwall and Sumburgh; and a stopping service Inverness - Wick - Kirkwall again daily except Sunday.

Finally, Inverness - Stornoway went daily, (except Sunday) for the first time, and Scottish Airways continued to operate the Renfrew - Belfast (Sydenham, or Harbour Airport) service three times daily now, and the Renfrew - Croydon (non-stop) service once daily each way, with new Avro XIX aircraft. However, in May, specially checked-out Scottish Airways' pilots took over the Belfast and Croydon services with three 20-seater Douglas C-47A Dakotas (G-AGZA, 'GZB and 'GYZ) delivered to Railway Air Services. The Belfast route stayed at three services a day, and Croydon stayed at once daily - (This was now the longest non-stop service in the UK).

Bill Baillie had been the first Scottish Airways' pilot to convert onto the C-47As, starting a course of instruction under the tuition of Capt. Nigel Pelly (of Midland & Scottish Air

SCOTTISH AIRWAYS LIMITED

Time Table — commencing 15th April, 1946, until further notice

SERVICE 1

GLASGOW—INVERNESS—WICK—KIRKWALL—SHETLAND
Daily Except Sundays
NORTHBOUND

			a.m.	a.m.	a.m.	p.m.
GLASGOW—Central Station	...	dep.	—	—	—	12.40
Renfrew Airport	...	dep.	—	—	—	1.10
INVERNESS—Airport	...	arr.	—	—	—	2.20
Station Square	...	arr.	—	—	—	2.30
Station Square	...	dep.	8.40	9.00	11.50	2.15
					p.m.	
Airport	...	dep.	9.00	9.25	12.10	2.35
WICK—Airport	...	arr.	—	—	12.55	—
Station Hotel	...	arr.	—	—	1.20	—
Station Hotel	...	dep.	—	—	12.45	—
Airport	...	dep.	—	—	1.10	—
KIRKWALL—Airport	...	arr.	—	10.30	1.30	3.40
7 Broad Street	...	arr.	—	10.50	1.50	4.00
7 Broad Street	...	dep.	—	—	—	3.25
Airport	...	dep.	—	—	—	3.55
SHETLAND—Airport]	...	arr.	10.50	—	—	4.40
Queen's and Grand			p.m.			
Hotels, Lerwick	...	arr.	12.00	—	—	5.50

SOUTHBOUND

			a.m.	a.m.	a.m.	p.m.
SHETLAND—Queen's and Grand						
Hotels, Lerwick	...	dep.	8.00	9.50	—	—
Airport	...	dep.	9.00	11.05	—	—
KIRKWALL—Airport	...	arr.	9.45	—	—	—
7 Broad Street	...	arr.	10.05	—	—	—
7 Broad Street	...	dep.	9.30	—	10.15	1.15
Airport	...	dep.	10.00	—	10.45	1.45
WICK—Airport	...	arr.	—	—	—	2.05
Station Hotel	...	arr.	—	—	—	2.30
Station Hotel	...	dep.	—	—	—	1.55
Airport	...	dep.	—	p.m	—	2.20
INVERNESS—Airport	...	arr.	11.05	12.50	11.50	3.05
					p.m.	
Station Square	...	arr.	11.15	1.00	12.00	3.15
Station Square	...	dep.	11.00	—	—	—
Airport	...	dep.	11.20	—	—	—
			p.m			
GLASGOW—Renfrew Airport	...	arr.	12.30	—	—	—
Central Station	...	arr.	1.00	—	—	—

SERVICE 2

INVERNESS—STORNOWAY
Daily Except Sundays
WESTBOUND

							a.m.
INVERNESS—Station Square	...	...	...	...	...	dep.	9.40
Airport	...	...	...	...	...	dep.	10.00
STORNOWAY—Airport	...	...	...	...	...	arr.	10.50
Town Hall	...	...	...	...	...	arr.	11.10

EASTBOUND

							a.m.
STORNOWAY—Town Hall	...	...	...	...	...	dep.	10.40
Airport	...	...	...	...	...	dep.	11.10
							p.m.
INVERNESS—Airport	...	...	...	...	...	arr.	12.00
Station Square	...	...	...	...	...	arr.	12.10

GLASGOW—LONDON and GLASGOW—BELFAST
Operated in association with RAILWAY AIR SERVICES LIMITED.
See separate TIME TABLE.

SERVICE 3

GLASGOW—CAMPBELTOWN
Daily Except Sundays
WESTBOUND

			a.m.	pm.	p.m.
GLASGOW—Central Station	...	dep.	8.50	1.00	4.20
Renfrew Airport	...	dep.	9.25	1.40	4.55
CAMPBELTOWN—Airport	...	arr.	10.00	2.15	5.30
Royal Hotel	...	arr.	10.30	2.45	6.00

EASTBOUND

			a.m.	p.m.	p.m.
CAMPBELTOWN—Royal Hotel	...	dep.	9.30	1.45	5.00
Airport	...	dep.	10.15	2.30	5.45
GLASGOW—Renfrew Airport	...	arr.	10.50	3.05	6.20
Central Station	...	arr.	11.20	3.35	6.50

SERVICE 4

GLASGOW—ISLAY
Daily Except Sundays
WESTBOUND

					a.m.	p.m.
GLASGOW—Central Station	...	...	...	dep.	10.25	3.40
Renfrew Airport	...	...	...	dep.	11.05	4.15
ISLAY—Airport	...	...	...	arr.	11.55	5.05

EASTBOUND

					p.m.	p.m.
ISLAY—Airport	...	...	...	dep.	12.10	5.25
GLASGOW—Renfrew Airport	...	...	...	arr.	1.00	6.15
Central Station	...	...	...	arr.	1.30	6.50

SERVICE 5 GLASGOW—HEBRIDES—STORNOWAY
NORTHBOUND

			Daily except Suns.	Daily except Suns.	Mons., Weds. & Fris. only	Tues., Thurs. & Sats. only
			a.m.	a.m.	p.m.	p.m.
GLASGOW—Central Station	dep.		8.25	8.50	12.40	12.40
Renfrew Airport	dep.		9.05	9.30	1.15	1.20
TIREE—Airport	...	arr.	10.05	—	—	2.20
Airport	...	dep.	10.20	—	—	—
BENBECULA—Airport	...	arr.	11.05	—	—	—
Airport	...	dep.	11.20	—	—	—
BARRA*	...	arr.	11.40	—	—	—
		dep.	11.50	—	—	—
			p.m.			
BENBECULA—Airport	...	arr.	12.10	—	—	—
Airport	...	dep.	12.50	—	—	—
NORTH UIST*	...		—	—	—	—
STORNOWAY—Airport	...	arr.	1.40	11.30	3.15	—
Town Hall	...	arr.	1.55	11.50	3.30	—

SOUTHBOUND

			Daily except Suns.	Daily except Suns.	Mons., Weds. & Fris. only	Tues., Thurs. & Sats. only
			a.m.	a.m.	p.m.	p.m.
STORNOWAY—Town Hall	dep.		9.30	11.25	3.00	—
Airport	...	dep.	10.00B	12.00	3.30	—
					p.m.	
NORTH UIST*	...	arr.	—	—	—	—
BENBECULA—Airport	...	arr.	10.50B	12.50	—	—
Airport	...	dep.	—	1.05	—	—
BARRA*	...	arr.	11.40B	a.m.	—	—
		dep.	—	11.50A	—	—
				p.m.		
TIREE—Airport	...	arr.	—	1.50	—	—
Airport	...	dep.	p.m.	2.05	—	2.35
GLASGOW—Renfrew Airport	arr.		12.00	3.05	5.30	3.35
Central Station	arr.		12.30	3.35	6.00	4.05

* SEE NOTES AT FOOT OF NEXT PAGE

ALL SERVICES SUBJECT TO ALTERATION OR CANCELLATION WITHOUT NOTICE

The Summer 1946 schedules operated by Scottish Airways - its last full season prior to nationalisation. (John Stroud Collection)

Ferries' fame, and later BOAC) at Liverpool on April 15th 1946. Bill had flown G-AGZB throughout April at Liverpool (Speke) and Renfrew, not merely for his own benefit but to help train the navigator that had now to be carried on these aircraft !

On April 30th Bill had actually flown one of RAS's new Avro XIXs, G-AGUE, on the Renfrew - Croydon - Renfrew non-stop day return service and again on May 3rd. Then it was back on the C-47As in May, instructing his colleagues Capt. Donald Prentice, and Capts. Martin, Ramsden and MacKenzie how to fly the C-47A, G-AGZB.

On May 11th Bill positioned the second C-47A, G-AGZA from Liverpool via Belfast (Sydenham) to Renfrew to get ready for starting the Renfrew - Belfast schedule (taking over from the Rapides). Both 'GZA and 'GZB were now at Renfrew and on May 12th Bill gave a special publicity flight for the Glasgow Press around the City and its shipyards.

The Renfrew - Belfast inaugural flight on the new C-47A Dakotas was flown by Bill Baillie on Monday May 13th 1946, in G-AGZA. The roundtrip took a mere 1hr 30 mins. and Bill took

out a party of 20, including Lord Provost Hector McNeill of Glasgow, and Sir Stephen Bilsland (the airline's Chairman). Next day Tuesday, May 14th Bill flew the first 'proving' flight on the C-47A G-AGZA from Renfrew to Croydon and back, in 4hrs. 25 mins. (the Avro XIX took 5hrs 15 mins). But Bill left the official 'inaugural' to be flown by another pilot on Monday May 20th. On that same day Bill flew all three roundtrips Renfrew - Belfast - Renfrew on the C-47A 'GZA, and this became a regular feature of his !

These Dakotas were based at Renfrew and maintained by Bill Mann, Chief Engineer of Scottish Airways. For the first time, Stewardesses were employed on board to look after the passengers and serve light refreshments. One of Ted Fresson's young traffic assistants from Inverness, Miss Robina ("Bobbie") Christie, transferred down to Renfrew to become one of the first such stewardesses (John Sword's airline, Midland & Scottish Air Ferries Ltd. had been the first scheduled operator in Scotland to use female stewardesses - back on August 22nd 1933).

David Barclay, now the Air Superintendent of the Southern

Left: A snapshot of Henry Vallance and his Radio Officer exiting Railway Air Services' Avro XIX G-AGUE, possibly at Croydon. (Henry Vallance)

Below: Seen at A.V. Roe's Yeadon factory prior to delivery, are Railway Air Services' three new Avro XIXs G-AGUX, 'GUE and 'GUD. (A.V. Roe and Co. Ltd)

Below left: Also used on Scottish Airways' routes with Scottish Airways' crews, were Railway Air Services' Dakotas. Here one such aircraft runs up its engines in preparation to leave Renfrew on 29th May 1946. (John Stroud Collection)

Section at Renfrew, did not himself convert onto the new C-47A Dakotas, for a very simple reason - with his shortened leg (from the crash at Hatston), and the force needed on the rudder pedals in the 'asymmetric engine' case, he found it too painful for him to sustain for long, and regretfully therefore stuck with his beloved Dragon Rapides. He did however, fly the Rapide G-AGLP up to Renfrew on April 17th 1946 from its overhaul at Liverpool, and starting on May 1st he had to instruct several new pilots on the Rapides, as his older ones had elected to be converted to the C-47As. One was called Affleck, one Fittall and another Stephens.

David in fact, found himself on instructional duties, and flying charters and air ambulance services through this last summer, and in fact did little line flying except for short trips to Tiree, Belfast or Campbeltown and back.

The Drama Unfolds

The political moves meanwhile, were still taking place to determine the future of UK civil aviation, and on April 2nd 1946, George Nicholson and Ted Fresson had to attend a meeting at Renfrew, in the Scottish Flying Club, with the new heads of BEA - Sir Harold Hartley (ex-Chairman of Railway Air Services) and Gerard d'Erlanger (ex-Air Transport Auxiliary and now back in his peacetime role as a Merchant Banker). Ted Fresson sensed that d'Erlanger was hostile towards him - probably for the lobbying he was conducting - and turned out to be correct in his estimation.

Then, on April 10th, Ivor Thomas, Parliamentary Secretary to the Minister of Aviation, made a statement in the House confirming that 'no existing airline companies in Scotland will be used in the Government air corporation to be set up. But staffs of all companies which were operating on November 1st 1946, will be offered employment in the new corporation on conditions of service not less favourable that those under which they have been previously employed'.

On May 16th 1946 the Civil Aviation Bill started to go through the Committee stages in the House and next day, May 16th, in the debate in the House, Eric Gandar Dower tried to push through an amendment seeking to set up a Fourth Corporation to service exclusively Scottish Aviation (together with the other three - BOAC, BSAA and BEA).

"I speak as an Englishman", he said, "a somewhat unusual person—half kilt, half trousers—who has emigrated to Scotland —and to Aberdeen of all places—to make (or lose) a living!

"After 16 years, I have been able to see how steadily England denies opportunity to Scotland.

"Scotland deserves its own separate Corporation on the airline pioneering alone. Scottish airlines began in 1933. To Scotland was awarded the first airmail contract. It fell to Scottish airline companies to face not only a loss on pioneering a new form of transport, but to build aerodromes and landing grounds along routes".

However, his pleas fell on deaf ears, and he was defeated by 27 votes to 16. Ivor Thomas' only concession was to say that a special Scottish Air Advisory Committee would be set up to act as a watchdog in Scottish aviation matters. Symptomatic of the way things were proceeding, was the fact that whilst Eric was actually uttering these words in the House, Ministry of Civil Aviation and Air Ministry officials were meeting at Dyce itself to discuss proposals for the airport's future—yet no-one had invited Eric— the original founder—to attend ! The Ministry regarded the entire land to be now "State-owned" or "Requisitioned" for their purposes!

In June 1946, Ted Fresson, on Scottish Airways' behalf, flew some County Council Surveyors to map out new, larger airstrips in the Orkney outer isles. They completed surveying such sites on North Ronaldsay, Stronsay, Sanday and Westray, obtaining three strips of 500-700 yards for use on each site (against the 400 yards or so in use previously). In between ferrying the surveyors back and forth to Hatston aerodrome, Kirkwall, Ted also flew a scientist, Mr Woodward, around the island shores in the Dragon G-ACIT, prospecting the best sites for seaweed collection . This project was for a company to use extracts of seaweed for making plastics—a new industry at that time.

Ted's survey for new airfields was approved by his Board in Glasgow, as was an estimate of £7,500 to put them into being (mostly levelling costs)—but when the matter was put up to higher level in BEA, the answer came back—not interested! And so the outer isles waited a long time after that until Loganair finally re-started scheduled inter-island air services again.

SCOTTISH AIRWAYS LIMITED.

PASSENGER & BAGGAGE LIST.

AIRCRAFT.. DATE *16/5/46* TIME *12-20*

FROM................*WICK*.................. TO..........*Inverness*..........

No.	NAME OF PASSENGER	TICKET NUMBER	Passengers Weight lbs.	No. of BAGS	WEIGHT OF BAGGAGE lbs.	EXCESS Charged lbs.	EXCESS Amount £ s. d.
1	*M.F. Stevenson*	*R61550*	*154*	*2*	*24*		
2							

At this time Ted heard of BEA's plans to operate three different types of aircraft on Scottish routes—all with too few back-up spares, non-interchangeable in passenger capacity, and hopelessly more expensive than the Rapides! And then he heard of the plan to allocate ex German wartime Junkers Ju 52/3m troop carriers to Scotland! After trying out a Ju52 at Renfrew with the Southern Section's Chief Pilot David Barclay, Ted branded them as wholly uneconomical in the projected 14-seat layout, with very unreliable BMW 450 hp radial engines (that had been produced for wartime use and a maximum 'life' of 100 hours only). He suggested if BEA must use them, to fit American Pratt & Whitney "Wasp" radials instead. No one took heed, and the Junkers were converted to BEA use at a cost (Ted later recollected) of £12,000 each—and soon proved their unreliability!

Also this Summer, the airline "unions" began rearing their ugly heads. A Pilot's Union and others representing the Engineers and Radio Operators made approaches about flying in the high winds in the North, or working overlong hours—but Ted merely rebuffed them, saying "what do you expect, up here?"

Later that Autumn, on October 7th 1946, Ted's Northern Section finally opened up the Aberdeen-Inverness sector of the new "through service" to Stornoway (which had been operating only from Inverness since it started in May 1944). This was the last new route it was to start under private enterprise. By the end of 1946, Ted's Inverness Division had carried 28,000 passengers (compared with 13,200 in 1945), and made a profit of £8,000 for the year. They would have doubled that in 1947, but Nationalisation was now about to take over in earnest, and there would be no more profits in the North until 40 years later!

So the last successful year of Scottish Airways' operations in the North ended on an all-time "high".

BEA formed; London - Glasgow - Aberdeen service.

On August 1st 1946 the Civil Aviation Act 1946 received Royal Assent, and on the same day British European Airways Corporation was established under the Act to provide civil air services in Europe and the British Isles and certain other parts of the world.

Sir Harold Hartley as its first Chairman then started to develop its European services, while he allowed the domestic services to continue, but being flown now 'on behalf of BEA'.

From September 2nd 1946, the Renfrew - London services were transferred to Northolt aerodrome (near which was BEA's new HQ at Ruislip). And on November 18th 1946 Scottish Airways' Dakota pilots began to operate a new Northolt - Renfrew - Aberdeen service.

Capt. Bill Baillie flew the Dakota G-AGZA from Renfrew to Aberdeen on Friday November 15th on a proving flight, taking George Nicholson with him, and on arrival at Dyce they met Ted Fresson who had flown over from Inverness in his DH Dragon G-ACIT. They then went into the City for a special Press Luncheon to announce the start on the following Monday (the 18th) of the actual service - often heralded in the past, long-awaited, but

never yet instigated.

George Nicholson told the Press that the service via Glasgow was only temporary, as eventually, when Edinburgh's Turnhouse aerodrome had civil facilities built there, the east coast route would then be used. Ted told them that the timings would be improved later on - as the present service didn't leave Dyce until after lunch ! After the lunch, was over, Bill Baillie flew George back to Renfrew.

On Sunday November 17th Bill positioned the Dakota 'GZA down to Northolt to start the service, and on Monday the 18th he flew it on the inaugural flight, Northolt - Renfrew - Aberdeen (Dyce), and then 'slipped' at Renfrew on the return, leaving another crew to go down to London with it.

Another bunch of pilots joined Scottish Airways at the beginning of these Winter schedules, including Capts. Day, Hadley, Woodward, Starling, Leask, and McDermott. Mostly they were to fill the gaps caused by the older Renfrew pilots gravitating south now to fly for the new BEA on international services out of Northolt, or on their Dakota fleet based there.

The accident at Milngavie

There were two accidents that clouded the otherwise excellent safety record of Scottish Airways Ltd during its last year of independent operations. One was fatal and involved passengers as well, and the other was non-fatal, only involved company personnel - but was absolutely unique in many ways.

The fatal one happened on Friday, September 27th 1946 at 13.30 hrs to the veteran Dragon Rapide G-AFFF, on its return flight to Renfrew from Islay. It was being flown by Capt. F. Stephens, D.F.C. aged 27, who had served during the war as a bomber pilot with the Royal Australian Air Force in England, flying Wellingtons, Stirlings and Lancaster bombers. After demob, he returned to Australia to fly with Australian National Airways as the second-pilot on Dakotas, but later came back to Liverpool to join the AAJC pilot's pool in August 1946, flying Rapides. He started a job with Scottish Airways on September 17th, and his wife had just moved up to Glasgow with him.

The Radio Officer in 'FFF was A. M. Calvert, of Inverness Street, Glasgow, a highly efficient and experienced wartime wireless operator in the RAF, aged 26. He had joined Scottish in December 1945, and had married a Belgian girl shortly after the liberation of Belgium.

The circumstances of the accident were unusual and very unfortunate, because they involved confusion with another aircraft of Scottish Airways (Rapide G-ADAJ) in the Renfrew area at the same time. As recounted in the Report (No C467) of the Accidents Investigation Branch of the Ministry of Civil Aviation, dated November 25th 1946, the events were:-

"The Rapide G-AFFF took off from Port Ellen, Islay at 12.26 hrs on a scheduled return flight to Renfrew. At 12.59 hrs it arrived in the vicinity of Renfrew and the pilot signalled Control that he was flying above cloud at 7,000ft and was winding in his trailing aerial. A weather report was passed to the aircraft at 13.02 hrs, and a series of Q.D.M.'s (magnetic course to steer, to reach the station) was commenced at 13.03 hrs. During this series of bearings the aircraft approached from an easterly direction and from a point approximately 12 miles away. It passed over the station at about 13.10 hrs. It then turned to port and flew south for about 9 miles when it again turned to port and approached the station from a south-easterly direction. It passed over the station at 13.20.5 hrs. On this occasion the aircraft was heard clearly but not seen, the indication being that it was flying in cloud at about 1,500 ft. At 13.30 hrs. the cloud base at Renfrew was 4/10 at 1,000 ft. and 10/10 at 1,200 ft. There was an intermittent drizzle and visibility was about 2 miles. The surface wind was S.S.W. 12 m.p.h. Q.B.I. was not in force. To the west and north of Renfrew there was a lowering of the cloud base. Six bearings (Q.D.M.'s) in 2.5 minutes were then given to the aircraft and these bearings showed that it was proceeding away from the station on a north-westerly track. At 13.23 hrs. the series of bearings was interrupted and the aircraft was given the signal "Wait." This signal was acknowledged. It was not, however, followed by any specific advice. The let-down procedure followed by Capt. Stephens in G-AFFF was in accordance with instructions issued by his chief pilot.

His initial approach to the Airport was, however, made at an altitude considerably higher than is customary. This necessitated monopolising the station for a much longer period than was usual, particularly in view of the actual weather conditions at the Airport. He had, in fact, received Q.D.M.'s almost continuously for twenty minutes. Two other aircraft due to land at Renfrew were thus kept waiting in the air during this time - G-ADAJ in the vicinity of the Airport and a Dakota over the coast near Ailsa Craig. The interruption of the bearings at 13.23 hrs. was the result of a message: "Petrol running out" received at this time by Renfrew Control from aircraft G-ADAJ. This was a D.H.89 (Rapide), also operated by Scottish Airways, which had left Inverness for Renfrew at 11.50 hrs. and had arrived in the vicinity of Renfrew about the same time as G-AFFF. This aircraft had repeatedly broken in on the bearings being passed to G-AFFF and it is probable that as a consequence at least three bearings from the last series had been lost to G-AFFF. Both the pilot and radio operator of G-ADAJ were annoyed at the delay in obtaining bearings from Renfrew, and following some remark by the pilot to the effect that if they continued like this their petrol would be running out, the radio operator sent the message: "Petrol running out" This was sent without the pilot's authority. The Captain of this aircraft was not at any time concerned about his fuel supply, but when the radio operator informed him that the message had been sent he did not countermand it because he thought it might lead to further confusion. On receipt of this message Renfrew rightly gave G-ADAJ immediate priority, and from 13.25hrs. a series of homing bearings was passed to that aircraft which brought it over the station from a south westerly direction at 13.29.5 hrs. It landed at 13.35 hrs. and was carrying sufficient fuel for about another hour's flight. Immediately the homing bearings to G-ADAJ were concluded, Control repeatedly called G-AFFF, but there was no reply and no further contact was made with the aircraft.

At 13.23 hrs. when the last bearing to G-AFFF was transmitted, the aircraft was approximately 5 miles north-west of the airport and, according to the bearings, was making a wide turn to port. At about 13.30 hrs. witnesses on 500 ft. high ground 5 miles north of the station caught glimpses of the aircraft through cloud flying north-eastwards at a very low height directly towards Craigton Hill on which it was later found to have crashed. Except for its low height the aircraft appeared to be flying quite normally. No one saw the accident occur because the hill was enshrouded in heavy mist and the visibility was limited to 50 yards. The wreckage was discovered by a farmer shortly after 14.00 hrs. It was stated in the report of the medical officer who was called to the scene that all the occupants had been killed instantaneously.

Inspection at the scene of the accident showed that the aircraft had struck the southern slope of Craigton or Tambowie Hill - the most easterly of the Kilpatrick Hills - at a point 900 ft. above sea level and about 250 ft. below the summit. The evidence of ground marks indicated that the aircraft had struck the hill on a bearing of 330 True and that at the moment of impact it was turning to port and climbing as though pulled up at the last moment. After ploughing up the grass surface with the wheels the aircraft had then bottomed and bounced twenty yards before coming to a violent stop against a steep rocky face. Except for the tail unit and the rear part of the fuselage the whole aircraft had been badly crushed and battered by the force of impact. Fire did not break out. An examination of the wreckage was carried out in situ. Both engines had been running under power at the moment of impact and no evidence was found to suggest that there had been any pre-crash failure of the airframe or its equipment.

Capt. Stephens had completed 730 hours in the Air Force, and a further 350 hours with A.N.A. before joining the AAJC. He had then transferred to Renfrew and between 17th and 27th September he had completed ten trips Renfrew-Belfast and return, six trips Renfrew-Campbeltown and return and two trips Renfrew-Islay and return. Although he had successfully brought aircraft into Renfrew under similar weather conditions to those obtaining on the day of the accident the available evidence suggests that he had on these occasions been in visual contact with the ground. His flying time as Captain in D.H.89 amounted to 45 hours. He had flown with Radio Officer Calvert on two previous occasions.

The Rapide G-ADAJ took off from Inverness with a total of 60 gallons of petrol in the tanks. After landing at Renfrew there was a total of 16 gallons left, 8 gallons in each tank. The pilot of G-ADAJ is 33 years of age and has been with Scottish Airways since July, 1944. Previous to that he had been an operational pilot in the R.A.F. His Service flying amounted to approximately 1,300 hours and he is said to have accumulated a total of about 2,300 hours in D.H.89s since joining Scottish Airways.

The radio operator is 23 years of age. After some experience at sea as a marine operator he became an instructor in wireless telegraphy and procedure at the Glasgow Wireless College. He joined Scottish Airways on 9th September, 1946, and on that day flew as Aircraft Radio Operator on a scheduled service. Before that date he had never flown as a member of an aircrew. His total flying time between 9th and 27th September amounted to approximately 60 hours.

In order to avoid any chance of collision when two aircraft are flying in cloud in the vicinity of Renfrew, it is the general practice for the radio operator of one aircraft to keep his pilot informed of the bearings being transmitted from the ground station to the other. It is

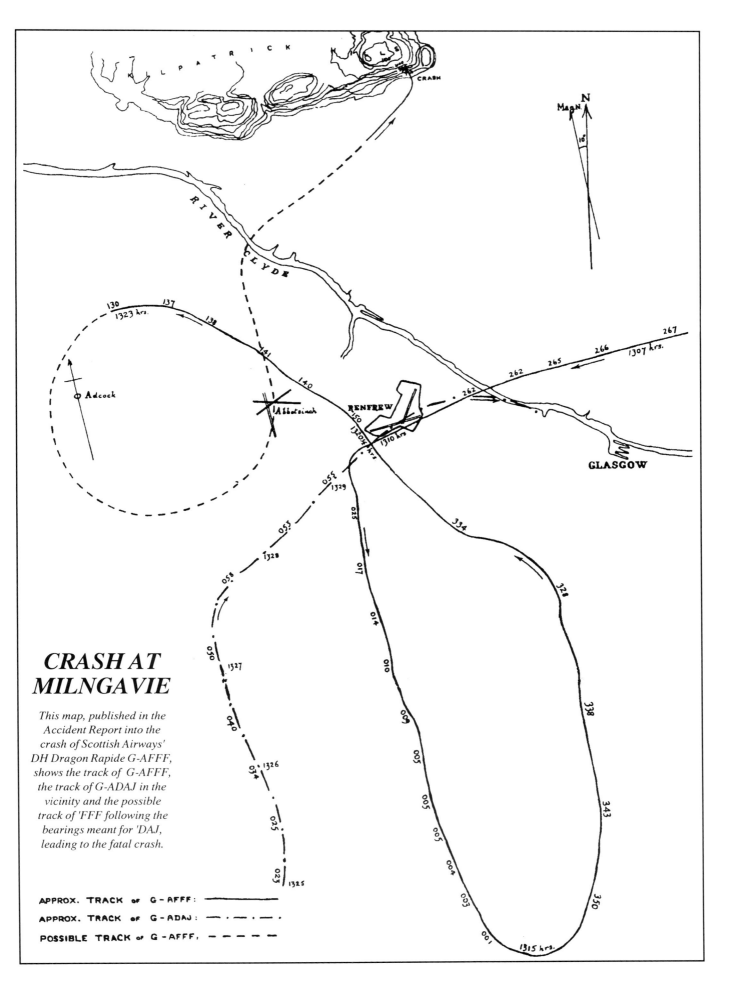

CRASH AT MILNGAVIE

This map, published in the Accident Report into the crash of Scottish Airways' DH Dragon Rapide G-AFFF, shows the track of G-AFFF, the track of G-ADAJ in the vicinity and the possible track of 'FFF following the bearings meant for 'DAJ, leading to the fatal crash.

APPROX. TRACK of G-AFFF: —————
APPROX. TRACK of G-ADAJ: — · — · —
POSSIBLE TRACK of G-AFFF: — — — —

Two DH89A Dragon Rapides (G-AJSK and G-AGUR) of the newly-formed British European Airways seen at Renfrew in 1947, with an ambulance patient being carried from 'GUR to a waiting ambulance. (Eric Starling)

G-ADAJ from 13.25 hrs. would have been verbally communicated to the pilot of G-AFFF by his radio operator, although they were not entered in the W/T log. The known track of G-AFFF shortly before it crashed bears a marked similarity to that of G-ADAJ in its approach to Renfrew from the south-west, i.e. both aircraft were flying on north-easterly tracks at the same time This suggests that the pilot of G-AFFF may have been flying on the Q.D.M.'s being passed to G-ADAJ. The radio operator could not have been confused in this respect since he acknowledged the signal to wait and would have continued to listen out until called again by the ground station. Moreover, he could not possibly mistake the bearings being given to any other aircraft for his own as he would not have been using his key.

It would, however, be possible for the Captain after a few minutes wait to believe that the bearings being given him by his radio operator were a resumption of his own—particularly a pilot who, with limited experience of Scottish Airways let-down procedure at this Airport, would be concentrating on this and on his blind flying instruments. The supposition that this was in fact the case is supported by the time, distance and direction factors from the moment G-AFFF was given the signal "Wait " until it crashed at about 13.30 hrs. Moreover, that the pilot then believed that he was being homed towards the Airport is an explanation for G-AFFF's north-easterly track towards high ground and at the same time for the low height of the aircraft in the vicinity of the hills.

When the Q.D.Ms to G-AFFF were discontinued at 13.23 hrs., the Captain had within the space of less than three minutes received a Q.F.G. (engines over the aerodrome) and six Q.D.M.'s. He should, therefore, have been aware of his position. He also knew his height and the local terrain.

As soon as the 'Petrol running out " message was received from G-ADAJ, there was a further signal from that aircraft asking for Q.D.M.'s which was immediately followed by a run for bearings.

Although the giving of some specific advice to the Captain of G-AFFF would have been a wise precaution, it is considered that under the circumstances Control was justified in the decision not to interrupt the series of bearings then being given to G-ADAJ."

The conclusion of the Accident Report was that:

"The accident was the result of flying into high ground in conditions of low cloud and poor visibility. The evidence strongly suggests that, following a break in the series of Q.D.M.'s which was being given him, the Captain, as the result of a misunderstanding between him and his radio operator, accepted as a resumption of his own. a series of bearings being transmitted to another aircraft. The following are considered to have been contributory factors:-

(i)   The sending by the radio operator of G-ADAJ of an unauthorised and erroneous message, as a result of which the series of Q.D.M.'s being given to G-AFFF was interrupted and priority transferred to G-ADAJ. The Captain of G-ADAJ cannot be considered blameless for his decision not to cancel this message.

(ii) The general air-operating inexperience of the radio operator of G-ADAJ.

(iii) The general flying inexperience of the Captain of G-AFFF."

The five passengers who were killed by the impact with Craighton Hill, Milngavie, seven miles north of Renfrew at 13.30hrs were: Sub. Lt. D. R. Mills of the Royal Navy Bomb Disposal Unit at Greenock, who had been to Islay on official duty; George Beattie, a representative of the Prudential Insurance Co. (on his first ever aerial round-trip); John McKay of Kirkintilloch; J. S. Crombie, an electrician from Glasgow working on a job on Islay, who had seen service in the Army throughout the war; and Cpl. A James of the Royal Engineers.

As *The Glasgow Herald* of Saturday September 23rd stated:

"FARMER'S DISCOVERY

The first intimation of the accident was from a lonely farmhouse in the Stockiemuir Hills. A farmer, Mr Andrew Graham, tending cattle on the slopes of the 1,500ft Tambowie Hill, saw the wrecked machine in the momentary lifting of the mist which surrounded the countryside.

He sent his son back to the farmhouse with instructions to summon the Police and within a few minutes the Police and Ambulance workers were on their way from Milngavie and Glasgow.

Mr Graham, first to reach the wreck, told *"The*

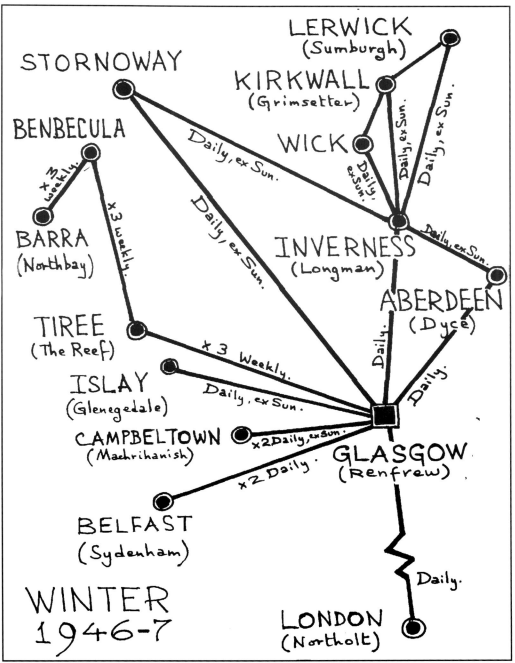

STORNOWAY

LERWICK
(Sumburgh)

KIRKWALL
(Grimsetter)

WICK

BENBECULA

Daily, ex Sun.

Daily, ex Sun.

Daily, ex Sun.

BARRA
(Northbay)

x3 weekly.

x3 weekly.

Daily, ex Sun.

INVERNESS
(Longman)

Daily, ex Sun.

ABERDEEN
(Dyce)

TIREE
(The Reef)

x3 Weekly.

Daily.

Daily.

ISLAY
(Glenegedale)

Daily, ex Sun.

CAMPBELTOWN
(Machrihanish)

x2Daily, exSun.

GLASGOW
(Renfrew)

x2 Daily.

BELFAST
(Sydenham)

WINTER
1946-7

Daily.

LONDON
(Northolt)

The last network map of Scottish Airways - for winter 1946-47, showing the links with London (Northolt) and Belfast (Sydenham) flown for RAS. (Author)

Glasgow Herald" that it was only the chance of the mist lifting for a short time that revealed the accident.

During most of the afternoon the wreckage of the aircraft was visible only from a few feet away and Ambulance workers toiling up the hillside in pouring rain over patches of boggy ground had great difficulty in reaching the wreck. Their search was aided by whistles sounded by Police who had reached the scene first.

Bodies Scattered

It was apparent that all the occupants of the aircraft had been killed instantaneously. Only two bodies were found in the wreckage and the rest were scattered over the hillside. Two indeed, had been catapulted 75 yards and were found on the summit of the hill.

It appeared as though the pilot had seen the hillside just before impact and had endeavoured to gain sufficient altitude to clear the summit. The aircraft had bounced on the first impact, then 'pancaked' on the hillside, breaking up violently.

Record Ended

This tragedy brings to an end the long record of accident-free operation by Scottish Airways. It is, in fact the first fatal crash involving one of the machines on a regular passenger carrying flight, and the hazardous conditions in which the service has operated in the Western Isles, particularly on Ambulance missions is well known.

Policemen, Pressmen, Ambulance men and farm workers worked in relays carrying the stretchers over the miles of difficult ground to a point where the Ambulances were stationed.

Several hours elapsed before all the bodies were finally recovered. They were taken last night to the mortuary at New Kilpatrick Cemetery".

This accident obviously disturbed the British Airline Pilots' Association (BALPA), because the Association's Air Safety and Technical Committee studied the findings and reported in Autumn 1947 as follows:

133

"The committee was unable to find serious fault with the conclusions of the Inspector of Accidents, but considers it unlikely that the pilot of the crashed aircraft mistook the bearings given to the other aircraft for his own; it was, however, a possible assumption. The committee did consider that there was a lack of control in that two aircraft were allowed to fly blind and at a low level on various headings in the immediate vicinity of Renfrew. In view of the risk it was thought that Captain Stephens might have been anxious to break cloud. It was considered that the controller should have passed a safe height to fly, although, as the committee pointed out, at Renfrew even if control had arranged separation there was no satisfactory method of accurate navigation. The committee considered that ground facilities at Renfrew were inadequate and out of date, in fact, showed little improvement on the practice of fifteen years ago, and made the observation that there had been no improvement in aids since the accident occurred. The inadequacy was matched, in the opinion of the committee, by the out-of-date airborne equipment and weather reporting facilities. An urgent recommendation was made that additional radio aids should be provided on the ground and on Rapide aircraft to afford more than single channel working, some kind of airborne navigational equipment, and that a ruling should be made to forbid aircraft being flown for hire or reward unless equipped with those minimum radio aids."

It is ironic that the date of this first fatal accident to a Scottish Airways' passenger aircraft should be easily remembered by another aviation tragedy. The very same afternoon, Geoffrey de Havilland, the test-pilot son of Sir Geoffrey, died when his DH108 'Swallow' jet broke up at high speed over the Thames estuary, preparing for a world air speed record attempt.

Dakota on the roof...

The second of these accidents referred to above occurred at 12.05hrs on December 19th 1946, this time at No. 46 Angus Avenue, Ruislip, only 1/2 mile East of the runway at Northolt Aerodrome. The owners of this semi-detached suburban house, Mr and Mrs Levene, had just been married, and were in the process of furnishing No.46 and preparing to move in, to start occupying their new home in a few days time. Just after mid-day that day Mrs Levene received a telephone call from a neighbour in Angus Avenue, suggesting she ought to "cycle round to tend to a burst water tank" in her new house, and so she set off in the snow and ice which covered the ground at that time. She was not, however, prepared for the sight that met her eyes on turning into the Avenue! Perched on the roof of her new home was a large gleaming C-47A Dakota, G-AGZA, with its tail sticking right

out horizontally over the front porch and its nose protruding over the rear of the roof over the back garden. Not much was left of the wings, which had collapsed grotesquely over the edges of the two semi-detached houses.

The details of how 'GZA arrived in this 'drunken duck-like' position are best taken from the Accident Report No.C469 dated January 29th 1947:

"The aircraft was due to take off from Northolt at 10.04 hrs. on a scheduled service to Glasgow, but its departure was delayed until faults in its radio equipment had been rectified. At 11.15 hrs. the pilot taxied to the end of the runway where he was held up while other aircraft were landing. It was snowing heavily at the time, and after waiting 15 to 20 minutes the pilot returned to the tarmac where he instructed the maintenance personnel to sweep the control surfaces and spray them with de-icing fluid. While the work was in progress he received a message from another pilot who had landed at 11.17 hrs. after a test flight that icing was very slight up to 1,500 ft. and gave no trouble and that the snow had cleared from the wings of the aircraft during take-off. Shortly before 12.00 hrs. Capt. Johnson again taxied to the end of the runway where he had to wait while Dakota G-AICV (a Skyways aircraft) took off at 11.55 hrs. Capt. Johnson has stated that his own decision to take off was influenced by the normal take off of this aircraft which he had noticed was

A strange bedfellow! The amazing arrival of Dakota G-AGZA on top of No. 46 Angus Avenue, Ruislip at mid-day on December 19th 1946 created not a little astonishment!

Above: The sight greeting callers to the front door.

Left: The view of 'GZA from the back garden.

covered with snow and was apparently in the same condition as his own. When another aircraft had landed, G-AGZA finally obtained clearance to take-off at 12.04 hrs by which time it had ceased to snow. The runway in use (08) was 1,833 yards long and the take-off was in-a north-easterly direction. Capt. Johnson gave his First Officer instructions to maintain 40" boost and commenced a normal take-off. He attributed a slowness in unsticking to snow on the runway, which was at the time about 2 in. in depth. Almost as soon as the aircraft became airborne it was noticed to be in a tail-down attitude, all three wheels being the same height off the runway. As it passed the Control Tower, 1,300 yards from the take-off point, it was still in a very noticeably tail down attitude and was then about 6ft. off the runway; the undercarriage was retracting slowly. It was not until he reached the end of the runway that the Captain realised that the aircraft was not climbing at its normal rate. He was then easing back the pitch controls to climbing revs. but he immediately returned the pitch to fully fine. At the same time he noticed that boost and revs. were normal and he remembers noticing that the rate of climb was 300 ft./min. and the airspeed about 110mph. When it became clear that the aircraft was not making any height, the First Officer advanced the throttles to 43" boost, and Capt. Johnson almost immediately afterwards opened them to maximum boost; this had no effect on the climb.

The aircraft passed over the airfield boundary 250 yards beyond the runway at roof-top height and in a still more pronounced tail down attitude. In this direction the level of the ground rises gradually to about 30 ft. above the height of the runway and the aircraft appeared to maintain its relative height. The Captain managed to turn slightly to avoid Bourne School, but 400 yards farther on the tail wheel tore away some telegraph wires running alongside the railway line. A pilot witness near this point saw that the undercarriage was fully retracted and that the aircraft was in an unbelievably nose-up attitude. Three hundred yards beyond the railway the port wing struck the first building on the left-hand side of a street of semi-detached houses. The aircraft turned on the impact and slid sideways, starboard wing first, damaging the roofs of intermediate houses and finally coming to rest horizontally on the top of the third block of houses. All

four occupants escaped unhurt. Fire did not break out on impact and none of the occupants of the houses was injured."

In fact there were four crew and one passenger aboard(the Accident Report above contains an error, where it refers to 'four occupants') and after the silence which followed the long drawn-out pancaking sequence, the Stewardess, Miss Robina 'Bobbie' Christie and Radio Officer H Murdoch, together with the single passenger, John Livingston, ran aft to open the passenger door, only to discover that it overlooked a 20 feet drop to the snow-covered front garden!

Slowly the Dakota began to tip down ominously rearwards - so they hurriedly retraced their steps! They climbed out of the escape hatch onto the Port wing, and with the two pilots, lowered themselves from its stub remains into the house attic, crossed the landing, descended the stairs and walked out of the front door, dusting off their clothes. To the stunned neighbours, they looked unconcerned, but a little excited when they looked up and saw their means of conveyance in its unusual setting!

The Captain was 37 year old W.J. ("Willy Jig") Johnson, who had joined Scottish Airways in March 1942 and was very experienced in flying in the North.

First Officer Crosbie was an ex-Fleet Air Arm pilot, who joined Scottish in November 1946. As the report continues:

"Inspection at the scene of the accident showed the aircraft to be perched on the top of two semi-detached houses, the roofs of which had been demolished by the impact. Its tail protruded well out over the road. The port wing had been shattered and lay trailing over the side of the house. The starboard wing was still attached although the damage to it was very extensive. The fuselage was intact except where the port propeller had cut into it, and the tail unit appeared to be undamaged except for a tear in the port elevator, probably caused by telegraph wires, some of which were still entwined about the tail wheel. The starboard propeller had been torn away and was lying in the road.

An examination of the wreckage was carried out in situ. Both engines had been running under power at the moment of impact. No evidence was found to suggest that there had been any pre-crash failure of the airframe nor that there had been any error in the manipulation of the cockpit controls."

The port side of 'GZA, showing the exit hatches used by the crew to climb down into the attic of the house and thence downstairs and out of the front door!

Dakota's Rest!

G-AGZA rests under skies leaden with snow on the roof of 46 Angus Avenue.

It took more than a little ingenuity to dismantle it for removal - damaging the house even more!

As the conditions of snow and icing were crucial to the evidence, the Report commented upon the pre-take-off actions:

"At 11.35hrs on the day of the accident, the aircraft was taxied back from the runway to the tarmac where, on the instructions of the Captain, the control surfaces were swept and sprayed with de-icing fluid. One of the two men who carried out the work said that he could not brush off the snow because it stuck to the surface; the other said that the de-icer had to be used to clear the surface. Only the control surfaces were cleared; the wings were not swept. The two men estimated the amount of snow on the remainder of the aircraft to be from 1 inch to 2 inches thick when it taxied back to the runway to take off 10 minutes later.

Note: Evidence was obtained that Dakota G-AICV, which made a successful take-off, had been completely defrosted (i.e., all surfaces except the fuselage had been swept clear of snow and sprayed with de-icer fluid) just before it taxied to the runway. This work was carried out by the Skyways engineer, whose company's pre-flight check schedule included the item ' Aerofoil surfaces free from ice and snow.'

The evidence of the pilot that boost and revs. were normal rules out the possibility of carburettor icing and loss of power from any other cause.

It is accepted that very adverse aerodynamic characteristics can result from the adherence of ice, snow or frost to the surfaces of an aircraft, the effect of which may give rise to loss of lift and added drag in addition to increasing the weight.

The conditions on the morning of the accident were conducive to snow or ice adherence. The following is an extract from a statement by a professional meteorologist:—

"If the wing of an aircraft on the ground were at a temperature just above freezing and snow fell on it (especially if the snow was falling through air at a temperature just above freezing) the lowest layers of snow on the wing would very likely be wet with water at a temperature of 32 F. If the air temperature then fell below freezing there would be a probability that some of the water would freeze and so bind the snow on the wing."

It will be noted that the air temperatures at 11.00 hrs. and 12.00 hrs. were 33 F. and 32 F. respectively.

There is evidence that the snow was adhering to the surfaces of G-AGZA before it took off and that during take-off the aircraft, with the exception of the control surfaces, was covered with a layer of snow.

In October 1939 at a R.A.F. Station in Scotland, three Oxfords taking off individually on the first flight of the day all failed to become completely airborne as the result of the adherence of hoar-frost to the lifting surfaces.

As long ago as 1938, " Notices to Aircraft Owners and Ground Engineers " (No. 24) drew attention to the effects of hoar-frost on the aerodynamic characteristics of an aircraft and on the take-off speed and length of run. "

And so the Report concluded:

"OPINION - This accident was the result of the pilot taking off when the aircraft was almost entirely covered with snow. In doing this the pilot committed an error of judgment.

RECOMMENDATION - It is recommended that the dangers of the adherence of ice, snow or frost to aerofoil surfaces at take-off should again be brought to the notice of all pilots and aircraft maintenance engineers."

The sole passenger, John Livingston, was employed by BOAC at the time of the crash, although he had been 'lent' to BEA to work on their scheduled planning for the 1947 Summer Domestic services. He still lives in Ruislip to-day, and all he suffered was a bump on the head during the pancaking. He remembers standing on the stub of the port wing, congratulating the Captain on making such a fine landing!

The Levenes eventually moved into their new home after six months repairing the houses - the dismantling of the C47A caused more damage than its unscheduled arrival! But for another ten years afterwards, oil and fuel stains kept re-appearing on the ceiling as the rafters dried out. Appropriately the Levenes called their new house *Dakota's Rest* and still live there to-day. 'Willy Jig' Johnson, the Captain, - not surprisingly - subsequently became known within BEA as 'Rooftop' Johnson!

The Stewardess, 'Bobbie' Christie had been a Traffic Officer with Ted Fresson's Northern Section in Inverness, before transferring to Renfrew to become Scottish Airways' first female Flight Attendant - paving the way for all the many who came after her in Scottish, and later BEA and British Airways. She was unhurt, and went on flying, as did the Captain and First Officer.

And so the year 1946 ended on a sober note for the airline, and the end of its independent career was nigh at hand.

CHAPTER 15

The End

At the beginning of 1947 the Scottish Airways' Directors were asked down to London by BEA for a re-organisational meeting. George Nicholson took his company secretary, William Cumming and Air Superintendent Capt David Barclay, and Ted Fresson flew down from Inverness. Sir Harold Hartley presided (BEA's Chairman and previously Chairman of the LMS Railway) and Gerard d'Erlanger (BEA Managing Director) was there to propose the organisational changes, amongst other BEA directors (including Air Cmdre Whitney Straight (a friend of Ted Fresson's, who had run Inverness airport before the war), Wing Cmdr Arthur Measures and Ian Hayward.)

At the end of the meeting, d'Erlanger announced the new Management organisation for Scottish Airways, once BEA had completed the takeover. George Nicholson was appointed 'Scottish Divisional Director' (the most senior man in the North), William Cumming was to be 'Senior Executive' and Ted Fresson was made 'Area Manager - Northern Scotland' (under the other two, based at Renfrew and only offered a 6-month contract!)

While George was duly delighted to be in overall charge, Ted Fresson was so amazed at the result that he couldn't find it in himself to be angry - at first. He had already had a 'brush' with d'Erlanger, and sensed the hostility there. He was a qualified engineer and pilot, and a top class airline professional. He had operated his airline for 1 1/2 years prior to George starting up, was senior in age, and above all - had made a profit on his operations almost every year. In fact, his Northern Section had been subsidising the other!

Ted said he'd let d'Erlanger know whether he would accept, after reflection on it. All d'Erlanger said was just: "Take it, or leave it." In the event, Ted could not find another job in time, though he tried to move to BOAC through a friend of his, so he reluctantly accepted the offer after a few days.

BEA takes over

And so BEA took over Scottish Airways on February 1st 1947, but not Allied Airways at Dyce. That company had never joined

the AAJC during the war (it had negotiated a separate contract direct with the Air Ministry), and now it still soldiered on alone, legally under contract to BEA since February 1st, but not yet merged into the State Corporation. (In fact it was not until April 12th that BEA stepped in and took over Allied's routes at Dyce, as the airline had had all its aircraft go 'technical' the previous day, abrogating its agreement with BEA to 'keep all services running'.)

The last traffic and operating statistics of Scottish Airways were prepared up to January 31st 1947, therefore, and henceforward BEA assumed responsibility for the day by day events. They showed that the combination of George Nicholson's Northern and Scottish Airlines Ltd and Ted Fresson's Highland Airways Ltd, had, since August 1st 1937 (up to January 31st 1947) carried a total of 205,139 passengers, flown 8 1/2 million aircraft miles, and carried some 7.2 million lbs of freight and mail - a quite commendable undertaking.

What BEA took over on February 1st 1947 was in effect the services, staff and aircraft of the AAJC - made up as it was of: Railway Air Services Ltd., Scottish Airways Ltd., Isle of Man Air Services Ltd. and Great Western and Southern Air Lines Ltd. Non-operating pre-war companies also taken over included: Highland Airways (1939) Ltd., North Eastern Airways Ltd., West Coast Air Services Ltd., and Western Isles Airways Ltd. The total fleet acquired by BEA included 2 C-47As, 8 Junkers Ju.52/3ms, 13 Avro XIXs, 39 D.H. Rapides and 1 D.H. Dragon.

The finishing touches...

On Monday April 14th 1947, Ted was asked by the Renfrew HQ of BEA to drive over to Aberdeen to take over Allied Airways' affairs and hand them over to BEA. He was astonished at this onerous task, but proceeded to Dyce by car, and (as he recorded later):

"I found on arrival that Mr Gandar Dower was away at his favourite holiday resort in Switzerland, so in his absence the take-over was effected through his representative in charge.

"It was an unpleasant chore, and I would have preferred someone else to have carried out the job - but there it was! I have always felt that at that moment 'G-D', as he was commonly known to us all, and myself became friends in adversity. We had both been blatantly robbed of many years' hard work and effort!"

The Aberdeen *"Press & Journal"* next day reported the visit in the following terms:

"Captain Fresson, British European Airways' Scottish Director, commendably declined publicity - pictorial or otherwise - when he went to Dyce Airport for the preliminaries of taking over Allied Airways (Gandar-Dower) Limited on behalf of the Government. Somebody less decent, might have revelled in it. For MP Gandar Dower in whose absence in Switzerland the Northern airline has been taken into State hands, was Fresson's one and only keen rival in the pioneering days of the North of Scotland and Outer Islands air routes. Competition at times, was intense."

Ted had to make further visits in the next few days, to interview the Allied Airways' staff at Dyce to take on the best ones for BEA

Meanwhile both George and Ted were bombarded with never-ceasing strings of instructions from the new BEA HQ at

SCOTTISH AIRWAYS LTD

Aircraft Fleet - Summer 1946

Southern Section:

De Havilland DH89A Dragon Rapide	G-AFFF
De Havilland DH89A Dragon Rapide	G-AFOI
De Havilland DH89A Dragon Rapide	G-AFRK
De Havilland DH89A Dragon Rapide	G-AGIF
De Havilland DH89A Dragon Rapide	G-AGJF
De Havilland DH89A Dragon Rapide	G-AGLE
De Havilland DH89A Dragon Rapide	G-AGLP
De Havilland DH89A Dragon Rapide	G-AGLR
De Havilland DH89A Dragon Rapide	G-AGOJ
De Havilland DH89A Dragon Rapide	G-AGUR
De Havilland DH89A Dragon Rapide	G-AHLL
Douglas C-47A Dakota (op for RAS)	G-AGZA
Douglas C-47A Dakota (op for RAS)	G-AGZB
Douglas C-47A Dakota (op for RAS)	G-AGYZ

Northern Section:

De Havilland DH84 Dragon I	G-ACIT
De Havilland DH89A Dragon Rapide	G-AEWL
De Havilland DH89A Dragon Rapide	G-AGDG
De Havilland DH89A Dragon Rapide	G-AGIC
De Havilland DH89A Dragon Rapide	G-AGJG
De Havilland DH89A Dragon Rapide	G-AHLN

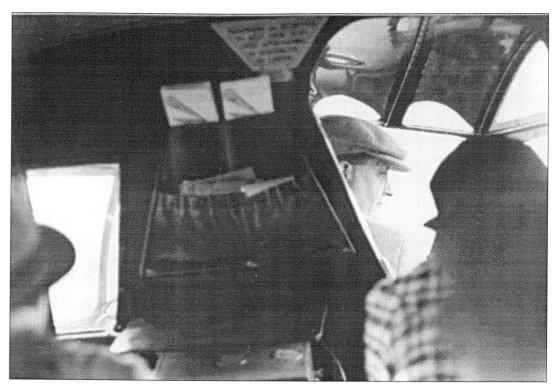

Ernest Edmund Fresson OBE, with his distinctive tweed cap, piloting one of Highland Airways' DH Dragons from Inverness. (Richard Fresson).

Ruislip. One of these was to tell Ted to prepare to move the BEA operations now from Longman Aerodrome at Inverness, out to RAF Dalcross. By now with much RAF and RN construction having taken place during the War years, Longman was as big as Dyce or Renfrew and so Ted felt that as Longman was so large now - and could yet be given hard runways - such a move was very premature and likely to be very costly, and he said so in the local paper! He had his knuckles rapped for that by BEA in London, and then he was asked to send back all the oldest registered Rapides to Glasgow, as German Ju. 52s would be sent to replace them!

The irrational thing was that Ted had worked for years to have his aircraft's woodwork 'dried out' during overhaul, and his oldest Rapides had a payload of up to 1,200 lbs - against the latest arrivals that could only carry 800 lbs! These and other equally disastrous decisions were being made by "faceless"men back at BEA HQ, and it was obvious the Scottish Division seemed to have no jurisdiction over its own affairs from Renfrew. Ted, in fact, was blistering in his criticisms, saying the men at HQ had as much idea of operating in the Scottish environment as "an ape had with a bad headache!" He wrote detailed letters to d'Erlanger laying out the extra costs in some of these decisions. The Ju. 52s proved a disaster, and had no ground equipment to adequately back them up. When the Inverness engineering staff were all moved down to Renfrew, Ted had to use his remaining Rapides on many occasions to stand-in for broken down Ju.52s!

Longman vs Dalcross

On the subject of Longman, Ted wrote to Gerard d'Erlanger as follows:

28th Jan 1947
"Dear Mr d'Erlanger,
The Inverness Town Council inform me they have received a letter from Mr G.S. Lindgren, Parliamentary Secretary, Ministry of Civil Aviation, stating that Longman Municipal Airport, Inverness, is to be given up and a transfer made to an alternative aerodrome at Dalcross at an early date.

Dalcross is a very fine aerodrome indeed. In fact, it is so good it would be suitable for a town the size of Manchester, Birmingham or Glasgow, but it is situated 8 miles further away from the centre of the town than is the case with Longman Airport. On the other hand, Longman Airport is quite suitable for any services that the Corporation can hope to operate into Inverness for many years to come. Undoubtedly, we reached the peak air traffic period during the war when there were many thousands of troops stationed at Orkney, Shetland and Lewis, and who were constantly on the move. Longman Airport coped with this peak quite easily, and, not only that, it provided services for the Naval Air Communications' Squadron and RAF sundry uses.

The dimensions of Longman do not compare unfavourably with that of Renfrew. For instance, our E & W strip is at present 1500 yards, but can be extended to 2000 yards at very little cost. SW x NE strip is 1100 yards, N x S strip is 1000 yards, and the SE x NW strip is 1300 yards. The E x W approach is excellent in both directions. The SW x NE approach is excellent from the North East and good from the South West. The N x S strip approach is good from the North but poor from the South. When the wind is blowing from the North we always use the approach from the South West corner. The SE x NW strip approaches are fair from NW, good from SE but this strip is not used a great deal. The visibility at Inverness is very good throughout the year and bears no comparison to the foul conditions pertaining at Renfrew. There are no tarmac strips on Longman, but the turf is firm and well drained, because the one foot of loam soil underneath the turf rests on gravel. During the war, Liberator and Flying Fortress aircraft landed and took off from this aerodrome, and Bristol Blenheims used it constantly. Whenever the weather is bad, the approaches are usually from the North or East, which are excellent. To end up this description, Longman has the wonderful advantage of being only five minutes' journey from the centre of the town.

Having given you a rough assessment of Longman Airport, I now want to tell you the disadvantages of what a move to Dalcross will mean for us.

1. The transport time will be increased by 25 minutes.

The interior (looking aft) of the new Avro 652A Anson XIX feederliner (probably G-AGNI) as demonstrated to Scottish Airways' pilots. Six seats are shown here, but a seventh was fitted in RAS aircraft on the Glasgow - Croydon run (flown by Scottish Airways' pilots). Entrance door was at the rear on the starboard side (left, here) behind the curtain. (John Stroud Collection)

This causes the passenger extra inconvenience, but chiefly it is going to spoil our centre to centre town time between Inverness - Aberdeen, Inverness - Glasgow, Inverness - Edinburgh. We are looking to cutting times between centres, and not increasing them, if we are going to wean the public away from surface transport.

2. The cost of operations is going up. Our present transport costs us during the winter months £25 per month. If we go to Dalcross it is going to be in the region of £250 per month, and during the summer it will possibly rise to as much as £350 per month.

3. The above increased costs only apply to passenger transport. Over and above this, we are going to be faced with transport for engineers and operating personnel. The Air Ministry are going to be faced with the same troubles regarding their Traffic Control, Teleprinter and Signals Staff.

4. There are no proper waiting room facilities at Dalcross, whereas the Air Ministry have only recently completed a very nice block of traffic offices for us at Longman. This means that new buildings will have to be put up at Dalcross.

5. At present we have three aerodromes on the route within five minutes of the centre of the town, namely Inverness, Wick and Kirkwall. I doubt whether there are three towns on any one route throughout the country which can boast such time saving aerodromes right up against the towns. I claim it would be a retrograde step to upset this happy trinity.

6. The close proximity of the aerodrome to Inverness is of great interest to visitors and as soon as restaurant tea rooms are functioning on this aerodrome, the local value along with the tourist trade can be greatly extended. Arising from these remarks, the publicity to air travel should not be overlooked.

7. The upkeep and maintenance of Longman Airport would cost the Government far less than that of Dalcross, and, as landings on turf aerodromes are far cheaper to the Corporation, than prepared air strips, a further saving in cost would be effected. You will remember at the lunch at Northolt at the beginning of the month Sir Harold Hartley stated he looked to

Scotland to make its own airways pay. If we are to do this, these economies cannot be overlooked.

8. Finally it is my opinion, and I have 14 years' experience to go by, that the heavy flow of traffic which will call for really large aircraft will go by Aberdeen and the Eastern coast.

Can you kindly therefore reconsider this matter to prevent a move at the present juncture?

Yours sincerely

E.E. Fresson"

However, he got absolutely nowhere, and services were eventually ordered to be transferred to Dalcross from August 1st 1947.

George made redundant

Meanwhile, there came a 'bolt from the blue'. On July 1st Gerard d'Erlanger was appointed Chairman of BEA to replace Sir Harold Hartley, who was moved across to become Chairman of BOAC, replacing Viscount Knollys. Sir Harold also took Whitney Straight with him as Managing Director and Chief Executive of BOAC.

At one fell swoop, both George Nicholson and Ted Fresson had lost the two men at the top of BEA whom they both knew and respected, and who in turn, had a great deal of respect for them.

Gerard d'Erlanger now had as his Deputy Chairman J.H. Keeling, and as Managing Director, John V. Wood. And almost immediately, George Nicholson received a call from Head Office informing him that the 'Scottish Division' (of which he was Director) was to be wound up at the end of September and George would be made redundant with it!

George rang Ted Fresson in Inverness to tell him, and Ted realised his own days were probably numbered now as well, although George indicated he hadn't yet been told about Ted.

In fact, as reported next morning in *The Glasgow Herald*, George tidied up his office at Renfrew for the last time on the afternoon of September 12th 1947. He cleared his desk, took a last look around the room from which he had built up, controlled and operated Scotland's largest airline over a period of almost thirteen years now, popped his head into the other offices as he walked down the corridors, shook hands and wished everyone "All the best", and finally said "Good-bye" to the crowd that had

A Last Goodbye! - probably the last occasion on which Ted Fresson and his wife Gwen spent some time together with George Nicholson (second from right) and his wife Ada (second from left). The year was 1947, the place - Oban. (Richard Fresson).

A group of Captains at Scottish Airways' Farewell Party (before Nationalisation) in Glasgow.
(Standing, Right to Left) Capt. Alec Appleby, Eric Starling, "Johnny" Afflec, Bill MacKenzie, "Windy" Martin, Tom Mackenzie, Bill Fittall, Eric Pooley and John Ramsden.
(Seated, Right to left) Donald Prentice, Stan Clayton, "Smokey" Hayes, Bill Baillie, David Barclay (Chief Pilot), "Willie Jig" Johnson and "Johnny" Wells. (Eric Starling)

gathered at the door. It was exactly 5.00 pm as he walked out of the building, got into his car and drove away for the last time. As yet, the realisation that his airline career in Britain had ended for good, had not properly penetrated his mind. That would take a long time yet, and indeed, was something he never did fully assimilate to his dying day.

And so, at the end of the Summer Season, George Nicholson retired to his home "Wemba", at Prestwick, to brood on what might have been. The 'Scottish Division', however, remained in being - probably with the force of all the Public lobbying that was going on to retain it.

By November 1947 a hail of protest was arising from all quarters about the way the services - or lack of them - were being run in the North of Scotland. There were no Orkney inter-island flights any more - unless an air ambulance was needed, in which case Ted himself usually flew 'CIT there to do it personally.

By the turn of 1948, all Ted's staff at Inverness had been relocated to Renfrew (Glasgow), and Dalcross had been in use as the new civil airport since the beginning of August 1947. He had been left with the Dragon G-ACIT for charters and ambulance work, and one of his engineers - Archie MacDonald - to maintain it. Ted's duties also entailed doing monthly checks on the

Aberdeen base, where he often saw his "friend in adversity", Eric Gandar Dower.

In February 1948 Ted Fresson received a ticking-off from BEA HQ for flying an ambulance flight in the Orkneys on the Dragon 'CIT (and saving a boy's life). Then he heard rumours circulating about a new wave of redundancies in BEA including himself, William Cumming, and even David Barclay at Renfrew. He went to see d'Erlanger himself at home about it, was kept waiting a long time, and left none the wiser.

Ted's complaints

Ted was also engaged at this time in a heated correspondence with the BEA Traffic Dept. about the inadequacies of the proposed 1948 Summer schedules. He wrote to the Dept.'s General Manager on February 4th as follows:

"Dear Waters,

Proposed Summer Timetable, 1948

A private line to you, along with a copy of letter I have addressed to Traffic Superintendent, S.D. àpropos forthcoming Summer Timetable.

Last month the original Summer Schedule was presented to us in rough form, and it was so unsatisfactory that I asked Swann to convene a meeting at Renfrew with the representatives from Northolt, interested in the Timetable, in attendance.

We prepared a plan which would give us an exceedingly good service throughout the North of Scotland, but one particular person, named Guy, seemed bent on wrecking it. Mr Wheatcroft, who was at the meeting, seemed very helpful, but, from what was said, it seemed evident that the proposal was to operate the Scottish services with one Dakota too few, and, at least, one DH.89.

		1947**	
SCOTTISH AIRWAYS*			
Traffic Statistics: 1946 - 1947			
	1946	**Jan 1st - 31st**	**TOTAL**
Passenger carried	32,958	1,800	34,758
Cargo (lbs)	384,521	35,000	419,521
Mail (lbs)	381,379	28,000	409,379
Aircraft miles	1,729,302	130,000	1,859,302

* Combined Scottish Airways Ltd and Western Isles Airways Ltd
** Estimate

The next step was, I believe, that Swann attended a meeting in London, where he was over-ruled seven to one on certain matters relating to the Timetable for this area.

If the schedule made out by the London committee, who seem to have very little knowledge of requirements in Scotland, and especially the Northern Area, is allowed to go through, the Corporation, I am certain, will lose traffic and will not fulfil the requirements of the travelling public.

There are four outstanding features in the Timetable, as shown in the copy of letter attached.

Can you use your influence in getting this matter put right in time?"

The core of the argument - which went on for some time - was that BEA HQ were extracting high utilisation out of their aircraft, but by so doing were not operating at the best times for the business traffic. Ted preferred full aircraft and lower utilisation - to empty aircraft being scheduled at great speed in every direction. But, as usual, the BEA HQ in Ruislip reckoned to know best ....

Ted Fresson redundant

The *"Sunday Express"* for February 22nd displayed a large banner headline on its front: "70 BEA pilots face sacking", and the article said that: "Three pioneers of the independent Scottish companies absorbed into BEA, to be dismissed." The Monday papers took up the news, and those in Scotland waxed indignant in their condemnation of BEA. Next Friday, the MP for Shetland and Orkney, Sir Basil Neven-Spence, accused BEA in Parliament of "waging a cold war on Scots, and the pioneers of Scotland's internal airways", and denigrated the Corporation for charging such high fares that there were few people able to afford to travel nowadays. (Interestingly enough, Mr Lennox Boyd, Conservative MP for mid-Bedfordshire, announced in the same debate that BEA would be de-nationalised when the Conservatives were back in power. They were - in 1951 - and Lennox Boyd became Minister for Civil Aviation, but failed to carry out his promise!).

A week after this, Ted, William Cumming and David Barclay reported to BEA's managing director, Mr. John Wood at Northolt on Thursday, March 18th 1948, to be given the Corporation's final decision about them.

Ted was to be made redundant and given a mere £2,000 compensation for all his efforts. He protested: "That amounts to the public theft of my business!"

Barclay reprieved

William was given the same treatment, but Capt. David Barclay was given a last-minute reprieve, and allowed to stay on to organise an Air Ambulance division of BEA in Scotland. Ted was to bow out on March 31st 1948, and so in the short time available, and neither having made any alternative plans, he and William agreed not to say anything to the Press. Ted stayed with George Nicholson that night at Prestwick, and the two reminisced about their dismissal, and the injustice of it all.

So Ted flew to Wick and Orkney on March 23rd, in 'CIT, to say goodbye to his staff, then on March 30th, to Aberdeen in his favourite old Dragon, to say farewell there.

Ted returned to Dalcross in the evening, and by next day a BEA crew came up from Renfrew and removed the aircraft back to Glasgow, before Ted even knew it had happened! (Ted was planning to buy it, and use it himself for charter and ambulance work in the Isles, to carry on his own business).

In fact, as BEA had already been informed of this wish of his,

Scottish Airways' Farewell Dinner - Capt Ted Fresson OBE (centre front) toasts his engineering team at Inverness (back standing) Arthur Gould and Arthur Dodds (front) Bert Farminer and George Griffiths OBE (Chief Engineer). (Richard Fresson)

it is highly likely that the last minute "reprieve" for David Barclay was indeed BEA's desire to keep Ted out of business by doing the ambulance work themselves!

As it happened, there came two calls for an air ambulance soon after the end of March, and BEA refused to supply one to the Orkney Island Council, for a flight from Westray.

BEA's press statement about Ted's dismissal was made on the evening of March 18th 1948, in the following terms:

"Due to the need to simplify the organisation of BEA, consequent on the present economic situation, the Corporation announces with regret it will have to dispense with the services of Mr W. Cumming, commercial manager, Scotland, and Capt. E.E. Fresson, North of Scotland area manager.

"The decision in no way affects the operational status and the responsibility of the Scottish Division."

And so with Ted Fresson's going, following George Nicholson's dismissal the previous Autumn, came the end of Scottish Airways as most people had known it in Scotland. A lot of the hard working staff who had grown up with it, either under George, or Ted, or both, remained in the BEA organisation to carry some of that special spirit on to new achievements. Many of the engineering staff stayed at Renfrew. Some of the pilots did,

---

SCOTTISH AIRWAYS*
Total Traffic
August 1st 1937 - January 1st 1947

Passengers	205,139
Cargo (lbs)	1,970,902
Mail (lbs)	5,239,990
Aircraft miles	8,514,467

*Combined Scottish Airways Ltd and Western Isles Airways Ltd.

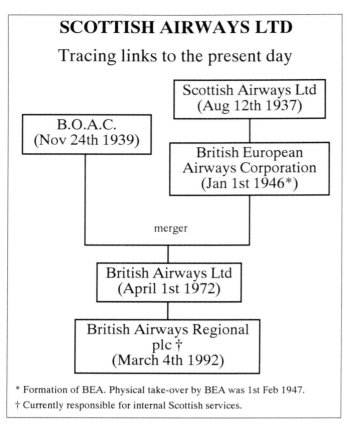

SCOTTISH AIRWAYS LTD

Tracing links to the present day

```
                    ┌─────────────────────┐
                    │  Scottish Airways Ltd │
                    │   (Aug 12th 1937)     │
                    └─────────────────────┘
┌──────────────┐              │
│   B.O.A.C.   │    ┌─────────────────────┐
│(Nov 24th 1939)│    │  British European   │
└──────────────┘    │ Airways Corporation │
       │            │   (Jan 1st 1946*)   │
       │            └─────────────────────┘
       │    merger         │
       └───────────────────┤
                    ┌─────────────────────┐
                    │  British Airways Ltd │
                    │   (April 1st 1972)   │
                    └─────────────────────┘
                            │
                    ┌─────────────────────┐
                    │ British Airways Regional │
                    │        plc †          │
                    │   (March 4th 1992)    │
                    └─────────────────────┘
```

* Formation of BEA. Physical take-over by BEA was 1st Feb 1947.

† Currently responsible for internal Scottish services.

and later worked their way up in the BEA hierarchy at Northolt. But some left to join KLM or Aer Lingus, and other carriers.

General uproar in Scotland

There was, of course, general uproar in Scotland over the dismissal of the pioneers and pilots. Perhaps this was put into the best perspective by the famous Orcadian writer, Eric Linklater when he wrote in *Time and Tide* on May 22nd 1948:

"Since 1933, we have been blessed in the North of Scotland with one of the first internal air services in Britain; and it paid its way. In Orkney and Shetland, where there are no railways, it lifted people from gigs and farm-carts into the speed and comfort of the sky - omitting altogether the usual intermediate stage of steam-driven locomotives and crowded third-class carriages - and as the service developed, and reached the smaller islands, it became a delight to see good solid farmers and their lively plump wives stepping contentedly from a de Havilland biplane for a day's shopping in Kirkwall. Captain Fresson was a great public servant in the north and he endeared himself to the islanders because he was not only a brilliant pilot and a business-like manager of his line, but a humane and charitable person who would always undertake a hazardous flight, if called upon, to fetch some desperate invalid to hospital.

His company was presently amalgamated with another that served the Western Isles and a larger area of Scotland and then, when our air services were nationalized, it was taken over by the British European Airways Corporation. Now Captain Fresson's pilots had flown for some fourteen years, to the general satisfaction of the public, without a serious accident, with a modest but efficient organization on the ground beneath them, and they had made a profit on their flights. The Corporation increased the fares, reduced the scale of service, showed a loss instead of a profit - and a couple of months ago, to our general rage and stupefaction, dismissed Captain Fresson.

There was a storm of protest, but the Corporation maintained a bureaucratic or totalitarian silence and would not explain its action. Mr Lingren absolved his chief, Lord Nathan, from the penalty of a public statement by the extraordinary assertion that the Minister had no control over the Corporation which his Government had established. Captain Fresson, a man in his fifties, had been deprived of his livelihood and his life's work; the north of Scotland had been deprived of a public servant of outstanding worth and ability; the Government looked nervously at the Frankenstein it had created - and Frankenstein wouldn't talk. Captain Fresson's claim for compensation is being urged, I believe, in the proper quarters, but my Highland and Island neighbours remain disconsolate in their loss. The Corporation declares that air services in Scotland are unremunerative and may have to be reduced - and anywhere north of Inverness you may hear angry voices saying: "If that's the way they treat Fresson, I'll have nothing more to do with them. The boats and the buses are still running, I can use them."

In the current number of *The Scots Review* there is a pertinent comment on the Government's disingenuous attempt to excuse its threatened abridgement of air service in Scotland by the assertion that Scots won't fly, and a reminder that the reason why Captain Fresson and Scottish Airways succeeded in making their service pay was that they were prepared to "take the public where

Seen on the apron of Glasgow's Renfrew Airport, in front of the old hangars used by Scottish Airways, Northern and Scottish Airways, and before that, Midland & Scottish Air Ferries, in turn, is Railway Air Services' C-47A Dakota G-AGYZ. The date is February 1st 1947, the RAS name has been painted out, and the new British European Airways (BEA) "Winged Key" symbol is already on the fin, signifying its new owner. (John Stroud Collection)

they wanted to go, when they wanted to go there". Private enterprise, in fact, had been the servant of democracy, but under Socialism's bureaucratic Frankenstein poor democrats must walk, not fly. How footsore we shall be if they nationalize the shoemakers !"

Parrots vs Eagles

One of Ted's old friends in Inverness, Robert Wotherspoon who had been Legal Director of Highland Airways up to the formation of Scottish Airways, made a remark in a speech in the Highland capital which drew much applause:

"To sack those who can fly and retain those who only talk, may encourage parrots, but it is a poor way to develop eagles!"

The last laugh however, was on George and Ted, for events had been happening 'behind the scenes', both in the State airline Corporations and in Whitehall, that created major management changes within BEA. This came to the public's notice in March 1949 with a sensation-seeking announcement in the *Daily Express:*

"BEA CHAIRMAN SACKED

The Government last night took its most drastic step in the re-organising of the heavily losing State airlines by sacking 42 year-old Mr Gerard d'Erlanger, chairman of British European Airways for the last eighteen months.

Mr d'Erlanger was told by Lord Pakenham, Civil Air Minister, that he wished to make a change in the chairmanship of BEA in June, when the young air executive's term of office expires.

Without waiting to complete his term, Mr d'Erlanger requested that his successor should be appointed at once"

It seems that 'the straw that broke the camel's back' had been when Gerard d'Erlanger had clashed with Lord Pakenham previously over the opening of a proposed Cardiff to Liverpool service. The Government had given high priority to a speedy opening of the route, but BEA thought it totally uneconomic and opposed it. In February Lord Pakenham had announced to the House of Lords that the service would open, despite BEA objections. But Gerard d'Erlanger loudly criticised the Goverment, claiming that it was interfering too much in the commercial freedom of BEA. Lord Pakenham would not budge, so d'Erlanger had now resigned in protest.

Thus, Lord Douglas of Kirtleside (Sholto Douglas of wartime Fighter Command fame) duly succeeded Gerard d'Erlanger as Chairman of BEA on March 14th 1949.

Lord Douglas, now 55 and Marshal of the Royal Air Force, had been recently appointed by the Government to investigate the inefficiences of the three state airlines and to recommend steps for their re-organisation. "It has..." said the *Daily Express* piece "...been known for a long time that the Government has been particularly sensitive over the £10 million losses of BOAC, BEA and BSAA."

Mr d'Erlanger, a member of the wealthy banking family, had thus been made the first scapegoat. As the *Daily Express* said: "He took over the chairmanship of BEA in 1947 when the airline had a trading loss for its first eight months of operation of £2,157,000. This worked out at a loss of £30 per passenger carried. In the next year BEA lost £3,284,000, and for the first six months of the present financial year the deficit has been £897,000 or £7 per passenger carried".

There were obvious signs, therefore, that d'Erlanger's efforts at cost reduction were bearing fruit now, but he was not given the

Gerard d'Erlanger

Merchant Banker, Commodore of the Air Transport Auxiliary, Board Member of the pre-war British Airways, Alternate Chairman of Scottish Airways, Chairman of British European Airways, Chairman of British Overseas Airways Corporation...

chance of taking them further. (Later he gained a second chance to show his cost-cutting expertise when he was appointed Chairman of BOAC in March 1956, being succeeded in turn on July 29th 1960 by Rear Admiral Sir Mathew Slattery. Sir Gerard's stint at BOAC was much more successful).

Sir Harold Hartley, K.C.V.O., C.B.E., F.R.S., M.C., retired from BOAC on June 30th 1949, and was succeeded by Sir Miles Thomas, D.F.C. Both Lord Douglas and Sir Miles were to bring back some financial stringency - and pride - to the airlines. But for George and Ted it was a generation too late. The route networks that had been founded at Renfrew and Inverness are still there, however, and still flown today by the new British Airways, or by Loganair as an associate airline. For that, George and Ted definitely have the last laugh !

The End

What happened to George Nicholson ? Well, disillusioned as he was with the 'Dead Hand' of Government taking over his lifetimes' work, he soon left Prestwick with his wife, son and daughter and emigrated to South Africa, with the intention of exploring the potentials for new air services there. He had hardly been there more than two years when his death was reported in Johannesburg on December 30th 1950.

William Cumming became the financial director of a large Charter company, and as for Ted Fresson, he settled in East Africa on two occasions, starting aerial enterprises there, but returning each time to Inverness to fly charters around the Highlands. He died in Inverness on September 25th 1963, knowing the route network of Scottish Airways, like a tenacious plant, was now recovering strongly after initially showing signs of withering in the early 1950s. He had already become a legend in his own lifetime for his flying skills. George was not a pilot, and so is not remembered quite so vividly, but because of his tenacity and acumen in building his Renfrew-based airline, he now shares the same Hall of Fame in the sky.

Scottish Airways' Managers and Pilots at Renfrew in 1944.

Back Row, Left to Right: Radio Officer "Paddy" O'Gorman, Radio Officer Andrew Ruthven, Engineer H.B. Murray, Engineer R. Young, Engineer J. McAvoy and Radio Officer J. Morrison.
Seated, Left to Right: Bill Mann (Chief Engineer), Capt. Bill Baillie, Capt. Jock Young, George Nicholson (Director and General Manager, Southern Section),
Capt. David Barclay MBE (Chief Pilot), Capt. William J. ("Rooftop") Johnson and Chief Radio Officer Jimmy Mitchell.

144

The Pilots and Radio Officers who braved all weathers

Before George Nicholson had properly established his second airline - Northern and Scottish Airways Ltd - at Renfrew for the 1935 Summer Season, he had already employed three pilots to help him get his new companies off the ground - **Edward Palmer, Charles Almond** and **Tom McNeill.** All three had worked for John Sword's airline, Midland & Scottish Air Ferries, and knew Renfrew of old.

"**Ted**" **Palmer** had, like Almond and McNeill joined John Sword's airline just before it was forced to close down (through the actions of the LMS Railway Co.). Ted had then joined George Nicholson's Northern Airways as its only pilot at Newcastle (Cramlington), to inaugurate the Newcastle - Carlisle - Isle of Man route on Monday July 30th 1934. He left at the end of the season and eventually became a Senior Captain in BOAC.

Charles Almond's family came from the Sunderland area, and he became a Director of the new company, Northern and Scottish Airways Ltd., when it was formed in November 1934, and its Chief Pilot when it moved to Renfrew. He left at the end of April 1935.

Tom McNeill took over from Charles as Chief Pilot at short notice at Renfrew on May 1st 1935, but after 3 months left on July 31st for new pastures, handing over to David Barclay.

David Barclay M.B.E., M.St.J.,
had also been flying for John Sword's Midland & Scottish Air Ferries Ltd in Summer 1934 and had been looking for a new job since M&SAF folded up. He had stayed at Renfrew as his home was at Bishopton nearby, and worked for the Scottish Flying Club through the Winter of 1934/35. He was suddenly offered a job as pilot  with Northern and Scottish Airways at the beginning of May 1935, under Tom McNeill and readily took it. With his previous knowledge of flying the Renfrew - Campbeltown/Islay services, he was very much at home with NSA, and when Tom left the airline at the end of July 1935, David Barclay was made Chief Pilot of NSA - a post he then held for some 10 1/2 years until February 1st 1946, when he was appointed Air Superintendent for the last 12 months - before Nationalisation on February 1st 1947.

David was born on April 1st 1905, and his family lived at 11 Roxburgh Street, Greenock at that time. As he grew up locally he watched the flying at nearby Renfrew (Moorpark) Aerodrome, and became very interested in learning to fly. He worked for a small local firm, George Barclay & Son, when he left school, and became a partner by 1927. Then on December 12th 1927 he started to learn to fly at the Scottish Flying Club at Renfrew, under the instruction of Flt. Lt. Jones, taking his first lesson on the DH. 60 Moth G-EBUU.

David had joined the Scottish Flying Club as a founder member and knew from the moment he became airborne that this was what he wanted to do.

He went solo after 4hrs 10mins of dual flying on March 2nd 1928, and carried on being instructed by "Bill" ("Red Hot")

Jones (as they nick-named his instructor). After 32hrs flying altogether, he was checked out by Flt. Lt. Jones for 'passenger carrying' and started to carry passengers for the first time on the Avro 594 Avian III G-EBTY on October 13th 1928. (On the 17th he up-ended the Avian on its nose while taxying over boggy ground, but no damage was done !)

After increasing his flying hours up to the 60 mark in August 1929, David decided to join the RAF and he enlisted at Uxbridge as a Pilot Officer on August 14th, doing a short square-bashing course and then starting flying training at the RAF's No.1 Flying Training School (FTS) at Netheravon, Wiltshire on September 13th. Here he went solo after 10 1/2 hours of dual flying Avro 504N "Lynx' trainers under the care of his instructor, Sgt. Baker. Later, he converted to the Armstrong Whitworth Atlas I bomber aircraft, and finally qualified for his 'B' licence on August 12th 1930, rated; "An exceptional pupil without any special faults".

David was now posted to 503 Squadron, RAF Waddington, to fly Avro 504Ns for a month, then he was posted out to India to join No.27 Squadron at Kohat, flying Westland Wapitis. He arrived there on November 14th and immediately began to fly the patrols along the North-West frontier area with Afghanistan. No.27 was classified as a Bomber Squadron, and David remained on active service with them until Spring 1933.

For the first three months of 1932 he was off flying with an injured hand, but from April was fully operational again. He carried out his first bombing raid on active service in Westland Wapiti J9746 on September 28th 1932, in the Chengai area northwest of Peshawar. More bombing raids followed on October 2nd and 6th.

In April 1933 he was posted to No.11 Squadron at Risalpur, flying the fast Hawker Harts, and promoted to Flying Officer by now. More bombing operations followed in the Kothai area, and some parachute supply dropping, with occasional visits south to Delhi. David began to lead the formation at times, and headed a special flypast over the Viceroy's Palace on December 4th 1933. Finally, he was posted back to the UK on April 23rd 1934, and decided to leave the RAF for civilian airline employment.

David re-joined the Scottish Flying Club at Renfrew on June 29th 1934 as an instructor, then on July 31st he took a job as a pilot with John Sword's airline there, Midland & Scottish Air Ferries. The airline was being wound up, but David started to fly the Renfrew - Campbeltown and Islay services, keeping them going through August and September until he flew the routes for the last time for M&SAF on September 27th 1934.

The Chief Pilot of M&SAF in this period was Charles F Almond, and David also carried out few charters for John Sword, flying His Grace the Duke of Montrose around, and on September 17th taking H.M. King George V in Fox Moth G-ACCU from Ballater to Dyce.

Out of a job again, David had to wait through the winter of 1934-35 until May 14th 1935 when he accepted a job as pilot with George Nicholson's new airline at Renfrew - Northern and Scottish Airways.

Charles Almond had probably secured the job for David, but just as David joined NSA, Charles left and was replaced as Chief Pilot by Tom McNeill.

David started immediately on the old routes to Campbeltown and Islay which George Nicholson had taken over from John

Pilots and Managers of Scottish Airways' Northern Section at Inverness in late 1944.

Standing, left to right are Jimmy Steen (Traffic Manager), J. H. Hayter (Traffic), A. Emerson (R.O.), Roy Stewart (R.O.) and Bill Gray (R.O.).
Seated, Mrs Margaret Chisholm (Secretary to Capt. Fresson), Capt. David MacFarlane, Capt. Henry Vallance, Capt. E.E. Fresson OBE
(Director and General Manager, Northern Section), Capt. B.T. O'Reilly, Miss Robina ("Bobby") Christie (Traffic, and later Scottish Airways'
first Stewardess and survivor of the Dakota crash at Ruislip), and Jean MacDonald (Sales). (Eric Starling)

Sword. He was flying the DH Dragons inherited from M&SAF and Northern Airways, and soon was flying to Hall Caine (Ramsey) on the Isle of Man, and places like Shiskine on Arran, looking for new scheduled route possibilities.

May 27th 1935 saw David fly his first Air Ambulance flight - to Islay and back in Sword's old Dragon G-ACJS. This was the first of more than 131 such mercy flights that David Barclay would fly during the existence of George Nicholson's Renfrew based airline (to January 31st 1947). But after the nationalisation and takeover by BEA David flew a great many more, giving him a final count of almost 10 times this total. This probably makes David the top Scottish Air Ambulance pilot ever, in terms of missions flown on fixed wing craft. These ambulance flights, of course, could take place at any time of the day - or night. David flew some in the early hours of the morning, and he frequently landed on the beach at Barra in the moonlight or by car headlights when there was no moon, and often arrived back at Renfrew in the dark as well. David was capable of flying anywhere, at any time, and many, many patients owed their lives to his efforts.

David flew King George V again on August 30th 1935 - this time from Balmoral to Dyce in the DH Fox Moth G-ACED, and he found his first airstrip on Skye in September - behind the Broadford Hotel. He landed on the sands there too, while he was on his honeymoon! Slowly that winter of 1935-36, he began to find airstrips on the land or beach, at Tiree, Harris, South Uist, North Uist, Oban, etc, and the best field he could find on Skye - at Glen Brittle. He also flew Lords and Ladies around on charters - My Lords Londonderry, Inverclyde, etc.

So David had paved the way with his 'recces' of the Western Isles for starting the scheduled services there in January 1936 that proved - over the years - to become the lifeline of the islanders in those parts. That the routes are still operating today is a tribute to David Barclay's skill and persistence in finding the right places to use as airstrips. Although Skye, South Uist (Askernish) and Harris (Northton) were later dropped from the network, the RAF stepped in during WW II and built runways at Campbeltown, Tiree, Islay, Benbecula and Stornoway. North Uist (Sollas) was dropped after the war, but David's early efforts had all borne fruit.

Something else David pioneered on these western routes was the use of radio on the aircraft, starting on October 26th 1935 when flying in the Dragon G-ACNH to Islay. From here sprang the fitting of radio to all aircraft in the fleet and the use of a separate Wireless Telegraphy Officer (W.T.O), later called just a 'Radio Officer' (R.O.), on each trip.

David had to hire new pilots and W.T.O.s, check the surface of the landing strips, make sure they were licensed, expand and improve the radio systems in use, test-fly the aircraft after maintenance or undergoing C of A renewals, etc, make sure the other pilots (and himself) were constantly kept in practice on blind flying and let-down procedures, etc, etc. The Chief Pilot is a very busy man, and as well as doing a lot of flying David had a lot of 'Admin' to look after, too.

On April 18th 1936 he flew several charters for V.I.P.s to let them view the amazing new liner undergoing trials off Arran - *R.M.S. Queen Mary.*

After the takeover by United Airways, and later British Airways, he flew all the new types of aircraft introduced into the airline - The Spartan Cruiser II and III, the De Havilland DH 84 Dragons I and II, and the De Havilland DH 89 and 89A Dragon Rapides.

Not often were flights ever cancelled on the Western Isles route - which David liked to fly most of the time - and he would land at Glen Brittle, that picturesque field at the foot (literally)of the famous Cuillin Hills, at Askernish, Barra or Sollas etc, in the most violent conditions. Twice during the turnaround at these strips his aircraft was badly damaged by violent squalls, but that was all in a day's work to David. Anyone who has ever flown over these wild, but beautiful parts will understand, however, how no single trip was ever the same - the sea or the sky and the mountains would look different every day in the contrasting sunshine or shade, and the cloud formations were infinitely variable. Heading westwards in the morning with the sun illuminating all the ground in front, or eastwards on the way back into the sun, and the shadowy side of the mountains, each flight was like a pilgrimage for David. In the mornings, the sea around the Uists could be turquoise green and the sands at Barra like shining coral; in the evening the inlets and islands near the mainland could be pools of deep purple in a blazing red and orange sky. This was part of the drama in flying these routes - the absolute beauty could frequently stun people into silence.

Until WW II broke out, each year was much the same for David. There would be occasional excitement, such as having to mount a search flight from Renfrew on February 4th 1937 to look for a missing DH Dragonfly aircraft belonging to the *Daily Express* newspaper group; flying a special 'Air Mail' flight on March 12th 1937 to Campbeltown and Islay; and flying photographic survey flights for the Air Ministry over Yorkshire, Northumberland and Fife, to help with the construction of new aerodromes for the conflict that lay ahead.

Apart from 'Air Ambulance Charters' David began to fly a number of 'Funeral Charters' in 1937, which became increasingly popular to carry citizens of the Western Isles back home on their last journey, after they had died on the Mainland. Relatives would accompany the coffin and David would fly them all out to places like Islay, Tiree, Barra and Askernish.

Every year, being on the RAF Reserve list David would attend a week's course of refresher flying on RAF types at Prestwick, etc., to keep him up to date with the Service standards of flying. When the War eventually started, David would inevitably have been called up to serve in a bomber squadron - but for his accident at Hatston on April 19th 1940 in the Dragon. He fractured his pelvis, an ankle, ribs and his nose when his aircraft was smashed into the airfield boundary by a violent downdraught while he was landing in a squall. At the time he was flying an Army General to Kirkwall, en route for Norway, and the general was taken to hospital with concussion. David's injuries left him lame, and unable to put much pressure on the rudder bar of an aircraft - thus relegating him to lighter aircraft, and exempting him from RAF service in WW II. He stayed with Dragon Rapides thereafter and could not fly the C-47A Dakotas that eventually arrived with BEA after the war - because of the force needed on the rudder pedals in an 'engine - out' case.

After he was married in 1935, David and his wife went to live at 31 Calder Street, Lochwinnoch, Renfrewshire for a time, but by 1939 they had settled at Primrose Bank, Bishopton, where his two daughters were brought up.

Like the other great pioneer pilots in Scotland, David had the honour to inaugurate an Air Mail service, in his case the Glasgow - Campbeltown run on October 2nd 1939, and he had the inevitable 'chore' of having to sign many of the envelopes carried!

Throughout the War years, David put up tremendous efforts in keeping the services going, flying anything up to 5 1/2 hours a day, every day of the week, to keep open the vital 'Air Roads to the Isles", despite his painful injuries. When the war broke out on September 3rd 1939 David had flown 585 hours in the RAF, 114 hrs 05 mins with Midland & Scottish Air Ferries, 2,437 hrs 50 mins with Northern and Scottish, and 1,711 hrs 35 mins with Scottish Airways (from August 1st 1937). By the time WW II finished in Europe on May 8th 1945, David had flown another 4,439 hrs 30 mins during the conflict (from September 3rd 1939) - or about 800 hours on average per year !

When BEA took over Scottish Airways on February 1st 1947 David had flown a total of 9,673 hrs 50 mins civilian time to that date - 9,492 hrs 55 mins of it being with Northern and Scottish/Scottish Airways, under George Nicholson, over a 12 year period.

With BEA David took responsibility for the Ambulance flights, and trained the pilots on the DH 89A Rapides who succeeded the old wartime pioneers now.

In May 1948, emulating Capt. Ted Fresson who had originally discovered all the airstrips in the Northern Isles, David took Fresson's old DH Dragon (G-ACIT) from its current Renfrew home and on May 21st he flew it to Prestwick and then out to Islay, Oronsay and Colonsay for the day, carrying Messrs Johnston, Carr and Adam of the Ministry of Civil Aviation (M.C.A) to survey new landing strips in the West and North of Scotland. Next day they flew out again from Prestwick, this time to Tiree and Coll, and then back again. On May 31st he was off to Tiree and Benbecula in 'CIT with the Ministry team, and the next day to Sollas, Northton Beach (Harris), Stornoway, Kirkwall (Grimsetter), Bay of Housby (Stronsay), Hamsbrooke (Sanday), and back to Kirkwall for the night. On June 2nd he flew to Garbo Field on Sanday, then to N. Ronaldsay, to a small field on Westray, and then to a better site at Aikerness on Westray, and finally back to Kirkwall. It was, however, for deciding on strips for ambulance usage that David was making this expansive 'recce' - not for scheduled services again. David had charge of all Scottish air ambulance services for BEA, and his first for the new Government airline was when he flew the Rapide G-AHGF on August 25th 1947 to Islay and back. His last was on April 29th 1965, when he carried his final patient to the mainland from Shetland in the DH Heron - G-ANXB. This was his 1,140th ambulance trip for BEA, or 1,271st in total ! (A whole book could be written about these ambulance exploits - the ghastly weather conditions they were often flown in, the types of patients - ranging from mental cases to babies - and the efforts to get them back to the mainland in time to save their lives. One day this story will be told).

The last time he flew Fresson's Dragon G-ACIT, incidentally, was on January 30th 1949 after he had spent over a week with it in the Orkneys, ferrying workmen back and forth from Hatston to North Ronaldsay to construct an airstrip suitable for regular DH 89A Rapide services. He flew 'CIT back via Inverness that day - the last time the Dragon was seen in the Highlands. He did, however, fly Ted Fresson again, when the latter boarded David's BEA Heron G-ANXA at Renfrew on January 10th 1958 to fly up to Inverness. They had a chat at each end, and a few reminiscences !

David had turned most of the Ambulance flying over to other pilots by January 1957, and had gone back onto line flying - much of it up to Inverness (and points North). He was then in charge of the Heron fleet and responsible for training all the new crews on the four-engined De Havilland aircraft. But he did continue to fly ambulance flights whenever needed.

David finally retired from BEA on April 30th 1965 at the age of 60, and he lived at his home at Primrose Bank, Gledstone Road, Bishopton until he died on February 24th 1981, leaving his wife, Nina, and daughters Patricia and Sheila. He had flown a grand total of 17,349 hrs 40 mins. in his civil career - almost entirely in Scotland, and the last 7,675 hrs 50 mins was with BEA. He had been appointed an M.B.E. in the King's New Year's Honours List of January 1944, and after the War while on his ambulance flight duties with BEA, he was made a Member of the Order of St. John of Jerusalem. But for a lifetime spent in the difficult skies over Scotland and for the incredible efforts in operating almost 1,300 ambulance flights - many in conditions most pilots today would never dream of operating in - these awards seem barely adequate. It seems that many Scottish pioneer pilots were to suffer a similar lack of adequate public recognition in the post-war years of nationalisation.

William ("Bill") Baillie M.V.O., O.B.E.

joined Scottish Airways at Renfrew on August 4th 1939. He followed Henry Vallance down from Allied Airways (Gandar Dower) Ltd at Dyce, Aberdeen, where he had been a line pilot since May 3rd 1937, with the task of flying the scheduled services from Aberdeen up to Shetland and Orkney.

Bill had learned to fly at Brooklands, going solo after 7hrs 30 mins dual there on June 27th 1934. Afterwards he returned to his home "Storrs", Whitecraigs, Renfrewshire, and joined the Scottish Flying Club, flying there and acting as an instructor until he joined Allied Airways in May 1937 (with 259 flying hours to his credit).

When he started flying the Renfrew - Inverness - Shetland service for Scottish Airways on August 4th 1939, he had 1,846 hours to his name and was becoming very experienced in the Scottish skies. When war broke out, he flew the Dragon G-ACNG and the Rapides G-AFEY and G-AFRK between Harwell and French airfields between September 2nd and 14th, and then from September 28th to November 14th he was continuously engaged in shuttling around French airfields in Northern France in the Rapide 'FRK for National Air Communications (NAC - later the AAJC). He carried out some charters in the Northern Isles for NAC, and only resumed line flying at Renfrew on December 7th - on the Campbeltown/Islay run, on Spartan Cruisers G-ACZM or 'CYL.

Bill then managed to get himself transferred to Ted Fresson's Northern Section from January 3rd 1940, to March 14th 1940, based in Inverness. He followed his colleague Henry Vallance up there, but had another spell at Renfrew again, flying Spartan Cruiser IIs on the Campbeltown run.

He was back in Inverness from April 14th 1940 on relief duty to April 22nd then down once more to Renfrew but flying the Rapide G-AFRK to Campbeltown now, as well as carrying out a few air ambulance charters on it. The first time Bill flew the Western Isles service was on May 14th 1940, landing the Rapide 'FRK at Tiree, Barra, Benbecula, Sollas and back via the same points. Bill flew the new Renfrew - Sollas - Stornoway service in Rapide 'FOI on May 20th and stayed on the Island routes until August 30th 1940, when he transferred back North to the Inverness station, flying to the Northern Isles for Ted Fresson for the next 2 1/2 years. On November 10th 1943, he returned to Renfrew and the Southern Section for the last time.

Bills first flight back at Renfrew was an ambulance trip to Sollas (North Uist) and back on November 13th - one of a total of 32 he was to fly for Scottish Airways between 1939 and 1947. (see Appendix 3 for details). Back on the Western Isles run, he often flew 8 sectors a day on the one roundtrip in a Rapide, and it could be a different Rapide four days running (the fleet consisting of G-AFFF, 'FOI, 'GIF and 'GJF in Spring 1944).

On July 29th, 1944 Bill flew a charter to Islay and back - carrying the Chinese ambassador from London. What political events were determined by this is not known, but the Chinese representative was probably loaded up with 'Islay Mist' whisky!

Usually Bill flew for six days running and had one day off. During one period of seven days in August 1944 he flew a total of 38 sectors, and 29hrs 45 mins to the Hebrides.

November 21st 1944 was a day Bill never forgot - he was flying the Rapide G-AGIF on the milk run from Renfrew to Tiree and Stornoway, but after taking off from Tiree for Stornoway on the second leg, just 12 miles south-west of Tiree, Bill suddenly spotted an RAF Halifax bomber wallowing in the sea, and obviously about to sink. He circled and flew nearer the aircraft and then spotted 8 or 9 survivors in a dingy nearby. They waved furiously at him, and Bill circled low to let them know he had seen them. Then he radioed to Stornoway to give them the details and position, and returned to Tiree to let them know about the survivors, and give the lifeboat the details. After this, he went off on his way to Stornoway.

In February 1945 Bill did a short conversion course at the ATA Advance Flying Training School at White Waltham between the 3rd and the 14th of the month. He was converted onto the Hudson VI, making practice landings and circuits at Cheddington, Chalgrove and Bedford and going solo on it. Then he travelled to Liverpool where he flew the Avro XII, G-AGNI, on February 17th 1945 to assess this prototype of the Avro XIX feeder-liner, and practice landings on it. Then he flew a new Rapide (G-AGLP) up to Renfrew to get himself home.

Bill's next date was a Beam Approach Training (BAT) Course at Prestwick from February 26th to March 4th where he flew Oxfords and carried out a lot of Link Trainer instruction, being passed out as 'Proficient in S.B.A.'. Bill then returned to Renfrew and the Hebrides 'Milk Runs'.

April 10th 1945 saw Bill fly the second southbound service on the new Renfrew - Prestwick - Liverpool - Croydon route, in Rapide G-AGLP, passing David Barclay on his way up. Bill overnighted at Croydon and returned North on the 11th. The next time he flew the Croydon Service was on April 23rd (in 'GLP), followed by April 28th in 'GIF and back on April 30th in 'GLR etc. On June 27th, however the service started to return the same day, Bill flying 'GLR to Croydon and back (via Liverpool each way) in a matter of 6hrs 45 mins. After arriving at Croydon, Bill now started on July 10th to be scheduled at times to fly Croydon - Guernsey - Jersey the same day, and overnighting in Jersey. He might even fly a further Jersey - Guernsey - Jersey flight too, before returning next day to Glasgow!

Bill went down to Liverpool in April 1946, and was given a conversion course onto the C-47A Dakota by the famous pioneer pilot Nigel Pelly (who had flown for Midland & Scottish Air Ferries and the pre-war British Airways). Bill was being picked to become one of the first band of Dakota Captains in the post-war Railway Air Services group of companies.

On April 30th 1946 Bill started to fly Anson XIXs on the daily roundtrips to Croydon, but on May 14th he switched to the Dakota to make a proving flight over the route - after inaugurating a Renfrew - Belfast service on the Dakota in the morning. His own first passenger schedule proper to London with the Dakota was on May 31st 1946.

But Bill now had to teach others how to fly the Dakota, and so he gave instruction to a number of Captains and First Officers, including Messrs. Prentice, Hillary, W. Mackenzie, Ramsden, Martin, Clayton, Pooley, Affleck, T. Mackenzie, Appleby, Welford, Wells and "Smokey" Hayes as the Summer of 1946 flashed by. Most of his own line flying on the Dakotas was to Belfast and back, but on August 18th he flew a Dakota charter up

to Kirkwall - probably the first visit of an airline C-47A. (No doubt Bill proudly showed it off to all his islander friends!)

On Saturday, September 28th he had the unenviable task of taking a party of his Renfrew officials up in the Rapide G-AGLE and flying around the scene of the fatal crash of 'FFF on Craigton Hill the previous day. And when he next flew a Renfrew - London service on the Dakota, on October 18th 1946, Bill found himself using Northolt aerodrome from now on, instead of Croydon.

Having trained up most of the old 'stalwarts' at Renfrew to fly C-47A Dakotas, Bill now had to help David Barclay convert an equal number of new pilots to fly the DH 89A Rapides in future. At the end of Summer 1946, therefore, he was busy putting Messrs. McDermott, Leask, Fittall, Hadley and Woodward through their paces.

As previously recorded, Bill few the inaugural Dakota flight on November 18th on the new Northolt - Renfrew - Aberdeen route (which in effect was the London - Glasgow service with an extension to Aberdeen and back, on a same day basis). After the inaugural, on which he piloted 'GZA from London to Aberdeen and back to Renfrew, it became the norm for the Renfrew crew to fly down to Northolt in the afternoon and back to Renfrew the next morning, and a different Renfrew crew to fly the aircraft up to Aberdeen and back to Renfrew.

The last new service that Bill was involved with at Scottish Airways was the re-opening of the Aberdeen - Inverness - Stornoway service. On November 29th 1946 he operated the Rapide 'GLE on a Renfrew - Stornoway - Inverness - Aberdeen flight and next day he flew Aberdeen - Inverness - Aberdeen, followed by a special check at Aberdeen (Dyce) of the S.B.A. landing system (Standard Beam Approach). On December 2nd he flew a reciprocal Aberdeen - Inverness -Stornoway - Renfrew service.

Finally, in the closing weeks of his existence with Scottish Airways, Bill was given the very doubtful privilege of being cleared to fly one of the BEA 'Jupiter" class Junkers 52/3ms, (G-AHOD) when it appeared at Renfrew flown by Capt. Johnson on December 23rd.

In the last month - January 1947 - of Scottish Airways' existence, Bill did have a little excitement. On the 10th he had the 'honour' to convert his past Chief Pilot in Allied Airways, Eric Allen Starling onto the Dakota G-AGZB. Eric had returned from War service in RAF Coastal Command and had recently been flying Rapides for Ted Fresson's Northern Section. On January 16th, Bill used the locally-based Junkers 52, G-AHOD, on a mercy mission to drop badly needed supplies to a storm-bound lighthouse near Colonsay. Let the *Daily Mail* report explain it:

"Bill Baillie goes wave-hopping

Drops supplies to lighthousemen

With 20ft waves breaking only a few feet below their three-engined aircraft, Scottish Airways' flyers yesterday dropped parcels of cigarettes and newspapers to lighthousemen on Dubh Artach, 18 miles west of Colonsay, isolated by storms for 11 weeks, nearly three times their usual spell.

Renfrew pilots had a "whip round" and collected sufficient cigarettes and newspapers for five weighted parcels which were loaded into a 12-seater Jupiter class air liner due for a training flight.

Captain William Baillie, Scottish Airways' senior pilot, who has flown over a million miles, said last night: 'In a way it was a routine flight. We swooped down over the lighthouse at a height of 40 to 50 feet.

'The seas were rising wildly and touched the undercarriage of the plane.

'We were afraid to go too near the light in case our wing-tips made contact, and as the rock itself is only about 50ft across, we had a minute target on which to concentrate.

'My radio-operator, Harry Seed, thought he scored four bull's-eyes by dropping all the parcels on the balcony.'

Later from Keeper A Fawns waiting at Eraid lighthouse off Mull to relieve the marooned men, I learned that only one parcel had been secured - the rest were washed away by the waves. "

At the end of January 1947, Bill's last flight of all as the Senior Pilot of Scottish Airways was in the Dakota G-AGYZ on the 30th, positioning it from Northolt to Renfrew. This completed his 6,504 hrs 30 mins flying for Scottish Airways, between August 4th 1939 and January 31st 1947 (his total hours were now 8,350).

With the creation on February 1st 1947 of BEA's new Scottish

Capt. Bill Baillie in BEA uniform, about to inaugurate the Edinburgh - London (Northolt) Dakota service after Nationalisation of Scottish Airways. (Audrey Baillie)

Division, Bill was made Chief Pilot, and then in 1948 he moved down to London, eventually becoming Chief Flight Captain of BEA in 1950. He was awarded the O.B.E. after flying a BEA Viscount in the London - New Zealand Air Race in 1953, and awarded the M.V.O. for services in flying many members of the Royal Family about in later years. He became General Manager and later Deputy Director of BEA Flight Operations, and then set up BEA Airtours Ltd., their first charter subsidiary at Gatwick, as Managing Director. He retired as Group Safety Adviser, British Airways in 1976, and died after a routine operation on March 11th 1981 at the age of 64, leaving a widow Audrey and a son and daughter.

Henry Vallance

joined Scottish Airways at Renfrew on March 1st 1939, having decided to leave Allied Airways in Aberdeen to fly for Capt. Ted Fresson in Inverness.

Henry was born at 984 Govan Road, Glasgow on December 6th 1915, later moving farther out with his family to live in Paisley. At the age of 18 he went to the College of Aeronautical Engineering at Chelsea and Brooklands, followed by the Brooklands

School of Navigation. He was well trained as pilot, navigator and engineer when he joined Aberdeen (later Allied) Airways at Dyce in April 1936, and by the time he joined Scottish, he had flown a total of 1,617 hours in all weathers, in the Northern Isles and around the Highlands, including operating a number of ambulance flights. (One of them being spectacular to say the least !)

Renfrew being the HQ of Scottish, Henry had to sign on there with the Chief Pilot, David Barclay. But he looked for an early transfer back North, to work for Fresson and set up home in Inverness with his wife, Dorothy (née Johnston, from 17 Affleck Street, Aberdeen).

When he started at Scottish, David Barclay gave him the Dragon 'CNG to practice on at Abbotsinch for a day, then converted him to flying the Spartan Cruiser II. They were using Abbotsinch at this time because of the boggy state of the ground at Renfrew.

Henry took Gilbert Rae with him to practice landings on the Rapide 'FEY at Tiree and Islay on March 3rd then he flew an ambulance charter to Islay and went onto line service on the Belfast run. That was his first week with Scottish!

He stayed at Renfrew, flying all the different routes including the Western Isles run and the Glasgow - Inverness - Shetland service (from May 16th 1939), as well as to the Isle of Man and even some sectors around the Orkney Islands and between Thurso (Claredon) and Kirkwall. From May 27th 1939 he based himself in Orkney with the Northern Section, and flew to and from Thurso, Longhope, Sanday, Stronsay, North Ronaldsay, Westray - and even down to Renfrew and back.

Most days would start with a Kirkwall - Thurso round-trip (0900 - 0920/0930 - 0945), followed by a Kirkwall - Longhope round-trip (1200 - 1210/1210 - 1220), then an inter-island service Kirkwall-Stronsay - Sanday - Westray - North Ronaldsay - Kirkwall, between 12.40 and 14.00. Another two - day pattern Henry operated from Orkney was; Kirkwall - Wick - Inverness - Perth - Renfrew/Renfrew - Belfast - Renfrew/Renfrew - Isle of Man - Renfrew (Day 1) ; and then the second day; Renfrew - Perth - Inverness - Wick - Orkney! This totalled some 8 hrs 20 mins over the two days, and 12 sectors.

Henry flew the last Kirkwall - Thurso scheduled service ever for Scottish Airways on August 31st 1939 - in the evening. Next day, September 1st, with War imminent, he was ordered to fly the Rapide G-AEWL to Renfrew, and he travelled back to Inverness by road to fly the Dragon 'CIT down the same evening (he took his wife with him on this flight).

Then, like the other pilots, on September 2nd he flew 'CIT down South to Harwell, shuttling across the Channel to French airfields to move British Service personnel around. He returned 'CIT to Renfrew on September 5th and flew back South again in Rapide 'FRK. He continued with the flights to Rheims, etc with S.P.&E. (Service Personnel & Equipment) until September 14th, returning to Renfrew to start operating Spartan Cruisers on the Campbeltown/Islay run from September 15th. He had another spell in the South, this time with the Dragon G-ACNG, between October 13th and 22nd, flying across the Channel and then he was back on the Western Isles routes out of Renfrew.

Henry finally got back North on December 19th 1939 and was based at Inverness over Christmas. From December 30th, however, he moved back up to Kirkwall to fly the early morning services down to Inverness each day (out of Hatston at this time). He moved to Inverness on February 16th, then back up to Kirkwall on March 5th.

He flew the last inter-island service out of Kirkwall on April 27th 1940 and then it was closed for the War - and a considerable time afterwards. Henry then re-located yet again down to Inverness, from May 3rd 1940 onwards. Duties here would normally consist of flying Inverness - Kirkwall - Sumburgh and back one day, then on alternate days flying Inverness - Wick (until it was dropped) - Kirkwall and back, or perhaps two Inverness - Kirkwall and return flights on the one day.

With the rigours of flying in those climates and constant pressure to keep flying, however ill you might feel, Henry went down with Pneumonia suddenly on November 6th 1940, but with some excellent attention from the Inverness Royal Northern Hospital and local G.P., recovered rapidly after two months, and was back flying again on January 2nd 1941!

On February 1st 1941 Henry suffered a broken con-rod in the port engine of Rapide G-AEWL between Kirkwall and Sumburgh, but landed safely. Bill Baillie flew up a relief (G-ADAJ) and 'rescued' the southbound passengers and Henry as well. The odd motor failure - due in many cases to the poor grade wartime petrol they were using - and tyre punctures afflicted the aircraft in the Northern and Southern Sections during the war. Suffice to say that on no occasion did any such failure result in a Rapide or Dragon having to ditch, or crash - a magnificent tribute to the skills of this devoted band of pilots - the best anywhere in the world.

There was a spot of excitement for Henry on February 15th 1941, on his way from Kirkwall (Wideford) down to Inverness in the Rapide G-AERN. First of all just after take-off his radio packed-up, closely followed by his gyro compass. In thick cloud, trying to avoid Scapa Flow, the warships down below suddenly started to open up with their Ack-Ack guns, and shell bursts appeared close to Henry. He made a rapid exit from the Orkneys and then flying in and out of cloud towards the Cromarty Firth a German aircraft appeared. Let the local newspaper record what happened (as related after the War finished);

"Junkers 88 was curious

A neck-and-neck flight between a Scottish Airways Ltd. machine and a Junkers 88, 700ft over Tarbat Ness, Ross and Cromarty, is one of the stories of Luftwaffe interference with civil aviation that can now be told.

It happened one morning early in 1941 when Captain Henry Vallance, of Inverness, was piloting his machine to Inverness, that the enemy plane suddenly appeared from a bank of cloud a mile away on his starboard side.

It flew ahead then came back. Not more than 100 yards separated the machines as they raced along together.

Then the Junkers swung away and left me to carry on home," said Captain Vallance yesterday. "Not a shot was fired. I think he was just curious. My six passengers knew nothing about it because the blacked-out windows were up against the wind."

Henry's last scheduled call at Wick (Hillhead Aerodrome) was on February 25th 1941, and because the RAF then moved in to enlarge the aerodrome and build hard runways, calls were discontinued for the rest of the War. In dire need, passengers could be (and were) flown to RAF Castletown aerodrome, close to both Thurso and Wick.

Henry remembers how, when they were flying up to Shetland on the last leg, they would often arrive just minutes after German marauders had flown in low over the sea, and shot up the airfield! It seemed to be a common occurrence. With the radios in use again, and carrying Radio Officers all the time, Henry remembers that for the rest of the War they frequently intercepted streams of radio warnings from Shetland and Orkney about the presence or arrival of German aircraft - yet despite keeping a close look out, Henry never saw an enemy aircraft again. The messages did, however, keep them constantly aware of the dangers they faced. If it was a clear day they would fly down 'on the deck', hoping the camouflaged wings would hide them from the Germans above. If it was cloudy, they would keep

Capt. Henry Vallance outside his 'castle' style house in Inverness with his 'Rudge' motorcycle. (Graeme Young)

in the clouds all the way.

Fresson's favourite Rapide G-ADAJ was in for a C of A overhaul from February 11th to April 17th 1941, and Henry gave it an air test and cleared it for use again on the latter date. (The Rapides G-AERN and 'EWL, with the Dragon 'CIT had given unceasing work in the meantime).

From October 7th 1941, Henry had to start using RAF Skeabrae (on the West Mainland of Orkney) for landing at Kirkwall, due to the state of the ground at their Wideford grass hilltop field. Then they obtained regular permission to use Hatston and from October 18th he called at the Naval base there on all the scheduled flights, up to November 24th when they moved back to RAF Skeabrae. Henry began to use the newly constructed RAF runways at Grimsetter (which is still the airport today) on December 20th. Ted Fresson had landed at Grimsetter the previous day (December 19th) and although the runways were not fully completed the schedules were now allowed to use this aerodrome - because Fresson's pilots had run into trouble with the new CO at Hatston who took a dislike to having civil aircraft around - especially more than one at a time (and on occasions all three Rapides could be there together !) Hence they had been 'banished' to Skeabrae again, but happily Grimsetter had just become available in the nick of time (and was only a few fields away from their long-used Wideford aerodrome). Wideford reverted to farm pastures, and was never used again.

Extremes of weather rarely affected flying in the North - so skilled and phlegmatic were the pilots, with their long experience. On November 1st 1941 for instance, Henry had to land temporarily at RAF Evanton (near Invergordon in the Cromarty Firth) on the way back to Inverness, due to very foggy conditions. Eventually he took off again, and used Fresson's old emergency landing strip on Culloden Moor (at Leanach Farm) to deplane and re-plane passengers, and refuel (from a motor lorry

RECORD OF FLIGHTS.

Date.	Aircraft Type.	Markings.	Engines Type.	H.P.	Journey From.	To.	Time of Departure Hrs.	Mins.	Time of Arrival Hrs.	Mins.	Time in Air Hrs.	Mins.	Pilot.	Remarks.
					Brought forward									
18.2.42	DH 89	G-AGDG	Gipsy VI	400	IV OY SJ OY	IV	8.10	45		1.10	2	50	self	Airline 3.40
19.2.42					IV OY Dalcross	IV	1.05	1.35			2	40		(Fog IV) 2.40
20.2.42					IV OY SJ OY	IV	1.05	45	50	1.05	3	45		3.45
21.2.42		G-ADAJ			IV OY IV OY	IV	1.05	1.00	1.05	1.05	4	15		4.15
23.2.42	DH 84	G-AELT	Gipsy Major	260	IV IV	IV				05		5		Petrol cocks up in port aircraft on take off 05
	DH 89	G-ADAJ	Gipsy VI	400	IV OY IV OY SJ	IV	1.00	1.05	1.05	45	5	40		5.40
24.2.42		G-AGDG			IV SJ OY	IV	1.45	45		1.05	13	35		3.35
25.2.42					IV OY SJ IV		1.00	45		2.05	3	45		3.45
					Carried forward							05		27.25

Two pages from Henry Vallance's log-books.

Above: The first recorded Scottish Airways' airline landing at Dalcross (then an RAF aerodrome) - albeit a diversion in fog on February 19th 1942.

Below: A laconic note in the 'Remarks' column for February 7th 1944 - "G over 100 mph SJ" (Gusting over 100 mph at Sumburgh) must be almost unique for any pilot flying a DH Rapide!
(Henry Vallance)

RECORD OF FLIGHTS.

Date.	Aircraft Type.	Markings.	Engines Type.	H.P.	Journey From.	To.	Time of Departure Hrs.	Mins.	Time of Arrival Hrs.	Mins.	Time in Air Hrs.	Mins.	Pilot.	Remarks.
					Brought forward									
28.1.44	DH. 89	G-AGIC	Gipsy VI	400	IV OY IV OY IV	IV	1.00	1.20	65	1.10	4	25	self	Airline 4.7
29.1.44		G-AEWL			IV SJ OY IV		1.20	1.10		1.16	3	45	L	3.4
1.2.44		G-AGIC			IV OY SJ IV		50	35		2.10	3	35	L	3.3
2.2.44		G-AEWL			IV OY IV OY	IV	1.00	1.15	65	1.20	4	30		4.3
3.2.44		G-AEWL			IV OY SJ IV		1.45	55		1.40	3	50	L	3.5
4.2.44		G-ADAJ			IV OY IV OY	IV	1.50	50	1.20	55	4	55		4.5
7.2.44		G-AGIC			IV IV SJ		50	1.35			2	25	NL	G. over 100mph SJ 2.0
8.2.44					SJ IV SJ IV		1.40	2.00	1.45		5	25	L	5.5
					Carried forward							50		32.

load of petrol drums), and take-off for Hatston again !

On February 19th 1942 very thick fog even covered Culloden, so Henry used RAF Dalcross for landing his passengers from Orkney (one of the first recorded uses of Dalcross by a scheduled service - as it subsequently became the civil airport for Inverness in August 1947, and still is today).

Winds could be gusting to fantastic levels - yet they would still fly and land with motors running, to be held still on the ground by Fresson's specially trained teams of ground handlers who held onto wings, tail-plane and fuselage until take-off again! In high winds the tail would be lifted onto the tail-board of a lorry and lashed down until ready to go - motors still running. Thus on November 11th 1941 Henry records leaving Inverness for Kirkwall in Rapide G-AGDG, but having (unusually) to return 90 minutes later due to "winds gusting to 90kts". On January 22nd and 23rd 1944, Henry had to overnight at Sumburgh after arriving from Inverness in G-ADAJ, and recorded for both trips "Gusts at Sumburgh over 90 m.p.h." On February 1st 1944 he went one better - he took off from Inverness for Sumburgh but was recalled to Inverness for a while due to extraordinarily high winds over Shetland; then he set off again and landed at Sumburgh - in winds that he noted had been "gusting to over 100 m.p.h."!

On Sunday May 14th 1944 Henry brought back the Rapide 'DAJ from Stornoway, after he and Ted Fresson had flown out in it to set up arrangements for starting the long-time awaited scheduled service from Inverness. Henry remembers that Sunday flight well, as in all ignorance and thinking they would score a point or two with the locals, they took out a load of Sunday newspapers for the inhabitants of Lewis and Harris. Unofrtunately, they forgot the strict religious views of the people of the Western Isles, which were brought home to them on arrival at the aerodrome at Stornoway. The airline's local agent came on board to greet them, but when they showed him the Sunday papers (the first time they had ever arrived on the island on the day of publication) he threw up his hands in horror, grabbed the bundles and threw them all into the passenger toilet at the back of the Rapide, locking the door tight behind them! He then whispered that he could not possibly sell them on a Sunday!

Ted Fresson started the schedule himself on Wednesday, May 24th 1944 in Rapide G-AGIC, and Henry flew it on Monday May 29th for the first time, in 'EWL (the service operated on Mon. Wed. and Fri. for the first year). Thereafter he flew to Stornoway regularly, as well as on the Shetland run (the roundtrip to Stornoway from Inverness would be around 2 hrs 10 mins altogether, compared with that to Sumburgh (non-stop) of around 3 hrs 50 mins.

One of the problems during the war, Henry remembers, was that of obtaining the little extra luxuries in the food line that people take for granted in peacetime. Even with everything tightly rationed, it was still possible in the Highlands to find the occasional dozen farm fresh eggs, or a chicken, turkey, pheasant or grouse! In fact food was not rationed in the Orkneys or Shetland, and so Ted Fresson used to get legs of lamb in Shetland and fresh eggs in Orkney, bringing them back to Inverness to share amongst staff and family alike. They often used to pickle the eggs, to preserve them for future use!

Henry remembers that Johnny Hankins became an expert at landing on Fair Isle (mid-way between Orkney and Shetland) to pick up poultry and game, but without logging the calls officially! Jock Young, on the other hand, was the fishing expert, and a deft hand with a 12-bore and used to load up with rods and guns when he went North. The normal shooting/fishing dates on the calendar meant nothing to him and Jock (Henry remembers) was a "fearsome person when armed with his fishing rods!"

During the war, they would hold parties in each other's houses or lodgings in Inverness, to relieve the strain and boredom - although there was seldom much of the latter! Ted Fresson would often hold 'Do's' at his bungalow in Mayfield Road, and Henry recalls what a magnificent pianist he was. His favorite piece was 'The Grand March' from Aïda (the opera), and this would always be played early in the evening. Henry once asked Ted to play some other music from Aïda, which he then did like a true professional.

Ted always used to refer to the two Greenhalgh brothers as 'Greensleeves' - eternally confusing them with the piece of music by Vaughan Williams, and he nearly always jokingly remarked to Bill Baillie at these parties *"I didn't hire you as a fire guard"* - because Bill unconsciously always used to stand with his back to the fire, blocking the heat from the poor war-time coal!

Henry rented a castle-style house in Inverness during the war, in Merlewood Road, on top of the hill overlooking the River Ness and the West. He was told later by neighbours that the house was supposed to be 'haunted', and at one corner of it was a Scottish-style rounded turret, with a spiral staircase and two upper rooms. Henry rarely went up there, but strangely, whenever he did, his hair stood on end, and it suddenly seemed extraordinarily cold!

What the house did have, however, was a large tree-covered estate at the rear, and lots of game in it. Henry kept a couple of shot-guns loaded up all the time in his bedroom, and on waking up in the morning he would empty the barrels at whatever moved

DH Dragon Rapide G-AGIC seen on the ground at a snow-covered RAF Hatston sometime during World War Two.

Capt. Henry Vallance, holding a sextant whilst flying with KLM after Scottish Airways was Nationalised. (Henry Vallance)

amongst the trees. One morning he could have sworn he had hit a very large rabbit, but suddenly it jumped up and ran a few yards again. Henry emptied a second gun at it - and the rabbit suddenly sprang up and vanished across the garden! Only later did he discover that his next door neighbour, a lorry driver, had rigged up a bundle of fur on the end of a long wire - and was almost paralytic with laughter at Henry's efforts!

Henry also remembers encountering some tricky weather conditions during the time he was with Scottish Airways - one particular occasion being in August 1939 while flying out of Sumburgh (Shetland) for Kirkwall (Orkney) on the way back to Inverness. On this occasion he was somewhere near Fair Isle when he ran into an almost inpenetrable black wall of cloud and torrential rain. For some reason the wireless operator promptly 'lost' his radio capability, and they could hear absolutely nothing from the ground stations.

Henry had his long trailing aerial line out, and tried his trick of descending slowly (until the lead weights on the end of the aerial wire struck the water, giving him adequate time to straighten out over the waves). But the murk was too dark, the headwind too boisterous, and so he climbed again, all the time trying to maintain his original course. They were getting short on fuel and then he suddenly saw a hole in the blackness, and, looking down, saw a small circle of sea at the bottom, with a bit of cliff at one edge. He put everything down, reduced speed and dropped in a steep spiral as quickly as he could down the small vertical funnel in the clouds. He caught the trailing aerial on the cliffs, and left it there, but he recognised the "Old Man of Hoy", set course over

Stromness and Scapa Flow, and made it into Wideford - just in time!

The second occasion was also in 1939, and Henry was flying the Inverness - Perth - Renfrew service (via the route across the Grampian Mountains and down the east side of Scotland, which was the best for weather conditions). He flew into a massive Cumulo-Nimbus cloud formation and found his Rapide being forced up in air currents and thrown around quite badly. The Pitot head became iced up, as did the Venturi tube and the small propeller driven generator. Suddenly he realised everything had gone very quiet and he was startled to see he had no airspeed on the clock at all. It was the classic case of: "There I was, with nothing on the clock "!.... Henry pushed the stick forward to get speed up in the up and down draughts, and suddenly seeing a gap with clear sky overhead, started a spiral climb up this narrow crevice in the massive clouds, until he came out over the top at 10,000ft or so. He then found his way around the tops, to descend into Perth unharmed.

Amongst Henry's air ambulance flights was one from Benbecula to Inverness in Rapide 'GJG on October 14th 1944. In March 1945, like Bill Baillie, Henry went down to White Waltham (near Maidenhead) for a two-week course on the Hudson V and VI, together with the other pilots Regan, Millis, O'Reilly and Sweeney, then it was back to Inverness to resume line - flying.

With the war over now, Henry flew into Dyce, Aberdeen on June 14th 1945 for the first time since his days with Gandar Dower's airline there, and on some days found himself even flying two roundtrips to Stornoway and back, such was the demand of traffic. He started to use Wick again - on charters - and on August 31st 1945 made a night air ambulance dash in 'GDG to Stornoway to pick up a patient and fly him to Renfrew.

Effectively his tremendous efforts for Scottish Airways came to an end on November 2nd 1945, when he was posted down to Liverpool to fly the Belfast and Dublin routes from Speke for Railway Air Services. Two Rapides he had used in Scotland, G-AERN and 'ERZ were back with the AAJC HQ there, and Henry flew these and also converted to the four-engined DH 86 again (for the Dublin run). On December 5th he also converted onto the new Avro XIXs, before being posted down to Croydon from December 13th 1945. He flew out his days in the UK with RAS, at Croydon, doing the runs to Belfast or Dublin on Avro XIX, or DH 86 or 89A aircraft. Between April 15th and May 24th 1946, he flew a few odd Renfrew-based services on Rapides to the Western Isles, on Avro XIXs to Belfast or down to Croydon, while he enjoyed a few days back in his native Glasgow. While there, he checked out Bill Baillie and Donald Prentice on the Avro XIX G-AGUE on April 21st. And his last flight for RAS was a Croydon - Liverpool - Belfast roundtrip on a DH 86 (G-AENR) on May 24th 1946.

Henry had run up a total of 8,496 hrs 25 mins flying by this time, exactly 6,431 hrs 45 mins being for Scottish Airways (between 1939 and 1945). Over the 7 years he had averaged over 900 hours flying per year. He had thus put up an amazing total of annual flying hours, spending, like David Barclay and Jock Young at Renfrew, and Ted Fresson and Bill Baillie at Inverness, the entire War years flying for Scottish Airways. Henry received the Kings Commendation for Valuable Services in the Air in August 1945 - a very well deserved award for his flying skills, but again, in hindsight a totally inadequate reward for all he had done.

Henry decided not to remain with the company that was taking over all the airlines now - BEA - and with several other pilots he applied for, and got a job with the newly re-established Dutch airline KLM in Amsterdam. John Michie went first, then Jock Young, and Henry Vallance followed soon after, with David MacFarlane.

Henry's career in KLM spanned the 1946 - 1971 period, and when he finally retired on September 28th 1971, he had flown all their piston and jet-engined types, was on the long-haul DC-8s, a Senior Captain of the highest grade (checked out on any airport worldwide), and had notched up an amazing final total of 28,123 flying hours. He lives now in retirement in the Isle of Man, with a grown up son and daughter in London and Amsterdam respectively. Dorothy sadly, died in 1992.

John ("Jock") Young

was another of the stalwart pilots who helped to make Scottish Airways great. He joined in 1936, and went right through the War up to April 1946, when he left to join KLM - Royal Dutch Airlines.

Jock was born on May 29th 1913 at "Rockline", 45, Loughborough Road, Kirkcaldy, Fife, and he grew up wanting to become a motor engineer. He dabbled in motor bicycles, sidecars, and small cars, and raced them in local meetings on field and beach in Fife.

The family later moved to 13, Stonefield Avenue Paisley, and Jock suddenly became very interested in flying when he took a 5s. 0d. flight in a local joy-riding aircraft one day; and liked it very much! Soon he had joined the Scottish Flying Club at Renfrew to learn how to fly, and he gained his pilot's licence there on August 24th 1934, just past his 21st birthday!

Jock was only 5ft 8ins in height, but with his fair hair and striking blue eyes, looked very handsome in an airline uniform. He flew with the S.F.C. as an instructor at Renfrew for another two years while earning money as a motor engineer nearby, and at the beginning of August 1936, having just obtained his Commercial Pilot's licence on August 8th, he joined Northern and Scottish Airways as a line pilot under David Barclay the Chief Pilot - just at the time when radio was starting to be placed in all the aircraft, and Wireless Officers recruited.

Jock was a highly talented pilot with a natural ease of flying, and never had anything that remotely approached an incident in his entire flying career. He had a tremendous sense of humour, and not a great liking for rules and regulations - except where safety was concerned. He was based at Renfrew, and flew the Western Isles and Argyll services continuously through the War years.

He took a great pride in his flying, always keeping the passenger's comfort foremost in his mind, so much so that he gained the reputation amongst his fellow pilots for always giving them a 'smooth ride, and soft landing' - whatever the weather.

Perhaps because of his respect for those he carried, Jock actually kept a record in his log-books of the number of passengers he flew on every flight. He totalled them up continuously, page by page, and so when he handed in his cards at Scottish Airways on April 11th 1946, he knew he had carried precisely 37,118 altogether, during his Renfrew career! He had also flown a total of 8,600 hrs 35 mins by then, some 6,202 of which were all on Rapides, 339 on Dragons, and 1,327 on Spartan Cruisers.

On May 15th 1946 Jock began flying with KLM following close on the heels of John Michie, and to be joined soon by Henry Vallance and David MacFarlane. First of all he was checked out on the four-engined Douglas C-54 then the twin-engined C-47. Soon he was off on runs around Europe, flying firstly as Second-Pilot, then by June 22nd he was able to fly as Captain on C-47s. At the end of August he began to crew as Second-Pilot on Far East services on C-54s now, changing over to Constellations in November 1946.

In January 1947 Jock began to crew as 2nd Pilot with John Michie, by now a Captain on the Constellation fleet, and they flew the North Atlantic routes to New York, via Prestwick. On one of these services, the Constellation suffered from sudden depressurization, and Jock had one of his eardrums burst. This took some time to mend and left Jock with constant ear problems. He went back to European routes, flying Dakotas by day and by night, in all weathers through the Summer of 1947.

He was now suffering constantly from ear problems, and so in November 1947, with great regret he left KLM and gained a temporary job with the Ministry of Civil Aviation (MCA) Airport Check Flight at Gatwick, flying an Avro XIX or Airspeed Consul around the UK to see all the approach lighting was properly set up at the civil airports. His ear problem was not going away, and after checking out the lighting at Tiree, Benbecula, Stornoway, Sumburgh and Dyce in July 1948, Jock Young had to finally retire from flying at the early age of 35, and hang up his flying gear for good. His final total of passengers carried reached 42,025 altogether and Jock's hours totalled some 9,400 hrs 40 mins.

Jock had a family of two sons and a daughter to look after (Iain, Graeme and Alison), and he retired now to live in Kennedy Road, Ardrossan, Ayrshire. He bought a local pub there, "The Horseshoe", and ran that for 10 years but Jock was well-enough endowed to be able to leave it, and enjoy complete retirement when his wife became ill and later died. Jock himself saw his children leave home to get married, and move down to live in North Surrey, but he stayed at Ardrossan and died at Saltcoats in 1978. He had been a 'Free Spirit' most of his life (as his children describe it), had thoroughly enjoyed his career in Scottish Airways and KLM, and had gained a reputation 'for safety and reliability' in flying second to none. The growth of aviation in Scotland owes a lot to those few pioneers like Jock Young.

No Smoking near the Aircraft!
Capt. John ("Jock") Young standing beside Northern and Scottish Airways' DH Dragon G-ACOR (still in its British Airways blue livery) at Renfrew. (Graeme Young)

TELEGRAMS:
SCOTAIRWAY, RENFREW

TELEPHONE:
RENFREW 2231 (4 LINES)

SCOTTISH AIRWAYS LIMITED

DIRECTORS:
SIR STEVEN BILSLAND, BT., M.C., D.L. (CHAIRMAN)
T. L. ADAM   E. E. FRESSON, O.B.E.   H. T. LEITH
G. NICHOLSON   J. W. RATLEDGE   C. H. SUTHERLAND
MAJOR MALCOLM S. SPEIR, M.C.   W. YEAMAN
WING COMMANDER A. H. MEASURES,
C.B.E., M.I.MECH.E. (MANAGING)

AIRPORT FOR GLASGOW
RENFREW

2nd April 1946.

TO WHOM IT MAY CONCERN

Captain John Young has been employed by this Company as a Senior Pilot since he joined in 1936 and has carried out all his Flying Duties up to date without accident.

He is leaving the Company in order to obtain wider experience on larger types of aircraft and more modern equipment than we have available at the present time . He has the knowledge and experience necessary to qualify for a suitable senior appointment.

Captain Young leaves the Company with the Best Wishes of myself and my Co-Directors.

Director.

Bernard ("Tug") Wilson, John Annesley Hankins, and other Captains joined the airline in turn from 1935 onwards. Some of them stayed on for a few years, others left for War service once hostilities broke out in 1939. Then there were some Royal Air Force and Fleet Air Arm pilots who were 'rested' by the Services from spells of duty in the 1940-45 period by being sent up to fly Rapides with Scottish Airways for some months at a time. Hardly a 'rest from ops'! Indeed, one pilot (he shall be nameless) came up to Inverness on such a 'rest' from the Royal Air Force, made one trip up to Orkney, then took such a dislike to the weather on the way back that he landed at RAF Evanton (on the coast of the Moray Firth near Invergordon), dispatched the passengers by bus to Inverness, abandoned the aircraft and disappeared, never to be seen locally again !

More Captains arrived before and during the war, who stayed some time with the airline - like **Donald Prentice, Bernard T. O'Reilly, Iain Ramsey, William J Johnson, J. Kennedy, John Michie, "Smokey" Hayes, Bill Mackenzie, Tom Mackenzie, Stan Clayton, Alec Appleby, Johnny Afflec, "Windy" Martin, Bill Fittall, Bill Pooley, John Ramsden, Johnny Wells,** and **Eric Allen Starling,** etc.

The most famous of these was **Eric Starling** who was one of the great pioneers of flying in Scotland, numbered alongside Ted Fresson, David Barclay, Bill Baillie and Henry Vallance. These five between them represent Scotland's longest serving pioneers, achieving more than many of the rest combined. Eric had been the Chief Pilot of Aberdeen (later Allied) Airways at Dyce from 1934 to 1939, and after distinguished RAF service in Coastal Command from 1940 to 1945, in the Atlantic and Indian Oceans had joined Scottish Airways at Inverness on January 2nd 1946. He flew the Northern routes under Ted Fresson until October 14th and then transferred South to Renfrew, for the rest of his career.

While based at Inverness he flew an ambulance case from Sumburgh via Dyce to Renfrew on February 7th in the face of severe gales. On February 23rd he was flying the nonstop Inverness - Sumburgh service in very heavy snow showers, and at Sumburgh the visibility was down to 200 yards. But short of petrol he had to land there and with all his previous experience of flying in such terrible conditions managed to pull off a beautiful landing. However, the same conditions prevailed at Kirkwall on February 27th, and Eric had to return to Inverness this time, without landing in Orkney. He succeeded in getting there later in the day.

Eric took his wife Eleanor (née Castell, from Aberdeen, and a previous Editor on *The Press & Journal*), eldest son Angus and daughter Zoe up for a joy-ride in the Rapide G-ADAJ at Inverness (Longman) on March 16th while carrying out an air test.

From April 15th 1946, at the start of the new 1946 Summer schedules, Eric used Hatston aerodrome at Kirkwall (the old R.N. airfield) while Grimsetter was closed for repairs. And on April 17th he flew the third service down to Renfrew of the re-opened North-South link (which had started again on April 15th after being closed since 1939). From May 11th Eric started to call

Capt. Eric Allen Starling, one of Scotland's greatest pioneer pilots, ranking alongside Ted Fresson himself, is seen here with Dan-Air Stewardesses Jane Summers and Julia Wall at Stavanger on the 50th Anniversary of his starting Allied Airways (Gandar Dower) schedules across the North Sea in 1937. (Peter Clegg)

at Wick aerodrome again (also closed for civil operations during the War). On May 29th even he couldn't get into Sumburgh in visibility of less than 150 yds, and he managed to get back to Hatston this time.

Eric took his son Angus with him on the occasional service to Stornoway and back - loads were lighter here, and the scenery more breathtaking. Then, after flying his family over to Aberdeen on October 12th in the Rapide G-AGDG and spending two days there on holiday, Eric flew them down to Renfrew on the 14th and started flying from George Nicholson's base on October 18th.

Eric flew all the island routes during October and on the 30th of that month took off from Renfrew in 20 yds visibility and landed at Campbeltown in 200 yds visibility ! With the start of the Winter schedules, he also found himself flying the new Renfrew - Aberdeen - Orkney - Shetland services from November 8th on Rapides.

Finally Eric flew as First Officer with Donald Prentice on the C-47A Dakota, G-AGZA on November 30th to Northolt and back to Renfrew, and after a spell of Rapide flying on Aberdeen - Inverness - Stornoway in December, found himself flying the new Dakotas as F.O. with Capts. Morton, Ramsden, Johnson, Martin and Baillie over the next few weeks - usually on the Northolt runs, but occasionally to Aberdeen.

As the last month of Scottish Airways' existence arrived, Eric finally converted to Captain on the C-47As in January 1947, flying them himself now and beginning to give instruction on them to new First Officers by February (under BEA jurisdiction from here on). He had tried out 'circuits and bumps' on a German Junkers Ju.52/3m on January 29th (G-AHOD), but was not very impressed!

Eric had only flown 939 hrs 50 mins with Scottish Airways, but had brought all the experience of his flying to this airline in its dying year.

After this Eric was quickly appointed BEA Flight Captain on the Rapide and Dakota fleets from July 1st 1947, and started to fly the new Viking aircraft that month (he did have to fly a few Ju.52/3m schedules, too, but these aircraft were all withdrawn from use on August 9th). He progressed rapidly in BEA, becoming Flight Manager, Scotland in 1949 and holding this post until he retired as BEA's oldest and most senior Captain on December 28th 1971. For his last four years (1968-1971) like David Barclay before him, Eric became the manager of the Air Ambulance Division, flying many trips to save patients' lives.

Eric finally finished with a grand total of 12,548 flying hours, 940 of which had been with Scottish Airways, 2,741 with Aberdeen Airways, (pre-war) and 6,505 hours with BEA up to his retirement. He and Henry Vallance have survived all the other pioneers, and Eric is now in his 83rd year, with a son in Ayrshire and two daughters in Sussex, all married. His wife Eleanor sadly died in 1977 not long after his retirement.

John Michie was the son of the Provost of Renfrew who had been involved in the effort to keep the aerodrome open in the mid-1930s and recognised as the major airport for South West Scotland (see earlier Chapter).

He had learned to fly with the Scottish Flying Club at Renfrew, and often joked later in life about his "mis-spent youth, spent at the billiard table or aircraft of the S.F.C." At the outbreak of W.W.II, he flew Lockheed Aircraft Co. warplanes across the Atlantic for a time, delivering their aircraft to RAF bases in the U.K. Then he joined Scottish Airways and flew from Renfrew for the rest of the airline's existence, leaving to go to KLM with Henry Vallance, Jock Young and Co. in 1946.

When John retired from KLM, he and his wife Mary went to live in Virginia Water in Surrey. He acted as Aviation Consultant for some years, but died suddenly in the late 1980's, leaving his wife and daughter (who currently lives near Uxbridge).

Capt John Michie, just after leaving Scottish Airways to work for KLM in 1946. His father was the Provost of Renfrew.
(Graeme Young)

John Philip Rae. "Johnny" Rae had first flown in Scotland with John Sword's Midland & Scottish Air Ferries at Renfrew from March 1st 1933 as the Deputy Chief Pilot of the airline (and Chief Pilot at Renfrew) under Sqn. Ldr. Harold Malet. When M&SAF ceased operations, he left in June 1934 and rejoined the De Havilland Aircraft Co. as a test pilot.

Capt John Philip Rae in his Highland Airways uniform. Note the cap-badge with the 'H.A.' motif.

He had been born in 1906, at Ilford, Essex, although the Rae family was descended from antecedents who lived in the Newmachar area of Aberdeenshire in the eighteenth century. John Rae's father was in the jute trade, and had come South to live in Essex during his career, and he tried to encourage John to become a jute merchant too.

However, John persuaded his parents to allow him to be apprenticed to the De Havilland Aircraft Co. at Stag Lane and there he duly passed out as a qualified engineer, and a member of the RAFVR, and budding pilot at the same time.

In 1927, the D.H. test pilot there was killed, and John Rae immediately applied for the vacant test-pilot's post, and was accepted. He then began a career in testing, and a few years later was sent out to Chile to help assemble and test-fly some D.H. Moth aircraft for the Chilean Air Force.

When he returned from Chile, John took a job for a short while with Aerofilms at Hendon, and then got married in 1932. After the more highly-paid job with M&SAF folded up, he worked for De Havillands again for some months, travelling to Rhodesia to help operate a new Moth flying club out there. But pay was bad, and so he returned to get a job with Ted Fresson and Highland Airways in Kirkwall from May 1st 1935 - where he remained through the take-over by United, then British Airways, (becoming Scottish Airways) until October 1937.

Johnny Rae became a noted Orkney-based pilot - like his successor Johnny Hankins - and flew some amazing ambulance trips during his memorable stay in Kirkwall.

Leaving the Highlands, John opened a garage in Shoreham with Adam Smith - another of Fresson's pilots - but this did not work out well and so he joined the Air Observers and Navigation School at Shoreham aerodrome to train pilots with the RAFVR.

When WW II broke out, John went to Canada with the Royal Air Force, joining Ferry Command to fly aircraft from the USA to the UK. But in fact he spent most of his time there helping to organise the Ferry Bridges, and he personally accompanied the senior officers who recc'd the new route down through the USA to the Caribbean, S. America and across to West (and thence North) Africa.

At the end of 1943 John returned to the RAF in Britain, and became C.O. of a Dakota squadron - No 512 - flying out of Broadwell. He trained his crews in the art of paratroop dropping, and glider-towing. He led the squadron across to Normandy in the hours before D-Day, and he cast off his own glider in "Operation Mullard", seeing it on its way down to French soil, and then he was hit badly by German flak. Two of his crew were wounded, and John used all his skills to ditch the Dakota in the Channel and get the crew into a dinghy. They survived, were picked up by an Air Sea Rescue launch and spent the night of D-Day on the Normandy coast!

In September of that year, he also led the squadron over Arnhem on the 20th, and dropped his load of paratroops without incident over the DZ to the West of the town.

When the war finished, John Rae joined Hunting Air Travel flying Vikings and Doves, and then he joined BEA in 1954 and flew with them on European routes until he had a sudden heart attack in 1959 (luckily not in the air), and died. He left two sons, John and Ian, who have both worked in Aviation, and who to this day still keep an eye on British Airway's activities in the Highlands!

John Annesley Hankins, was the elder son of Mr and Mrs G. Hankins of Wellington, New Zealand, and came to Britain at the beginning of the 1930's to join the RAF, gaining the rank of Flying Officer after a short service commission.

He left the RAF to join Scottish Motor Traction Co. (SMT) as a joy-riding pilot in 1933. Here he flew an exhausting programme of joy-riding flights at seaside and town locations

Incident at Rousay!
John Rae flew into a sudden downdraught in DH Dragon G-ADCT one afternoon, trying to cross the beach on Rousay in the Orkney Isles to land in a field nearby. This sequence of pictures shows 'DCT (above) as it came to rest in a hedge with its port lower mainplane crumpled.

The aircraft was carefully dismantled in situ (above left) and moved over a stone wall (above right) and through a garden. The Dragon was finally taken down to the beach and placed on a large rowing boat (bottom left), and conveyed in calm water to Kirkwall Harbour (bottom right). The aircraft was soon flying again. (John Rae)

around Scotland, bringing the delights of air travel for the first time to thousands of people who paid their 5s. 0d. for a 5 minute flip around the circuit.

In his second season, whilst based for a short time at Riverside Park, Dundee, F.O. John Hankins was chartered to take two passengers down to St. Andrews on Tuesday July 31st 1934, in his D.H. Fox Moth. He had taken off in a westerly direction from the Park, and was turning to port over the trees along the railway line, to fly across the Tay estuary, when he caught a violent downdraught in the strong wind. The nose of the Fox Moth dipped, and struck a big tree in the gardens of Binrock House. One wing crashed into the gardens, and the other hung over the Dundee - Perth railway tracks. The tail was suspended high in the air on the railway signal and telegraph wires.

The force of impact was such as to shatter the front of the Fox Moth, with the engine falling into the garden. The 16 - year old Dundee girl, Miss Nan Craighead, was rendered unconscious

and died later in hospital, while Mr Stewart Campbell, aged 29, son of a well-known Perth shop-keeper, was seriously injured in the legs and body and spent some time in intensive care. John Hankins was only slightly hurt, and was soon flying again.

In March 1936, John joined Northern and Scottish at Renfrew and soon made a name for himself there, being called by some of the aerodrome managers in Skye and the Western Isles: "The best pilot of the lot."

In November 1937 he was transferred to Ted Fresson's Northern Section, to become resident pilot at Kirkwall for the inter-island schedules, and ambulance and charter work (later also flying the Inverness route as well).

Ted Fresson personally flew him to Fair Isle on November 11th 1937, to check him out on landing there over the dangerous cliffs.

On February 28th 1939, Jonny Hankins was responsible for a particular Air Ambulance feat that Fresson later reckoned was

Capt. John Annesley Hankins and his wife Sheelah Daphne Annesley at their wedding in Kirkwall on March 4th 1939.

one of the bravest he remembered. He was called out in the late evening, on a dark night with a gale blowing up and rain squalls developing, to fly a doctor to Sanday.

Hankins took off in the Dragon, and without radio aids, not only found Sanday, but landed by the light of some car headlights on a 300 yard strip. This created a lot of publicity in the Orkney Isles, and a series of legends grew up around the work of "Johnny" Hankins (the motto of Scottish Airways was: "This plane must get through!").

On Saturday March 4th 1939, John married a pretty young girl from Rhodesia - Sheelah Daphne Annesley Lockwood. She had met John recently, while working on one of the islands in the Inner Hebrides to which he was flying from Renfrew at that time. Strangely enough, she came from the same original Irish family of Annesley as did John, going back a couple of generations, yet they had been respectively born in New Zealand and Rhodesia!

They were married in a solicitor's office in Kirkwall, and John promptly went off and flew the inter-island Schedule, before leaving on a brief honeymoon in the South on the 13.45 plane to Inverness.

John continued flying for Fresson until the War began and then joined the RAF again. He was eventually promoted to Squadron Leader, and was awarded the Air Force Cross (A.F.C.)

in 1944. It is believed that he was C.O. of a Dakota Squadron at the end of the War and he eventually re-joined Scottish Airways in November 1944.

He served with BEA for a time, and is then believed to have gone to live and fly, in Mexico. His wife is thought to have served in the WRNS with the Fleet Air Arm during WW II.

Charles Bernard ("Tug") Wilson, joined George Nicholson's Northern and Scottish Airways Ltd at Renfrew in January 1936, after service in the RAF. He flew the Western Isles routes mainly, and carried out a number of ambulance flights for NSA, before being transferred up to Inverness to fly for Ted Fresson's Northern Section in January 1938.

Here he became the Inverness - based pilot with Adam Smith for the Inverness - Kirkwall service (John Hankins was based in Kirkwall with John P. Rae, and John J Veasey was the resident pilot in Shetland).

"Tug" (as he was always called) was involved in a memorable operation to the island of Foula (west of Shetland Mainland) on Saturday February 5th 1938. Fresson sent him up from Inverness for this special flight, in the Northern Section's flagship G-ADAJ, as *The Sunday Post* for the following day recorded:

"Food Dropped to Starving Islanders.

Foula Relieved By 'Plane After 34 Days
Flour Bags used as parachutes

After being isolated for thirty-three days, Foula, one of the farthest-flung isles of the West of Scotland, was relieved yesterday.

In the afternoon ten packages of foodstuffs attached to parachutes were dropped on the island by a Highland Airways airplane after a thrilling flight against a 30-mile headwind.

The fishery cruiser Betty Bodie landed twelve tons of provisions, medical supplies, and mails.

The inhabitants of the island, which rises like a rock out of the storm-tossed Hebridean seas, have had an unfortunate time since the New Year.

Following an epidemic of influenza, which affected every family, came the long-continued storms, until the inhabitants were almost at starving point.

The 'plane - piloted by Captain C.B. Wilson - which relieved the isle left Kirkwall yesterday morning, and flew over 200 miles of storm-tossed waters against a 30-

G-ADAJ, the flagship of the Northern Section of Scottish Airways seen low over Inverness. This aircraft was put to good use in what became known as the "Foula Food Drop".

Capt. Bernard ("Tug") Wilson (in the doorway of the DH Dragon Rapide G-ADAJ), together with the helpers at Sumburgh and the food parcels that were dropped on Foula!

mile-per-hour head wind.

The intrepid pilot, who was accompanied by Mr J.J. Johnson, from Highland Airways' Kirkwall Aerodrome, reached his objective, and was able to drop much-needed supplies to the marooned inhabitants of the little island before returning safely to Kirkwall.

Five parcels, weighing 5 lb each, were dropped by Mr Johnson by means of flour-bag parachutes he fashioned for the occasion.

Failed To Open

Mr Johnson lay on the 'plane floor, his legs tied to the seats in case he was bumped out, and released the parcels through the open door.

The first parachute failed to open, but the groceries did not appear to suffer.

The other four parachutes all opened and floated gracefully to the heather, where islanders retrieved them and waved their thanks to the 'plane which spent half an hour over the island.

The total distance covered was about 440 miles, and the outward journey was accomplished in less than two hours.

On reaching Foula the aeroplane circled round and made a complete survey of the island looking for a possible landing-place.

The island cliffs rise almost sheer out of the water and the island slopes up to a central peak.

The only possible landing-place was a small field but the pilot decided should he try to make a landing there a crash was probable.

Moreover, there would be no possiblity of taking off again as the field was not long enough for a run. Only an auto-giro could have landed and taken off again successfully.

The welcome spectacle of the aeroplane with its much-needed supplies must have given heart to the islanders as at the hour it was still not possible to approach Foula by sea.

Later in the day the Betty Bodie reached the island.

Foula, wild and picturesque, was brought into prominence in a romantic fashion recently when the film "Edge of the World" was shown. The wonderful pictorial scenes were shot on Foula."

During WW II "Tug" flew as a test-pilot for the USAF at Burtonwood, Lancs., and Liverpool (Speke), test-flying fighter aircraft like the Lockheed Lightning, Republic Thunderbolt and North American Mustang, that were shipped to Liverpool by sea from the USA, and then assembled locally for delivery to USAF squadrons. On one occasion he had to bale out of a fighter by the banks of the Mersey estuary, but survived to keep on flying!

Radio Officers were far more numerous than pilots, in NSA and Scottish Airways service - they tended not to stay very long and consequently changed frequently. Some came from the RAF, some from the Navy or Merchant Navy, and some were civilians. All braved the weathers just like the pilots, and were often the only means of getting the pilot to his destination in very bad weather - and the principal means of getting him down. A

Radio Officers all!

Clockwise, above: J.C. ("Jimmy") Mitchell, J. Morrison and "Paddy" O'Gorman.

THE MAIL MUST GET THROUGH!

A bad winter in Inverness just before World War Two - the mail-bags are loaded into DH Dragon Rapide G-ADAJ that is still in the Highland Airways silver and green scheme, despite now being part of Scottish Airways! (Authors Collection)

few did stay a long time with the airline - like the first R.O. (or W.T.O. - as they were then called) **F.R. Hughes,** who was the first Chief Radio Officer. He was followed by men like **Hugh Black** and **J.C. ("Jimmy") Mitchell,** (the next Chief R.O.), and **Messrs T. Hedley, William ("Bill") Gray, Andrew ("Andy") Ruthven, Morrison, Roy Stewart, McGinlay, Ritchie, McPherson** and **Edmonston,** etc.

All the R.O.s put up a sterling display alongside the pilots, and must be equally remembered, for the part they played in guiding their pilots into safe landfalls in the foulest of weathers. Not usually being as keen or as dedicated about flying as were the pilots, they put up with the discomfort of the job, and with the awkward seating arrangement in the aircraft, without complaint.

Andrew ("Andy") Ruthven typifies that courageous band of early Radio Officers that were taken on by Scottish Airways to assist their pilots to navigate between Renfrew and the out-stations in all weathers.

Like some of the other R.O.s, Andrew had been in the Merchant Navy at the turn of the 1930's after qualifying as a Radio Officer. He had been born at Larkhall, just South of Hamilton (on the old A74) in April 1912, and had always wanted to go away to sea - perhaps stired by seeing the ships on the Clyde on boyhood excursions - as were many of his school chums.

Sailing firstly to India, then the USA, and finally in the Union Castle Liners from Southampton to South Africa, Andrew had come to notice the swarms of yellow - coloured training biplanes

(Avro's) buzzing around Hamble airfield, whenever he sailed up or down the Southampton Water.

One day he took a friend to investigate, and they talked to the Chief Instructor at Air Service Training (A.S.T) - a Hawker Siddeley Group company - about the chances of converting to become aerial radio officers.

The upshot was that Andrew then took a short conversion course to gain an air radio operator's licence and after a few more sea trips the Superintendent at Hamble rang him up one day, and offered him a job at A.S.T. as an instructor, teaching young cadets how to navigate. (This took the form of classroom teaching on the one hand, and taking them aloft to fly Army Co-operation flights at night, to help the Ack Ack gunners and search light operators to learn how to predict onto targets).

Andrew "rubbed shoulders" at Hamble with many famous pilots who appeared there at that time like Amy Johnson, Gordon Olley etc. Two of the aircraft he flew in frequently were the original two Avro 652s built for Imperial Airways (*Avalon* and *Ava* - the forerunners of the Anson series).

Then he was offered a job at the new No. 1 Air Navigation School at Prestwick, nearer home - but he was unsure whether to take it. He mentioned it to his Superintendent at Hamble - the "Wee McGillivray" - who promptly took it himself! But it wasn't long before "Mac" was on the 'phone asking Andrew to join him up in Ayrshire - and he did so, promptly!

So Andrew became an instructor with the No 1 A.O.N.S (run by Scottish Aviation for the RAF), and when that School left for Southern Rhodesia when the war broke out, Andrew stayed behind for a time, instructing on some other Ansons at the base - as he was arranging to get married.

When Andrew was at Prestwick, for instance, there was a certain Sergeant Pilot in the RAF who flew the Anson trainers in which Andrew checked out the budding navigators all around the Western coasts of Scotland. They often flew around the Islands

Scottish Airways's DH Dragon Rapide G-AFRK basks in the summer sun under a dramatic skyscape.

Lochs and Bays at 500 ft, and when this pilot turned to Andrew on one flight and said: "You don't mind if we do a little low flying?", Andrew said "No". However, when he looked up to see the Connel Bridge (near Oban) flashing by overhead, he thought better of it. In fact he asked not to be rostered with this pilot again - as did two other instructors - and when the C.O. asked them why one muttered: "He flies under all the bridges he sees ...!" (A short time after this, the pilot concerned flew some top instructors and pupils into a hill and nobody survived).

He now looked around for another job, and approached Scottish Airways at Renfrew in the Autumn of 1940, and was immediately taken on by David Barclay, the Chief Pilot.

Andrew stayed with Scottish Airways now from November 1940 to January 1946, being based at Renfrew most of the time, but acting as "Relief R.O." up at Inverness with the Northern Section in August 1941, July, August and December 1942 and January 1943. (There, he came to know Ted Fresson very well, both as the General Manager and Chief Pilot).

Andrew had nothing but praise for George Nicholson, and he remembers they got on well together. "George was always ready to listen to anybody who had any good points to make," he says, "and his door was always open. He was a man you could easily talk to - very forthright, mind you - but very fair and I never ever saw him lose his temper at any time."

The first flight Andrew made with Scottish was on November 11th 1940 to Campbeltown and Islay and back with Geoff Greenhalgh, and then he was flying most days to the Hebrides. The Captains he flew with in the first few months included Geoff, Jock Young (for whom he developed an immediate friendship, and flew with as often as possible - not least because they lived opposite each other in Paisley, and Jock would often give Andrew a lift to work in his car), S. Clark, Wood, S. Coleman and David Barclay (the Chief Pilot).

There were also quite a few Ambulance flights through that winter of 1940-41 that Andrew flew on, with different pilots.

On June 14th 1941 he was flying with David Barclay in the Rapide G-AFRK to Campbeltown and Islay and Andrew

recorded in his log that one of the other pilots crashed on Islay in Rapide G-AERZ that day. And on November 26th 1941 he recorded: "Rapide lost in 95 mph gale at Stornoway."

On June 7th 1942 Andrew flew a relief service with Geoff Greenhalgh to Stornoway, as the Rapide G-AGED had hit a patch of soft ground landing at Benbecula, and ended up on its nose there - but was fortunately repairable.

Ambulance flights continued to occur regularly for Andrew - who was considered one of the best R.O.s in the business - and alone of most of the crews he usually recorded the medical reason for each flight in his log book. Thus there were a succession of flights to bring 'Appendicitis', 'Peritonitis', 'Fractured leg' etc, patients to the mainland. But there were also odd cases of 'gunshot wounds', 'injuries due to bomb explosions' (at RAF bases), and on October 11th 1942 a 'Spinal Tuberculosis' patient from Stornoway, for which Andrew's wife Mary flew out with them (Jock Young being the pilot,) to act as stewardess on the way back with the unfortunate patient.

There were charter flights too - some by the RAF, Admiralty, etc (to carry bomb or mine disposal teams out to the islands to deal with unexploded munitions, etc), some for civic dignitaries (Eg the Lord Provost of Glasgow to visit Belfast) and then there were the increasing number of ENSA Charters to take entertainers out to see the troops - people like Beverley Nichols and Anne Shelton, etc. There were other occasional charters - to take Lord Bridgeman (C-in-C, Home Guard), Lord and Lady Astor and their doctor, the Earl of Airlie, Lady Hamilton, etc, to the Isles, or for the Ministry of Supply or for Admiralty wreck inspection teams, etc.

On the late afternoon of March 10th 1941, Andrew was returning with David Barclay from a flight in Rapide G-AFOI to Campbeltown and Islay and they were diverted to Prestwick for a

Andrew Ruthven, Radio Officer outside Henry Vallance's home at Inverness, with his motor-cycle. (Graeme Young)

163

time because there was a German air raid in progress on Clydebank. A few days later, there was a devastating blitz on Clydebank by the Luftwaffe, and on each of the morning flights on March 13th and 14th, Andrew and Geoff Greenhalgh flew over the destruction around the shipyards to look at the effects of the bombing - and they let their passengers up into the cockpit to take a peek as well (the rear windows were all doped silver to prevent them seeing things they shouldn't in Wartime!)

Andrew made a unique entry in his logbook on July 23rd 1941 - the date of his marriage to Mary. He entered: "July 23rd P.M. A/c Type - "Taxi". Pilot - "Rev. M. Stewart". Duty - "Bridegroom" - Remarks - "QBI, QFO, QDT clear !!!"

He had several cases of a motor cutting out in flight with different pilots - one over the Isle of Arran - and a few examples of bursting a tyre on landing (usually at Islay, Campbeltown or Tiree it seemed). Then there were a few " coffins" and/or "corpses" to fly to Barra and the Western Isles.

One thing Andrew remembers vividly was their highly 'unofficial' method of finding their way back into Renfrew by air from the West, in low cloud and bad weather. Normally flying with Jock Young when they used this means, Andrew would receive a continuous series of QDM's as they approached the airport. But when they were in cloud or couldn't see the ground at all, they would open their nearest cockpit windows - Jock the sliding one on his left, and Andrew the right hand one. Then, both constantly sticking their heads into the airflow, they would "sniff" the breeze. The moment they suddenly smelt cornflour dust - from the famous Brown & Polson custard powder factory on the Renfrew approach - they would start their descent procedure! It always worked perfectly!

The weather, of course, could be atrocious, but even in the 80, 90 and 95 mph gales they encountered, the pilots would fly the Rapides into the airstrips, where teams of helpers would be waiting to grab onto the wings and tail of the aircraft to hold it steady for the passengers to change round (under almost full power) - before letting go to see the aircraft rocket up vertically like a helicopter! On one such occasion, Andrew remembers Geoff Greenhalgh touching down on the main runway at Stornoway - but pointing across the width of the runway (not along it)! He took off again across the runway ! On only one occasion did Andrew's Captain have to land to avoid a storm in flight - at Turnberry on August 30th 1944, with Jock Young on the way back from Islay.

On another occasion at Stornoway, Andrew remembers vividly how Jock Young and he landed there, and discharged their passengers. Then, suddenly without warning, a German Heinkel He.111 flew low across the RAF aerodrome, spraying machine gun bullets everywhere. Andrew and Jock dived out of the Rapide and huddled under one wing as bullets ricochetted around the aircraft. Fortunately, they were not hit, nor was the Rapide - but in hindsight they both wondered if crouching so close to the fuel tanks had been the best thing to do!

Flying with Bill Baillie on November 21st 1944 in Rapide G-

AGIF to Stornoway, Andrew and Bill sighted the floating shape of a crashed Halifax in the sea near Tiree, and promptly radioed off the position to the Authorities and circled for some time to direct help to the scene.

Between January 18th and 26th 1945 the weather was so cold that Renfrew was completely icebound, and no flights could be made. Andrew eventually got airborne again with John Michie on the 26th to Belfast - where it wasn't much better!

During this time with the airline Andrew flew with most of the pilots. But inevitably the R.O.'s had their own ideas of who they trusted most, and usually flew with a specific pilot more often than not. In Andrew's case these were Ted Fresson and Henry Vallance in Inverness and at Renfrew - Jock Young, Geoff Greenhalgh, and David Barclay. Conversely there were some they didn't have much faith in - but fortunately these were few and far between, and never lasted very long in the organization concerned!

At Scottish Airways there was one pilot Andrew never forgot - Bob Pepper. The latter came to Scottish from the Fleet Air Arm in September 1942 and Andrew flew with him occasionally up to February 1943. On February 2nd - the day before his wife Mary's birthday - Andrew was rostered with Capt. Robert M Pepper again to fly to Stornoway in the DH 89A Rapide G-AGED. They started their take-off run at Renfrew towards the West, gathering speed as they rolled past the cemetery (to their port side). But suddenly they hit a patch of very soggy ground, and slowed appreciably.

Andrew looked into the cockpit and through the windscreen, and noted the boundary embankment coming up. He also saw that the pilot seemed to be sitting bolt upright, and still held the throttles wide open. He made no attempt to throttle back and abandon take-off, and suddenly they bounced into the air, but struck the earth bank with their undercarriage.

The next thing Andrew knew was that they had flipped upside-down with a tremendous "crash", and then there seemed to be a sudden silence, through which he slowly became aware of a hissing noise. Suddenly registering the fact that this could be petrol falling on the hot engine, he sprang into action, felt his feet on Bob Pepper's shoulders in the wreckage of the shattered cockpit, and he pushed Bob through the broken triangular window on the side. He broke two of Bob's ribs in the process but got him out, following through the window himself (afterwards, it looked far to small to have used it as an exit!)

The six passengers were extracted from a largely intact fuselage, and miraculously there was no fire at all.

George Nicholson had driven across the grass in his car, arriving at the crash just after the fire brigade. He saw Bob Pepper into an ambulance, but then took a rather dazed Andrew into his car and drove him to the Scottish Flying Club and gave him a large Scotch at the bar there!

Andrew must have appeared to be all right after that, and George said he would get a taxi to take him back home to Paisley (Andrew and Mary lived diagonally opposite Jock Young's

Crash at Renfrew!

The wrecked Scottish Airways' DH Dragon Rapide G-AGED lies upside down after striking the boundary hedge on take-off. (Andrew Ruthven)

Two more snapshots of the Renfrew crash, showing 'GED's crushed cockpit that demonstrates just how lucky Andrew Ruthven and Capt. Bob Pepper were to escape with minor injuries.

Interestingly, these pictures show the wartime registration markings, underlined with Red, White and Blue stripes, including the registration letters under the wings, which is not often recorded in photographs...

...the fuselage letters were outlined in white, and it can be seen that despite the aircraft being painted in low visibity colours, the fuselage cheat line was still retained. Another view of the accident with 'GED, with Scottish Airways' engineers standing on top of the wreck. It was a write-off. (Andrew Ruthven)

house there). Andrew didn't want to scare Mary by turning up in a taxi at his front door, so he insisted on taking the normal bus home - and George rather reluctantly let him go.

So Andrew arrived back home, having to walk some 75 yds from the nearest bus-stop, and Mary answered the door bell, asking him in astonishment why he'd come home so early ! Andrew began to explain, and then he fainted dead away in the hall, with delayed shock!

He was back flying again on February 8th, with his favourite pilot, Jock Young. Pepper was also back in action on March 6th and begged Andrew to fly with him again - which he did on a number of occasions up to June 24th 1943. (After this, Pepper had to face the crash inquiry, and Andrew believes he then lost his licence).

At this stage in the War, several new pilots were arriving to take over the flying in Scottish Airways. After Bob Pepper's accident in G-AGED in February 1943 and his subsequent Inquiry in June, a replacement for him arrived in the shape of Bernard T. ("Paddy") O'Reilly. He was followed by H. Riley-

Sawdon in September 1943, and the return of John Michie and John Hankins in October and November 1944, with an H.V. Morton. Then in 1945 came a bunch of newcomers - Capts. E. Pooley, E Elgey, David Prentice, J.S. Leslie, David MacFarlane, B. Youell, D.F. Williamson and D Prowse (both employed on the new Renfrew - London run).

Andrew made his first Renfrew - Croydon run with Bill Baillie in Rapide G-AGLP on April 10th 1945, returning on the 11th, via Prestwick and Liverpool. His next similar trip was with John Michie in G-AFEP on April 24th/25th. His trip with Bill Baillie was the second service on the route as David Barclay and the Chief R.O., Jimmy Mitchell, had inaugurated the new route the day before (April 9th) and passed Bill and Andrew on the 10th flying the opposite way back to Renfrew.

The end of the War in Europe came on May 8th 1945, and saw Andrew and Jock Young flying to Stornoway and back. Then on July 7th Andrew and John Annesley Hankins took part in another "first" - they flew on the first official Railway Air Services' scheduled flight into the Channel Islands after the end of the

German occupation. (Jersey Airways had begun services already on June 21st, leasing RAS aircraft). They flew Rapide G-AGLR down to Croydon, and then took 'GLP and flew to Guernsey and then on to Jersey, where they overnighted. They retraced their steps in reverse next day, the flight Jersey - Guernsey - Croydon taking 2 hours and Croydon - Renfrew just over 3 hours.

Andrew repeated this operation to Jersey on July 11th/12th, 16th/17th, 23rd/24th and 27th/28th - but after that he never flew there again, merely overnighting at Croydon.

From August 17th Andrew flew the Renfrew - Croydon - Renfrew round trip in the same day, as the flights were re-timed to enable this to happen - but he had a different Scottish Captain on each sector. Evidently this did not work very well for in September he went back to overnighting at Croydon again (as the Captains from Renfrew had always done). They were struck by lightning on the northbound, return flight on September 20th (the Captain was D. Prowse and the Rapide was 'GLR).

Andrew was introduced to the Avro XIX aircraft at Renfrew on September 24th (G-AGPG), and on the 25th flew in 'GPG to Stornoway and back with John Michie, as a trial service.

The Avro stayed with them for a time, and in October Andrew and John Michie flew a number of services to Stornoway and Belfast (in later years "Aggie-Paggie" was used by Avros as their own company "hack" and it would visit Stornoway frequently on business, taking Sir Thomas and Lady Sopwith up to their castle and estate at Amhuinnsuidhe on the Isle of Harris, as well as a succession of business guests to stay with them.

Andrew flew his last flight with Scottish Airways on January 21st 1946, and bowed out with a trip with Jock Young around the Western Isles in Rapide G-AGOJ. He had accepted a new job with British South American Airways (BSAA) down at Heathrow, and on February 28th he entered a new world of trans-Atlantic flying. He had flown a total of 5,291 hrs 45 mins as a R.O. with George Nicholson's Renfrew - based airline (including a small number of hours as a 'relief' R.O. with Fresson in Inverness).

When Andrew finally left Scottish Airways, his cousin, Iain Kirk took his place there as a Radio Officer, later serving with BEA for many years.

His time with BSAA included operating on their very first Lancastrian flight out of Heathrow - on a quick hop up to Avro's spare's depot at Waddington in G-AGWI on February 28th 1946.

He went on to fly Lancastrians, Yorks and Tudor IVs on a total of 54 trans-Atlantic services to South America and the Caribbean; made a complete survey of the Caribbean as R.O. to BSAA's Managing Director, Air Vice-Marshal Don Bennett flying in Lancastrian G-AGWI; flew Ernest Bevin across to Paris to a Peace Conference; broke the record on Bermuda - London by being re-fuelled in flight on Lancastrian G-AHJT on June 8th 1947 - amongst many other things.

He lost a very good friend of his, however, later on in BSAA. This was Bob Tuck who had been at Hamble with Andrew, and who had also joined BSAA at its inception. Bob was "very fast on the keys" indeed, and disappeared without trace with the rest of the passengers and crew when the Tudor IV "Star Tiger" was lost in the Atlantic. The fact that two Tudor IVs were lost without any radio call for help being made, makes Andrew certain that both incidents were due to the petrol heaters in the cockpit and cabin exploding (troubles had been experienced with them on the ground when being tested). Only something sudden and catastrophic could have accounted for the disasters - yet it was very strange that no items of wreckage were ever recovered from the sea in each case! Andrew himself was involved in a protracted search next day for his friend, Bob's, Tudor.

Andrew went onto the Berlin Air Lift with BSAA's Tudor Is, then when BSAA was taken over by BOAC, he was taken onto the latter's payroll, eventually becoming one of the last six R.O.s employed by the airline. In fact he was later transferred onto International Aeradio's payroll, but continued to operate from his office at Heathrow, as Route Communications Manager until he retired in 1973. He was involved with the first Argonaut Flights, then the Comet 1 and 4s on the trans-Atlantic routes, and Andrew Ruthven can certainly be said to have had a long and interesting career, since he decided to switch over from the Merchant Navy at Hamble before the War! He had come a long way since it was customary to take a packet of chewing gun aloft in the Spartan Cruisers - to plug the hinge lines in the roof exits where the rainwater dripped through !

Today, Andrew and Mary live in busy retirement at Ickenham, Middlesex, and their two daughters Shona and Morag in their turn carried on the aviation tradition - both working for British Eagle at first, and later BEA and British Airways (in Morag's case), and Monarch Airlines (in Shona's).

Railway Air Services' Dakota G-AGZA takes off from Renfrew towards the East, in 1946, on the Belfast service. Although maintained by Scottish Airways at Renfrew, and flown by their crews, the aircraft were kept in the RAS red and green livery. In the background can be seen the famous cemetery at Renfrew. Nowadays the M8 motorway runs along the site of this runway. (John Stroud Collection).

The Aircraft that winged over the Glens

1. de Havilland D.H. 84 Dragon

The DH Dragon was originally formulated to requirements by the Royal Iraqi Air Force, and later on by Hillman's Airways for a suitable airliner for its London - Paris service. The prototype, G-ACAN, first flew on November 24th 1932 at Stag Lane.

a) Northern, and Northern and Scottish Airways Ltd

George Nicholson purchased an early Dragon I, G-ACFG in July 1934, (as his first aircraft) from the de Havilland Aircraft Co. who had used it as a demonstrator since it was built in June 1933. He used this aircraft in Northern Airways, and then in Northern and Scottish Airways at Renfrew.

As he was taking over some of John Sword's routes, George also bought Midland & Scottish Air Ferries' Dragon, G-ACJS (the initials of John Sword), and with the merger of NSA into the United Airways' group in May 1935 came the allocation from its new 'pool of aircraft' of Dragon IIs G-ACMO, 'CNH and 'CMC (all originally delivered to Jersey Airways). The Mk II merely had individually framed windows. Sword's Dragon had been fitted out as a VIP version and to take ambulance stretcher cases, and was used to carry on this work.

All these aircraft were left in basic silver livery, with the name of the airline on the nose, and the registration letters, painted in cobalt blue. There were no cheat lines, but the engine cowlings, interplane struts, and undercarriage legs were also painted in cobalt blue. In 1937, for a brief period, Dragon's 'COR and 'CNG acquired from the British Airways 'pool' were left in all-blue livery, with fin and rudder, propellers, interplane struts, lettering and window frames in silver.

b) Highland Airways Ltd

Fresson first seemed to become aware of the DH Dragon when he visited John Sword (of SMT) at Renfrew in July 1933, when desperately seeking temporary replacements for the damaged Monospar G-ACEW. Sword had some Dragons in use, but could not spare one.

Fresson then saw some at Brian Lewis Ltd at Heston, and negotiated to buy his first Dragon G-ACIT through them.

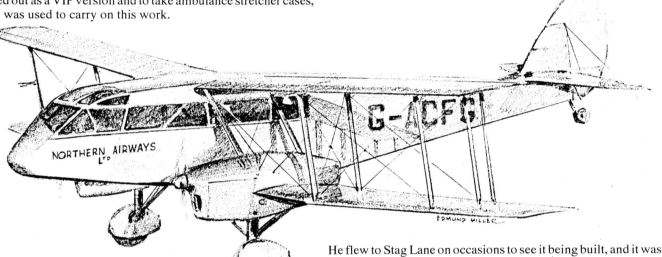

He flew to Stag Lane on occasions to see it being built, and it was delivered to him on July 30th 1933, at Edinburgh.

Thereafter he acquired four more, over the next three years. These were:

G-ACIT	(c/n 6039)	*"Aberdeen"*	(Mk I).
G-ACCE	(c/n 6010)	*"Caithness"*	(Mk I).
G-ACGK	(c/n 6033)	*"Loch Ness"*	(Mk I).
G-ACET	(c/n 6021)	*"Kirkwall"*	(Mk I).
G-ADCT	(c/n 6095)	*"Orcadian"*	(Mk II).

All aircraft were finished in silver, with mid-green cheat lines, lettering, and engine and wheel cowlings.

2. de Havilland D.H. 83 Fox Moth

The DH 83 Fox Moth G-ACED appears to have been used regularly by NSA as a company 'hack' and for the odd ambulance charter to more remote strips. The Fox Moth was a four-seat biplane with the pilot in an open cockpit on top, and a lower, enclosed cabin for three passengers to his front.

3. de Havilland D.H. 85 Leopard Moth

The DH 85 Leopard Moth G-ACUO was also acquired as a company 'hack' for some time, and for ambulance work etc. This was a totally enclosed three-seat aircraft for luxury travel, with a high wing braced to the lower fuselage.

Type: D.H. 84 Dragon I and II	
Particulars of aircraft:	
Built by:	De Havilland Aircraft Company Limited, Stag Lane, Edgware, Middlesex.
Designer:	A.E. Hagg
Registration (and Constructor's Number):	
	G-ACFG (c/n 6027), and G-ACJS (c/n 6042) fitted out for ambulance duties, and as a VIP transport- both Mk Is. G-ACMO (c/n 6062) a Dragon I and G-ACNH (c/n 6070) and G-ACMC (c/n 6053) Mk IIs allocated from United Airways 'pool' in 1935. Later, G-ACNG (c/n 6069) and G-ACOR (c/n 6073) also allocated in 1937 from British Airways 'pool' (Mk IIs).
Powered by:	Two D.H. Gipsy Major I, 4-cylinder inverted in-line engines (130 hp).
Price:	From £2,500 ex-works (excl. furnishings).
Capacity:	Eight passengers, baggage and freight.
Production:	A total of 115 Dragons were made at Stag Lane in the 1932-35 period, and 87 more were made in Australia. Some 53 made in the UK were of a Mark II version, with individual cabin windows.
Speed:	134 mph (max). Cruising: 109 mph.
Altitude:	14,500 ft (max).
Range:	400 miles.

4. Spartan Cruiser II and III

As part of the re-allocation of group aircraft when George Nicholson merged his Northern and Scottish Airways Ltd with United Airways Ltd (later British Airways Ltd), some Spartan aircraft previously used by other members of the group were now give to NSA to operate the Western Isles routes from Renfrew. These included four Cruiser IIs and three Cruiser IIIs - a total of seven altogether.

They had variously been operated by Spartan Air Lines, by United Airways (with whom it merged) or by the new name for the Group - British Airways and it took some time for the colourings/markings to be changed to "Northern and Scottish Airways". It also took time to change NSA for "Scottish Airways" after mid - 1937, when Scottish Airways became the new name in the North (and indeed the name was never changed in one case before the aircraft was written off!).

The Spartan Cruisers were normally used on the services to the inner and outer Hebrides where their short take-off and landing runs came into advantage in these areas.

The Spartan Cruiser design owed its origins to the Saro-Percival wooden mailplane built at Cowes to the design of Edgar Percival in 1931. Subsequently the Spartan Aircraft Co. converted the design to a passenger aircraft (the Cruiser I) with a new metal fuselage and tailplane of longitudinally corrugated skinning.

The Cruiser II retained the wooden wing, but had a stronger, re-designed fuselage. Later, the Mk III had a slightly longer fuselage, but now of smooth metal panels at the front, and fabric covered welded steel tube at the rear. This model had a heavily 'trousered' cantilever undercarriage.

These aircraft were very robust, and ideal for Northern and Scottish Airways' use on the Hebridean routes, but the salt water environment - particularly on the beach strips at Barra and Northton - took its toll on the metal parts of the aircraft's structure with time.

Shortly after the start of World War Two, almost all of the surviving Cruisers had to be scrapped prematurely because of corrosion.

A typical advertisement for the Cruiser II, emphasising its excellent payload over medium ranges.

Type: Spartan Cruiser II	
Particulars of aircraft:	
Built by:	Spartan Aircraft Ltd., Cowes, Isle of Wight.
Designer:	Based on an original design by Edgar Percival.
Registration (and Construction Numbers):	
	G-ACYL (c/n 12).　　G-ACVT (c/n 11).
	G-ACSM (c/n 10).　　G-ACZM (c/n 14).
Powered by:	Three 130 hp de Havilland Gipsy Major engines.
Capacity:	6 passengers, luggage and some cargo.
Production:	A total of 12 Mk IIs were produced in 1933-34 after a prototype Mk I had been built and tested (following on from the Saro-Percival Mailplane - originator of the Series).
Speed:	Max - 140 mph. Cruising - 118 mph.
Altitude:	Max - 15,000 ft.
Range:	Max - 650 miles.

Performance and Adaptability

THE first consideration in the choice of an air-line aeroplane is its pay load over a definite range.

The "Cruiser" is particularly suitable for operation over long and medium distance routes. With standard tanks it can carry pilot, mechanic, five passengers, 265 lbs. of luggage and full-size wireless set for 620 miles. If half this distance will suffice, the passengers can be increased to seven (or more) and the luggage allowance to 390 lbs. The use of metal airscrews and toilet arrangements are included in these figures, which give the machine an all-up weight of 6,200 lbs.

The "Cruiser" will fly easily on any two of its three engines.

The particular suitability of the "Cruiser" for Private Charter work was well shown at the end of last year when a "Cruiser" flew from England to Australia and back. The 32,000 miles covered on this trip still constitute the longest charter flight on record.

SPARTAN CRUISER
THREE-ENGINED CABIN MONOPLANE
SPARTAN AIRCRAFT LTD., COWES, ISLE OF WIGHT

Type: Spartan Cruiser III	
Particulars of aircraft:	
Built by:	Spartan Aircraft Ltd of Cowes, I.O.W.
Designer:	Based on an original design by Edgar Percival.
Registrations (and Construction numbers):	
	G-ADEM (c/n 103) G-ACYK (c/n 101)
	G-ADEL (c/n 102)
Powered by:	Three D.H. Gipsy Major 130 hp engines.
Capacity:	8 passengers, baggage and some cargo.
Production:	Three aircraft only.
Speed:	Max - 135 mph, Cruising - 115 mph.
Altitude:	Max - 15,000 ft.
Range:	Max - 550 miles.

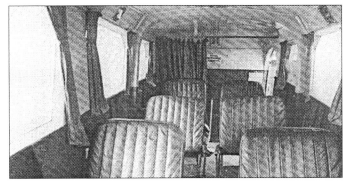

A view looking to the rear of the cabin of a Spartan Cruiser II, showing the six car-type passenger seats with no seat-belts!

5. de Havilland D.H. 89 and 89A Dragon Rapide

a) Highland Airways Ltd.

The DH 89 Dragon Rapide (initially known as the Dragon Six) was a scaled-down version of a larger, four-engined biplane - the DH 86 - that had been designed for use on the Singapore-Australia route. The twin-engined Rapide was produced to Hillman's Airways requirements - as the launch customer - but Ted Fresson had a considerable influence on the eventual design, liaising with de Havilland during the testing of the prototype and during the initial stages of construction. Highland Airways' requirements, indeed, had just as much bearing on the aircraft that eventually went into production, as Hillman's Airways had in initiating the design.

Fresson, when he was in the throes of acquiring a fleet of the earlier Dragons, knew at an early stage of de Havilland's ideas for the Dragon Rapide (originally named the Dragon Six). The newer aircraft was faster (hence the name), and - more important for Fresson - had a better single-engined performance if one engine failed. Over the longer sea crossing to Shetland from Aberdeen, this was very important indeed. But the greatest asset was its extra load carrying capacity - this meant the difference between profit and loss to Highland Airways.

Fresson arranged to borrow one of the early production models G-ACPO for a few days in November 1934, and it was during this time that he decided that, whilst take-off performance exceeded that of the Dragon, the landing took farther because of the higher approach speed and higher wing loading.

Either DH would have to modify the aircraft - or Ted would have to lengthen his airfields! Thus was born the idea of fitting flaps to the Rapide, and Fresson's suggestions were accepted by DH and within six months they had a flapped model ready for test (April 1935). Fresson checked the results of this with DH, and promptly placed an order for delivery in Summer 1936. In the event Fresson's requirements crystallised earlier - in Spring 1936 - as he wanted to start the new Aberdeen (Kintore) - Shetland service, and as a result of the rush, an earlier production model, G-ACPN was delivered whilst still in British Airways' livery

and leased to him from April 30th to August 9th.

All Highland Airways' Rapides were finished in all-silver colour, with mid-green cheat lines, engine and wheel cowlings (à la Dragons).

b) Northern and Scottish Airways Ltd

George Nicholson for his part, needed more aircraft in the Summer of 1936 to fly the route network that his airline NSA took over from United Airways. The new British Airways group thus allocated two of the new Dragon Rapides to Renfrew, G-ADBU from United, and G-ADDF from Hillman's Airways (both part of the Group). And before the Summer was out, two more had been allocated to NSA, G-ADAG and G-ADAH (both ex-Hillman's). The latter was kept for a short time in its British Airways all-blue livery with silver fin and rudder, interplane struts, propellers and lettering. But all NSA Rapides were standardised in silver finish with cobalt blue lettering, and cheat lines down fuselage and engine cowlings.

c) Scottish Airways Ltd.

After Northern and Scottish Airways and Highland Airways combined to form Scottish Airways Ltd in August 1937, the British Airways group went on allocating more Dragon Rapides to the Scottish subsidiary (or taking them away for re-deployment !) up to the start of World War Two. The aircraft so used were G-AFEY (acquired brand new from the manufacturers to open the Renfrew - Perth - Inverness - Northern Isles service, and based in Glasgow) G-AEOV, 'FFF, and 'FRK (all acquired in 1939 for the Renfrew base). During the war, the AAJC in Liverpool allocated a number of Dragon Rapides from their pool of machines to both the Renfrew and Inverness Sections of Scottish Airways, although most of these were to the Renfrew base (see box for details). Even after the war, more Dragon Rapides were bought, acquired or allocated by Railway Air Services to Scottish Airways until the airline ceased to exist (on paper) on February 1st 1947.

Type: De Havilland D.H. 89 and 89A Dragon Rapide

Particulars of aircraft:

Built by: De Havilland Aircraft Co. Ltd. Hatfield, Herts. and Brush Coachworks of Loughborough, Leics

Registrations and Constructor's Numbers:

a) Highland Airways Ltd.

G-ACPN	(c/n 6252)	on short lease.
G-ADAJ	(c/n 6276)	*"Inverness"*.
G-AEWL	(c/n 6367)	*"Zetland"*.

b) Northern and Scottish Airways Ltd.

G-ADBU (c/n 6280)		G-ADDF (c/n 6284)
G-ADAG (c/n 6266)		G-ADAH (c/n 6278)

c) Scottish Airways Ltd

G-AFEY	(c/n 6402)	for Renfrew base.
G-AEOV	(c/n 6342)	for Renfrew base.
G-AFFF	(c/n 6386)	for Renfrew base.
G-AFRK	(c/n 6441)	for Renfrew base.

During WW II: Aircraft allocated under auspices of the A.A.J.C.

G-AERN	(c/n 6345)	for Inverness base.
G-AFOI	(c/n 6450)	for Renfrew base.
G-ACPP	(c/n 6254)	for Renfrew base.
G-AERZ	(c/n 6356)	for Renfrew base.
G-AGDH	(c/n 6548)	for Renfrew base.
G-AGDG	(c/n 6547)	for Inverness base.
G-ACYR	(c/n 6261)	for Renfrew base.
G-AGED	(c/n 6621)	for Renfrew base.
G-AGEE	(c/n 6622)	for Renfrew base.
G-AGIC	(c/n 6522)	for Inverness base.
G-AGIF	(c/n 6509)	for Renfrew base.
G-AGJF	(c/n 6499)	for Renfrew base.
G-AGJG	(c/n 6517)	for Inverness base.
G-AGLE	(c/n 6784)	for Renfrew base.

after the end of WW II:

G-AGLR	(c/n 6781)	for Renfrew base.
G-AGOJ	(c/n 6850)	for Renfrew base.
G-AGUR	(c/n 6910)	for Renfrew base.
G-AGLP	(c/n 6780)	for Renfrew base.
G-AHLL	(c/n 6576)	for Renfrew base.
G-AHGI	(c/n 6935)	for Renfrew base.
G-AHLM	(c/n 6708)	for Renfrew base.
G-AHLN	(c/n 6754)	for Inverness base.
G-AIHN	(c/n 6498)	for Renfrew base

Powered by:	Two 200 h.p.D.H. Gipsy Six 6-cyl inverted inline engines.
Price:	£3,500.
Capacity:	Pilot and Radio Operators, and up to 8 passengers.
Production:	The Prototype, E-4 (later CH-287), flew at Hatfield on April 17th 1934. The second production aircraft was G-ACPN (used for a time by Fresson), and a total of 730 aircraft were eventually built. The D.H.89A variant was produced to Fresson's requirements in 1935, incorporating landing flaps, a landing light in the nose and cabin heating.
Speed:	157 mph (max level). Cruising - Approx 130 mph.
Altitude:	19,500 ft.
Range:	578 miles.

6. Avro 652A XIX Series 1

The Avro 652A Anson Mk XIX was a version of the ubiquitous wartime Anson produced with 9 passenger seats for post-war civil use. It was converted in response to the Brabazon Specification for a Feeder-liner, and the first aircraft turned out for this purpose by Avro's Yeadon factory was a Mk XII MG 159, which was later extensively modified for civilian airline use, registered G-AGNI, and loaned to the A.A.J.C. at Liverpool for the pilots of various operating airlines to evaluate it (including Scottish Airways).

Railway Air Services (R.A.S.) was the airline primarily interested in the Avro XIX, for use on its new Croydon - Belfast/Glasgow services (amongst others), and to take over from the long serving D.H. Dragon Rapides.

As noted earlier (Chapter 14), Capt. Bill Baillie had flown down from Renfrew to be checked out on G-AGNI at Speke in February 1945. David Barclay then flew the first production Avro XIX, G-AGPG, in September 1945 at Renfrew.

In the event, R.A.S. then ordered and took delivery of no less than 14 Avro XIXs in all over the next year, placing them on most of the longer sectors from Croydon. These aircraft were not maintained by Scottish Airways (unlike the C-47A Dakotas - see below), but because they were used on the Renfrew - Croydon service (in seven-seat configuration) between April 16th and

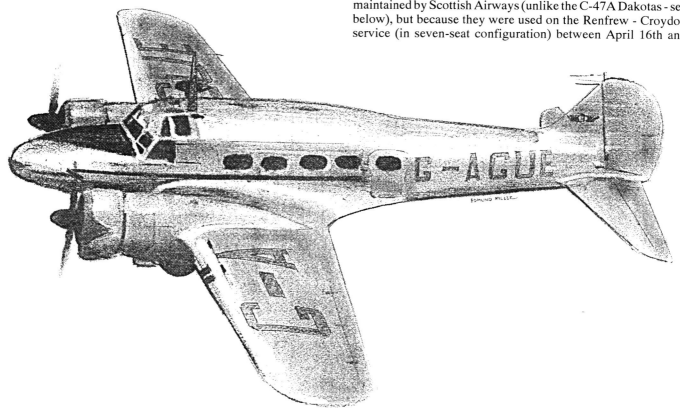

The prototype Avro Anson XIX G-AGNI, seen on the apron at Liverpool (Speke) in November 1945. Converted from an Anson Mk.I to a Mk. XII and then to the forerunner of the passenger-carrying feeder-liner Mk.XIX models, 'GNI was lent to the AAJC for the emerging post-war airlines such as Scottish Airways to evaluate. Railway Air Services, in fact, did order fourteen of these seven-to-nine seat airliners. (John Stroud Collection)

Type: Avro 652A Anson Mk XIX, Series 1 (Civil)

Particulars of aircraft:

Built by:	A.V. Roe & Co. Ltd. Yeadon.
Designer:	Roy Chadwick, C.B.E., and his design team at Yeadon under Stuart Davies.
Registrations (and Construction Numbers):	
	G-AGUD (c/n 1275), G-AGUE (c/n 1276), G-AGUX (c/n 1277), G-AGVA (c/n 1278).
Powered by:	Two 420 hp Armstrong Siddeley Cheetah 15 engines.
Capacity:	Crew of 2, and up to 9 passengers, luggage and cargo. (R.A.S. aircraft had 7 seats).
Production:	A total of 37 of these civil Series 1 Avro XIXs (with wooden wings) were produced. Other military versions were later converted to civil use, too.
Speed:	190 mph (max).
Altitude:	15,000 ft (max).
Range:	610 miles.

May 19th 1946 - prior to the Dakotas taking over - and flown by Scottish Airways' pilots, these early Avro XIXs (G-AGUD, 'UE, 'UX, and 'VA) deserve a place in this history of Scottish Airways.

They were all finished in aluminium colour, with the R.A.S. red and green cheat lines and insignias.

7. Douglas C-47A Dakota

Railway Air Services, the principal airline company in the LMS group, acquired several C-47A Dakota transports in 1946, but although painted in RAS colours, most of the fleet were actually based at Renfrew and looked after by Bill Mann, Scottish Airways' Chief Engineer, and his staff. Indeed they flew the Renfrew - Belfast, Croydon (later Northolt) and I.O.M. routes for RAS but crewed entirely by Scottish Airways' pilots and cabin crews.

The C-47As based at Renfrew were G-AGZB, 'GZA, and 'GYZ, in order of appearance there in 1946.

Type: Douglas C-47-A Dakota 3

Particulars of aircraft:

Built by:	Douglas Aircraft Co. Long Beach, California, USA.
Registrations:	G-AGZB (ex FZ 624 as delivered to RAF in Canada in 1944); G-AGZA (ex KG 420 ditto); G-AGYZ (ex FZ 681 ditto).
Powered by:	2 x 1,200 hp Pratt & Whitney R-1830-92 Twin Wasp 14 cyl. air-cooled radial engines.
Capacity:	Crew of 4, and 20 passengers.
Production:	Some 10,655 civil and military versions produced in USA altogether, with more in USSR and Japan.
Speed:	160 mph
Range:	1,600 miles (max).

Scottish Airways' staff group picture at Renfrew in late 1944.

Front row (seated) left to right: Secretary to Bill Cumming, Accountant, Engineer, William Cumming (Company Secretary), George Nicholson (Director and General Manager - Southern Section), David Barclay (Chief Pilot), Jimmy Mitchell (Chief Radio Operator), Secretary to George Nicholson. Middle Row (standing): Marconi representative, William Mann (Chief Engineer), Jock Bain (Traffic), Engineer, Andrew Ruthven (Radio Officer), Capt. Bill Baillie, Barry Murray (Engineer), Capt. W.J. Johnson, Bill Barden, Bill Palmer, Jock McAvoy (Engineer), Jock Bain (Traffic), Engineer, Andrew Ruthven (Radio Officer), Capt. Bill Baillie, Barry Murray (Engineer), Capt. W.J. Johnson, Radio Officer Paddy O'Gorman, Young (Engineer), Capt. Jock Young, Radio Officer Jimmy Morrison, Accounts. Back Row: Second from left, Mary Kelso (Accounts). The rest are Secretaries, Accounts Staff, Apprentice Engineers and female hangar staff. (Henry Vallance).

APPENDIX 1

PRINCIPAL EMPLOYEES

In approximate chronological order of joining.*

I - NORTHERN AIRWAYS:

1934

June 1st **Edward F. ('Ted') Palmer.** - Joined John Sword's Midland & Scottish Air Ferries in March 1934 at Renfrew (Glasgow). Left in May 1934 to join as Chief (and only) Pilot of George Nicholson's Northern Airways at Cramlington, Newcastle on Tyne. From August 1934, also acted as Instructor at John Sword's Flying School at Blackpool (Stanley Park) until November, when moved to Renfrew with George Nicholson's newly formed Northern and Scottish Airways to operate to Campbeltown and Islay from December 1st. Left NSA in 1935, joined Imperial Airways, later BOAC, becoming a Senior Capt. in BOAC post WWII.

Nov 21st **Charles F. Almond.** - of 66 John Street, Sunderland. Chief Pilot of Midland & Scottish Air Ferries, then a Flying Instructor with the Scottish Flying Club at Renfrew (Glasgow) in Autumn 1934. Had taken over the operation (on demand) of John Sword's Air Ambulance DH84 Dragon, until Dec 31st 1934. Joined George Nicholson as a Director of the former's newly formed Northern and Scottish Airways Ltd on November 21st. Flew inaugural flight of NSA's Renfrew - Campbeltown - Islay service on Dec 1st 1934. First to land a Dragon on Colonsay. Left April 30th 1935.

II - NORTHERN & SCOTTISH AIRWAYS:

1934

Nov 21st **William Douglas Thompson ('Bill') Gairdner.**

- Recruited from Brian Lewis Ltd (De Havilland aircraft sales agents of Heston, Hooton Park and Renfrew). A pilot himself, Bill became Air Superintendent of NSA, and later Scottish Airways, giving up the post in 1940 when WWII broke out. Went to Australia to work for QANTAS in 1947.

1935

April ? **William B. ('Bill') Mann.**

- Taken on as Chief Engineer of NSA by George Nicholson when the aircraft fleet expanded from one to five DH84 Dragons between April and May 1935. Bill Mann stayed at Renfrew until BEA took over all operations in 1947, maintaining a growing fleet of aircraft up to DC-3 size in very difficult conditions. Became BEA's Chief Engineer for Scotland before moving to London in senior capacity.

May 1st **Capt. T. A. McNeill.** - Joined NSA to take over as Chief Pilot from Charles F. Almond, who had just left. Had flown for Midland & Scottish Air Ferries from Aug 1933 to May 1934. Licensed Engineer also. Left NSA on July 31st 1935

and place taken by David Barclay.

May 4th **Gilbert Rae.** - Taken on as NSA's first Apprenticed Ground Engineer. Later acquired pilot's licence at Scottish Flying Club, Renfrew, and flew as pilot for NSA/Scottish Airways. Later joined Imperial Airways, delivered Spitfires, etc., for ATA when war broke out, then joined BOAC and posted to Leuchars in Fife to fly the un-armed passenger flights to Sweden. Shot up by FW.190 and crash-landed in Sweden. Later attacked again over North Sea, but escaped. Ditched Mosquito in sea near Leuchars August 18th 1944, after structural failure. All crew drowned.

May 14th **Capt. David Barclay MBE, M.St.J.** - Joined NSA as a pilot under T.A. McNeill (Chief Pilot). Took over as Chief Pilot when McNeill left on July 31st 1935. Remained Chief Pilot until Feb 1946, then appointed Air Superintendent and Operations Director. After nationalisation on 1st Feb 1947 made General Manager of BEA's Air Ambulance Division in Scotland, and later Chief Pilot and Training Pilot of Heron fleet. Flew a total of 17,350 hrs in his civil career and over 1,271 ambulance flights - more than any other pilot.

Dec 15th **Capt. Charles Bernard ('Tug') Wilson.** - Joined NSA as an experienced pilot for the Argyll and Western Isles services. Flew Ambulance services. Transferred to Northern Section of Scottish Airways in Inverness from Jan 1938. Remained in Inverness or Kirkwall until WWII, when became a Test Pilot at Liverpool (Speke) and Burtonwood on USAAF fighters assembled locally.

1936

Mar 5th **Capt. John Annesley Hankins.** - After service in the RAF as a Flying Officer, joined Scottish Motor Traction (SMT) as a joy-riding pilot. Crashed in a Fox Moth on July 31st 1934 at Riverside Park, Dundee, killing one passenger and seriously injuring another. Joined NSA and flew from Renfrew until Nov 1937, when he transferred to the Northern Section of Scottish Airways, based at Kirkwall. (Flew inter-island and Ambulance services, as well as services to Inverness and Shetland). Famous for some of his inter-island ambulance flights and regarded as one of the finest pilots in the airline. Re-joined RAF at the start of WWII, rose to Squadron Leader and became C.O. of a Dakota Squadron. Air Force Cross (AFC) awarded in 1944. Returned to Scottish Airways at Renfrew in Nov 1944, later to BEA. Went to live in Mexico.

Mar 7th **Capt. J. Johnstone.** - Flew with NSA at Renfrew until Jan 1938, when transferred to Northern Section of Scottish Airways, as resident pilot at Kirkwall. Left at start of WWII.

Mar ? **J. P. W. Hepburn.** - Ground Engineer at Renfrew.

Mar 23rd **WTO. F.R. Hughes.** - Employed as company's first Wireless Telegraphy Officer to use new Marconi sets installed in the aircraft. Appointed Chief W.T. Officer, when others taken on later. (The title W.T.O. was later changed to R.O. [Radio Officer] when radio set usage took over from Morse Code transmission)

May 1st **John Swann.** - Traffic Officer. Joined at Renfrew. Sent across to IoM in July for summer season, to assist at Hall Caine. Became Traffic Superintendent at Glasgow, and later Traffic Manager. To BEA.

May ? **Colin McPhail.** - Local Manager, Tiree.

May ? **James MacGeachy.** - Local Manager, Campbeltown.

May ? **Tom Caskie.** - Local Manager, Islay.

May ? **Ewen MacRae.** - Local Manager, Glen Brittle, Carbost, Skye.

May ? **A.F. Martin.** - Local Agent, North Uist.

May ? **F. S. Mackenzie.** - Local Agent, South Uist.

---

* Date shown is either known starting date, or earliest date of employment available from records/log-books etc.

Signatures of some of the Directors and staff of Scottish Airways are displayed above. Most are recognisable, and they include George Nicholson (top centre), W. Gairdner, (top left), T. McNeill, Radio Officer R.A. Stewart, Radio Officer A. M Ruthven, Capt E.E. Fresson, Capt. J.P. Rae, Capt. J.M. Hayes, etc...

Dragons at Renfrew! Five DH 84 Dragons of the Northern and Scottish fleet are shown here, when they were operating the United Airways' routes (Eric Starling).

May ? **W.H. Chapman.** - Local Agent, IoM.

July 1st **J. W. S. Spinner.** - Station Superintendent, Hall Caine Airport, IoM.

July 1st **D. L. Robertson.** - Base Engineer, Hall Caine Airport, IoM.

July 1st **A. Kelly.** - Traffic Officer, Hall Caine Airport, IoM.

July 1st **C. Collister.** - Traffic Officer, Hall Caine Airport, IoM.

July 1st **Capt. G.E. Mustard.** - Resident Pilot, Hall Caine Airport, IoM for 1936-37 period.

Aug 7th **Capt. John ('Jock') Young.** - Learned to fly, and became an Instructor at Scottish Flying Club. Joined Scottish Airways to fly DH Dragons and Spartan Cruisers to Western Isles. Flew throughout WWII and left in Jan 1946 to join KLM. Retired early due to ear trouble following a rapid de-pressurisation in a Lockheed Constellation over the Atlantic. Owned a hotel in Ardrossan, before retiring to live locally in Ayrshire. Never had an accident in entire flying career.

Aug 27th **Capt. Slocum.** - Joined as a pilot for a time.

Sept 12th **W.T.O. Butterfield.** - Wireless Telegraphy Officer

Oct ? **John Macpherson.** - Local Agent, Barra.

Oct ? **Donald MacGillivray.** - Local Agent, Benbecula.

Oct 29th **W.T.O. W. Bitchimo.** - Wireless Telegraphy Officer

Dec 8th **Capt. Prickett.** - Joined as pilot.

Dec 18th **W.T.O. Eadie.** - Wireless Telegraphy Officer

1937

Jan 28th **W. Wyatt.** - Ground Engineer.

Feb 12th **Tubb.** - Ground Engineer.

Apr 19th **Hoose.** - Ground Engineer.

May 29th **W.T.O. A. Tingle.** - Wireless Telegraphy Officer

June 9th **W.T.O. Hugh Black.** - Wireless Telegraphy Officer. Later to BEA. Native of Shetland and retired to live there.

III - HIGHLAND AIRWAYS LTD:

1933

Apr 12th **Cyril Pugh.** - Engineer and mechanic. Previously worked for General Aircraft Co. at Croydon. Left Fresson soon after George Griffiths took over (Summer 1934)

Aug 1st **Capt. G. Bernard Holmes.** - Experienced joy-riding pilot (ex-RAF, ex Scottish Motor Traction). Taken on to fly new DH Dragon G-ACIT on the Inverness - Kirkwall run.

1934

Apr ? **Capt. J. A Greenshields.** - Experienced pilot (ex-RAF). Taken on to open new Aberdeen-Orkney service using Dragon G-ACIT.

Apr ? **Capt. Eric Coleman.** - Experienced pilot (ex-RAF). Taken on to fly Inverness-Kirkwall service. Had two unfortunate accidents, writing off Dragons G-ACCE at Kirkwall and G-ACGK at Inverness. Left in 1935.

July ? **George Griffiths, OBE.** - Licensed Engineer (ex-SMT) who joined Highland Airways and became Chief Engineer of the Northern Section of Scottish Airways. Remained until BEA took over in 1946, and joined Rolls-Royce in Glasgow. Retired back to Inverness, and killed in car accident near Bunchrew.

1935

May ? **Bert Farminer.** - Engineer and ex-apprentice with Sopwith Aviation Co. Became aero-engine expert at Inverness for

Northern Section of Scottish Airways, staying until BEA take-over.

May ? **Archie MacDonald.** - Mechanic and fitter at Inverness. Stayed on with BEA at Glasgow after 1946.

May ? **Theo Goulden.** - Radio Mechanic/Operator at Inverness. Stayed on with BEA at Glasgow after 1946.

May 1st **Capt. John Philip Rae.** - Experienced pilot with Midland & Scottish Air Ferries and ex-De Havilland test pilot. Taken on by Highland Airways as resident Kirkwall pilot. Left Oct 1937, joined RAF. Became C.O. of No. 512 Squadron (Dakotas) and flew missions on D-Day and at Arnhem. (was shot down on D-Day, after dropping paratroops in the dark, ditching in the Channel. Crew saved and spent D-Day in Normandy!) After war joined Hunting Air Travel, then BEA. Died 1959 of heart attack.

? ? **Capt. Adam Smith.** - Experienced pilot. Opened new Aberdeen (Kintore)-Shetland service on June 3rd 1936. Left in 1937. Ran a motor garage for a short time with John Rae at Shoreham. After WWII ran a Timber Merchant's business at Troon, Ayrshire.

1936

May ? **Miss Jean Macdonald.** (later married surname was McManus) - Sales and office administration. Remained

Oops!. Two views of Highland Airways' DH84 Dragon G-ACIT parked on its nose at Kirkwall after hitting soft ground. No-one was injured, but just how the passengers climbed out is not revealed... Without seatbelts they must have all ended up in a heap at the front! (Gilbert B. Archer).

with Northern Division of Scottish Airways Ltd until after WWII.

May ? **Capt. John Joshua Veasey.** - Burly ex-South African airline pilot who kept pigeons.

May ? **Capt. Johnny Fielden.** - Both he and Veasey replaced Rae and Smith.

IV - SCOTTISH AIRWAYS LTD:

1937

Sept 1st **W.T.O. Cane.** - Based at Renfrew.

Oct ? **J. McCallum.** - Local Agent, Harris.

Dec 14th **H. Willoch.** - Ground Engineer at Renfrew.

1938

Mar ? **Alexander ('Sandy') Cumming.** - Traffic Superintendent at Inverness.

Apr 29th **W.T.O. J. Pickles** - Wireless Telegraphy Officer at Renfrew.

May ? **A. Maclennan.** - Expert woodworker at Inverness who became Foreman of aircraft repairs. To BEA later.

May ? **Arthur Dodds.** - Mechanic and Fitter at Inverness. To BEA later.

May ? **Robert ('Bob') Jamieson.** - Porter and Baggage Handler at Inverness.

May ? **Miss L. B. McDougall.** - Publicity Manager at Renfrew.

July ? **Capt. T. H. ("Jock") Wilson.** - Pilot at Renfrew.

Bill Gairdner stands by the nose of a DH89A Dragon Rapide at Glasgow's Renfrew Airport, whilst the signwriter paints out the old "Northern and Scottish Airways" name, and replaces it with the new "Scottish Airways" titling after August 12th 1937.
(DH/BAe)

1939

Feb 15th **Capt. Donald Prentice.** - Joined as a pilot at Renfrew until WWII broke out. Left to join Services. Re-joined Scottish Airways in August 1945, after war ended. Converted to Dakota May 5th 1946. To BEA.

Mar 1st **Capt. Henry Vallance.** - Experienced pilot from Allied Airways in Aberdeen. Joined at Renfrew and transferred to Northern Section on May 27th 1939 to be resident Orkney pilot. He then moved to Inverness for the rest of the war on Apr 27th 1940. On Nov 2nd 1945 he was transferred down to RAS at Liverpool and Croydon until 1946 when he joined KLM for the rest of his career. He retired from KLM in 1971 to live in the Isle of Man.

Mar 7th **R/O. J.C. ('Jimmy') Mitchell.** - Radio Officer. Joined at Renfrew, later succeeded F.R. Hughes as Chief Radio Officer of Scottish Airways at Renfrew. Joined BSAA in 1946, later BOAC. Retired to live in Aberdeen.

Mar 12th **Capt. B. T. ('Paddy') O'Reilly.** - Joined as pilot at Renfrew from Services. Based in Inverness from Aug 31st 1943. Was married with five children. Left in November 1945 (To Aer Lingus?)

Mar 24th **Capt. Markam.** - Joined at Renfrew.

Apr 4th **R/O. T. Hedley.** - Radio Officer at Renfrew.

May 6th **R/O. William M. ('Bill') Gray.** - Radio Officer at Inverness. Later to BEA. Then to Air Traffic Control at Heathrow.

June 4th **R/O. Bradley.** - Radio Officer at Renfrew.

June 26th **R/O. McGill.** - Radio Officer at Renfrew.

July 1st **R/O. Lansdale.** - Radio Officer at Renfrew.

July 15th **Capt. William ('Bill') Baillie OBE, MVO.** - Came from Allied Airways at Aberdeen, following Henry Vallance. Based at Renfrew from Aug 1st 1939. Then to Inverness, Aug 30th 1940 - Nov 10th 1943. Back at Renfrew, then to BEA, becoming Chief Pilot - Scotland Feb 1st 1947. Chief Flight Capt. BEA (in London) in 1950, General Manager, later Director of BEA Flight Operations, then Managing Director BEA Airtours at Gatwick. Retired in 1976 and died after routine operation Mar 11th 1981 aged 64.

Aug 26th **R/O. Ball.** - Radio Officer at Renfrew.

1940

Feb 2nd **J. Ferguson.** - Ground Engineer at Renfrew.

Feb 9th **R/O. J. Dufferin** - Radio Officer at Renfrew.

May ? **Norman McIver.** - Local Manager, Stornoway.

Nov 11th **R/O. Andrew M. Ruthven.** - Radio Officer at Renfrew. Ex-Merchant Navy and AST at Hamble and RAF No.1 A.O.N.S. at Prestwick. In January 1946 he joined BSAA at Heathrow and later with BOAC until retiring in 1973 as a Route Communications Manager.

Nov 20th **Capt. C.W.S. Clark.** - Joined at Renfrew. Left for RAF service Feb 14th 1941 and returned to Scottish on Oct 16th 1943.

Nov ? **Capt. Geoffrey Greenhalgh.** - Joined as a pilot with Northern Section at Inverness. Left for RAF service November 1943.

? ? **Mrs Margaret Chisholm. (née Green)** - Secretary for Capt. Fresson at Inverness. Joined 1940, left 1945 after marriage. Her office was in Macrae & Dick's Garage, on the first floor.

1941

Feb 18th **Capt. S. S. Coleman** - Joined Scottish as experienced pilot. Left for RAF service March 5th 1941, returned Sept 5th 1943.

Mar 4th **R/O. Garside.** - Radio Officer at Renfrew.

May ? **Norman McIver** - Local Manager, Stornoway.

July 29th **R/O. J. Morrison.** - Radio Officer at Renfrew.

Aug 18th **R/O. Roy A. Stewart.** - Radio Officer, ex-Merchant Navy. Joined from RAF. Based at Inverness until Nov 27th 1945, when relocated to Renfrew. Left July 22nd 1946. Bought a Petrol Filling Station at Culcabock, Inverness. Died 1971.

Aug 19th **R/O. Frederick.** - Radio Officer at Renfrew.

Sept 25th **Capt. J. E. Kennedy.** - Joined as a pilot at Renfrew. Left for RAF service Sept 30th 1942.

Nov 28th **R/O H. B. Seed.** - Radio Officer at Renfrew.

1942

Mar 1st **Capt. William J. Johnson.** - Flying Officer RAF, Test Pilot MU. Released from RAF to Scottish Airways in April 1942. Remained at Renfrew with Scottish A/W, later BEA. Pilot of Dakota which crashed on roof of a house in South Ruislip, Dec 19th 1946. (Thereafter known as "Willy Jig" or "Rooftop Johnson").

June 24th **R/O. Sallas.** - Radio Officer at Renfrew.

July 27th **R/O. Hay.** - Radio Officer at Renfrew.

Sept 5th **Capt. Robert M. Pepper.** - Ex- Fleet Air Arm. Crashed Rapide G-AGED at Renfrew. Left company June 24th 1942.

Sept 9th **R/O Bennison.** - Radio Officer at Renfrew.

Oct 20th **R/O Crann.** - Radio Officer at Renfrew.

Nov 7th **Murray.** - Ground Engineer at Renfrew.

Dec 11th **Capt. William A. ('Bill') Cash.** - Joined as a pilot at Inverness. Left to join Services on Feb 8th 1944.

Dec 22nd **R/O Anderson.** - Radio Officer at Renfrew.

Engineers and staff of Scottish Airways' Northern Section at Inverness in late 1944.
Front Row (seated): Arthur Dodds, Bert Farminer, Theo Goulden, George Griffiths (Chief Engineer), Archie MacDonald,
Alex MacLennan. Back Row (standing): All engineering apprentices. (Richard Fresson)

1943

?   ?   **James D. Steen. -** Traffic Officer, Inverness (16 years old). Remained with Scottish Airways, BEA and BA until retired in May 1981. Now lives in Stornoway

Feb   19th   **Capt. J.E.D. Scott. -** Pilot for short time on rest from Services.

June   5th   **R/O P. D. O'Gorman.** - Radio Officer at Renfrew. To BEA, later BEA Helicopters on Scilly Isles service.

July 17th   **Capt. T. K. Breakell** - Pilot at Renfrew.

Sept 26th   **Capt. H. Riley-Sawdon.** - Joined as pilot at Renfrew from RAF. Left to re-join RAF Feb 5th 1944.

Dec 22nd   **R/O 'Archie' Emerson. -** Radio Officer at Inverness.

1944

?   ?   **H. B. Murray. -** Ground Engineer at Renfrew.

?   ?   **R. Young. -** Ground Engineer at Renfrew.

?   ?   **J. McAvoy. -** Ground Engineer at Renfrew.

?   ?   **Miss Robina L. ('Bobbie') Christie.** Traffic officer at Inverness. Later became Scottish Airway's first Stewardess, flying on Dakota fleet from Renfrew in 1946. Was in Dakota crash on house in South Ruislip on 19th December 1946. To BEA.

?   ?   **J.H. Hayter. -** Traffic Officer at Inverness.

?   ?   **R/O. J. Macaulay. -** Radio Officer at Inverness.

Feb   16th   **Capt. David MacFarlane. -** Joined as a pilot on release from Services as replacement for Bill Cash. Based at Inverness until Jan 12th 1946. Left to join KLM.

June   1st   **Capt. John F. ('Smokey') Hayes. -** Posted in from RAF. Had instructed Spitfire pilots in Canada. Based at Inverness. Stayed with BEA later. Now lives near Wantage

Oct   1st   **Capt. John Michie. -** Son of Provost of Renfrew. Pilot in South Africa 1937-1939. Served with Lockheed Aircraft Co. on North Atlantic ferry run prior to joining Scottish Airways. Went to KLM Apr 19th 1946. Retired to live in

Surrey. Died in late 1980's at Virginia Water.

Nov 11th   **R/O Wilkinson. -** Radio Officer at Renfrew.

Nov 30th   **Capt. W. H. Morton. -** Joined as a pilot at Renfrew for a short time. Left March 1st 1945.

1945

?   ?   **John Watson. -** Station Superintendent, Kirkwall for Northern Section, Scottish Airways.

?   ?   **H. Fisher. -** Traffic Officer, Kirkwall.

?   ?   **Robert Bain. -** Driver at Kirkwall.

?   ?   **Kenneth Wards. -** Airport Assistant, Kirkwall.

Mar 14th   **R/O Laughlan. -** Radio Officer at Renfrew.

Mar 18th   **R/O Norrington. -** Radio Officer at Renfrew.

Apr 17th   **R/O J. M. Wilson. -** Radio Officer at Renfrew.

May   ?   **Capt. E. Elgey. -** Joined as pilot at Renfrew. Left August 1945

May   ?   **Capt. Eric Pooley. -** Joined as pilot at Renfrew. Left June 1945.

Sept   5th   **Capt. J. D. Greenhalgh. -** Joined as a pilot at Renfrew. Later to BEA. Brother of G. Greenhalgh.

Sept 12th   **Wing Commander R.J. Ralph. -** Joined as a pilot from RAF. Left July 17th 1946.

Sept 19th   **Capt. D. F. Williamson -** Pilot at Renfrew.

Sept 20th   **Capt D. Prowse. -** Pilot at Renfrew.

Dec   ?   **R/O Calvert. -** Radio Officer at Renfrew. Ex-RAF (1938-1945). Killed in crash of Rapide G-AFFF.

Dec   2nd   **R/O Maher. -** Radio Officer at Renfrew.

Dec   5th   **Capt. J. D. Youell. -** Joined at Renfrew as pilot. To BEA.

Dec   8th   **Capt. J. S. Leslie. -** Joined at Renfrew as pilot. To BEA.

Dec   8th   **R/O T. R. McCorkindale. -** Radio Officer at Renfrew.

1946

?   ?   **Agnes F. Latimer. -** Engineering Clerk at Renfrew.

?   ?   **R/O. P.D. Chrisp. -** Radio Officer at Inverness.

?	?	**R/O. Christie.** - Radio Officer at Inverness. Later became Traffic Officer with BEA at Dalcross.
?	?	**Miss I Cooper.** - Traffic Clerk, Kirkwall.
?	?	**R. McKenell.** - Scottish Airways' Manager, Orkney.

Jan 2nd **Capt. Eric Allen Starling.**- Ex-Chief Pilot, Aberdeen Airways 1934-9. Joined RAF Coastal Command May 1940. 292 Sqdn (Wellingtons) N. Ireland; Iceland on Atlantic Patrols. N. Africa. N Ireland (No. 3 Sqdn). Islay (304 Ferry Training Unit) on Beaufighters, then C.O. 292 Sqdn with ASR Warwicks in Far East. Joined Scottish Airways on demob. Based at Inverness until Oct 14th, then Renfrew. To BEA, becoming Flight Manager - Scotland (1949 - 1968). Air Ambulance Pilot, 1968 - 1971. Retired Dec 28th 1971 as BEA's oldest and most senior pilot. Lives at West Kilbride.

Jan 2nd **R/O Fraser.** - Radio Officer at Renfrew.

Jan 11th **R/O Sutton.** - Radio Officer at Renfrew.

Jan 22nd **R/O Hamilton.** - Radio Officer at Renfrew.

Feb 10th **R/O Brodie.** - Radio Officer at Renfrew.

Feb 23rd **R/O Nicoll.** - Radio Officer at Renfrew.

Mar 4th **R/O McGinlay.** - Radio Officer at Renfrew.

Mar 11th **Capt. Stanley Clayton.** - Converted to Dakota May 16th 1946 at Renfrew.

May 8th **Capt. William ('Bill') Mackenzie.** - Converted to Dakota fleet.

May 8th **Capt. Tom Mackenzie.** - Converted onto Dakota fleet.

May 9th **Capt. John Ramsden.** - Converted to Dakota fleet.

May 11th **Capt. 'Windy' Martin.** - Converted to Dakota at Renfrew.

May 29th **Capt. William ('Bill') J. Pooley.** - DH89 Fleet.

May 29th **Capt. D. Ross.** - Joined at Renfrew as pilot. Left July 18th 1946.

June 3rd **Capt. Alec Appleby.** - Converted to Dakota fleet.

June 3rd **Capt. Welford** - Converted to Dakota. Great practical joker, renowned for his tricks played on passengers and colleagues alike!

June 13th **F/O 'Johnny' Afflec.** - Joined at Renfrew. Converted to Dakota June 1st 1946.

June 21st **R/O Ritchie.** - Radio Officer at Renfrew.

June 25th **Capt. Johnny Wells** - DH89 Fleet.

July 22nd **Capt. Fittall.** - Joined at Renfrew.

July 23rd **R/O Kirk.** - Radio Officer at Renfrew.

July 26th **R/O McPherson.** - Radio Officer at Renfrew.

Aug 20th **R/O Cunningham.** - Radio Officer at Renfrew.

Jean McManus (neé Macdonald) was the Northern Section Sales Manager. (Richard Fresson)

"Jock" Young, one of the Renfrew based Captains who stayed with Scottish Airways throughout the war. (Alison Mills)

Aug 22nd **R/O Morton.** - Radio Officer at Renfrew.

Sept 4th **R/O Banks.** - Radio Officer at Renfrew.

Sept 11th **R/O Byrne.** - Radio Officer at Renfrew.

Sept 20th **R/O Collyer.** - Radio Officer at Renfrew.

Oct 4th **R/O Quigley.** - Radio Officer at Renfrew.

Oct 7th **Capt. McDermott** - DH89 Fleet.

Oct 8th **Capt. Jack Leask** - DH89 Fleet. Later BEA Chief Pilot, Aberdeen.

Oct 8th **Capt. R. C. Day.** - Joined at Renfrew. Converted to Dakota.

Oct 10th **Capt. Bill Fittall.** - DH89 Fleet.

Oct 10th **Capt. G. C. Woodward.** - Joined at Renfrew. Converted to Dakota Oct 22nd.

Oct 14th **Capt. Hedley.** - DH89 Fleet.

Oct 18th **R/O Walker.** - Radio Officer at Renfrew.

Oct 18th **R/O McLevy.** - Radio Officer at Renfrew.

Oct 23rd **Capt. Wood.** - Joined at Renfrew.

Nov 4th **R/O Millar.** - Radio Officer at Renfrew.

Nov 13th **R/O H. Murdoch.** - Radio Operator at Renfrew.

Nov 19th **R/O More.** - Radio Officer at Renfrew.

Nov ? **F/O I. Crosbie.** FAA pilot, June 1943-Nov 1946. Joined at Renfrew. Aboard Dakota that crashed onto house in South Ruislip, Dec 19th 1946. Uninjured.

Dec 12th **Capt. Gibson.** - At Renfrew.

Dec 12th **Capt. Brown.** - At Renfrew.

Dec 12th **Capt. Black.** - At Renfrew.

Dec 14th **R/O Edmondston.** - Radio Officer at Renfrew.

Dec 30th **Capt. Forbes.** - DH89 Fleet.

APPENDIX 2
AIRCRAFT FLEET
(In order of acquisition or use)

I - NORTHERN AIRWAYS

G-ACFG   (July 1934*) c/n 6027. De Havilland DH84 Dragon I. First C of A 28th June 1933, DH Aircraft Co. Ltd. To Northern Airways July 1934. Sold abroad February 1937. To Australia as VH-UZG.

II - NORTHERN AND SCOTTISH AIRWAYS LTD.

G-ACJS   (January 8th 1935*) c/n 6042. De Havilland DH84 Dragon I. First C of A 4th August 1933 for Midland & Scottish Air Ferries. Fitted with toilet and radio. Registration letters chosen for it comprised John Cuthill Sword's initials. Remained at Renfrew after M&SAF ceased trading. To Northern and Scottish Airways on 8th January 1935. Registration cancelled during November 1936. No further details known.

G-ACMO   (June 1st 1935*) c/n 6062. De Havilland DH84 Dragon II. First C of A 31st January 1934 for Jersey Airways. Aircraft named *St Ouen's Bay*. To Northern and Scottish Airways on June 1st 1935. Sold to Australia on 27th January 1938 and registered as VH-ABK for South Queensland Airways during March 1938. Impressed into Royal Australian Air Force as A34-4 on 4th July 1940 and delivered to 3 Elementary Flying Training School, subsequently to 1 Air Observers School, to 2 Air Observers School, Mount Gambier. Converted to Air Ambulance. To 33 Sqdn and 35 Sqdn. Restored to civil register as VH-ABK on 29th March 1944 on loan for McRobertson Miller Aviation Co, Perth. Believed aircraft scrapped, listed as struck off charge 12th September 1944.

G-ACNH   (June 1st 1935*) c/n 6070. De Havilland DH84 Dragon II. First C of A March 26th 1934 for Jersey Airways Ltd, named *Bouley Bay*. To Northern and Scottish Airways on 1st June 1935. Registration cancelled 1st March 1937.

G-ACED   (June 1st 1935*) c/n 4064. De Havilland DH83 Fox Moth. First C of A May 6th 1933. Delivered to Scottish Motor Traction, Turnhouse May 1933. To Northern and Scottish Airways June 1st 1935. Sold to Australia in March 1937 as VH-UZL.

G-ACMC   (August 15th 1935*) c/n 6053. De Havilland DH84 Dragon I. First C of A 24th November 1933 for De Havilland Aircraft Co Ltd. Prototype Mk II. To Jersey Airways Ltd, named *St Brelades Bay*. To United Airways. To Northern and Scottish Airways August 15th 1935. To Airwork on 23rd January 1936. Sold to Australia as VH-UXK during August 1936. Reported crashed en-route Cairns - Brisbane while operated by Queensland Airways. Listed as repaired and restored. Crashed at Mindoo, Queensland on 29th August 1938.

G-ACYL   (February 19th 1936*) c/n 12. Spartan Cruiser II. First C of A October 24th 1934 for United Airways. To British Airways December 1935. To Northern and Scottish Airways February 19th 1936. Impressed into RAF on 2nd April 1940 as X9431. To No. 6 AACU on 7th April 1940. To No.7 AACU on 3rd May 1940. Struck off charge as beyond repair by No.7 AACU after a total of 3,310.40 hours flying time. To No. 284 ATC Sqn at Cheadle (Cheshire Wing) on 28 August 1941.

G-ACVT   (May 17th 1936*) c/n 11. Spartan Cruiser II. First C of A August 2nd 1934 for Spartan Air Lines. To British Airways December 1935. Crashed Isle of Man March 23rd 1936. To Northern and Scottish Airways May 17th 1936. Crashed Skye July 25th 1936, no injuries to crew or passengers, but written off when over-ran on wet grass and struck wall.

G-ACUO   (May 19th 1936*) c/n 7081. De Havilland DH85 Leopard Moth. First C of A September 24th 1934. To Northern and Scottish Airways May 19th 1936. Impressed into RAF July 11th 1940 as AX865. Struck off charge June 6th 1944 at Hooton Park.

G-ACSM   (May 22nd 1936*) c/n 10. Spartan Cruiser II. First C of A. June 13th 1934 for Spartan Air Lines Ltd. To British Airways February 1936. To Northern and Scottish Airways

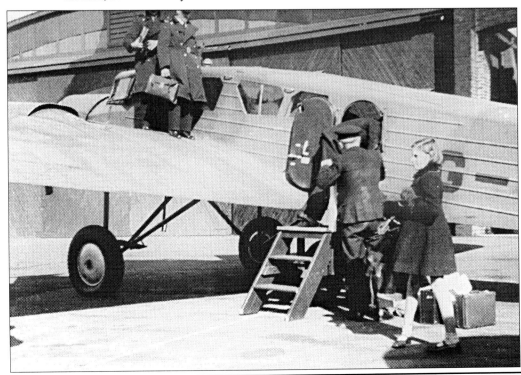

*Renfrew turn-around!
The flight crew dis-embark
from this Spartan Cruiser at
Renfrew, whilst groundstaff
unload the luggage.
(John Stroud Collection).*

* Date of acquistion, or first known date of airline use of aircraft.

May 22nd 1936. Impressed into RAF as X9433 April 2nd 1940. To No.6 AACU 7th April 1940. To No.7 AACU on May 3rd 1940. Struck off charge 4th July 1940 when airframe found to be in advanced state of decay.

G-ADBU (June 11th 1936*) c/n 6280. De Havilland DH89 Dragon Rapide. First C of A 29th April 1935 for United Airways. To British Airways on 1st October 1935. Transferred to Northern and Scottish Airways, Renfrew on 11th June 1936. Damaged beyond repair during November 1936.

G-ADDF (June 29th 1936*) c/n 6284. De Havilland DH89 Dragon Rapide. First C of A 8th August 1935 for Hillman Airways. Transferred to British Airways during December 1935. To Northern and Scottish Airways, Renfrew on 29th June 1936. Sold by Airwork Ltd to Lejeune Aviation before 7th September 1937. Possibly used in Spanish Civil War. No further details known.

G-ADEM (July 6th 1936*) c/n 103. Spartan Cruiser III. First C of A June 3rd 1935 for Spartan Air Lines. To British Airways March 1936. To Northern and Scottish Airways 6th July 1936. Crashed into hangar at Stanley Park, Blackpool on November 20th 1936 whilst attempting to take-off in thick fog. Pilot (Capt. O'Connell) and passenger killed.

G-ADAG (July 30th 1936*) c/n 6266. De Havilland DH89 Dragon Rapide. First C of A 6th February 1935 for Hillman Airways. Transferred to British Airways during December 1935. Sold to Airwork Ltd, Heston during January 1936. To Northern and Scottish Airways on 30th July 1936. Impressed into RAF under civil contract with 6 Civil Air Navigation School Shoreham. Damaged in landing at Oakhampton Landing Ground on 24th November 1939 when stalled holding off to avoid rising ground. Wing struck ground and skidded on nose. Allocated serial Z7264 on 15 July 1940. To Headquarters Ferry Pilots' Pool on 19th June 1941. Damaged Cat AC/FA at Prestwick, to De Havilland's Witney on 10 January 1942. To Headquarters Ferry Pilots' Pool on 14 March 1942. Damaged Cat B on 20th August 1943, re CatE/FA on 13th September 1943.

G-ADAH (August 10th 1936*) c/n 6278. De Havilland DH89 Dragon Rapide. First C of A. 19th February 1935 for Hillman Airways. Transferred to British Airways during December 1935. To Northern and Scottish Airways, Renfrew on August 10th 1936. To Allied Airways (Gandar Dower) Ltd, May 26th 1938 named *Thurso Venturer* later *Pioneer*. Sold

to Air Ministry. Later bought back for £2,036. Stored at Dyce from 1947 until 1967 when moved by road to Booker Airfield, High Wycombe for re-build. To Northern Aeroplane Society during 1970. Loaned to Royal Scottish Museum, East Fortune during 1974. Loaned to Manchester Museum of Science and Technology in 1980s. Aircraft currently on static display and under restoration.

G-ACZM (October 24th 1936*) c/n 14. Spartan Cruiser II. First C of A December 23rd 1934. To Spartan Air Lines. Absorbed into United Airways, then to Northern and Scottish Airways on 24th October 1936. Withdrawn from use on January 9th 1940 at Renfrew, and scrapped in April 1942.

G-ACNG (February 17th 1937*) c/n 6029. De Havilland DH84 Dragon II. First C of A 23 March 1934 for Jersey Airways, named *Portelet Bay*. To Spartan Air Lines during June 1935, transferred to British Airways on 1 October 1935. To Northern and Scottish Airways February 17th 1937. Written off when crashed at Hatston on 19 April 1940. (injuring Capt David Barclay and an Army General, with R.O. Gray on board).

G-ACOR (April 24th 1937*) c/n 6073. De Havilland DH84 Dragon II. First C of A 19 March 1934 for Graham McKinnion, named *Fiona*. To British Continental Airways, aircraft named *St Christopher*. To British Airways Ltd on 1 August 1936. To Northern and Scottish Airways on April 24th 1937. To Australia on 2 March 1938 and registered as VH-AEA on 26 June 1938 for Wewak Air Transport, later Parer's Air Transport. Damaged New Guinea during November 1938 but repaired. Aircraft set on fire at Salamaua on 21 January 1942 during Japanese air raid. The owner, Kevin Parer was sitting in the cockpit awaiting take-off when the Japanese aircraft attacked, hitting the aircraft. Parer was wounded, but stumbled across the airfield until hit and killed by another burst of gunfire.

G-ACYK (June 11th 1937*) c/n 101. Spartan Cruiser III. First C of A April 16th 1935 for Spartan Air Lines Ltd. To United Airways, then Northern and Scottish Airways on June 11th 1937. Crashed in poor visibility and downdraughts on hills East of Largs on January 14th 1938, after charter flight to deliver films. Pilot uninjured.

G-ADEL (June 16th 1937*). c/n 102. Spartan Cruiser III. First C of A April 18th 1935. To Spartan Air Lines. To United Airways then Northern and Scottish Airways on June 16th 1937.

Longman Line-up - Capt. Fresson's four different aircraft types in use by Highland Airways in the winter of 1936: (front to rear) his personal DH Gipsy Moth G-AAWO, the first DH Rapide G-ADAJ 'Inverness', the DH Dragon G-ADCT 'Orcadian', and the airline's first aircraft, General Aircraft ST4 Monospar G-ACEW 'Inverness'. (Leslie Serjeant)

Impressed into RAF as X9432 on April 2nd 1940. To No. 6 AACU on the 7th April 1940, then to No. 7 AACU on May 3rd 1940. Struck off charge 26th July 1940 when airframe and main spar found to be in advanced state of rot.

III - HIGHLAND AIRWAYS LTD.

G-ACEW (April 8th 1933*) c/n 11. General Aircraft Ltd GA ST-4 Monospar II. First C of A April 6th 1933. To Highland Airways April 8th 1933. Re-built at Croydon following accident at Wideford, Kirkwall on July 3rd 1933. Sold June 20th 1937 to Mr. Tutt. Crashed North of Cramlington. Wreckage shipped to Croydon. Struck off December 1937.

G-ACIT (July 30th 1933*) c/n 6039. De Havilland DH84 Dragon I. First C of A 24th July 1933 for Highland Airways, named *Aberdeen.* Used to inaugurate Highland Airways' Aberdeen (Seaton) - Kirkwall service on May 7th 1934. Later named *Orcadian* in 1939 as based in Kirkwall for inter-island services. To BEAC February 1st 1947. To Air Navigation and Trading Co during January 1952. To British Executive and General Aviation Ltd (Beagle Aircraft) during March 1962. To Airways Flying Club, Booker. To J Beaty during September 1969. To Southend Air Museum, C of A expired on 25 May 1974 and cancelled from register as withdrawn from use on 19 August 1981. Restored to register by Science Museum 26 May 1983. Currently in Science Museum out-station at Wroughton as part of the Air Transport Collection as Britain's oldest surviving airliner.

G-ACCE (April 24th 1934*). c/n 6010. De Havilland DH84 Dragon I. First C of A 21 April 1933 for The Honourable Brian Lewis. First leased to Highland Airways 14 -19 July 1933. To Highland Airways, named *Caithness.* Aircraft operated first-ever official British internal air mail service on 29th May 1934 (Inverness - Kirkwall). Written off on 29 August 1934 when machine crashed at Kirkwall following a downpour. Aircraft failed to take-off and hit a stone wall. The pilot and C of A assengers were not badly hurt, but aircraft written off.

Capts. Adam Smith and John Hankins of Scottish Airways try to keep warm at Inverness by a coke brazier during the severe winter of 1937/38. (The Fresson Trust).

G-ACGK (July 11th 1934*) c/n 6033. De Havilland DH84 Dragon I. First C of A 30th June 1933 for E C G England. To Highland Airways 11 July 1934, named *Loch Ness.* Written off on 8th January 1935 when aircraft ditched into the Moray Firth after taking off from Longman Aerodrome. The aircraft lost height, forcing the pilot to land in the sea about 20 yards offshore at about 45 mph. The aircraft's wheels came to rest on the sea-bed with the top wing just clear of the surface. The pilot hauled his two passengers onto the fuselage top, and after a short wait, they were rescued by a fishing boat. The aircraft was later salvaged, but was scrapped because of the effects of the sea water. The cause of the accident was later traced to severe ice accretion on the wings and control surfaces.

G-ACET (September 26th 1934*) c/n 6021. De Havilland DH84 Dragon I. First C of A 3 June 1933 for Scottish Motor Traction Co. To Midland & Scottish Air Ferries on 15 February 1934 to be kept at Renfrew and later Hooton Park. Sold to Highland Airways, 26th September 1934, named *Kirkwall.* To DH Co. Ltd 24th June 1937 in exchange for DH 89A Rapide G-AEWL. To Air Dispatch Ltd, February 1940. Impressed into RAF as AW171 at RAF Ringway on 7 July 1940. To 6 AACU on 13 July 1940. To De Havillands for major inspection but struck off charge as Cat E1 on 22 October 1941. Remains passed to No 328 Sqdn, ATC. To Capt Mike Russell 1989 for restoration to flight.

G-ADCT (June 2nd 1935*). c/n 6095. De Havilland DH84 Dragon II. First C of A 26 May 1935. To Highland Airways, named *Orcadian.* Crashed into trees at Westness, Island of Rousay, Orkneys September 6th 1935 in violent downdraught, with no injuries to pilot or five passengers. Dismantled, returned by rowing boat to Kirkwall and repaired. Flying again by November 10th 1935. Crashed at Longman Aerodrome on take-off on 14 December 1939. Written off by 14 February 1940.

G-ACPN (April 19th 1936*) c/n 6252. De Havilland DH89 Dragon Rapide. First C of A 2 August 1934 for Hillman's Airways. Transferred to British Airways during December 1935. Sold to Airwork Ltd, Heston during January 1936. Used by Highland Airways on some services from April 19th 1936. Inaugurated Aberdeen (Kintore) - Kirkwall - Shetland service on June 3rd 1936. Returned to British Airways on August 9th 1936. Listed as 'sold abroad' during September 1936. Bought by Juan de la Cierva and Louis Bolin for the Nationalist side in Spanish Civil War (registration/serial unknown). Arrived in Spain on 13 August 1936. Either shot down on 27 August 1936 or destroyed by fire at Aragon on 13 September 1936.

G-ADAJ (December 26th 1936*) c/n 6276. De Havilland DH89 Dragon Rapide. First C of A 5 June 1935 Hillman's Airways. Transferred to British Airways during December 1935. To Highland Airways, December 26th 1936, named *Inverness.* Inaugurated Inverness - Aberdeen service on May 31st 1937. First aircraft to land at Kirkwall (Grimsetter) on December 10th 1941. Taken over by BEAC 1st February 1947. Sold to France during November 1947 as F-BEDY. Used by Air France in Madagascar, later registered F-OADY. To Société Autrex, Hanoi as F-BADY during October 1950. Registration cancelled on 22 May 1953, believed withdrawn from use.

G-AEWL (June 25th 1937*) c/n 6367. De Havilland DH89A Dragon Rapide. First C of A 18 June 1937 for North Eastern Airways. To Highland Airways, named *Zetland,* June 25th 1937 in exchange for Dragon G-ACET. To BEAC 1 February 1947. Sold to C Allen 25 April 1948. To M J Fletcher 27 September 1948. To Wing Commander H C Kennard 13 April 1950. To Air Kruise (Kent) Ltd 13 April 1955, named *Nichole.* To Aviation Supplies Co Ltd 14 December 1955. Sold to French Ivory Coast as F-OATT 24 January 1956.

The Northern Section's DH Rapide G-AEWL 'Zetland' at Sumburgh, illustrating how beautifully clean the aircraft were kept by the Inverness staff. (John Rae)

IV - SCOTTISH AIRWAYS LTD

G-AFEY (April 15th 1938*) c/n 6402. De Havilland DH89A Dragon Rapide. First C of A March 7th 1938. To Scottish Airways (Renfrew Base) on April 15th 1938. Used to open Renfrew - Perth - Inverness and Northern Isles service on May 2nd 1938. Crashed at Wideford, Orkney on 18th March 1940.

G-AEOV (May 1st 1939*) c/n 6342. De Havilland DH89 Dragon Rapide. First C of A 3 March 1937 for The Right Hon The Viscount Forbes. The first DH89 fitted with flaps. To Scottish Airways (Renfrew) May 1st 1939. Impressed into RAF as W6456 with 24 Sqdn, RAF Hendon 10 January 1940. Damaged CatB/FA when port tyre burst at RAF Hendon during taxiing on 11 April 1942. The machine swung off the taxi track and onto soft grass. The aircraft was conveyed to De Havilland's for repair on 16 April 1942, but later struck off charge as Cat E1.

G-AFFF (May 26th 1939*) c/n 6386. De Havilland DH89A Dragon Rapide. Registered/First C.of A. 16 March/July 27th 1938 for the De Havilland Aircraft Co Ltd, Hatfield. Sold to Scottish Airways (Renfrew) May 26th 1939. Crashed into Craigton Hill, Milngavie, 27 September 1946, killing Pilot, R/O and 5 passengers.

G-AFRK (July 19th 1939*) c/n 6441. De Havilland DH89A Dragon Rapide. Registered/First C. of A. 9th March/May 8th 1939 for Isle of Man Air Services. To Scottish Airways Ltd (Renfrew) July 19th 1939. To BEAC February 1st 1947, named *Rudyard Kipling*. Sold to Airviews Ltd during May 1956. Withdrawn from use and broken up at Christchurch during March 1959.

G-AFOI (May 9th 1940*) c/n 6450. De Havilland DH89A Dragon Rapide. Registered/First C of A 28 July/28 August 1939 To AAJC. Scottish Airways (Renfrew) May 9th 1940. To

BEAC 1 February 1947. Leased to Gibraltar Airways 1948/49. To Airmotive (Liverpool) Ltd January 1950. To Handley Page Ltd Radlett June 1952. Withdrawn from use and scrapped at Sywell 20th September 1957.

G-AERN (July 1st 1940*) c/n 6345. De Havilland DH89A Dragon Rapide. Registered/First C of A 13th January/24 March 1937 for Blackpool and West Coast Air Services. To Scottish Airways (Inverness) from AAJC Pool on July 1st 1940. Returned to AAJC at Liverpool January 5th 1944. Used by Railway Air Services at Liverpool. To BEAC 1 February 1947. Leased to Gibraltar Airways 17 November 1947. Sold to Metamar S.A. Barcelona as EC-AKO during January 1954. Aircraft still current and flown occasionally.

G-AERZ (February 1st 1941*) c/n 6356. De Havilland DH89A Dragon Rapide. Registered/First C of A 10th March/7th May 1937 for Air Commerce Ltd. To AAJC. To Scottish Airways (Renfrew) November 15th 1940, later to Inverness February 1st 1941. Transferred to Renfrew May 15th 1941, following the return of G-ADAJ from maintenance. Returned to AAJC June 26th 1941 and flown back to Renfrew September 17th 1942, and kept until August 26th 1943. To AAJC. To Railway Air Services Ltd. Written off when crashed in fog at Belfast 1 April 1946 when crew of two and six passengers were killed.

G-ACPP (February 22nd 1941*) c/n 6254. De Havilland DH89 Dragon Rapide. Registered/First C of A 20th February/12 March 1935 for Railway Air Services, named *City of Bristol*. To Great Western and Southern Airlines on 31 January 1939. Impressed into RAF with 24 Sqdn at RAF Hendon on 18 September 1939. To Speke on 21 October 1939. To 24 Sqdn, RAF Hendon on 30 November 1939. Returned to Great Western and Southern Airlines under

Scottish Airways' DH Rapide G-ADAJ 'Caithness' at Sumburgh, beside the passenger reception hut. (Shetland Museum)

AAJC during June 1940. To Scottish Airways (Renfrew) February 22nd 1941. Returned to AAJC June 26th 1941, Back to Renfrew January 2nd 1942. Returned to AAJC September 16th 1942. To BEAC on 1 February 1947. To Aircraft & Engineering Services on 16 April 1946. To Yellow Air Taxis Ltd on 22 June 1948. To Air Couriers Ltd on 4 September 1951. To Hawker Aircraft Ltd on 7 May 1952. To W H Wyton on 3 January 1958. To Aviation Traders Ltd, Southend on 23 April 1959. To Air Navigation and Trading Ltd on 30 November 1960. Sold to Canada on 19 June 1961 in crates. To North Air Services Ltd, stored at Toronto Airport. Current with J R Bowdery, St Johns Newfoundland as CF-PTK.

G-ACYR (March 4th 1941*) c/n 6261. De Havilland DH89 Dragon Rapide. Registered/First C of A 15th October/27th December 1934 for Olley Air Services Ltd. Chartered from Olleys to fly General Franco from the Canary Isles to Morocco at the start of the Spanish Civil War, flown by Charles Bebb. To AAJC. To Scottish Airways (Renfrew) March 4th 1941. Returned to AAJC 25th April 1942. To Air Couriers Ltd, stored at Desford after WWII when presented to General Franco by Air Couriers Ltd during 1954. Restored to static display for preservation in Spanish Air Force Museum, Madrid. Aircraft current.

G-AGDH (October 13th 1941*) c/n 6548. De Havilland DH89A Dragon Rapide. Built under Contract number B104592/40. RAF serial X7388. To 18 MU Dumfries 20 July 1941. To Director General of Civil Aviation for AAJC 7 September 1941. Registered G-AGDH, First C of A 10 September 1941. To Scottish Airways (Renfrew) October 13th 1941. Damaged beyond repair when wrecked in a 95 mph gale at Stornoway, 25 November 1941.

G-AGDG (October 16th 1941*) c/n 6547. De Havilland DH89A Dragon Rapide. Built under Contract number B104592/40. RAF serial X7387. To 18 MU Dumfries 29 July 1941. To Director General of Civil Aviation for AAJC 7 September 1941. Registered G-AGDG, first C of A 11 September 1941. To Scottish Airways (Inverness) 16th October 1941. To BEAC 1st February 1947. Sold to Air France as F-BEDX, used in Madagascar. Re registered after sale as F-AODX October 1950. Sold to Société Autrex, Hanoi as F-BAHX. Registration cancelled after expiry of C of A 5 July 1953.

G-AGED (April 25th 1942*) c/n 6621. De Havilland DH89A Dragon Rapide. Built under Contract number B104592/40. RAF serial X7504. To Speke for AAJC 3 April 1942. Registered G-AGED, first C of A 21 April 1942. To Scottish Airways Ltd 25th April 1942, as replacement for G-ACYR. Crashed and written off at Renfrew 2 February 1943. Aircraft hit soft ground on take-off, failed to get airborne and hit boundary fence, tipping upside down. Pilot slightly injured, R.O. and passengers unhurt.

G-AGEE (February 5th 1943*) c/n 6622. De Havilland DH89A Dragon Rapide. Built under Contract number B104592/40. RAF serial X7505. To Speke for AAJC 3 April 1942. Registered 16 April 1942 as G-AGEE, first C of A 15 May 1942 for Great Western and Southern Airways. To Scottish Airways (Renfrew) as replacement for G-AGED on February 5th 1943. Returned to AAJC July 7th 1943. To BEAC 1 February 1947. Leased to Gibraltar Airways 26 November 1947. To Thytur Flying School (Iceland) 1 July 1953 as TF-KAA. To Daniel Petursson 3 July 1961. C of A expired 18 May 1963. Broken up and burnt 1966.

G-AGIC (May 18th 1943*) c/n 6522. De Havilland DH89A Dragon Rapide. Built under Contract number B104592/40. RAF serial X7349. To Headquarters Ferry Pilots' Pool 5 May 1941. To 10 Ferry Pilots' Pool 16 May 1941. To De Havilland's 3 February 1942, awaiting collection 17 April 1943. To 18 MU Dumfries 23 April 1943. To AAJC. Registered 6th July 1943 as G-AGIC, first C of A 20 August 1943. To Scottish Airways (Inverness) May 18th 1943. Inaugurated Inverness - Stornoway scheduled service on May 24th 1944. To BEAC 1 February 1947. Sold to France as F-OADZ during November 1947. Re-registered F-BAHZ. Used by Air France in Madagascar. No further details known.

G-AGIF (July 19th 1943*) c/n 6509. De Havilland DH89A Dragon Rapide. Built under Contract number B104592/40. RAF serial X7336. To 18 MU Dumfries 20 March 1941. To 614 Sqdn, Macmerry 8 April 1942. To 225 Sqdn, Macmerry 15 December 1942. To RAF Macmerry 31 December 1942. To De Havilland's Cat B 13 February 1943, awaiting collection 10 May 1943. To 18 MU Dumfries 6 June 1943. Some references indicate aircraft registered G-AGIF, first C of A 20 July 1943 for Great Western and Southern Airlines. However, others indicate C of A date 15th July. Aircraft known to have been allocated to Scottish Airways (Renfrew) July 19th 1943. To BEAC 1st February 1947. Broken up at Newtownards October 1950.

G-AGJF (October 10th 1943*) c/n 6499. De Havilland DH89A

G-AGIC seen at a Hebridean airstrip towards the end of World War Two. (John Stroud Collection)

Dragon Rapide. Built under Contract number B104592/40. RAF serial X7326. To 18 MU Dumfries 14 September 1940. To 6 MU, Brize Norton 15 September 1940. To Air Transport Auxilliary 31 December 1941. To De Havilland's 3 May 1943, awaiting collection 23 July 1943. To 18 MU Dumfries 24 August 1943. To Scottish Airways (Renfrew) 10th October 1943. Registered G-AGJF, first C of A issued on 29 October 1943. To BEAC 1 February 1947. Written off in crash at Barra, Hebrides 6 August 1947.

G-AGJG (February 7th 1944*) c/n 6517. De Havilland DH89A Dragon Rapide. Built under Contract number B104592/40. RAF serial X7344. To 9 MU, Cosford 16 April 1941. To 1 Communications Flight, RAF Hendon 10 May 1941. Damaged Cat AC/FA 5 June 1942. Repaired on site 2 July 1942. To 18 MU Dumfries 10 October 1942. Registered G-AGJG 25 October 1943 for AAJC. To Scottish Airways February 7th 1944 at Inverness. Used in North. To BEAC 1 February 1947. To Addie Aviation Ltd, Croydon 14 October 1948. Sold to Mediterranean Air Services, and listed to them 10 January 1949. To Ernest Arthur Taylor 9 June 1953. To Island Air Services Ltd 2 April 1954. To Thomas Hutton Marshall 13 March 1959, used by Morton Air Services. To Earnest Percy Jones, t/a Swansea Airways 26 September 1960. To Thomas Hutton Marshall 18 December 1961. To Gerry Dromett, Thruxton 11 May 1962. Damaged at Christchurch Aerodrome, Hants on 20 May 1962 whilst practising landings during gusty conditions. The aircraft bounced after touchdown and wing touched the ground. To John Alexander Galt 8 June 1967. To Aerial Enterprises Ltd, Booker March 1968 until company ceased trading. C of A cancelled during November 1974 when withdrawn from use at Halfpenny Green. Transferred by road to IWM Duxford, owned by D Wein. Ownership transferred to David & Mark Miller, Cambridge. Currently under restoration.

G-AGLP (February 27th 1945*) c/n 6780. De Havilland DH89A Dragon Rapide. Brush built under Contract number a/c2580/C20a. RAF Serial NR681. To De Havillands Witney 11 August 1944 for AAJC. Registered G-AGLP October 28th 1944, first C of A issued on 2 February 1945 for Railway Air Services. To Scottish Airways (Renfrew) February 27th 1945. (To Jersey Airlines May 1945 to June 1945). Back to Scottish Airways at Renfrew April 17th 1946. To BEAC 1 February 1947. To International Airways July 1948. To Jersey Airlines during April 1949 to May 1949. Withdrawn from use at Croydon September 1950.

G-AGLE (March 14th 1945*) c/n 6784. De Havilland DH89A Dragon Rapide. Built by Brush Coachworks, Loughborough, under Contract number a/c2580/C20a. RAF Serial NR685. To 5 MU, Kemble 28 July 1944. To

AAJC. Registered G-AGLE, first C of A December 14th 1944, for Railway Air Services, but operated by Scottish Airways at Renfrew from 14th March 1945. To BEAC 1 February 1947. To International Airways July 1948. Leased to Jersey Airlines 1949. Withdrawn from use at Croydon during December 1951.

G-AGLR (May 2nd 1945*) c/n 6781. De Havilland DH89A Dragon Rapide. Built by Brush Coachworks, Loughborough under Contract number a/c2580/C20a. RAF Serial NR682. Registered G-AGLR, first C of A 13 January 1945 for Railway Air Services. To De Havillands Witney 23 January 1945 for AAJC. Operated by Scottish Airways at Renfrew from May 2nd 1945. To BEAC 1 February 1947. To Lees-Hill Aviation during June 1948. To Don Everall Aviation Ltd September 1951. Written off 7 October 1956 at Berkeswell, Warwickshire.

G-AGOJ (October 17th 1945*) c/n 6850. De Havilland DH89A Dragon Rapide. Built by Brush Coachworks, Loughborough under Contract number a/c2580/C20a. RAF Serial NR774. To De Havillands Witney 20 February 1945. Registered G-AGOJ, first C of A issued on 27 September 1945 for AAJC. To Scottish Airways October 17th 1945 at Renfrew. To BEAC 1 February 1947. To Lancashire Aircraft Corporation July 1948. To Skyways Ltd September 1955. Written off at Lympne 1 May 1961.

G-AGUR (Jaunaury 12th 1946*) c/n 6910. De Havilland DH89A Dragon Rapide. Built by Brush Coachworks, Loughborough under Contract number a/c2580/C20a. RAF Serial NR846. To De Havillands Witney 20 July 1945. Returned to Brush Coachworks for conversion 10 August 1945. Registered G-AGUR November 9th 1945, first C of A 20 December 1945 for AAJC. To Scottish Airways at Renfrew January 12th 1946. To BEAC 1 February 1947, named *Lord Roberts*. To R Myhill. Crashed at Frankfurt Rhein Main 2 August 1954.

G-AGZB (April 20th 1946*) c/n 12180. Douglas C-47A Dakota 3. Ex 42-92385 USAAF, ex-RAF FZ624. First C of A February 21st 1946. To Railway Air Services but operated at Renfrew by Scottish Airways from April 20th 1946. To BEA February 1st 1947, named *Robert Smith-Barry*. Crashed at St Boniface, near Ventnor, Isle of Wight May 6th 1962.

G-AHLN (April 26th 1946*) c/n 6754. De Havilland DH89A Dragon Rapide. Built by Brush Coachworks, Loughborough under Contract number a/c2580/C20a. RAF Serial NF883. To A.T.A. White Waltham 13 June 1944. To 32 MU 23 November 1944. To 1680 Flight, Prestwick 27 December 1945. To Ministry of Supply for AAJC, Prestwick 16 April 1946. Sold to Scottish Airways, Registered G-AHLN, first C of A issued on May 8th 1946 for Scottish Airways

Anything to Anywhere!
Of all the photographs located, this has to be the strangest - and is certainly an unusual load. The picture shows Capt E.E. Fresson (right) and Capt Adam Smith carrying an intriguing trophy from Dragon G-ADCT at Inverness. (The Fresson Trust)

(Inverness). To BEAC 1 February 1947. To Ulster Airways 1948. Sold to France as F-BGOQ during April 1953. No further details known

G-AGZA (May 11th 1946*) c/n 12455. Douglas C-47A Dakota 3. Ex 42-92633 USAAF, ex-RAF KG420. First C of A February 18th 1946. To Railway Air Services, but operated at Renfrew by Scottish Airways from May 11th 1946. Crashed at South Ruislip, Middlesex on December 19th 1946 onto roof of house. No injuries to crew or single passenger. Accident caused by snow accretion on wings before take-off. Written off.

G-AGYZ (May 26th 1946*) c/n 12287. Douglas C-47A Dakota 3. Ex 42-108843 USAAF, ex-RAF FZ681. First C of A February 6th 1946. To Railway Air Services, but operated at Renfrew from May 26th by Scottish Airways. To BEA February 1st 1947, named *Sir Charles Kingsford Smith*. Sold to Sudan Airways September 1953 as SN-AAG, later ST-AAG. To Sudan Air Force as '421' during 1957. To Ethiopian Airlines June 8th 1977 as ET-AGQ. Damaged at Degahabour 25 October 1978.

G-AHLL (August 15th 1946*) c/n 6576. De Havilland DH89A Dragon Rapide. Built under Contract number B104592/40. RAF serial X7416. To 20 Maintenance Unit 17 October 1941. To 24 Sqdn, RAF Hendon 1 ADF 28 January 1942. To RAF Redhill 6 January 1944. To De Havilland's Witney 19 March 1945. Awaiting Collection 25 May 1945. To 18 MU 20 June 1945. To 1680 Flight 14 December 1945. To Ministry of Supply for AAJC, Prestwick 16 April 1946. Registered as G-AHLL May 8th 1946, First C of A 28 June 1946 for AAJC. To Scottish Airways (Renfrew) August 15th 1946. To BEAC 1 February 1947, named *Sir Henry Lawrence*. (Name later transferred to G-AJCL). Damaged beyond repair at St Just, Cornwall 21 May 1959. Listed at broken up by February 1960, but remains still at 3 Civil AACU Exeter October 1968.

G-AHGI (September 9th 1946*) c/n 6935. De Havilland DH89A Dragon Rapide. Built by Brush Coachworks, Loughborough under Contract number a/c2580/C20a. RAF Serial RL953. To De Havillands Witney 2 January 1946. To AAJC 5 April 1946. Registered G-AHGI 18 March 1946, first C of A May 2nd 1946 for Railway Air Services. To Scottish Airways September 9th 1946. To BEAC 1

February 1947. To Patrick Aviation, Birmingham during June 1948. Sold to Société Indochinoise de Plantations Réunies de Mimot, Saigon during November 1952 as F-OANF. To Companie Veha-Akat as F-LAAF. Written off 1 May 1958.

G-AHLM (October 23rd 1946*) c/n 6708. De Havilland DH89A Dragon Rapide. Built by Brush Coachworks, Loughborough under Contract number a/c2580/C20a. RAF Serial HG723. To 18 MU Dumfries on 18 March 1944. To 1680 Flight on 17 October 1945. Transferred to AAJC on 16 April 1946. Registered G-AHLM May 8th 1946, first C of A issued on 13 July 1946 for AAJC. To Scottish Airways October 23rd 1946. To BEAC on 1 February 1947. To Marshalls Flying Services, Cambridge. To Mayflower Flying Services during June 1961. Written off at St Mary's Airfield, Scilly Isles on 20 July 1963 whilst on scheduled service with seven passengers and pilot. During take-off in calm conditions the aircraft bounced a number of times, then swung left and right. It became airborne, then banked to the right. The starboard wing was seen to cut through gorse bushes then hit a rock, then the aircraft cartwheeled and caught fire before coming to rest with the rear fuselage overhanging a cliff. All occupants escaped through the emergency hatches, the seriously injured pilot being removed from cockpit wreckage by fire service.

G-AIHN (November 13th 1946*) c/n 6498. De Havilland DH89A Dragon Rapide. Built under Contract number B104592/40. RAF serial X7325. To 9 MU, Cosford 4 September 1940. To 7 Ferry Pilots Pool 17 January 1941. To 18 MU Dumfries 5 March 1941. To Headquarters Ferry Pilots Pool 15 April 1941. To 10 MU 3 October 1941. To 2 Signal School 3 August 1942. To 18 MU Dumfries18 February 1944. To 1680 Flight 19 March 1944. To Ministry of Supply, and sold to AAJC, Preswick 14 June 1946. Registered G-AIHN September 5th 1946, first C of A issued on 25 October 1946 for Railway Air Services. To Scottish Airways November 13th 1946. To BEAC 1st February 1947. Leased to Gibraltar Airways. Sold to General Mining Ltd as ZS-DJT. To African Air Photo. To Drakensburg Air Services. Crashed at Ladysmith 10 November 1953. The remains were stored in the South African Air Force Museum for eventual restoration.

NOTES ON AIRCRAFT LISTING

The reader should be aware that there are known minor discrepencies in the aircraft histories recorded here. To compile this listing, information has been gathered from a number of primary sources - the British Civil Aviation Authority Registration Files, Certificate of Airworthiness information and the Royal Air Force Form 78's (Aircraft Movement Cards). When this information is collated consecutively, inconsistencies of data appear. Much of these inconsistencies can be explained by the difficulties in keeping accurate paperwork in wartime. Where two dates appear it has been assumed that the earlier is the date the registration was allocated, the latter being the date of C of A.

ABBREVIATIONS USED IN THIS BOOK

AACU	Anti-Aircraft Co Operation Unit (RAF)	GA	General Aircraft
AAJC	Associated Airways' Joint Committee.	IOMAS	Isle of Man Air Service.
ATA	Air Transport Auxiliary.	IOM	Isle of Man
ATC	Air Training Corps	LMS	London Midland & Scottish Railway Co.
AONS	Air Observers & Navigators School (RAF)	M.D.	Managing Director
BEAC	British European Airways Corporation	MU	Maintenance Unit (RAF)
BOAC	British Overseas Airways Corporation	M&SAF	Midland & Scottish Air Ferries Ltd.
BSAA	British South American Airways Corporation	NAC	National Air Communications.
Cat	Category - RAF Aircraft Damage Categorisation	NSA	Northern and Scottish Airways Ltd.
	Prefix that has a number of suffixes thus.	RAF	Royal Air Force.
Cat AC/FA	Aircraft/Flying Accident.	RAS	Railway Air Services
Cat B	B = Damaged beyond capability of Unit.	R.O.	Radio Officer.
Cat B/FA	Damaged beyond capability of Unit/Flying Accident.	R/T	Radio Transmission
Cat E1	Write off	SMT	Scottish Motor Traction Co.
Cat E/FA	E = Write off/Flying Accident	USAAF	United States Army Air Force.
C OF A	Certificate of Airworthiness.	W.O.	Wireless Operator.
C/n	Construction number (Allocated by manufacturer).	W.T.O.	Wireless Telegraphy Officer.
DH	De Havilland.	W/T	Wireless Transmission
		WSAS	West of Scotland Air Services.

APPENDIX 3

AMBULANCE FLIGHTS KNOWN TO HAVE BEEN CARRIED OUT BY THE AIRLINES.*

I - Northern and Scottish Airways Ltd:
Flown by Capt. David Barclay M.B.E, M.St.J.

Year	Date		Aircraft Type	Regn	Trip	Total Round-trip Time
1935	May	27th	DH84 Dragon I	G-ACJS	Renfrew - Islay - Renfrew	2 hrs 10 min
	June	4th	DH84 Dragon I	G-ACJS	Renfrew - Arran (Shiskine) - Renfrew	1 hr 20 min
	Sept	9th	DH83 Fox Moth	G-ACED	Renfrew - Skye (landed rear of Broadford Hotel) - Renfrew	2 hrs 50 min
	Nov	19th	DH84 Dragon I	G-ACFG	Renfrew - Campbeltown - Renfrew	1 hr 30 min
1936	March	11th	Spartan Cruiser II	G-ACYL	Renfrew - Campbeltown - Renfrew	1 hr 10 min
	May	4th	DH84 Dragon II	G-ACNH	Renfrew - Tiree - Renfrew	2 hrs 30 min
	May	26th	Spartan Cruiser II	G-ACSM	Barra - Renfrew	N/A
	June	12th	DH84 Dragon I	G-ACJS	Renfrew - Islay - Renfrew	2 hrs 00 min
	July	6th	Spartan Cruiser III	G-ADEM	Renfrew - Sollas - Renfrew	3 hrs 00 min
	July	10th	DH89 Dragon Rapide	G-ADDF	Renfrew - Islay (night landing) - Renfrew	1 hr 10 min
	Aug	24th	DH84 Dragon I	G-ACFG	Renfrew - Tiree - Renfrew	2 hrs 05 min
1937	April	8th	DH84 Dragon II	G-ACMO	Renfrew - Sollas - Renfrew	4 hrs 50 min
	May	28th	DH89 Dragon Rapide	G-ADAG	Renfrew - Campbeltown - Renfrew	1 hr 00 min
	June	30th	DH89 Dragon Rapide	G-ADDF	Renfrew - Sollas - Renfrew	2 hrs 55 min

II - Highland Airways Ltd:
Flown by Capt. E.E. Fresson O.B.E.

1937	Feb	9th	DH84 Dragon I	G-ACIT	Inverness - Stornoway	0 hrs 50 min
	June	30th	DH89A Dragon Rapide	G-AEWL	Inverness - Stornoway - Inverness	1 hr 30 min

Flown by Capt. John Philip Rae

1935	June	7th	DH84 Dragon II	G-ADCT	Kirkwall - Glasgow - Kirkwall (19 pax total)	6hrs 30 min
	Aug	14th	DH84 Dragon II	G-ADCT	Kirkwall - Aberdeen - Stronsay - Kirkwall (14 pax total)	3 hrs 40 min
	Sept	30th	DH84 Dragon I	G-ACET	Kirkwall - Sanday - Kirkwall (11 pax total)	2 hrs 00 min

NB - John Rae flew with Highland Airways up to October 2nd 1937 - but he did not record details of trips in his log-books after 1935, so it is quite likely he flew more ambulance services.

III - Scottish Airways Ltd:
Flown by Capt. David Barclay M.B.E., M. St. J.

1937	Sept	11th	DH84 Dragon II	G-ACNG	Renfrew - Sollas - Renfrew	3hrs 30 min
	Oct	25th	DH84 Dragon II	G-ACMO	Sollas - Northton (stretcher case)	N/A
	Nov	16th	DH84 Dragon II	G-ACMO	Renfrew - Coll - Renfrew	2hrs 10 min
	Dec	17th	Spartan Cruiser II	G-ACYL	Renfrew - Campbeltown - Renfrew (Dep 02.15hrs)	1 hr 20 min
1938	Jan	10th	DH84 Dragon II	G-ACOR	Renfrew - Renfrew (bad weather - returned)	1hr 00 min
	Jan	29th	Spartan Cruiser II	G-ACYL	Renfrew - Islay - Renfrew	1 hr 55 min
	Feb	19th	Spartan Cruiser II	G-ACZM	Renfrew - Barra - Renfrew (night flight)	3 hrs 05 min
	March	4th	DH84 Dragon II	G-ACNG	Renfrew - Islay - Renfrew	1 hr 40 min
	March	6th	DH84 Dragon II	G-ACNG	Renfrew - Sollas - Renfrew	4 hrs 35 min
	March	10th	DH84 Dragon II	G-ACNG	Renfrew - Islay - Renfrew	2 hrs 00 min
	March	11th	DH84 Dragon II	G-ACNG	Renfrew - Coll - Renfrew	2 hrs 30 min
	March	27th	Spartan Cruiser II	G-ACSM	Renfrew Islay - Renfrew (Night flt: 00.20-04.30hrs)	3 hrs 15 min
	April	20th	DH84 Dragon II	G-ACNG	Renfrew - Skye - Renfrew	2 hrs 45 min
	May	9th	DH84 Dragon II	G-ACNG	Renfrew - Askernish - Renfrew (Twins born dead over Mull)	3 hrs 10 min
	May	14th	DH84 Dragon II / Spartan Crusier II	G-ACNG/ G-ACZM	Renfrew - Campbeltown - Renfrew	1 hr 30 min
	Nov	28th	Spartan Crusier II	G-ACSM	Sollas - Abbotsinch - Renfrew	2 hrs 40 min
1939	Jan	14th	Spartan Crusier II	G-ACSM	Renfrew - Campbeltown - Colonsay - Renfrew	2 hrs 05 min
	Jan	18th	DH89A Dragon Rapide	G-AFEY	Abbotsinch - Campbeltown - Abbotsinch	1 hr 10 min
	Jan	21st	Spartan Crusier II	G-ACSM	Sollas - Abbotsinch - Renfrew	2 hrs 00 min
	Feb	12th	DH89A Dragon Rapide	G-AFEY	Renfrew - Barra - Renfrew	2 hrs 35 min
	March	13th	DH89A Dragon Rapide	G-AFEY	Renfrew - Tiree - Renfrew	2 hrs 10 min
	March	28th	DH89A Dragon Rapide	G-AFEY	Renfrew - Islay - Renfrew	1 hr 30 min
	March	28th	DH89A Dragon Rapide	G-AFEY	Renfrew - Campbeltown - Renfrew	1 hr 15 min
	July	16th	DH84 Dragon II	G-ACNG	Renfrew - Islay - Renfrew	1 hr 45 min
	July	22nd	Spartan Crusier II	G-ACSM	Renfrew - Islay - Renfrew	1 hr 50 min
	Aug	11th	DH89A Dragon Rapide	G-AFEY	Renfrew - Islay - Renfrew	1 hr 40 min
1940	Feb	14th	Spartan Cruiser II	G-ACYL	Renfrew - Islay - Renfrew	1 hr 35 min
	March	11th	Spartan Cruiser II	G-ACYL	Renfrew - Islay - Renfrew	1 hr 50 min
1941	March	8th	DH89 Dragon Rapide	G-ACPP	Renfrew - Campbeltown - Renfrew	1 hr 10 min
	March	11th	DH89 Dragon Rapide	G-AFOI	Renfrew - Campbeltown - Renfrew (Maternity)	1 hr 15 min
	April	18th	DH89 Dragon Rapide	G-ACPP	Renfrew - Islay - Renfrew	1 hr 30 min
	May	5th	DH89 Dragon Rapide	G-ACPP	Renfrew - Islay - Renfrew	1 hr 30 min
	May	21st	DH89A Dragon Rapide	G-AERZ	Renfrew - Islay - Renfrew	1 hr 20 min
	June	5th	DH89A Dragon Rapide	G-AFOI	Renfrew - Barra - Renfrew	2 hrs 15 min
	July	1st	DH89A Dragon Rapide	G-AFOI	Renfrew - Campbeltown - Renfrew	1 hr 05 min
	July	2nd	DH89 Dragon Rapide	G-ACPP	Renfrew - Campbeltown - Renfrew	1 hr 10 min
	July	17th	DH89A Dragon Rapide	G-AFRK	Renfrew - Tiree Renfrew	2 hrs 00 min
	July	22nd	DH89 Dragon Rapide	G-ACPP	Renfrew - Islay - Barra - Renfrew (Maternity)	2 hrs 50 min

* Only those ambulance flights recorded in the available logs of Pilots and Radio Officers have been noted here.

	July	26th	DH89A Dragon Rapide	G-AFRK	Renfrew - Islay - Renfrew	1 hr 25 min
	Aug	1st	DH89A Dragon Rapide	G-AFRK	Renfrew - Sollas - Renfrew	2 hrs 55 min
	Aug	3rd	DH89A Dragon Rapide	G-AFOI	Renfrew - Islay - Renfrew	1 hr 45 min
	Sept	14th	DH89A Dragon Rapide	G-AFRK	Renfrew - Inverness -Sumburgh - Inverness - Renfrew (Leg Fracture)	6 hrs 35 min
	Dec	8th	DH89A Dragon Rapide	G-AFOI	Renfrew - Campbeltown - Renfrew	1 hr 10 min
	Dec	10th	DH89A Dragon Rapide	G-AFRK	Stornoway - Sollas - Stornoway	1 hr 10 min
	Dec	30th	DH89A Dragon Rapide	G-AFRK	Campbeltown - Prestwick	0 hr 30 min
1942	Feb	11th	DH89A Dragon Rapide	G-AFRK	Sollas - Benbecula - Renfrew	1 hr 40 min
	March	11th	DH89A Dragon Rapide	G-AFRK	Prestwick - Islay - Renfrew	1 hr 30 min
	March	30th	DH89 Dragon Rapide	G-ACYR	Renfrew - Islay - Renfrew	1 hr 35 min
	April	2nd	DH89 Dragon Rapide	G-ACPP	Renfrew - Campbeltown - Renfrew (Brain Tumour)	1 hr 15 min
	April	23rd	DH89 Dragon Rapide	G-ACYR	Renfrew - Benbecula - Abbotsinch - Renfrew (Bomb Explosion - RAF Personnel)	3hrs 15 min
	May	9th	DH89A Dragon Rapide	G-AFOI	Renfrew - Campbeltown - Renfrew (Jaundice)	1 hr 10 min
	June	3rd	DH89 Dragon Rapide	G-ACPP	Renfrew - Islay - Renfrew	1 hr 25 min
	July	7th	DH89 Dragon Rapide	G-ACPP	Renfrew - Islay - Renfrew	1 hr 25 min
	July	10th	DH89A Dragon Rapide	G-AFOI	Renfrew - Barra - Renfrew	2 hrs 30 min
	Aug	16th	DH89A Dragon Rapide	G-AGED	Renfrew - Islay - Renfrew	1 hr 25 min
	Sept	27th	DH89A Dragon Rapide	G-AGED	Renfrew - Campbeltown - Renfrew	1 hr 15 min
	Oct	5th	DH89A Dragon Rapide	G-AFRK	Renfrew - Islay - Renfrew	1 hr 35 min
	Oct	14th	DH89A Dragon Rapide	G-AERZ	Renfrew - Islay - Renfrew	1 hr 35 min
	Dec	13th	DH89A Dragon Rapide	G-AFOI	Renfrew - Turnhouse - Campbeltown - Renfrew	2 hrs 05 min
1943	Jan	10th	DH89A Dragon Rapide	G-AFRK	Renfrew - Islay - Renfrew	1 hr 30 min
	March	13th	DH89A Dragon Rapide	G-AGEE	Renfrew - Islay - Renfrew	1 hr 30 min
	June	1st	DH89A Dragon Rapide	G-AFOI	Renfrew - Campbeltown - Renfrew	1 hr 20 min
	June	11th	DH89A Dragon Rapide	G-AERZ	Renfrew - Campbeltown - Renfrew	1 hr 00 min
	July	8th	DH89A Dragon Rapide	G-AFOI	Sollas - Renfrew	1 hr 20 min
	July	11th	DH89A Dragon Rapide	G-AFOI	Renfrew - Grangemouth - Renfrew - Abbotsinch	2 hrs 50 min
	July	28th	DH89A Dragon Rapide	G-AFRK	Renfrew - Islay - Renfrew	1 hr 45 min
	July	28th	DH89A Dragon Rapide	G-AFRK	Renfrew - Prestwick - Islay - Renfrew	1 hr 45 min
	Aug	17th	DH89A Dragon Rapide	G-AFOI	Renfrew - Islay - Renfrew	1 hr 40 min
	Aug	31st	DH89A Dragon Rapide	G-AGIF	Renfrew - Islay - Renfrew	1 hr 30 min
	Sept	10th	DH89A Dragon Rapide	G-AFRK	Renfrew - Islay - Renfrew	1 hr 40 min
	Oct	16th	DH89A Dragon Rapide	G-AFOI	Renfrew - Tiree - Benbecula - Renfrew	3 hrs 45 min
	Dec	28th	DH89A Dragon Rapide	G-AGJF	Campbeltown - Renfrew	N/A
1944	Jan	9th	DH89A Dragon Rapide	G-AFOI	Renfrew - Stornoway - Turnhouse - Renfrew	4 hrs 25 min
	March	17th	DH89A Dragon Rapide	G-AGJF	Renfrew - Campbeltown - Renfrew	1 hr 10 min
	March	18th	DH89A Dragon Rapide	G-AGJF	Renfrew - Stornoway - Renfrew	4 hrs 10 min
	April	12th	DH89A Dragon Rapide	G-AGJF	Renfrew - Barra - Renfrew	2 hrs 40 min
	May	14th	DH89A Dragon Rapide	G-AGJF	Renfrew - Campbeltown - Stornoway - Renfrew	4 hrs 05 min
	June	8th	DH89A Dragon Rapide	G-AGIF	Stornoway - Sollas - Stornoway	1 hr 05 min
	June	13th	DH89A Dragon Rapide	G-AGJF	Renfrew - Campbeltown - Islay -Renfrew	1 hr 30 min
	Aug	4th	DH89A Dragon Rapide	G-AGIF	Renfrew - Islay - Renfrew	1 hr 30 min
	Aug	6th	DH89A Dragon Rapide	G-AGIF	Renfrew - Stornoway - Renfrew	3hrs 25 min
	Aug	17th	DH89A Dragon Rapide	G-AGIF	Renfrew - Islay - Renfrew	1 hr 20 min
	Aug	22nd	DH89A Dragon Rapide	G-AGJF	Renfrew - Barra - Renfrew	2 hr 25 min
	Aug	28th	DH89A Dragon Rapide	G-AFOI	Renfrew - Campbeltown - Renfrew	1 hr 15 min
	Sept	13th	DH89A Dragon Rapide	G-AFOI	Renfrew - Barra - Renfrew	2 hr 40 min
	Sept	16th	DH89A Dragon Rapide	G-AFRK	Renfrew - Benbecula - Renfrew	3 hr 10 min
	Oct	5th	DH89A Dragon Rapide	G-AFFF	Renfrew - Islay - Renfrew	1 hr 35 min
	Nov	7th	DH89A Dragon Rapide	G-AFRK	Renfrew - Islay - Renfrew	1 hr 40 min
1945	March	9th	DH89A Dragon Rapide	G-AGJF	Renfrew - Barra - Renfrew	2 hrs 40 min
	April	8th	DH89A Dragon Rapide	G-AFFF	Renfrew - Islay - Renfrew	1 hr 30 min
	April	22nd	DH89A Dragon Rapide	G-AGJF	Renfrew - Benbecula - Renfrew	2 hr 55 min
	May	13th	DH89A Dragon Rapide	G-AGJF	Renfrew - Islay - Renfrew	1 hr 55 min
	June	28th	DH89A Dragon Rapide	G-AFRK	Renfrew - Tiree - Renfrew	1 hr 55 min
	July	4th	DH89A Dragon Rapide	G-AGJF	Renfrew - Benbecula - Renfrew	3 hrs 15 min
	July	29th	DH89A Dragon Rapide	G-AFFF	Renfrew - Belfast (Sydenham) - Renfrew	1 hr 55 min
	Sept	9th	DH89A Dragon Rapide	G-AGJF	Renfrew - Campbeltown - Renfrew	1 hr 15 min
	Sept	18th	DH89A Dragon Rapide	G-AGLE	Renfrew - Islay - Renfrew	1 hr 30 min
	Oct	2nd	DH89A Dragon Rapide	G-AGJF	Renfrew - Barra - Renfrew	2 hrs 25 min
	Oct	13th	DH89A Dragon Rapide	G-AFOI	Renfrew - Campbeltown - Renfrew	1 hr 10 min
	Oct	19th	DH89A Dragon Rapide	G-AGJF	Renfrew - Islay - Renfrew	1 hr 30 min
	Nov	8th	DH89A Dragon Rapide	G-AFFF	Renfrew - Campbeltown - Renfrew	1 hr 10 min
	Dec	29th	DH89A Dragon Rapide	G-AFRK	Renfrew - Barra - Renfrew	2 hr 25 min
	Dec	30/31st	DH89A Dragon Rapide	G-AGOJ	Renfrew - Prestwick - Stornoway - Renfrew	3 hrs 45 min
1946	Feb	12th	DH89A Dragon Rapide	G-AGOJ	Renfrew - Benbecula - Renfrew	3 hrs 20 min
	Feb	17th	DH89A Dragon Rapide	G-AGUR	Renfrew - Inverness - Renfrew	2 hrs 15 min
	Feb	17th	DH89A Dragon Rapide	G-AFRK	Renfrew - Sollas - Renfrew	3 hrs 05 min
	April	21st	DH89A Dragon Rapide	G-AFRK	Renfrew - Barra - Renfrew	2 hrs 40 min
	April	22nd	DH89A Dragon Rapide	G-AGLP	Renfrew - Tiree - Barra - Renfrew	3 hrs 00 min
	April	29th	DH89A Dragon Rapide	G-AGLR	Renfrew - Barra - Renfrew	2 hrs 35 min
	May	6th	DH89A Dragon Rapide	G-AGLE	Renfrew - Barra - Renfrew	2 hrs 30 min
	May	9th	DH89A Dragon Rapide	G-AGLP	Renfrew - Tiree - Renfrew	2 hr 10 min
	May	28th	DH89A Dragon Rapide	G-AGOJ	Renfrew - Barra - Renfrew	2 hrs 20 min
	July	26th	DH89A Dragon Rapide	G-AGLR	Renfrew - Islay - Campbeltown - Renfrew	1 hr 35 min
	Aug	21st	DH89A Dragon Rapide	G-AGUR	Renfrew - Tiree - Renfrew	1 hr 55 min
	Sept	17th	DH89A Dragon Rapide	G-AGUR	Renfrew - Campbeltown - Renfrew	1 hr 15 min
	Sept	23rd	DH89A Dragon Rapide	G-AGOJ	Renfrew - Campbeltown - Renfrew	1 hr 05 min
	Nov	11th	DH89A Dragon Rapide	G-AHGI	Renfrew - Campbeltown - Renfrew	1 hr 05 min

Flown by Capt. E. E. Fresson O.B.E.

1938	March	3rd	DH89A Dragon Rapide	G-AEWL	Inverness - Kirkwall - Inverness (60 mph SW winds)	2 hrs 10 min
	Sept	30th	DH84 Dragon II	G-ADCT	Inverness - Wick - Kirkwall -Westray - Kirkwall - Wick - Inverness Carried Mail, Newspapers, 3 pax + Ambulance case	2 hrs 40 min
1941	Feb	25th	DH84 Dragon I	G-ACIT	Inverness - Hatston - North Ronaldsay - Hatston - Inverness	3 hrs 15 min
1942	July	6th	DH84 Dragon I	G-ACIT	Inverness - Grimsetter - Inverness Carried Newspapers and mail + Ambulance case	2 hrs 35 min
1943	May	5th	DH89A Dragon Rapide	G-AEWL	Inverness - Brim Ness - Grimsetter - North Ronaldsay - Grimsetter - Inverness 12 passengers carried over trip length	2 hrs 55 min
	Aug	21st	DH89A Dragon Rapide	G-AGDG	Inverness - Stornoway - Inverness (stretcher case + 7 Pax)	1 hr 35 min
	Nov	26th	DH89A Dragon Rapide	G-AEWL	Inverness - Sollas - Inverness (2 patients)	2 hrs 00 min
1945	July	26th	DH89A Dragon Rapide	G-AGIC	Inverness - Benbecula (2 patients + 1 pax)	1hr 15 min
	July	26th	DH89A Dragon Rapide	G-AGIC	Benbecula - Barra (2 patients + 1 pax)	0 hr 15 min
	July	26th	DH89A Dragon Rapide	G-AGIC	Barra - Inverness (2 patients + Nurse)	1 hr 15 min
	Nov	15th	DH89A Dragon Rapide	G-AGJG	Inverness - Sollas - Benbecula	2 hrs 15 min
1946	May	27th	DH89A Dragon Rapide	G-AGDG	Inverness - Wick - Inverness	1 hr 25 min
	June	18th	DH89A Dragon Rapide	G-AGDG	Kirkwall - North Ronaldsay - Kirkwall (Doctor & 2 patients)	0 hr 40 min
	Aug	19th	DH84 Dragon I	G-ACIT	Kirkwall - Stronsay - Kirkwall	0 hr 30 min
	Aug	22nd	DH84 Dragon I	G-ACIT	Kirkwall - Stronsay - Kirkwall	0 hr 30 min
1947	April	22nd	DH89A Dragon Rapide	G-AGLN	Orkney - North Ronaldsay - Orkney (Man with crushed hand)	0 hr 35 min
	Sept	13th	DH84 Dragon I	G-ACIT	Inverness - Orkney - Sanday - Orkney - Inverness (I patient)	2 hrs 55 min
1948	Feb	11th	DH84 Dragon I	G-ACIT	Orkney - Westray - Stronsay - Orkney (1 small boy as patient)	1 hr 00 min

Flown by Capt. Henry Vallance

1939	March	4th	DH84 Dragon II	G-ACNG	Renfrew - Abbotsinch - Islay - Abbotsinch - Renfrew	1 hr 55 min
	June	30th	DH84 Dragon II	G-ADCT	Wideford - Westray - Wideford	0 hr 35 min
	July	12th	DH84 Dragon II	G-ADCT	Wideford - Westray - Wideford	0 hr 25 min
	Aug	29th	DH84 Dragon II	G-ADCT	Wideford - Stronsay - Wideford	0 hr 20 min
	Sept	22nd	DH89A Dragon Rapide	G-AFRK	Renfrew - Islay - Renfrew (with R/O Black)	1 hr 20 min
	Oct	23rd	DH84 Dragon II	G-ACNG	Renfrew - Islay - Renfrew (with R/O Mitchell)	1 hr 45 min
	Nov	29th	Spartan Cruiser II	G-ACSM	Renfrew - Campbeltown - Renfrew (with R/O Black)	1 hr 05 min
1943	Dec	25th	DH89A Dragon Rapide	G-AERN	Inverness - Renfrew - Inverness	4 hr 15 min
1944	Oct	17th	DH89A Dragon Rapide	G-AGJG	Inverness - Benbecula - Inverness	2 hr 55 min
1945	Aug	31st	DH89A Dragon Rapide	G-AGDG	Inverness - Stornoway - Inverness	2 hrs 30 min

Flown by Capt. "Bill" Baillie

1939	Dec	29th	DH89A Dragon Rapide	G-AFRK	Renfrew - Islay - Renfrew	1 hr 25 min
1940	Jan	11th	DH84 Dragon II	G-ADCT	Kirkwall - Hatston - Stronsay - Stronsay local - Hatston - Kirkwall This was an Admiralty Ambulance Charter	0 hr 40 min
	April	30th	DH89A Dragon Rapide	G-AFRK	Renfrew - Islay - Renfrew	1 hr 35 min
	July	21st	DH89A Dragon Rapide	G-AFRK	Renfrew - Islay - Renfrew	1 hr 25 min
	Sept	6th	DH89A Dragon Rapide	G-AERN	Kirkwall - North Ronaldsay - Kirkwall	0 hr 50 min
	Oct	7th	DH89A Dragon Rapide	G-AERN	Kirkwall - Sanday - Kirkwall	0 hr 30 min
1941	May	8th	DH89 Dragon Rapide	G-ACPP	Renfrew - Barra - Renfrew	2 hr 45 min
1943	Sept	25th	DH89A Dragon Rapide	G-AGIC	Inverness - Barra - Inverness	2 hr 15 min
	Nov	13th	DH89A Dragon Rapide	G-AFRK	Renfrew - Sollas - Renfrew	3 hr 30 min
	Nov	20th	DH89A Dragon Rapide	G-AGJF	Islay - Renfrew	0 hr 50 min
1944	April	3rd	DH89A Dragon Rapide	G-AFRK	Renfrew - Barra - Renfrew	3 hr 05 min
	May	30th	DH89A Dragon Rapide	G-AFRK	Campbeltown - Renfrew - Campbeltown	1 hr 40 min
	June	7th	DH89A Dragon Rapide	G-AFFF	Renfrew - Islay - Renfrew	1 hr 35 min
	June	20th	DH89A Dragon Rapide	G-AGIF	Renfrew - Tiree - Stornoway - Benbecula - Sollas - Renfrew	5 hr 50 min
	July	14th	DH89A Dragon Rapide	G-AGIF	Renfrew - Islay - Renfrew	1 hr 25 min
	July	27th	DH89A Dragon Rapide	G-AGIF	Renfrew - Islay - Renfrew	1 hr 20 min
	Aug	4th	DH89A Dragon Rapide	G-AFOI	Renfrew - Campbeltown - Renfrew - Campbeltown - Renfrew - Islay - Renfrew - Campbeltown - Renfrew	5 hrs 35 min
	Aug	31st	DH89A Dragon Rapide	G-AFOI	Renfrew - Sollas - Renfrew	3 hrs 05 min
	Dec	24th	DH89A Dragon Rapide	G-AFRK	Renfrew - Stornoway - Renfrew	4 hrs 10 min
1945	April	16th	DH89A Dragon Rapide	G-AGIF	Renfrew - Tiree - Renfrew	2 hrs 05 min
	April	22nd	DH89A Dragon Rapide	G-AGIF	Renfrew - Turnhouse - Doncaster - Croydon - Doncaster - Turnhouse - Renfrew	7 hrs 00 min
	May	14th	DH89A Dragon Rapide	G-AGLR	Renfrew - Barra - Renfrew	2 hrs 55 min
	May	19th	DH89A Dragon Rapide	G-AGIF	Renfrew - Islay - Renfrew	1 hr 30 min
	Aug	13th	DH89A Dragon Rapide	G-AGIF	Renfrew - Barra - Renfrew	2 hrs 35 min
	Aug	18th	DH89A Dragon Rapide	G-AFOI	Renfrew - Campbeltown - Renfrew	1 hr 15 min
	Oct	7th	DH89A Dragon Rapide	G-AGJF	Renfrew - Islay - Renfrew	1 hr 45 min
	Oct	12th	DH89A Dragon Rapide	G-AERN	Renfrew - Islay - Renfrew	1 hr 35 min
1946	Jan	25th	DH89A Dragon Rapide	G-AGUR	Renfrew - Barra - Renfrew	2 hrs 30 min
	Feb	7th	DH89A Dragon Rapide	G-AGUR	Renfrew - Campbeltown - Renfrew	1 hr 15 min
	June	25th	DH89A Dragon Rapide	G-AFFF	Renfrew - Benbecula - Renfrew	2 hrs 50 min
	Dec	20th	DH89A Dragon Rapide	G-AGLE	Renfrew - Campbeltown - Renfrew	1 hr 05 min
1947	Jan	4th	DH89A Dragon Rapide	G-AGLR	Renfrew - Islay - Renfrew	1 hr 30 min

Flown by Capt.David MacFarlane

1945	March	22nd	DH89A Dragon Rapide	G-AGDG	Inverness - Sumburgh - Dyce - Inverness	4 hr 50 min
	Oct	31st	DH89A Dragon Rapide	G-AGLP	Renfrew - Benbecula - Renfrew (Gastric Ulcer)	3 hrs 10 min
1946	Jan	3rd	DH89A Dragon Rapide	G-AGOJ	Renfrew-Belfast-Renfrew-Campbeltown-Renfrew(Amb last sect)	3hrs 30 min
	Jan	12th	DH89A Dragon Rapide	G-AGUR	Renfrew - Benbecula - Renfrew	3 hr 10 min

Flown by Capt. Eric Allen Starling

1946	Feb	7th	DH89A Dragon Rapide	G-AGIC	Inverness - Sumburgh - Dyce - Renfrew - Inverness	6 hr 30 min
					(with R/O/ Sutton & Nursing sister - Stretcher case Sumburgh-Renfrew)	
	Nov	25th	DH89A Dragon Rapide	G-AHGI	Renfrew - Campbeltown - Renfrew	1 hr 15 min

Flown by Capt. "Jock" Young

1941	Feb	13th	DH89A Dragon Rapide	G-AFOI	North Uist - Benbecula - Renfrew	2 hrs 00 min
	April	15th	DH89 Dragon Rapide	G-ACPP	Renfrew - Islay - Renfrew	1 hr 35 min
	Aug	23rd	DH89A Dragon Rapide	G-AFFF	Renfrew - Campbeltown - Renfrew (Boy with leg fracture)	1 hr 10 min
	Sept	24th	DH89A Dragon Rapide	G-AFOI	Renfrew - Campbeltown - Renfrew (Maternity case)	1 hr 10 min
	Dec	13th	DH89A Dragon Rapide	G-AFRK	Stronoway - North Uist - Renfrew	4 hrs 05 min
1942	Jan	11th	DH89 Dragon Rapide	G-ACPP	Renfrew - Benbecula - Renfrew (Male epileptic)	3 hrs 25 min
	June	19th	DH89A Dragon Rapide	G-AGED	Renfrew - Campbeltown - Renfrew	1 hr 50 min
	June	22nd	DH89 Dragon Rapide	G-ACPP	Renfrew - Campbeltown - Renfrew	1 hr 15 min
	Aug	25th	DH89 Dragon Rapide	G-ACPP	Renfrew - Islay - Renfrew (Boy, Appendix)	1 hr 40 min
	Sept	15th	DH89A Dragon Rapide	G-AFRK	Renfrew - Islay - Renfrew (Appendix)	1 hr 35 min
	Sept	15th	DH89A Dragon Rapide	G-AFRK	Renfrew - Islay - Renfrew (Fractured leg)	1 hr 40 min
	Oct	11th	DH89A Dragon Rapide	G-AFOI	Renfrew - Stornoway - Renfrew	3 hrs 55 min
					(Spinal T.B. Andrew Ruthven's wife Mary acts as Stewardess)	
1943	March	12th	DH89A Dragon Rapide	G-AGEE	Renfrew - Tiree - Renfrew	1 hr 55 min
	April	28th	DH89A Dragon Rapide	G-AFFF	Abbotsinch - Campbeltown	1 hr 10 min
	May	5th	DH89A Dragon Rapide	G-AFFF	Abbotsinch - Islay - Renfrew (Maternity)	1 hr 45 min
	July	26th	DH89A Dragon Rapide	G-AFRK	Renfrew - Islay - Renfrew (Appendix)	1 hr 30 min
	July	29th	DH89A Dragon Rapide	G-AFRK	Renfrew - North Uist - Renfrew (Maternity)	3 hrs 00 min
	Aug	5th	DH89A Dragon Rapide	G-AFOI	Renfrew - Campbeltown - Renfrew	1 hr 20 min
	Oct	10th	DH89A Dragon Rapide	G-AFFF	Renfrew - Campbeltown - Renfrew	1 hr 20 min
1944	Jan	21st	DH89A Dragon Rapide	G-AFRK	Renfrew - Belfast - Renfrew - Islay - Renfrew (Amb last sect)	3 hrs 35 min
	March	23rd	DH89A Dragon Rapide	G-AGJF	Renfrew - Islay - Renfrew - Islay - Renfrew (Amb last sect)	5 hrs 20 min
	May	13th	DH89A Dragon Rapide	G-AFRK	Renfrew - Islay - Barra - Renfrew	4 hrs 25 min
	July	2nd	DH89A Dragon Rapide	G-AFOI	Renfrew - Stornoway - Renfrew	3 hrs 30 min
	July	21st	DH89A Dragon Rapide	G-AFFF	Renfrew - Belfast - Renfrew - N. Uist - Renfrew (Amb last sect)	7 hrs 00 min
	Oct	1st	DH89A Dragon Rapide	G-AFRK	Renfrew - Benbecula - North Uist - Renfrew (Amb first sect)	3 hrs 45 min
	Oct	9th	DH89A Dragon Rapide	G-AFRK	Renfrew - Belfast - Renfrew - Tiree - Campbeltown - Renfrew	5 hr 10 min
1945	June	1st	DH89A Dragon Rapide	G-AGJF	Renfrew - Islay - Renfrew	1 hr 30 min
	Sept	30th	DH89A Dragon Rapide	G-AGIF	Renfrew - Barra - Renfrew (Appendix)	2 hrs 35 min

Flown by Capt. Donald Prentice

| 1945 | Sept | 4th | DH89A Dragon Rapide | G-AGLG | Renfrew - Belfast - Renfrew - Islay - Renfrew (Amb last sect) | 5 hrs 05 min |

Flown by Capt. S. Clark

| 1941 | Feb | 14th | DH89A Dragon Rapide | G-AFRK | Renfrew - Islay - Renfrew | 1 hr 55 min |

Flown by Capt. S. Coleman

| 1941 | Feb | 26th | DH89A Dragon Rapide | G-AFRK | Renfrew - Islay - Renfrew | 1 hr 50 min |
| | March | 5th | DH89 Dragon Rapide | G-ACPP | Renfrew - Campbeltown - Renfrew | 1 hr 20 min |

Flown by Capt. G. T. Greenhalgh

1941	June	3rd	DH89A Dragon Rapide	G-AFOI	Renfrew - Tiree - Renfrew (Jaundice)	2 hrs 05 min
	June	21st	DH89 Dragon Rapide	G-ACPP	Renfrew - N. Uist - Benbecula - Renfrew (Compound fracture)	3 hrs 30 min
	July	3rd	DH89 Dragon Rapide	G-ACPP	Renfrew-N. Uist-Benbecula-Stornoway-Renfrew (Gunshot)	4 hrs 35 min
	Aug	24th	DH89A Dragon Rapide	G-AFFF	Renfrew - Stornoway - Renfrew (Liver trouble)	4 hrs 40 min
1942	Feb	17th	DH89 Dragon Rapide	G-ACYR	Renfrew - Islay - Renfrew (Pneumonia)	1 hr 40 min
	Feb	17th	DH89 Dragon Rapide	G-ACYR	Renfrew - Belfast - Renfrew (Brain Tumour)	1 hr 55 min
	March	4th	DH89 Dragon Rapide	G-ACYR	Renfrew - Islay - Renfrew (Maternity case)	1 hr 55 min

Flown by Capt. W. J. Johnson

1942	June	1st	DH89 Dragon Rapide	G-ACPP	Renfrew - Benbecula - Renfrew (Prostrate gland)	4 hrs 15 min
	July	19th	DH89A Dragon Rapide	G-AGED	Renfrew - Islay - Renfrew (Peritonitis)	1 hr 35 min
1943	June	10th	DH89A Dragon Rapide	G-AFFF	Renfrew - Islay - Renfrew (Epileptic)	1 hr 50 min

Flown by Capt. Robert M. Pepper

| 1942 | Dec | 1st | DH89A Dragon Rapide | G-AERZ | Renfrew - Campbeltown - Renfrew (Maternity case) | 1 hr 10 min |
| 1943 | March | 13th | DH89A Dragon Rapide | G-AFRK | North Uist - Stornoway - North Uist | 1 hr 20 min |

Flown by Sqn Ldr John Annesley Hankins

| 1945 | Feb | 10th | DH89A Dragon Rapide | G-AGIF | Renfrew - North Uist - Stornoway | 2 hrs 35 min |
| | Feb | 11th | DH89A Dragon Rapide | G-AGIF | Stornoway - Renfrew | 2 hrs 25 min |

Flown by Capt. John Michie

1945	Feb	27th	DH89A Dragon Rapide	G-AGLP	Renfrew - Campbeltown	1 hr 20 min
	April	23rd	DH89A Dragon Rapide	G-AFFF	Renfrew-Belfast-Renfrew-Campbeltown-Renfrew (amb last sect)	6 hrs 30 min
	Nov	5th/6th	DH89A Dragon Rapide	G-AGIF	Renfrew - Doncaster - Coningsby - Loughborough - Renfrew	7 hrs 05 min

APPENDIX 4

SUMMARY OF PRINCIPAL EVENTS IN GEORGE NICHOLSON'S AIRLINE CAREER

1905 April 15th - George Nicholson born, and brought up by his family in Ebchester, near Consett, Co. Durham.

1923 - George joins his father's accountancy practice in Midland Bank Chambers, Consett, and studies to become an accountant.

1934 July 1st - George Nicholson registers "Northern Airways" as a business with its address at Cramlington Aerodrome, Newcastle. (It was not a 'Limited Company').

1934 July 30th - Northern Airways inaugurates a Newcastle (Cramlington) - Carlisle - Isle of Man (Castletown) air service, with DH Dragon G-ACFG flown by Edward F. (Ted) Palmer. Flights were daily after August 1st.

1934 August 23rd - Frequency of flights reduced due to poor results, and stopped on October 29th.

1934 September - Nicholson agrees to take over Glasgow - Campbeltown - Islay service from John Sword's airline Midland & Scottish Air Ferries (which is closing down), also the Air Ambulance service at Glasgow.

1934 November 21st - Nicholson registers "Northern and Scottish Airways Limited" with himself, Charles Almond (pilot) and his wife Ada Nicholson as Directors.

1934 December 1st - NSA inaugurates Renfrew - Campbeltown - Islay services on a three times weekly basis.

1935 January 1st - NSA took over responsibility for the Scottish Air Ambulance services from Renfrew, and bought John Sword's DH Dragon, G-ACJS.

1935 March 15th - Renfrew - Campbeltown - Islay service stepped up to twice daily, Monday to Friday.

1935 May 23rd - NSA, and Highland Airways Ltd of Inverness were taken over by United Airways Ltd of London and Blackpool, as part of a scheme by Whitehall Securities Ltd to create a large new domestic airline. New capital was injected into the two Scottish carriers who kept their old names. NSA took on more staff, opened a three times weekly Renfrew - Hall Caine (I.O.M.) route (daily by May 31st), and was allocated three more DH Dragons by United Airways. Note: The summer schedules started on May 17th by which time the mergers must have been agreed. News was only released to the public on May 23rd however.

1935 June 1st - NSA acquired DH Fox Moth G-ACED from SMT, for use as an air ambulance on difficult terrain.

1935 September 30th - "Allied British Airways Ltd" -a holding company - is formed by Whitehall Securities to take over United Airways from October 1st (as well as Spartan Air Lines Ltd). NSA and Highland Airways are thus part of this new group from October 1st.

1935 October 26th - David Barclay inaugurates the use of radio on NSA flights, by carrying a Wireless Telegraphy Officer (W.T.O.) on Dragon G-ACNH to Islay.

1935 October 29th - Name of this new holding company changed to just "British Airways Ltd".

1935 December 5th - NSA started a twice weekly service Renfrew - Skye (Glen Brittle). David Barclay flew Dragon G-ACFG on the 1 hr 35 min inaugural trip.

1935 December 11th - British Airways Ltd takes over full control of Hillman's Airways Ltd., and both Whitehall Securities and the d'Erlanger banking interests (behind Hillmans) each put up £50,000 of its new capital.

1935 December 17th - NSA extended the Skye service to Askernish in South Uist for the first time (but officially opened scheduled services to South Uist on January 21st 1936).

1936 January 3rd - David Barclay and George Nicholson land at Sollas, North Uist for the first time on a 'recce'.

1936 January 21st - Official inaugural of Renfrew - South Uist (Askernish) schedules, operating twice weekly (Tuesday and Thursday) via Skye.

1936 February 5th - David flew George to Barra for the first time, landing on the sands at Tàigh Mhór.

1936 February 27th - David Barclay inaugurated scheduled services to Sollas (North Uist) with a Spartan Cruiser II G-ACYL supplied from British Airways group 'pool'.

1936 May 26th - David Barclay makes final survey flight to Barra, and to a new site at Benbecula.

1936 June 1st - Tiree was added to the scheduled service network (via Islay) for the first time, on a regular basis. Barclay flew the Spartan Cruiser II G-ACSM on the inaugural.

1936 June 2nd - Barclay inaugurated schedules on Spartan Cruiser II

G-ACSM to both Northton, (Harris) and Benbecula for the first time, adding these calls 'on demand' to schedules from now on.

1936 June 10th - Scheduled calls to Barra ("on demand") commenced on this date, incorporated in the Western Isles services.

1936 July 1st - United Airways Ltd hands over most of its Northern route network for NSA to operate from this day. Routes include - Liverpool (Speke) - Belfast (Newtownards) - Renfrew; Liverpool - Blackpool (Stanley Park) - Isle of Man (Hall Caine) - Renfrew; Belfast (Newtownards) - Renfrew; Belfast (Newtownards) - Isle of Man (Hall Caine); and Isle of Man (Hall Caine) - Carlisle.

NSA also took over the Air Mail contract on the Isle of Man (Hall Caine/Castletown) - Liverpool (Speke) route.

Aircraft allocated from the British Airways 'pool' to NSA to operate these services included 3 x Spartan Cruiser IIs, 1 x Spartan Cruiser III, 4 x DH Dragon Rapides and 1 x DH Leopard Moth.

1936 July 1st - Major J.R. McCrindle, Managing Director of British Airways Ltd., appointed to Boards of NSA and to Highland Airways.

1936 July 25th - NSA's Spartan Cruiser II G-ACVT crashed at Glen Brittle, Skye, on landing, but no one badly injured. Aircraft written off.

1936 July 30th - By now NSA had a personnel strength of 14 pilots and 100 other staff, and Hall Caine Airport, I.O.M. (near Ramsey) had become NSA's busiest station.

1936 September 12th - David Barclay had to divert a scheduled service from Harris (Northton) to Stornoway (Melbost Sands) for the first time, due to bad weather.

1936 October 4th - NSA's Glasgow city-centre terminal changed from Hope Street to: The Grosvenor Restaurant, 74 Gordon Street, G.2.

1936 November 20th - NSA's Spartan Cruiser III G-ADEM crashes on take-off (in fog) into a hangar at Blackpool (Stanley Park). Pilot and only passenger killed.

1937 January - NSA's own new radio station at Sollas, North Uist went 'live'.

1937 February 17th - Two DH Dragon IIs, and two Spartan Cruiser IIIs arrived from British Airways group 'pool' to join NSA's fleet.

1937 May 20th - NSA gave up operating its ex-United Airways routes to/from Liverpool, Belfast and the Isle of Man (with the exception of Renfrew - Hall Caine) and passed these services (with all passenger reservations) over to Railway Air Services (as part of British Airways group rationalisation plans under the Maybury Committee recommendations).

A number of its aircraft returned to the British Airways 'pool'.

1937 August 1st - A new company, Scottish Airways Ltd, formed by NSA and Highland Airways on the one hand (representing the British Airways Group) and by the LMS Railway and David MacBrayne on the other, started to trade in Scotland combining the operations and staff of NSA and Highland Airways into one unit hereafter, with HQ at Renfrew.

1937 August 12th - The above company came into legal being (although trading had already started). The Share Capital of 80,000 £1 shares was divided into NSA (31.9%), Highland (18.1%), LMS (40%) and David MacBrayne (10%). Chairman was W.D.L. Roberts (Vice Chairman of British Airways Ltd), and George Nicholson was made Managing Director of the Southern Section (at Renfrew) while Capt. Ted Fresson was Managing Director of the Northern Section (at Inverness). Wing Cmdr Arthur Harold Measures, Air Superintendent of Railway Air Services was appointed 'effective Managing Director' of Scottish Airways Ltd, and a subsidiary that was created to look after operating to the Western Isles - Western Isles Airways Ltd. HQ was at the Renfrew offices of NSA.

1937 October 1st - New hangar constructed and made ready at Sollas, N. Uist to house the overnighting aircraft in the Winter season.

1938 January 14th - Spartan Cruiser III G-ACYK crashed on high ground East of Largs, Ayrshire, after delivering films to cinema. Pilot uninjured.

1938 May 2nd - Start of daily scheduled service Renfrew - Perth - Inverness - Kirkwall - Sumburgh. David Barclay and Ted Fresson flew Rapide G-AFEY on the inaugural service.

Services to Skye (Glen Brittle) ceased after the last day of the previous Winter 1937/38 time tables.

Inauguration of scheduled services between Renfrew and Tiree (The Reef Airport).

1938 November 1st - All domestic air services have to be licensed from this date by the newly created Air Transport Licensing Authority.

1939 January 1st - The UK Government began to pay subsidies to domestic airlines. £100,000 for the year 1939 was to be allocated among 11 different airlines, - including Scottish Airways, and Western Isles Airways.

1939 January 16-19th - Applications for long-term licences for the scheduled routes of the airlines operating within, and to, Scotland, were heard in Edinburgh by Mr Trustram Eve, Chairman of the new Air Transport Licensing Authority.

1939 February 12th - Decisions on the air transport licences sought by the airlines operating in Scotland were made known. Scottish Airways lost its Aberdeen - Wick/Orkney/Shetland route (to Allied Airways), gained Kirkwall - Thurso and Aberdeen - Inverness - Stornoway, and kept the rest of its routes, (with the proviso it had to share frequencies equally between Kirkwall and Sumburgh).

1939 February 20th - Army co-operation flights start, to provide out of hours utilisation for the airline's aircraft in the evening.

1939 March 1st-12th - Several new experienced pilots arrive, including Henry Vallance and Donald Prentice.

1939 May 15th - Summer schedules included twice daily Glasgow - Perth - Inverness - Kirkwall - Sumburgh services - one in each direction (with the exception of the Kirkwall - Sumburgh sector, shared with Allied Airways on alternate days). A new Kirkwall - Thurso (Claredon) service was operated. The aerodrome at Askernish (South Uist) was dropped from scheduled services from the last day of the previous Winter 1938-39 time-table.

1939 May - Two more newer DH Dragon Rapides, followed by a third in July, acquired from British Airways aircraft 'pool'.

1939 June 12th - A Bill introduced into the House of Commons providing for the merger of British Airways Ltd with Imperial Airways Ltd into a new Government controlled airline, British Overseas Airways Corporation (B.O.A.C.). All British Airways' domestic routes would have to be relinquished to another airline (or airlines).

1939 August 4th - The above Bill receives Royal Assent.

1939 August 25th - Stornoway Aerodrome opens for use (financed by Scottish Airways and Stornoway Trustees). Only two charters are flown in by Ted Fresson from Inverness and on August 31st the Air Ministry takes over the aerodrome for enlargement.

1939 September 1st - Air Ministry orders Scottish Airways to close down its radio station at Sollas, North Uist. An organization called National Air Communications (N.A.C.) formed by the Air Ministry to manage all civil airlines. It was set up at Exeter Airport under Wing Cmdr. A.H. Measures.

1939 September 3rd - War declared on Germany. An Air Navigation Order promulgated, banning all Civil Aviation movements, unless specially authorised. All en route radio facilities closed.

Scottish Airways ceased all scheduled operations but flew some Government charters, until September 11th, when scheduled flights were allowed to resume. (Those to the Western Isles were not re-started yet and the Glasgow - Inverness link ceased for the War).

1939 September 2-14th - Many of Scottish Airways aircraft were ordered to fly Service Personnel & Equipment (S.P.&E.) flights around Northern France, for the Services.

1939 October 2nd - David Barclay flew Air Mail between Renfrew and Campbeltown for the first time on a new contract for the Post Office. Spartan Cruiser II G-ACYL was used.

1939 November 24th - BOAC finally established. Chairman: Sir John Reith. Deputy Chairman: Hon Clive Pearson (Managing Director of Whitehall Securities and Director of British Airways).

1940 April 1st - Arrangements finally concluded for BOAC to divest itself of its domestic network. The shares in Scottish Airways Ltd (40,000 'A' shares of £1) were taken over by the LMS Railway Co, and The North of Scotland & Orkney & Shetland Steam Navigation Co Ltd, who paid 11s. 0d. for each £1 share. These two companies, and David MacBrayne, now jointly owned Scottish Airways, the LMS Co. being the major partner.

1940 April 19th - David Barclay crashes in DH Dragon G-ACNG on the edge of Hatston aerodrome, Kirkwall. An Army general gets concussion, and David fractures his pelvis, ankle and ribs, not flying again until February 18th 1941.

1940 May 5th - The NAC was replaced by the Associated Airways Joint Committee (AAJC) at Liverpool (Speke) Airport. This controlled all the aircraft in the fleets of the seven airlines concerned and operated a central overhaul and maintenance facility at Speke.

1940 May 14th - Services to the Western Isles are re-started for the first time since the War began. Services to Perth and Inverness from Glasgow are not re-started until after the War is over.

1940 May 20th - Bill Baillie operates the first flight on the new Renfrew - Sollas - Stornoway service using the latter's new RAF aerodrome for the first time.

1940 May 22nd-31st - Air Ministry stopped all airline flights again and ordered aircraft South to prepare for Dunkirk evacuation. They were not used, however, and sent back.

1940 June 14th-20th - All Scottish Airways' Renfrew services suspended again, and aircraft sent to France to evacuate troops, etc. One Rapide, G-AFOI, only returned after the crew changed an engine themselves in Jersey.

1941 February 18th - The Chief Pilot, Capt David Barclay, resumes flying after recovering from his accident.

1941 November 25th - While David Barclay was on the ground at Stornoway in a new Rapide G-AGDH, a 95 mph gale blew it over and wrecked it.

1942 July 7th - Scottish Airways' pilots started to operate Renfrew - Belfast (Sydenham); on behalf of Railway Air Services.

1943 February 2nd - Scottish Airways' DH Dragon Rapide G-AGED crashed at Renfrew, and was written off. No injuries to crew.

1943 July 27th - Capt E.E. (Ted) Fresson is awarded the O.B.E. for his services running the Northern Section of Scottish Airways.

1944 January - Capt David Barclay, Chief Pilot of Scottish Airways at Renfrew, appointed an M.B.E. in the King's New Year Honours.

1944 May 24th - Inauguration of Inverness - Stornoway service by Ted Fresson, flying Rapide G-AGIC, on a three times weekly basis.

1945 April 9th - David Barclay inaugurated a Renfrew - Prestwick - Liverpool - Croydon service for Scottish Airways (on behalf of R.A.S) flying DH Rapide G-AGLE.

On May 15th the service went non-stop in each direction.

1945 April 9th - With the start of the Summer time-tables, some of the Glasgow - Stornoway flights were scheduled non-stop, for first time.

1945 August - Capt Henry Vallance, Chief Pilot of Scottish Airways at Inverness, awarded the King's Commendation for Valuable Services in the Air, for his services throughout WW II.

1945 October 8th - With the start of Winter services, Scottish Airways henceforward discontinued using Sollas, North Uist on scheduled services.

1945 November 1st - The newly elected Labour Government announces in the House its intention of nationalising all British air transport services.

1946 April 15th - The Glasgow - Inverness service re-starts, but without calling at Perth.

1946 May - Miss Robina ("Bobbie") Christie, a traffic assistant from Fresson's Inverness Section, becomes the first air stewardess to fly for Scottish Airways - on the C-47A Dakotas.

1946 May 13th - Newly acquired C-47A Dakotas (flown on behalf of R.A.S.) were placed on the Renfrew - Belfast service and on May 14th Capt Bill Baillie flew the first C-47A flight to Croydon (although the 'official' inaugural was kept for May 20th).

1946 August 1st - British European Airways Corporation came into existence, to take over all domestic scheduled airlines.

1946 September 2nd - Scottish Airways Renfrew - London (Croydon) service transferred to Northolt Aerodrome - BEA's new base in the South.

1946 September 27th - Scottish Airways DH Rapide G-AFFF crashed into Craigton Hill, Milngavie killing the crew of two and five passengers. The pilot, Capt. F. Stephens D.F.C., was an ex-RAAF Lancaster bomber pilot, on loan from the A.A.J.C.

1946 October 7th - Inauguration of Aberdeen - Inverness - Stornoway service.

1946 November 18th - Scottish Airways' Capt. Bill Baillie inaugurates a Northolt - Renfrew - Aberdeen (Dyce) service on Dakota G-AGZA.

1946 December 19th - C-47A Dakota G-AGZA crashed onto the roof of a house in S. Ruislip after taking off from Northolt on the Renfrew service. All the Scottish Airways' crew, and one passenger, escaped uninjured. Capt W.J. Johnson was the pilot, and Miss Robina Christie was in the crew.

1947 February 1st - BEA takes over full control of Scottish Airways, its staff and fleet of aircraft. George Nicholson made 'Scottish Divisional Director' of BEA, Ted Fresson 'Area Manager, Northern Scotland', and William Cumming 'Senior Executive'.

1947 September 30th - George Nicholson made redundant by BEA. He decides to take his family to South Africa in search of new opportunities.

1948 March 31st - Ted Fresson and William Cumming made redundant by BEA. Capt David Barclay retained as BEA's Air Ambulance Divisional Manager in Scotland.

1950 December 30th - George Nicholson's death announced in Johannesburg newspapers.

1963 September 25th - Ted Fresson dies in Inverness.

AUTHOR'S ACKNOWLEDGEMENTS

Much material used in the compilation of this book has been drawn from Richard Fresson's collection of books, documents and photographs about his father's life, from Mrs Sheila Harper's collection of log-books and papers of her father, Capt. David Barclay, MBE, M St. J, and from the original British European Airways Corporation archives - now incorporated into the British Airways historical collection.

Equally, the book owes a great deal to the photographs and time-tables supplied by the aviation historian John Stroud, Capt. Henry Vallance and Capt. Eric Starling, to the information supplied by Peter Ward (Shetland Islands historian), by Peter Connon, Cumberland historical aviation researcher and publisher, by Iain Hutchison and Charles MacKay and by Graham Simons ("International Friends of the DH89"), who is also the publisher of *Wings over the Glens'*.

Apart from those principal sources, the compilation of this book would never have been possible without the generosity of many of those described within the previous chapters, and thanks are also due for the loan of photographs, and the assistance provided by the following:

British Airways p.l.c.
British Airways Regional p.l.c.
British Aerospace p.l.c.
Loganair Ltd.
The Highland Regional Council (Development Department).
The Orkney Islands Council.
The Western Isles Island Council.
The Stornoway Trust.
Highlands and Islands Airports Ltd.
The Shetland Museum.
Inverness Museum.
Mrs Alison Mills (neé Young).
Graeme Young.
Iain Young.

Andrew Ruthven.
Mrs Jean Wotherspoon Cook (wife of Roy Stewart).
Mrs Audrey Baillie (wife of Capt. Bill Baillie).
Ian Rae.
William Sword.
Nan Orrell (wife of Capt. "Jimmy" Orrell).
Capt. Eric Coleman.
Brian Watt, MBE.
Capt. Bill Reid.
Ewen MacRae.
Mike McLennan.
Rodney Long.
James Steen.
James Shaw Grant.

All drawings of aircraft used in this book, and the cover painting *"Wings over the Glens"* (reproduced in the centre-spread), are by Edmund Miller G.Av.A. Photographs are credited to those who took them originally, (or if unknown, to those supplying them).

Further copies of this book, or individual colour reproductions of the painting *"Wings over the Glens"* can be obtained at any time through your local bookshop, or direct by application to:
GMS Enterprises, 67 Pyhill, Bretton, Peterborough PE3 8QQ
Tel & Fax (01733) 265123